# A TRAVELLER
# IN
# SOUTHERN ITALY

*by the same author*

★

A TRAVELLER IN ITALY
A TRAVELLER IN ROME
A STRANGER IN SPAIN

IN THE STEPS OF THE MASTER
IN THE STEPS OF ST PAUL
THROUGH LANDS OF THE BIBLE
WOMEN OF THE BIBLE
MIDDLE EAST
IN THE STEPS OF JESUS

I SAW TWO ENGLANDS
IN SEARCH OF ENGLAND
THE CALL OF ENGLAND
IN SEARCH OF SCOTLAND
IN SCOTLAND AGAIN
IN SEARCH OF IRELAND
IN SEARCH OF WALES
IN SEARCH OF SOUTH AFRICA

IN SEARCH OF LONDON
THE HEART OF LONDON
THE SPELL OF LONDON
THE NIGHTS OF LONDON
H. V. MORTON'S LONDON
A LONDON YEAR
GUIDE TO LONDON
GHOSTS OF LONDON

ATLANTIC MEETING
BLUE DAYS AT SEA
OUR FELLOW MEN
I, JAMES BLUNT

# A TRAVELLER IN SOUTHERN ITALY

BY

## H. V. MORTON

DODD, MEAD & COMPANY, INC.

NEW YORK

First published 1969
Paperback edition first published 1987
in the United States of America by
Dodd, Mead & Company, Inc.
Copyright © 1969, 1983 H. V. Morton

ISBN 0–396–08926–7

Printed in Great Britain

# CONTENTS

v

# ILLUSTRATIONS

B   An 18th century impression of a Calabrian earthquake
32A   The ruins of Locri
B   Norman nave of Byzantine columns, the Cathedral,
        Gerace, Calabria

Except where otherwise acknowledged, and those copied from old
prints, the photographs are by H. V. Morton.

# ACKNOWLEDGEMENTS

My thanks are due for help and advice to Count Sigmund Fago-
Golfarelli of the Italian State Tourist Department in Rome, also to
the Inspector General of the Ministry of Public Instruction and his
staff everywhere in the south of Italy. Among those who gave me
the benefit of their local knowledge are Dr N. Durano of Bari, Dr
Franco Molinari of Matera, Dr Gustavo Valente of Cosenza, and
Dr Carmelo Cavallaro of Reggio di Calabria. I am grateful to the
Director of the E.P.T. of Salerno who despatched a photographer
to the mountain top behind Paestum to obtain for me the
excellent, and rare, photograph of the Madonna of the
Pomegranate, reproduced in plate 26C.

My warmest gratitude is due to Mr John Greenwood, of the
Italian State Tourist Office in London, for his inexhaustible kindness, and to Avv. Fernando Savarese of Vico Equense for much
Neapolitan lore. I should like to thank Mr John Cullen of
Methuen for his unobtrusive editorial skill and his always percep-
tive and useful comments. The list of books printed at the end of
this volume implies my debt to others who have written on
this subject.

I must offer thanks, so often expressed in private, to my wife
for her invaluable help in the tiresome task of proof-reading and,
above all, for her index.

H.V.M.<br>1969

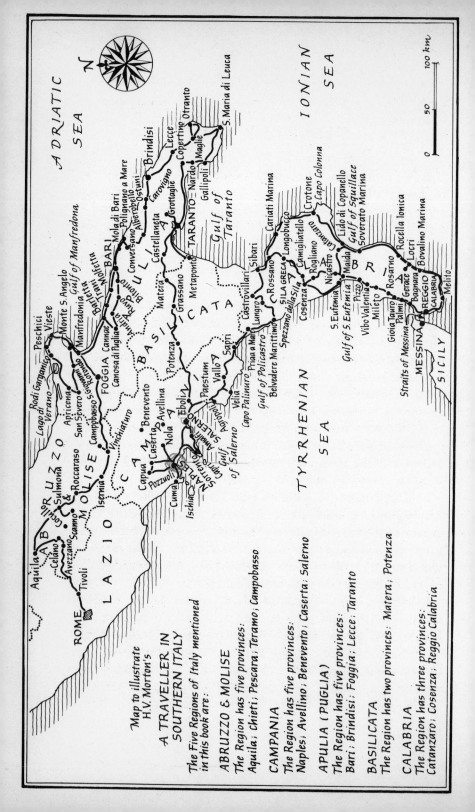

Map to illustrate
H.V. Morton's

A TRAVELLER IN
SOUTHERN ITALY

The Five Regions of Italy mentioned
in this book are:

ABRUZZO & MOLISE
The Region has five provinces:
Aquila; Chieti; Pescara; Teramo; Campobasso

CAMPANIA
The Region has five provinces:
Naples; Avellino; Benevento; Caserta; Salerno

APULIA (PUGLIA)
The Region has five provinces:
Bari; Brindisi; Foggia; Lecce; Taranto

BASILICATA
The Region has two provinces: Matera; Potenza

CALABRIA
The Region has three provinces:
Catanzaro; Cosenza; Reggio Calabria

# CHAPTER ONE

*The Five Southern Regions of Italy – On the way to the Abruzzi –
the Land of Wizards – The Castle of Celano – Aquila – The Capital
of the Abruzzi – the hermit Pope – Sulmona, the birthplace of Ovid –
Cableway to the Gran Sasso – Memories of Mussolini – the snake
ceremony at Cocullo*

§ 1

Leaving Rome early one morning in May, I arrived at
Tivoli before the baker's boy. Chairs were still piled on the
tables of the café, and the room, littered with the evidence
of last night's dinners – the unremoved bottle, the filled ash-tray –
wore that raffish air which the freshness of early sunlight bestows
upon such scenes. An elderly waiter, a broom in one hand, a
cigarette in his mouth, turned peevishly as I entered, then, recog-
nizing the day's first customer, his Italian professionalism asserted
itself and he said, bowing, that if the signore could return in, say,
half an hour the baker's boy would by then have arrived and he
would set a table for me outside in the sun.

I thanked him and walked about Tivoli watching the fine,
strapping market women erecting their stalls and umbrellas and
unpacking the vegetables. At that time of the morning, before the
streets are invaded by the hideous din of traffic, Tivoli is filled
with a sound like that of wind in a forest: it is the rush and rustle
of water from the fountains of the Villa d'Este.

I remembered Liszt and thought how wonderful it was to have
sent that sound rippling round the world; and I recalled an infinitely more ancient musical memory of Tivoli, a curious story
which is told by Ovid, Livy and Plutarch. It seems that the Roman
Guild of Flute-players, angered by some by-laws and regulations,
went on strike and exiled themselves in Tivoli in the year 311 B.C.
The Senate, irritated to find that the temple services were

I

disorganized by amateur flautists, ordered the magistrates of Tivoli to send the musicians back at once, but they refused to move. The Tivoli municipality then entertained the strikers to a banquet, and, having drugged their wine, loaded them into carts and deposited them by night in the Roman Forum.

When I returned to the café the waiter had put on a white apron and had prepared a table for me. I ate the usual Continental apology for breakfast, and was soon upon the first stage of a journey that was to take me through the South of Italy.

§ 2

Except for a brief holiday many years ago in Naples, Capri and Sorrento, I had never been south of Rome. I had often contemplated such a journey, but somehow the time, the money and the season had never coincided. Among those who cheered me on my way was one of the most fastidious of my Italian friends who, to his own astonishment, had returned full of enthusiasm from a visit to Calabria.

'You must go and see this new Italy,' he said, 'before it is ruined by tourism. Forget all you have ever read about bad roads, about bug-infested inns and horrible food. In all the larger towns you will find new, modern hotels, most of them air-conditioned. But – go quickly while it is still possible to recapture something of the enthusiasm which François Lenormant expressed in *La Grande-Grèce*.'

He described the *Autostrada del Sole*, which begins at Milan and now ends at the Straits of Messina, as the finest example of road engineering since the Via Appia and the military roads of ancient Rome. Rather to my surprise he was not cynical about the billions which the *Cassa del Mezzogiorno* – the Southern Development Fund – continues to pour into the southern regions, inaugurating industries, making roads, developing land and generally attempting to solve the notorious *problema* of the South with its long history of poverty and emigration.

What my friend had described as 'this new Italy' is also the oldest of all Italies, a region whose cities were famous for their wealth and luxury before anyone had heard of Rome. The Greek colonies of the coast, which were settled seven hundred years before Christ, rose, declined and fell, to be followed centuries later by the Norman Conquest of the South.

'You will find,' said my friend, 'that thousands of southern Italians worship in Norman cathedrals, that the ruins of Norman castles still crown a hundred hill-tops, that the peasants still remember the *paladini* – the knights, the paladins – that memories of King Arthur and Morgan le Fay are still alive.'

It was an attractive prospect.

The South of Italy should be defined. It is that part of the country, once known as the *Regno*, which was subject to the Kingdom of Naples and Sicily. It incorporates five of the nineteen administrative regions of Italy. They are: the Abruzzi, Campania, Apulia (the older name, which I prefer to the modern Puglia), Basilicata and Calabria. Though some might object to the inclusion of the Abruzzi, I think this would be a mistake since that wild mountain land has more in common with the *Regno* than with the northern half of Italy. Of these five regions one only is familiar, Campania, whose capital is Naples. Its charms, which include Pompeii, Capri and the Sorrento Peninsula, are as well known as any in Europe. But southward and eastward lie four regions with their ancient provinces which are still virtually unknown, except for Calabria, which attracted a few travellers in the last century and the beginning of this, most of them English: Henry Swinburne, Keppel Craven, Craufurd Tait Ramage, Edward Lear and, more recently, George Gissing, Norman Douglas, whose *Old Calabria* is a classic, and Edward Hutton.

The impression left upon the mind by the writings of these travellers is of an almost forgotten world locked up in its mighty geological formations, once the richest and most famous portion of the Peninsula and now the poorest and most neglected. The nineteenth century conception of the South was depressingly but accurately defined by Augustus Hare, who wrote:

'The vastness and ugliness of the districts to be traversed, the bareness and filth of the inns, the roughness of the natives, the torment of *zanzare* (mosquitoes), the terror of earthquakes, the insecurity of the roads from brigands, and the far more serious risk of malaria or typhoid fever from the bad water, are natural causes which have hitherto frightened strangers away from the south.'

Improvements were slow until after the last war when the first miracle was the abolition of malaria. The importance of this cannot be exaggerated. It meant that for the first time since the seventh century, when malaria and Saracen pirates drove the population inland to the mountain-tops, it is now possible for men to cultivate and live in health along the exquisite Tyrrhenian and Ionian sea-coasts.

The road led upward into the mountains of the Abruzzo and Molise.

§ 3

The Abruzzi is a curious word which has never been satis-factorily explained. It is used indiscriminately in the singular and the plural, though, as the region contains a southern portion called Molise, I think it is correct to say Abruzzo when you refer to the north and Abruzzi when you wish to include Molise. The name fits the region well. It suggests a harsh land of mountains, remote from modern life: there is even a hint of antique dialects in the sound of it, and certainly, to my mind, bleak summits where snow lies until summer and woods in which wolves and bears are to be met with. Equally suitable is the name Molise, which seems to express in its gentler sound the nature of the southern Abruzzi where the mountains descend to the Adriatic Sea and the Apulian plain. In the charming valley of the Aniene, a few miles from Tivoli, the hills became wild and precipitous, each one crowned with its Sabine town. The land was poor and rocky, such vines as there were lay miles from the nearest habitation, but the mountainsides shone everywhere with gold. From April until midsummer the *genistra*, or broom, covers the hills of Italy from Lombardy to Calabria.

I passed a side road that led to the ancient town of Saracinesco, and in a mile or so I came to the turning for Anticoli Corrado. Glancing towards the mountains, I saw both towns against the sky. Lanciani traced the name of Saracinesco to a raiding party of Saracens who settled there in the eighth century, and I have read somewhere that Anticoli Corrado takes its name from Conrad of Antioch. A year ago I climbed to both of these towns when I was visiting the source of the Acqua Marcia, which lies in an adjacent valley, and I found, after winding round the mountain several times, that the road to Saracinesco expires below the town and the only way onward is by mule or on foot. The town seemed to be stricken by poverty as if by a plague; half the houses were vacant and the inhabitants had left for Rome to seek work. In contrast, Anticoli Corrado was quite a cheerful little place that was proud of its association with the Arts. Most of the artists' models who in the last century plied for hire on the Spanish Steps and were described by every traveller to Rome, notably by Dickens, came from this eyrie; and even today a great-grandmother can be produced whose youth still lives in canvases which often appear in Roman auction-rooms, depicting a flashing beauty with an amphora upon head or hip; and old men may be found who in their day were famous as Apollo, or even the Creator.

I pulled up at a level crossing behind a lorry crammed with sheep whose pitiful faces protruded from the network which confined them, and whose miserable bleating and general plight aroused vegetarian resolutions in my mind. However, I realized that the animals were to be envied rather than pitied. Seated next to the driver was a shepherd with his dogs, and I knew that before sunset the animals would be released to gambol all summer on mountain pastures. This is the modern version of the great migration which has taken place for centuries, as sheep from the Campagna are moved to the mountains of the Abruzzo. Roman friends have often described to me how sometimes in the old days they were awakened by an eerie, stealthy pattering at dead of night and, glancing out of the window, have seen the street filled with a grey, moving wave of wool, as the flocks went past in the darkness, led (not followed as in England) by the shepherd and his dogs. I remembered that someone once told me that the goats, who brought up the end of the procession, showed their mental superiority over the sheep by lying down and resting during any hold-up in the progress. I looked at the shepherd and wondered if he welcomed the new age and whether he had sold his pipes to a folk museum and had bought himself a pocket radio.

The road led upwards where I saw at a bend the picturesque town of Arsoli, standing above a gorge, with mountains in the background, each holding aloft its crested town. I stopped and, spreading my map on a stone wall, tried to identify the peaks. While I was doing this a young woman strode past carrying upon her head a basket in which sat two hens, one white, the other black. In passing, she gave me the look one warrior might be expected to bestow upon another, and this appraisal seemed to be seconded by the fiery glances of the birds. When I arrived at Arsoli I found myself the centre of one of those confusing situations so common in Italy, due to the Italian desire to please and help the stranger. The castle of Prince Massimo, which is an impressive architectural conglomeration begun in the eleventh century, occupies an outstanding position in the town, and I was told that the guardian would show it to me; but he could not be found, and as everyone in the crowd had a different idea of his whereabouts, I could see that I might stay there until afternoon before he was discovered; so, with many thanks and salutations, I motored higher into the mountains.

Rome is the only capital city I know which has retained the Middle Ages on its doorstep. The city was not two hours away by car, yet as I went on through the Sabine country I passed muleteers upon the road, and I saw them watering their animals at springs; old women clothed in black were descending the mountain tracks with burdens upon their heads, and at wayside fountains stood young women filling their water-pots. The Sabine landscape remains as it was a century ago. There is nothing here that would surprise John Evelyn, Goethe, or Charles de Brosses, and the merest touch of colour at a head or waistbelt would transform the muleteers into the characters so delightfully painted by Pinelli. A few miles from Arsoli I crossed from the region of Lazio into that of the Abruzzo and found myself in mountains which grew bleaker with every mile. Some frontiers are made by politicians and are lines drawn upon a map, and others are defined by Nature, in this instance by the highest mountains in the Apennines. Upon a pass sliced into the side of a mountain called the Colli di Montebove, I became aware of something sinister that I had never before encountered in Italy. For miles around the land was unnaturally contorted and twisted. Rocks which appeared to have been hurled down from the mountain-tops were lying in the valley or protruding from the side of the mountains. This was my first sight of earthquake land, and for the first time I heard the awful word *terremoto*, which I was to hear again so often in Southern Italy. In January, 1915, an earthquake in which thirty thousand people perished in nearly four hundred parishes devastated this part of the Abruzzo. Whole villages vanished and even now, more than half a century later, the landscape remains unnatural and distorted. As I travelled through the pass, a bend of the road revealed an astonishing vista ahead. Stretched across the sky was a shining band of white, the mountains of the Gran Sasso d'Italia, the highest mountains in the Apennines, still covered in snow. The road through the pass reached a height of nearly four thousand feet; the air came, cold and crisp, from the snowfields.

I descended to the town of Avezzano, where I found it impossible to distinguish between those streets which had been rebuilt after the earthquake of 1915 and those rebuilt after the bombing of the last war. A policeman on point duty advised me to lunch at the railway restaurant, which I did. The pasta, even to one who avoids it when possible, was excellent, so was the red wine. The room had an unusual quality. Many of the town dignitaries were there, calling each other formally by their titles and picking their teeth with zest, while a few yards away, beyond the glass window, huge electric locomotives hissed and panted, as if worn out and angry after their climb through the Apennines.

§ 4

The most interesting thing about Avezzano is that it lies in the country of the Marsi, a people famous in ancient times for witches, wizards, and snake-charmers. When Cleopatra was dying of snake venom, Augustus rushed a member of the Psylli to her in an attempt to save her life, but it was too late. These people had the same reputation in Africa as curers of snake-bite, that the Marsi had in Italy, indeed some authorities have seen a connection between them.

The heart of the country of the Marsi was the lakeside at Fucino, but their villages straggled over the mountains across the central region of the Abruzzo. The Avezzano district is still known as La Marsica and the tribe is perpetuated in countless place-names all over the area – Ortona dei Marsi, Magliano dei Marsi, Lecce dei Marsi, Scarcolo Marsicana, Luco de' Marsi, and Gioia de' Marsi, just to take a few names at random. In addition, one of the mountains of the Abruzzo is called Monte Marsicano.

Avezzano stands on the western boundary of the Plain of Fucino, once the ancient Lake of Fucino. It is also the most important town on the perimeter of the plain. The enormous bowl of flat land, every part of which is cultivated, looked as if sixty square miles of Holland had been set down amid the Apennines. It is the largest lake in the world to have been artificially drained.

When it was a lake, Fucino's peculiarity was that it had no outlet, and after the melting of the winter snows the surrounding country was frequently flooded. The Marsi begged the Romans to do something to prevent this, and Julius Caesar was about to tackle the problem when he was assassinated. Nothing was then done until the time of Claudius, who, nine years after his invasion of Britain, completed an outlet tunnel nearly four miles long, designed to drain the lake by carrying the waters into the adjacent valley of the Liri. Ancient historians have described the extraordinary scenes which occurred in the year A.D. 52, when Claudius, wearing a superb suit of armour and accompanied by Messalina in a robe of spun gold, presided over the opening of the Fucino outlet in the presence of spectators who surrounded the lake and occupied the slopes of the mountains. First, a mechanical Triton emerged from the centre of the lake and blew a trumpet, the signal for a naval battle to begin between warships manned by condemned criminals. When sufficient blood had been shed, Claudius stopped the fight and the outlet tunnel was opened with unfortunate results. Owing either to miscalculation or to bad workmanship, the volume of water was too great for the outlet and many thousands of spectators, including the imperial party, were nearly drowned.The lake was never successfully drained until our own times. In the Middle Ages it became a malarial marsh and it was not until 1875 that the banker, Prince Torlonia, drained the land with Swiss and French engineers, on the condition that it should belong to him. He then settled farmers on it from his various estates, and so it remained until 1951 when the Government expropriated the land and handed it over to the peasants as small-holdings. They grow a great amount of sugar beet, potatoes, wheat, and vegetables of every kind, a remarkable contrast to the bare and rugged uplands which rise all around.

Attracted by this enormous artificial plain, I went to S. Bene-detto dei Marsi on the eastern side, where a few stones mark the site of the capital of the tribe, a town called Marrubium. Though there is little to see, my imagination responded to the idea of a city of wizards and soothsayers; and a fascinating memory of the Marsi may be found in a field on the western side of the plain, where the goddess Angitia, who presided over the magic books, the incantations and the herbs from which the Marsi made their potions, had her sanctuary.

Knowing this reputation for necromancy, I looked with interest into the faces of those whom I met in mountain passes and in the villages, but they bore little sign of their secrets. That they are descended from the Marsi is strongly suggested by the belief in witches and werewolves and in amulets which is still one of the leading characteristics of the Abruzzo. The most interesting of their links with the ancient Marsi is the cult of the serpent. Motor buses and television have had no effect on the practices of the *serpari* – the snake-charmers – in the remote mountain villages. The *serpari* are mostly young men.

In the northern boundary of the plain I came to a small town called Cerchio, which bears into modern life the name of the enchantress Circe. She was the legendary ancestress of the Marsi and here once stood a temple dedicated to her. How strange that within easy distance of Rome there exists this enchanter's country where Circe was revered and for all one knows may still be revered, and where such Circean transformations as man into wolf are still believed. I looked everywhere for a snake-charmer, but in vain. Could I have understood the local dialects, which sometimes vary from village to village, I might have fared better. Keppel Craven wrote that in his time, 1835, snake-charmers from the Abruzzo were sometimes seen in Italian cities. He noticed them near Naples, 'carrying boxes full of serpents of all sizes and colours; offering at the same time, for a very trifling remuneration, to render the spectators invulnerable as themselves'.

Successive earthquakes have spared many fine things like the beautiful Romanesque church at Magliano dei Marsi, the magnificent Cosmatesque pulpit as fine as anything in Rome, of S. Pietro in Alba, and the carved Gothic pulpit of S. Maria, in Rosciolo. I thought the most interesting of all the towns around the plain was Celano, whose houses rise in terraces towards a square castle with a machicolated tower at each corner, which resembled a toy fortress, the kind which children build on a seashore.

The town's most distinguished son was Thomas of Celano, the first contemporary to write an account of S. Francis of Assisi, which he did at the bidding of another of the saint's contemporaries and admirers, Pope Gregory IX. Not much else is known of Brother Thomas save that he is believed to have been one of the first Franciscans in Germany. As I walked about Celano noting one of the characteristic scenes of Southern Italy, women clothed in black, sewing, knitting and lace-making, seated on rush-bottomed chairs in the doorways of their houses, an ominous cloud obscured the sun but enhanced the colours of April trees and grass, of roof tiles, lime-washed houses and green shutters. I climbed to the castle, which was locked, and as I stood regretting the absence of the horn which in romance and ballad is generally available to visitors in such circumstances, there was a crash of thunder, and rain fell. I was about to turn away to find shelter when an upper casement opened and a man shouted that he would come down and open the main gate. This he did in the time it takes to descend three or four spiral staircases, and I entered a fine castle, newly restored, of the fifteenth century. The rain now fell in blinding torrents enclosing us in this dripping world of brown stone; it poured from the mouths of gargoyles and curved down in a wave from the steeply pitched roofs to splash into courtyards.

The custodian told me that he had come from Elba and had been in his present job for only a fortnight. He had been reading up the history of the castle and, like a good guide, was concentrating on horror stories. He told me of a Renaissance heiress who had married a Colonna and left him to marry, or live with, her own nephew. When the son of this marriage grew up he seized the castle and locked his mother in the dungeons for some years until she was rescued by the intervention of Pius II. In revenge, she left her estates to the Pope's family, the Piccolomini of Siena.

These dark doings have, however, left no detectable gloom behind, at least none that I could sense as the custodian led me up every spiral stairway, sparing me nothing, as he practised his newly acquired patter on me. He showed me with pride the flat that had been contrived for him in the massive halls. A hundred men might have dined in his drawing room where a suite of veneered Italian furniture designed for a suburban villa stood cowed against the walls. Reclining against satin cushions upon a couch was one of those enormous blonde dolls in frilly dresses which sell so readily at country fairs throughout Italy. They all have terrifying smiles, some can close their eyes with a faint click if inclined backwards, and some can even totter about and say 'Mama'. No child could possibly like anything as large and unmanageable, therefore I assume that they must be made for adults.

This specimen sat with her chubby legs in white socks, grinning like a ventriloquist's dummy, seated in the place of honour, the chatelaine of Celano. In such mediaeval surroundings Horace Walpole would have imagined as the height of terror an iron gauntlet grasping a dagger; Alfred Hitchcock would, I think, have made the doll, with her relentless smile, pursue one through vaulted corridors crying 'Mama', an infinitely more frightening spectre.

The rain stopped. Old women in black were once more sewing, and I noticed in the streets a breed of small white dogs, the image of the helpful little dog in the centre of Carpaccio's picture of S. Jerome in his study (now, however, believed to be S. Augustine).

§ 5

That Italy is a bitterly cold country for a large part of the year is a secret which has been well kept. The Alps, the Dolomites, and the Apennines send freezing blasts across the mountainous peninsula from autumn until late in spring. Some of our ancestors who innocently wintered there were appalled by the lack of warmth in the average Italian palazzo. Anyone who has spent a chilly winter in Milan or Venice is still appalled. Nevertheless, with the arrival of the peach blossom and the nightingale all is forgiven and forgotten. At such moments who can doubt that Italy is indeed the land of eternal sunlight?

There are, however, a few places which never really look warm, no matter how high the temperature may be: they retain well into the year an air of having been recently defrosted. And one of these is the capital of the Abruzzo, the town of Aquila. I came to it over mountains and through valleys and saw it in the evening when the streets were full of people wearing overcoats, the sunlight lingering pink upon the snowfields of the Gran Sasso. My first thought was to find, if possible, a warm hotel and in this I had no difficulty. I was given a well-heated bedroom with a private bathroom and took possession, thinking how times have changed since travellers of the last century described the primitive inns and hotels of the region.

I dined in a restaurant which might have been in Switzerland or Austria. The walls gave the effect of pickled pine; so did the settles with their tables covered with red and white checkered cloths. Here for the first time I tasted the characteristic dish of the Abruzzi, *pasta alla chitarra*, the 'guitar' being a wooden board strung with wires over which the pasta is pressed, emerging in unusually thin strips. It was excellent. Every home in the Abruzzi has a '*chitarra*', and I was told that the housewife's first task of the day is to make the pasta and press it into the wires.

One's first aimless wandering in a strange town at night is nearly always a memorable experience and, like a woman's instinct, first impressions are often surprisingly accurate. I found it difficult to believe that Rome was only a hundred and nine miles away, its inhabitants dining out of doors on a warm night. In Aquila such café life takes place behind closed doors. From most points of the town I could see the enormous curves of the surrounding mountains, with the stars above them. I came to a wide piazza which sloped to a cathedral, an open space that is a market in the daytime. Italians say of the people of the Abruzzo that they are *forte e gentile* – strong and courteous – and that is the impression given by the people of Aquila, the capital and the largest town of the region. Like all mountain towns there is a lot of flint and granite in its make-up and, like most mountaineers, the Aquileans appear mild and gentle until, as history reminds us, they are angered. The town is pear-shaped, tapering to the south and completely dwarfed by the gigantic mountains which surround it. The hill upon which it stands appears trivial until you begin to walk and find yourself descending steep streets into a valley, with the prospect of a stiff climb back.

The origin of Aquila is unusual. It was one of the 'arsenals' created about 1240 by the Emperor Frederick II during his struggle with the Papacy. Either because the first citizens were drawn from ninety-nine neighbouring villages, or because ninety-nine communities came to the rescue of Aquila after one of its frequent wars or earthquakes, this number is etched on the memory of the town. Every evening the town bell peals ninety-nine times, and the inhabitants tell you that once there were ninety-nine *piazze* and the same number of churches; and even should this be an exaggeration, it is true that there is a fountain from which water pours from ninety-nine moss-incrusted faces, so worn and old that you cannot tell whether they are human or animal. This is one of the most unusual mediaeval fountains in Italy. It is approached by steps which lead into a sunk courtyard whose high walls are decorated with a chequerwork of ancient tiles beneath which, along three walls, protrude the ninety-nine spouts. I saw the fountain on a Sunday and was the only person there. I resolved to return one day in the hope of seeing the courtyard filled with women busy with the week's washing.

To Aquileans, January is not a popular month since most of the many earthquakes recorded since the fourteenth century have occurred then. They say 'when the cold is at its greatest, the earthquake is at its strongest'. However the earthquake of 1915 which devastated the district was comparatively kind to Aquila, whose worst earthquake was in 1703, in which year, I was told, people slept in the piazza, preferring to meet death in the open rather than in the ruins of buildings. John Wesley once said that 'there is no divine visitation which is likely to have so general an influence upon sinners as an earthquake', and while one feels that the virtuous might also be included, both good and bad often combine in acts of thankfulness after such experiences. The stairs to S. Maria in Aracoeli, in Rome, are an instance, and so is the church of S. Tommaso in Aquila.

The piazza is, as I have said, enormous. There are identical fountains at either end, each displaying what appears to be the same bronze-green athlete standing above the basins. On most days the statues rise above an encampment of canvas stalls filled with merchandise of every kind. There are hand-made agricultural implements, rakes, forks and spades, and vegetables, fruit in season, furniture and clothes. The Italian plastic industry now fills country fairs and markets with garish objects of every type, but I was glad to see that the coppersmiths of Aquila still make the large two-handled water-pots of beaten copper called *conche*, which women all over the region are to be seen carrying to and from the local wells and fountains.

Even a single day in the Abruzzo fills one with wonder and admiration for the amount of needlework the women, who never seem to enjoy a moment's idleness, manage to produce: lace, embroidery, even rugs and carpets, and most of it accomplished in gossipy family groups outside cottage doors. I found a shop under an arcade in Aquila full of local work of this kind. There was everything from lace bedspreads to jewellery.

I thought that probably this was the last time one would be able to buy such merchandise, for, with life changing so rapidly everywhere, in ten years' time probably little will be made; indeed the shop window already has the appearance of a museum.

The real museum in Aquila is housed in the massive castle which the Spaniards constructed in 1534 to keep Aquila in order; now, tamed, it stands above its grassy moat and is entered by way of what was once a drawbridge; above the main gate is to be seen an escutcheon bearing the imperial eagle of Charles V. The castle is full of Roman fragments and mediaeval Madonnas from the churches of the Abruzzo. The most popular exhibit is the skeleton, discovered locally, of what I took to be a mammoth until I was sharply rebuked by the guide who said it was the only complete specimen in existence of *Elephas meriodionalis,* truly an astonishing apparition complete, as far as I could judge, save for one tusk. Each foot was the size of a card-table.

Among the finest palaces in the town is the Palace of Justice, which was built for that remarkable woman who had more than her share of male hormones, Margaret of Austria, the natural daughter of Charles V. Even his admirers must find it hard to forgive the emperor for marrying her while still in her 'teens to the repulsive illegitimate Medici, the mulatto Duke Alessandro, who was assassinated soon after the marriage. The second marriage of this forceful young woman, to Ottavio Farnese of Parma, was not a happy one. They lived separate lives, he struggling in his duchy, and she in her turbulent Netherlands, where as Regent she had succeeded her half-brother, Philip II of Spain. Tough as she was, she was no match for the Dutch Protestants and willingly resigned her regency to the famous Duke of Alva and retired to Rome and Aquila. Keppel Craven, who visited Aquila early in the last century, wrote an unflattering description of her which may have been handed down by eye-witnesses. 'She is described as having been harsh in her manner, fidgety in her habits, which led her to be always riding (not on a side-saddle) about the country, and masculine as well as ordinary in her form and visage; which aspect was considerably aggravated by a huge pair of bushy yellow mustachios.' In 1572, in her palace in Aquila –

the year after the Battle of Lepanto – Margaret met, for the first and perhaps for the last time, her half-brother, Don John of Austria, also a natural child of Charles V and her junior by twenty-three years. He had been in the habit of writing to her in a lyrical and sentimental style to confess his many love affairs; and it must indeed have been a strange, and in its way, pathetic meeting, the woman of fifty so uncouth and unloved, and the man of twenty-three, so handsome, so elegant and so admired. The family provides a wonderful study in the mysteries of genetics: Charles V, himself the son of Joan the Mad of Spain ('Crazy Jane'), his legitimate son, Philip II, and Margaret and Don John.

These famous characters do not by any means exhaust the strange persons who have occupied the stage at Aquila. To the north of the town, in a church far finer than the cathedral, is the tomb of S. Bernadino, the patron saint of Siena, and to the south is another fine church in which lies the body of the hermit pope, Celestine V, one of the few pontiffs who have abdicated.

Pope Celestine's name was Peter Angeleri, though he was better known as Peter of Morrone, the name of the mountain on which he lived in a cave. He was the son of a peasant of the Molise, the southern region of the Abruzzi, who, driven by mystical longings, decided to renounce the world and live a life of prayer and meditation. He was nearly eighty years old when the College of Cardinals, following the death of Nicholas IV in 1292, failed to elect a successor and the Church remained without a head for two years. Worldly candidates put forward by rival factions failed to obtain the necessary votes until, at a conclave held in Perugia, Cardinal Latinus happened to mention the saintliness of the old hermit and suggested that he might make a better pope than most. Amazingly the Conclave, in a mood of mingled exasperation and exaltation, acclaimed Peter of Morrone as Pope on July 5, 1294.

Towards the end of the month a cavalcade of cardinals, prelates, princes and knights set out for the Abruzzo to find the pope-elect. An eye-witness, Jacopo Stefaneschi, described in verse what then happened. The delegation, after ascending Monte Morrone by goat and sheep tracks, came at length to the hermit's cave. They saw an unkempt and aged man with a long beard, hollow cheeks and frightened eyes, before whom they knelt while some, to his bewilderment, kissed his sandals. He must have believed the scene to be another of his disturbing visions. When the parchment announcing the decision of the Conclave was placed in his hands, the hermit tried to run away, but was respectfully restrained and eventually persuaded to accept the papal crown. The poor old man, ignorant of the world, accepted everything at its face value. Mounted upon an ass, still in his hermit's habit, and with King Charles of Anjou holding the bridle on one side and his son on the other, he was conducted to Aquila, while choirs sang and knights jingled past. It must have reminded some of the entry into Jerusalem.

The hermit was made a bishop in the beautiful church of S. Maria di Collemaggio where, later, he was consecrated as Pope Celestine V. The Cardinals were then shocked by what they had done. They saw that they had elected a septuagenarian child to the pontifical throne. Washed, barbered, and clothed in splendid vestments, the poor old Pope believed everything that was said to him and obeyed implicitly the wily courtiers and politicians, including Charles of Anjou, whom he regarded as a true friend and under whose influence he agreed to live, not in Rome, but in Naples. Here a cell was built for the guileless pontiff in the fastness of the Castel Nuovo, where he prayed and meditated and sighed for the sun and storms on Monte Morrone, while a committee of cardinals conducted the affairs of the Church.

It was not long before the ineptitude of the pontiff brought the problem of abdication into the open. It was only too obvious that a good man can be a bad pope. It was said at the time that the ambitious Cardinal Caetani, who became Boniface VIII, arranged a speaking tube in the Pope's cell into which he whispered at dead of night, urging the unhappy hermit to renounce the Papacy. This he did before the year was out. With tears of thankfulness in his eyes, the poor old man put aside the insignia of the greatest dignity upon earth and stood once more in the rough garments of an anchorite.

All might have gone well for Celestine V if, in their pathetic longing for goodness and spirituality in the Church, the people had not taken the Pope's part and begged him to remain on the throne. This did not suit his successor, Cardinal Caetani, now Boniface VIII, who could not afford to allow a popular rival to remain at large. After an attempt to return to his old cell on the mountain, and an unsuccessful flight to Dalmatia, the ex-Pope was captured and imprisoned by Boniface in the castle of Fumone, among the mountains of Alatri, where he died in two years' time, aged eighty-one. Now that he was safely in heaven, the Church canonized him as S. Celestine within seven years. His body was brought back to Aquila and interred in the church in which he had been crowned.

The walk to the church of S. Maria di Collemaggio is a delightful one through a park on the southern outskirts of Aquila. At the end of a long avenue of trees I caught sight of an imposing façade sheeted in red and white marble, arranged in the form of crosses and pierced by a noble Romanesque entrance with a smaller door on either side; above each door was a rose window.

The long, high nave beneath a fine ceiling of carved and painted wood was empty save for a small group of men who shuffled towards me with a curious gait, and as they drew near I saw they were carrying a coffin and were followed by a priest. In front of the high altar I noticed a gruesome pall on which the coffin had rested, decorated at each corner with a skull and cross-bones.

I found the tomb of the hermit Pope at the end of the aisle on the right, a beautiful and delicate Renaissance work by Girolamo of Vicenza, which was paid for by the wool merchants of Aquila in 1517, two centuries after the Pope's canonization. I was puzzled to see a wax effigy of Celestine lying behind a grille, wearing a mitre and vestments. The face was that of a fairly young man and the ex-Pope had been, of course, over eighty. I asked a passing Franciscan why the figure had been placed there. He said that it had been made in 1944 when the six hundred and fiftieth anniversary of Celestine's coronation had been celebrated in the church. He asked me to admire the admirable frescoes on the walls of the tomb chapel which illustrated the life and death of the saint, painted, he told me, by a pupil of Rubens named Ruter; there was one which showed the hermit in the act of taming a bear. The friar took me to the left side of the church and pointed out an architectural feature which is rarely to be seen outside the major basilicas of Rome. This is a Holy Door of the thirteenth century and was, so the story goes, made for the coronation of Celestine V in 1294.

A church even finer than S. Maria is that of S. Bernadino, which is approached by a noble flight of steps on the eastern boundary of the town. I made a point of going there before breakfast to enjoy a sight that never palls by repetition. That I should have found it so unusual and so moving implies how far the world has slipped away from faith, reverence and discipline. It was the sight of school-boys and girls of all ages, from small creatures grotesquely gowned and with floppy ties like miniature Latin Quarter artists of the last century, to young men and women ready for the university, who entering the church, their books beneath their arms, knelt and said a prayer, before going to school. This devotion, whether decreed by priest, parent or custom, or whether, as I like to think, a personal act of devotion, raised the young people of Aquila in my estimation. Sometimes they came alone, sometimes in groups of two or three, and in the most businesslike way sought out the place where they preferred to pray, then rose and hurried out to school.

If anyone had asked me where S. Bernadino was buried I should have said in Tuscany, because it is there that memories of the emaciated little Franciscan are so frequently to be met with, and his emblem, the letters IHS with the sunburst, is so often seen. In Siena a portrait of him exists that was painted during his lifetime and all portraits and statues represent the same slight, ethereal figure, with bald skull, hollow cheeks (he had lost every tooth by the time he was forty), pointed chin, and eyes which reflect a blend of suffering and humour. To come across his splendid Renaissance tomb in Aquila surprised me. Why had he come to the Abruzzo? How did he happen to die in Aquila? I found the answers in Iris Origo's *The World of San Bernadino*.

The saint was sixty-four years of age and was suffering from a complexity of ailments which, says Iris Origo, included 'gravel, dysentery, inflamed kidneys and piles, as well as from gout and podagra', and with the feeling that his life was ending, he decided to go to the only region of Italy in which he had never preached, 'the vast and wild Kingdom of Naples and Sicily, often called simply "the Kingdom".' The poor invalid, who according to modern ideas was not old yet looked eighty, struggled on through the mountain passes on the back of a donkey, but was sometimes so racked by pain that he was obliged to dismount and lie flat on the earth. As he approached Aquila, it is said that he saw an old man approaching dressed in a hermit's gown of white, wearing on his head a peculiar hat in the form of a triple crown upon which a dove was resting. This was Pope Celestine V, 'who now appeared in a vision to this other friar, as pure in heart and as unworldly as he himself had been. In silence he embraced Fra Bernadino and gave him his blessing, and then disappeared again into the shadow of the rocks'.

S. Bernadino was carried dying into Aquila. As his end approached, he asked, as S. Francis had done, to be placed upon the bare ground to die. Fra Girolamo of Milan, who was there, wrote, 'If this is how men die, then death is sweeter than sleep.'

It is a tribute to the respect inspired by the toughness of the Abruzzesi that Siena's attempts to obtain the body of her saint were unsuccessful, even after an appeal to the Pope. The most that Siena received was the gown S. Bernadino was wearing at the time of his death and certain objects from his cell. So you will find Siena's patron saint in the mountains of the Abruzzo, together with another holy man, the hermit pope Celestine. Both shared the rare distinction of rapid canonization: Bernadino six years after his death, and Celestine seven. I like to think that someone visiting Aquila in the future may find the schoolchildren with their books under their arms still slipping into church before hurrying off to their classrooms.

§ 6

I know of only two books in English about the Abruzzi; one is Keppel Craven's *Excursions in the Abruzzi* (1835), which is a straightforward account of a horseback tour, and *Through the Apennines and Lands of the Abruzzi*, by Estella Canziani (1928), which describes a sketching expedition undertaken by the young artist and her father in the autumn of 1913. The author was interested in persuading the women to sit for her, and in gathering stories, legends and poems, in which she was successful. Reading this admirable narrative one is astonished by the changes which have taken place in the Abruzzi during the fifty odd years since the author was there. Estella Canziani saw a mediaeval society. All the women, old and young, wore regional costume, and there were few roads. She and her parent travelled by train, then on to the mountain villages by carrier's cart or by mule or on foot. Hotels did not exist in most places, the food was foul and often bedrooms swarmed with vermin. The author never reflects that she was in the country of the Marsi, indeed she appears to have been unaware of it; nevertheless the uninhibited way her casual acquaintances discussed the spells and incantations, witches and sorcery, werewolves, and *malocchio*, the Evil Eye, proved that the region possessed its ancient link with magic, as it still does.

This is how some villagers not far from Aquila greeted the author: 'By this time it had gone round that two strangers had come, and that one of them (myself) wore a strange white hat, and the whole village came to inspect us, saying nothing like my panama had ever been seen before. While our things were being carried up, they felt me all over, both my skirt and clothes and hat, and then they picked up the pencil, knife and scissors which hung on a chain from my belt, and wished to know if I were a tailor. Next they wanted to see my hair, so to satisfy them I took off my hat, and to their amazement they found it was not black like theirs, and that my cheeks were not nearly so brown. They tried to pull down my hair, because they were surprised to see that it was not all worn away by tight nets and head-dresses, but I escaped by saying "*Un' altra volta*". They promptly said that I must come from a very long way to be so different, that I should certainly be ill in their barren and rough ugly mountains, for there was no beautiful food.'

Since that extraordinary scene there have been two wars, new roads have been built over the mountains, the village motor bus has arrived, and so have radio and television. It is inconceivable that such a scene could ever occur again, even in the most remote village of the Abruzzo.

The author describes the frightful sleeping quarters which she and her heroic parent often endured. 'I went to bed early, but I had been only in bed ten minutes when I felt something nibbling my toes, and I caught five large bugs. I got up, and put up the *livinge,* a kind of calico sack one ties onself in, with a mosquito curtain top with canes to keep it away from one's face, and I got into it and went to bed again. But it was suffocatingly hot, and I spent nearly the whole of the night watching thirty bugs rushing up and down in the moonlight trying to find a hole through which they could get at me. I do not know what happened to my father.' She mentions a photographer who had to fly for his life from villages because soon after he had taken a photograph a thunderstorm broke over the mountains, followed by hail that flattened the crops, which the peasants put down to the Evil Eye of his camera.

The area of Estella Canziani's explorations was confined to Aquila and Sulmona and a few of the neighbouring villages. Among those which the author painted and described were S. Stefano and Castel del Monte, both of them only a few miles from Aquila. Thinking that I should like to see what these places are like today, I set off one afternoon and motored east to a little town called Barisciano, where a secondary road winds and twists over the lower slopes of the Campo Imperatore, with the snow-dusted mass of the Gran Sasso d'Italia beyond. What a landscape it is! To the north there was nothing but the uninhabited wilderness of the Campo Imperatore above whose tough grasses two peregrine falcons were hunting, while to the south rolled pointed hills, each one bearing upon its summit a white village like an illustration from a *Book of Hours*. I was never out of sight of these picturesque hill towns and villages, and I rarely travelled a mile without meeting peasants with their mules or seeing them in the small fields, packing meagre crops of hay into sacks which were then loaded upon the backs of mules or donkeys. And women, always women, were working away with rakes or sickles, their heads tied in handkerchiefs, their black skirts blowing in the wind, their legs in thick black knitted stockings, and their feet in hob-nailed boots. Old and lined at thirty, and bearing upon their shoulders, with apparent willingness, the whole burden of life, those patient women amazed me by their industry. Sometimes they would be seen walking behind a laden donkey, not idly but knitting as they walked. As the road climbed, long stretches which are subject to snowdrifts in the winter were marked out with lines of tall striped poles. How different, I thought, are the gentle hills of Tuscany from this wild Abruzzo land, all the difference between a man of the Renaissance and a man of the Middle Ages.

On this beautiful late spring afternoon with the warmth of summer in it, I came at last to the little mountain village of S. Stefano, piled on a height whose slopes descended almost sheer into the valley. In 1913 Estella Canziani said it 'looked like a fairy town', and to me on this afternoon fifty-three years later it had the same look, indeed I thought of the palace of the Sleeping Beauty, for everywhere was silence. I drove to an embattled gateway where I had to leave the car. I saw upon the archway a shield of the Medici, six *palle* beneath a ducal crown once the entrance to a palace. Mediaeval and Renaissance buildings stood everywhere in narrow lanes, silent and deserted, some with de-lightful stone window frames, others with balconies. I recognized the oriental-looking street of archways painted by Estella Canziani in which she shows a group of women, each one in regional costume. Now there was not a soul to be seen. That life still existed in the village was proved by hens and chickens which ran about the streets and by a mule or a donkey in a stable whose gateposts were of marble. While I was admiring the picturesque flights of steps that led to some of the houses, I saw an old man watching me. He wore a battered felt hat, and he looked a cheerful kind of person, I spoke to him but could not understand his reply. Then he replied with obvious delight in what was, remotely, English, or rather American-Irish. He was what is known as an 'Americano', one who had spent some years in South America or the United States and had returned home. He told me his name was Domenico Necco and that he was seventy-three years old. He had worked in the United States for twenty-six years, for some of the time as a coal miner in Pittsburgh.

I told him that I had read a book written about fifty years ago in which S. Stefano was described as a town full of people. Yes, he said, that was so, but now the inhabitants had descended to the valley and only a few like himself and his wife continued to live in the old houses. He stood aside and indicated a stone stairway that led up to his house and asked if I would like to enter. An old woman came out wiping her hands on her apron and asking who I was, at the same time rebuking her husband for introducing me at a moment when she was so untidy and so busy, though I was not intended to hear this. I entered a small room whose window was set in a wall about two feet thick. In front of a wood fire sat a speckled hen that had recently hatched a clutch of eggs. Some of the first-born were peeping out from her wing feathers, and one ran lost about the kitchen peeping miserably while the hen clucked in maternal dismay. Though the room was so old there was electric light, and, an incongruous touch, a spotless white electric stove.

I was shown into an adjoining sitting-room whose window offered a splendid glimpse of the distant valley. There were pictures of saints upon the walls, but the chief decoration was one of the large dolls with its foolish smile, the sister of the doll in the castle of Celano, still in its cardboard box, upright upon a chair. I looked at its mass of brassy blonde curls and thought what an odd possession it was for an aged couple.

We sat at a table while Domenico produced two glasses and his wife entered with a jug of pink juice which he told me he had pressed from his own grapes in a vineyard in the valley. She refused to join us and bustled away. I thought the drink was fruit juice, but it was more potent. Domenico was full of reminiscences, none of them really of interest, about the United States and the money that could be earned there, but he knew nothing about the history of S. Stefano. He had heard that there was once a splendid castle there – perhaps the Medici gateway had been a part of it –

and he thought that some of the old houses may have been formed from its rooms and built in its courtyards.

I told him I was going on to Castel del Monte and he said he would like to accompany me. His wife objected, saying he was far too untidy, whereupon he vanished for some moments to reappear wearing a new felt hat. This appeared to mollify the old woman, and we set off across the mountains.

From a distance Castel del Monte appeared to be an enchanted town from the world of Merlin, but when we arrived the magic soon disintegrated in a depressing, but not unexpected, way, and we found ourselves trudging up steep cobbled streets between stark stone houses where children played in the gutter and lean cats slunk swiftly from door to door.

It was here that Estella Canziani was awakened at two o'clock in the morning by a screaming girl and, thinking that she had been attacked by wolves, flew to her bedroom window and asked the girl if she needed help. She replied that she had been delayed in the mountains and was only trying to awaken her family. 'I could see from my window,' wrote Estella, 'the carcass of a sheep which a wolf had killed and half eaten. We were told it was left for the dogs to finish.' I saw neither wolves nor sheep in Castel del Monte, but I did see a fine selection of dogs which included a Dobermann Pinscher with a long tail, a liver-coloured retriever that might have ingratiated himself out of an eighteenth century aquatint, a number of the little Carpaccio dogs and, most interesting of all, a tough Abruzzo sheepdog like a white St. Bernard, wearing a spiked collar to protect him from wolves. 'But we have them only in the winter,' said a local man, speaking of wolves, as if referring to influenza.

Estella Canziani had a gruesome story about the church here. She wrote that there were caves below in which the dead were buried dressed and seated on cane chairs. One day a man making some alterations to his cellar broke into one of the caves and was horrified to see a dead priest seated there, wearing a big hat, his chin supported by a wooden fork. In 1912 bricklayers at work in the church broke into the caves by accident and were so appalled by what they saw that they ran for the schoolmistress. She lighted a piece of paper and threw it into the cave to illuminate the scene and so set fire to the skeletons, which burned so furiously that a hose had to be laid on from the public fountain. But the fire was not put out until every skeleton had been destroyed. The caves were then filled with earth and lime. The villagers I spoke to had no memories of this, or did not wish to discuss it, or believed that I may have had some ulterior motive in mentioning it. I began to wish that I could meet some of the uninhibited creatures who spoke so freely to Estella Canziani half a century ago. This town was then completely isolated. The village bus which drew up in the piazza was still in the future; the television aerial which sprouted from the roof of a café was an unimaginable revelation, and the parents and grandparents of the modern inhabitants belonged to another world. While I was wondering whether they were any better off, or happier, than their fierce and arrogant forebears, old Domenico was greeted fulsomely, slapped on the back and kissed by a friend of his, a lorry driver, who insisted that we should visit his house. He was a much younger man and, I think, a relative. We descended from the town and walked up a steep hill on the outskirts, coming at last to a stone cottage with a superb view of the town, lifting itself, tier upon tier, to culminate in the dome and campanile of the church, now outlined against the sunset. I wondered what to expect as we mounted some stairs to a room on the first floor. Was I to see one of those picturesque peasant gatherings visible half a century ago? I entered a spotless suburban parlour where three women were chatting while their children played on the floor. I never discovered who they were, for there burst into the room an elderly woman of such exuberant vitality that she entirely dominated everything and everybody. She was the lorry-driver's mother. After a few questions about me, she opened her arms and greeted me as if I were a long lost member of the family. She darted away and returned with a bottle of anisette and some small glasses. Her expressive eyes in her lined face gave the impression that a gay young woman of twenty was entombed within an old woman. I could not understand a word she said, but her gestures and expressions were a language anyone could read. I thought that she was the type of peasant woman who sometimes in history has ruled kings and held the destiny of nations in her hands, given intellect; without it, of course, such vivacious females can become a public nuisance.

It was dusk when I dropped Domenico in his silent mediaeval town. He stood wearing his new hat, a small cigar between his lips. He looked as if he had been up to no good, yet I was witness to the blamelessness of our little outing. It was dark when I reached Aquila.

§ 7

I thought at the time, and I still think, that the rescue by air in 1943 of Mussolini by Hitler from the top of Italy's highest mountain was one of the most fantastic stories of the last war. Every day as I saw from the end of Aquila's streets the Gran Sasso towering into the sky, I began to feel curious about the Dictator's detention in that remote spot, and to wonder if anyone who saw him rescued still remained in the mountain hotel on the Campo Imperatore.

Fifteen miles from Aquila a cableway links the valley with a point on the mountains some seven thousand feet above. In winter the cable cars ascend bearing sportsmen to the ski runs of the Gran Sasso, while in summer the mountains offer a retreat from the heat and attract climbers to the peaks which culminate in the highest Apennine, the Corno Grande, some nine thousand five hundred feet above the sea.

On a spring morning as warm as if it were summer, I drove out to the cableway. Birds which had miraculously evaded the *cacciatore* were singing happily in the new leaves of oak and chest-nut trees. There was the music of a mountain stream at the pleasant old town of Assergi which one passes on the way to the station. Here I found an attractive place to wait for the ascending car. There was a café-restaurant with a pleasant garden in which one could sit and drink a glass of wine or, if addicted to the national vice, a thimbleful of bitter coffee. The aluminium-coloured towers of the cableway diminished in the distance as they ascended the mountain, the cable swaying above precipices and vanishing amid the lingering snowfields. As one car ascends, its companion descends and they meet half-way, rocking slightly over appalling gorges.

No other passengers were visible at departure time and I began to wonder, as the winter sports season had ended and the mountain climbing had not yet begun, whether the hotel would be open at the top. The man in the ticket office assured me that it was, and I took my place, the only passenger in a steel and glass car that could hold about twenty people. The bored young conductor rang a bell which was the signal for us to glide upwards towards the mountains. He told me that the cable cars were new since the war; indeed as we looked down we saw the old ones lying abandoned beside the cable station. They were the cars in which the fallen Dictator had been taken up the mountain on the afternoon of September 5, 1943. The event has been described in statements by the manager and manageress of the Albergo Campo Imperatore and printed at the end of Mussolini's *Memoirs*. How strange it was that a man who was in considerable danger, and might have been handed over to the Allies as a war criminal, should have asked when he saw the cable car, 'Is this funicular safe?' Then he hastily added, 'Not for my sake, for my life is over, but for those who accompany me.' Thoughtlessly I asked the conductor if he had any memories of this event. He replied that in 1943 he had not been born. To the south the view beyond Aquila to Monte Morrone above Sulmona was stupendous. Half-way up, the cable car slid into a little platform where I had to change cars and take an even more aerial one. It was now bitterly cold and I was glad that I had put on warm clothes. I saw the snow lying, now quite close, melting in the sunlight, but frozen in the valleys.

This second part of the ascent was superb. The distant landscape, splendid as it was, lost its interest as the car, swinging on its cable over enormous distances from tower to tower, revealed rocks and corries known only to eagles; and I looked down upon jagged pinnacles and lonely valleys above the vegetation line, while the cold struck even through the plate-glass windows. I stepped out at the cable station into a temperature that seemed to me to be below freezing point. A long covered passage designed to protect visitors from wind and snow led to the hotel, a large building with double doors and windows that stood on level land, with mountains rising all round it. It had the air of a prison or a penitentiary, or perhaps some ship that lay ice-bound in the Arctic.

After the cable station and the open air, the hotel was like a furnace. As far as I could see it was empty save for one old lady seated in a basket chair reading a book, and a young man and a girl in a dark corridor so much in love that they sat looking into each other's eyes and occasionally touching hands to assure themselves that they were real.

Through the windows of the semicircular dining-room I saw the hazardous rocky space on which Hitler's gliders landed and from which the German escape plane carried off Mussolini. The director of the hotel, Signor Amilcare Tiberti, pointed out Mussolini's table to me and invited me to have lunch with him at an adjoining one. He was in the hotel at the time of the escape and had many recollections. Though Mussolini, who was on a diet because of a duodenal ulcer, ate in his rooms, he generally appeared in the dining-room to play cards – *scopone* – with three of his guards. He asked if I would like to see Mussolini's bedroom. We went upstairs where he unlocked rooms 201–2, a double room with bathroom, dark and prison-like, whose small windows preserved the occupant from icy blasts.

'He was not allowed to listen to the radio,' said Signor Tiberti, 'but he managed to find a small battery set which he put under his pillow at night.'

He described the excitement of the rescue operation which has been told many times and will, I think, go down as one of the great escape stories of history.

Hitler acted with astonishing speed, also with commendable loyalty to a fallen partner. The day after the Fascist Party had rejected its founder, July 25, 1943, Hitler summoned a young commando captain, Otto Skorzeny, from Berlin to his head-quarters and said: 'I have an important task for you. Mussolini, my friend and our loyal comrade in arms, was betrayed by his king and arrested by his own countrymen. I cannot and will not fail Italy's greatest son in his hour of need. To me, the Duce is the incarnation of the ancient grandeur of Rome. Italy under the new Government will desert us. I will keep faith with my old ally and dear friend. He must be rescued promptly.'

Skorzeny reeled out, dazed from the hypnotic presence, and went to Italy where he had first to discover Mussolini, who had vanished. He had been held captive on various islands, and it was not until September that the Germans were able to pinpoint him on the Gran Sasso. The rescue plan was immediately put into action. Mussolini was looking through the miserable little window of his room on Sunday, September 12th when German planes swooped over the mountain and cut loose eleven gliders which crash-landed on the rocky plateau in front of the hotel. In a few moments German commandos had surrounded the building. The Italian guards, soldiers and police, put up no resistance as Skorzeny found his way up to rooms 201-2 and explained to Mussolini what was happening. 'I knew that my friend Adolf Hitler would not desert me,' said the Duce.

Skorzeny was shocked by Mussolini's appearance. He looked old, ill and unshaven. He wore a shabby suit that did not fit. Skorzeny hurried him outside where a Fieseler-Storch spotter plane had been landed with difficulty and with a damaged under-carriage, by a German flying ace, Captain Gerlach. The airman did not think he could take off with a passenger. When he knew that he would have two passengers, since Skorzeny insisted on accompanying Mussolini, he said that it would be impossible to lift the machine into the air from the small rocky pleateau. How-ever, there was no time to argue or to think. Mussolini, wearing an overcoat and a wide-brimmed felt hat, said farewell to the hotel servants as they lined up on the steps, and once again looking like a dictator, entered the plane; so did Skorzeny. Twelve Germans held the plane back, grasping ropes as the engine raced, then suddenly let go at a sign from the pilot, and the Storch leapt ahead and dashed for the edge of the precipice, but did not leave the land. Just as those who knew anything about flying expected to see the machine go tumbling into space, one of the wheels hit a rock, which sent the plane into a spin over the edge of the gulley and by what looked like a miracle the pilot pulled out of the dive, straightened up and flew. That night Mussolini slept in Vienna.

It was interesting to talk of these events while lunching next to the table where Mussolini once played *scopone*. The Duce was obviously at his best in uniform, standing with jutting chin upon the balcony of the Palazzo Venezia, or seated at his desk in the long marble room there, ready to impress visitors with a calculated scowl. His act was evidently not so good when he was dressed in an old coat and a black hat, and while Signor Tiberti told me how ill-favoured the Dictator was – the word he used was *brutto* – my mind went back to the hysterical repetition of the word 'Duce' written on walls in the nineteen-thirties, and 'The Duce is always right', those first lessons in mass hypnotism which have been so well taken to heart by the political father figures of other lands.

I descended in a cable car that felt like a refrigerator. The mountains were pink in the afternoon sunlight. I looked back at the white gulleys and peaks. Even Elba's story seems commonplace compared with the melodrama acted upon those dispassionate snowfields.

§ 8

I had heard of the snake ceremony at Cocullo when I was in the village of Scanno, not far from Sulmona. Until recently Scanno was approachable only by way of a mule track through a gorge, but now a road has been cut into the mountain on which one winds and twists through magnificent scenery, with a river, the Sagittario, sliding from pool to pool below. The little town has now parted with its isolation and has gladly accepted the modern world of bus services and television.

The houses of Scanno climb the side of a mountain in a way which prepared me for the maze of narrow streets, many in semi-darkness like an eastern souk. The village is chiefly famous for the splendour of the regional dresses worn by the women, though I did not see this. I did see, however, a great number of old women in bunchy black dresses wearing coloured scarves on their heads, but I saw nothing remotely approaching the magnificence of the illustrations in books on Italian costume. The young women of Scanno were dressed like young women everywhere, and I imagine that it would not be easy to persuade them to wear the heavy, stuffy and costly regalia of their grandmothers.

The jewellers of Scanno, whose work has been celebrated for centuries, are still to be found tapping away in underground cellars, making gold buttons, earrings, and various objects of female adornment which were once bought exclusively by the splendidly attired women of the town. Some of the designs perhaps go back to the time of the Marsians. I bought a pair of drop earrings which I watched a jeweller make in a small dark workshop and I believe they could be introduced into a case of Roman jewellery in a museum and rouse no question in the mind of an expert.

The day I arrived in Scanno was one of annual importance. In the first week of May a rain goddess is carried from a chapel near the Lake of Scanno, about two miles away, and placed above the altar in the village church, where she remains for a month. She is the Madonna del Lago, or L'Annunziata, and is of great antiquity. In appearance she is a small doll no more than a foot high, dressed in vestments like a Spanish Virgin, and covered with gold chains and other gifts. The frescoed chapel where she is to be seen for the rest of the year is on the edge of the charming lake. It is partially hewn out of the rock and was once a cave.

A local artist, Elia Ubaldi, who paints recognizable pictures of Scanno which are bought by winter visitors, told me how 'the good rains' begin to fall immediately the Madonna arrives in Scanno, and, as if to prove this to be so, the sky clouded and a determined mountain drizzle settled over the little town. We went to see the Madonna. She stood above a hedge of candles in the old church while women faced her on their knees in prayer, gazing up at her in the candlelight.

After dark we made a tour of the town on foot, exploring the narrow mediaeval streets, climbing up and down cobbled alleys and coming to many a fine arched doorway which carried above it an armorial escutcheon carved in stone, for Scanno was a wealthy wool town in the fifteenth century. All these mountain towns and villages now have electric light, and so have advanced at one step from the world of candlelight into that of electricity, radio, television and refrigeration. Stranger still, the snow which once completed the isolation of Scanno has now made it popular in winter; the local people have ceased to marvel at the chair-lift which carries winter sports visitors to the snowfields. While we explored the old streets, Ubaldi paused before a stone building and asked if I would like to see the library. Upstairs we found several rooms where shelves held a good selection of modern Italian fiction, several sixteenth- and seventeenth century folios, and various town records. Among these we came across the visitors' book of a now defunct hotel called, I seem to remember, the Albergo Pace, in which, said the librarian, an Englishman had once written something. Eventually we discovered the following entry: 'I have stayed on two occasions at this hotel and have been thoroughly satisfied; it compares most favourably, in regard to accommodation and food, with the hostelries in other Italian places of the size of Scanno. The landlord is most obliging. Norman Douglas. Aug. 23. 1910.'

Lured by dreams of comfort I stayed not in the town of Scanno but two miles away in the hotel by the lakeside. This was built for winter sports visitors and wore that vague air of Austria or Switzerland which such places assume, either deliberately or by association. I was the only guest, the season having ended. The air became bitterly cold after sunset, blowing chilled from the still whitened mountains. Fortunately the hotel clientèle were obviously insistent on warmth and even the corridors were full of electric oil heaters. There were two in my bedroom. In the morning I opened the double windows and saw the blue lake lying below in the early sunlight, and opposite, upon the water's edge, was the chapel of the Madonna del Lago, now without its presiding deity. It was a curious little shrine, frescoed from ceiling to floor and with a vault of deep blue scattered with golden stars.

One afternoon I noticed with surprise, in itself an indication of the isolation of the Abruzzo, a dusty car bearing an English number-plate standing outside the hotel. Later, I met an Englishman and his wife who were motoring home through Italy and France after a holiday in Sorrento. They told me they had made a détour to see the women of Scanno in their gorgeous costumes. Such pilgrimages are caused by out-of-date information in guidebooks and by the romantic haze in which the compilers of tourist literature are obliged to exist. When I told him that he would see no gorgeous costumes, the couple seemed annoyed, and the woman produced some postcards in colour.

'Oh, but they *must* be visible!' she said. 'I bought these in the hotel.'

I told her that the sight of a camera is enough to send the old women in black scurrying into archways and vanishing from balconies, even in their working attire, and I suggested that the beautiful postcards had been made by a photographer who had brought a model or a good-looking wife or daughter with him. Such cynicism seemed faintly outrageous to the Englishwoman, and she produced in support of her argument the 1962 edition of Baedeker's *Touring Guide to Italy*, in which we read that 'the women wear a curiously severe costume and sit on the floor in church, in Oriental style'. On Sunday morning we attended the eleven o'clock Mass in the hope of witnessing this scene, but, instead, found the church full of old women in black with coloured head-scarves, all sitting on benches. But they did sit on the floor as recently as 1913, when Estella Canziani described them.

'In church they always sit cross-legged,' she wrote, 'only instead of being on the ground they balance on their ankles and lean their elbows on their knees, and in their houses they usually sit like this without using chairs.'

Shortly after the English couple had departed a wedding reception was held in the hotel, or rather a wedding luncheon which continued into the late afternoon. I hoped that at last I should see Scannese womanhood in their regional costumes, but save for one little old lady everyone wore modern clothes. The bride, a powerfully built girl whose fairy godmother was absent when the dangerous gift of beauty might have been bestowed, had been pressed into a white wedding dress: the bridegroom, a man of mature years and, I was told, a bureaucrat, wore hired morning dress. The old lady who was wearing regional dress had the appearance of having strayed into a commonplace gathering from an age of leisure and elegance. She wore upon her head, above a white-frilled cap, the kind of peaked hat which Mary Stuart wears in most of her portraits; her dark dress had large puff sleeves; she wore a decorative apron and upon her feet were black shoes with steel buckles. A feature of the feast was a gigantic white cake which, contrary to the usual custom, was never cut. After interminable speeches, the party converged upon a small berib-boned car. There was an orgy of kissing during which the bride-groom kissed the priest twice, and I thought, as the newly-married couple disappeared round the lake, that a sensible financial trans-action had been arranged which would probably turn out at least as well as a union founded on passion. When Ubaldi dined with me we sat in an otherwise empty room facing a fine television set which was switched on for our benefit. We had lake trout, followed by *pollo diavolo*, and we drank a jug of honest red wine. His father had emigrated to America, where his brother had been born, and his great desire was to go to a land which so many Italians think of as *el dorado* – the golden. He had been haunted towards the end of the war, when he was in the army, by the thought that he might be ordered to fire upon or fling a grenade at an American. 'It might have been my brother,' he said. There was something of the horror of civil war in this divided loyalty.

It was strange to sit in this once remote place and watch a sophisticated floor show beamed from Milan or Rome. There were girls dressed chiefly in ostrich feathers, and the usual songs and jokes. I wondered what the old women in black thought about it, if they were watching. Did they enjoy it or did they look upon the dancers as something from a world stranger and more macabre than the world of wizards, soothsayers and werewolves into which they had been born?

I asked my acquaintance whether country people had forsaken their superstitions with the coming of the bus service, the chair-lift and television. He lit a cigarette and hesitated before he replied. 'It takes more than that to change the mental background of centuries. Of course, their lives are still largely ruled by superstition. I don't say that everyone believes in *lupi minnari* (werewolves), but if anyone met a strange man in peculiar circumstances in a lonely place on a winter's night, it is highly probable that the idea of a *lupo minnaro* would flash into his mind. Everyone, of course, believes in omens, and quite a lot of people are celebrated as fortune-tellers – witches, if you like. And everyone wears amulets to ward off the Evil Eye. I have one myself.' He produced a ring with his car keys on it from which dangled a small red hand, the fingers making the sign that wards off the Evil Eye.

We talked of the Marsi and their reputation for magic which was mentioned by Ovid, Horace and Pliny, and other ancient writers; and I brought up the subject of snake-charming.

'There's still plenty of that,' he replied. 'The whole of the Abruzzi is full of *serpari*, serpent men who have power over snakes and believe themselves immune to snake venom and to possess power to cure those who have been poisoned.'

'Just like the ancient Marsi?'

'The same. But you can see this for yourself next Thursday, which is the first Thursday in May when the *festa* of S. Domenico is held at Cocullo. This is a village about twelve miles away. If you go there, you will see the statue of the saint, covered with live snakes, carried in procession through the streets.'

§ 9

I rose early on Thursday and was soon on my way to Cocullo. It was a sweet May morning, the vines, like fingers in green gloves, were sprouting on the sloping hills; the lake of Scanno, a mile-long sheet of blue, reflected the mountains, and where the water ended, the beautiful gorge of the Sagittario began. I recollected it as a lonely pass save for the odd lorry or two, but now I passed cars, a few motor coaches and farm carts, all on their way to the *festa* of S. Domenico. The pilgrims of the Abruzzo no longer

36

march on foot, led by someone carrying a wooden cross: they travel in vans, cars and coaches.

In Scanno I had heard a great deal about S. Domenico. His memory is revered there as elsewhere in the Abruzzo and even farther afield. He has no connection with the founder of the Dominican Order but was a Benedictine monk, born at Foligno in A.D. 951, who spent a wandering life, travelling on muleback from place to place, founding a monastery, then moving on, doing good and occasionally performing a miracle. His mule understood him perfectly. It is related that one day, having begged a smith to shoe the animal 'for the love of God', the holy man was reviled by the smith, who demanded money. S. Domenico, who was penniless, then ordered the mule to return the shoes, which it did by shaking them off, nails and all. One of the shoes is among the most revered possessions of Cocullo. It is said to confer upon men and animals immunity from hydrophobia, and the shepherds of the Abruzzo still take their big white sheepdogs to the church, where the shoe is produced and a prayer is said over them.

Another prized relic of S. Domenico is a tooth which, it is said, the saint himself removed and left as a gift to the people of Cocullo. Now enclosed in a silver reliquary, it confers relief from toothache, and today, when the dentist visits a mountain village perhaps once a week or a fortnight, it is consulted almost as often, as it was in the Middle Ages. S. Domenico's third gift, safety from snake-bite, is certainly a survival of ancient Marsican practice, and the annual display of snakes, which I was on my way to witness, is really a pagan festival which, like so many others, has been incorporated into the festivals of the Church.

Round a bend of the mountain road I came in sight of Cocullo clustered upon its hill, white, picturesque and shining in the sun. I managed to park in the piazza among coaches, farm wagons and bicycles. A noisy fair was in progress. Crowds, mostly of villagers, had come from near and far and during the whole day I never heard a word of English. Two *carabinieri* in dress uniform, red cockades in their Napoleonic hats, cotton-gloved hands folded on sword hilts, stood in a little island of official calm while the excited crowds circulated round them.

Motor vans from Aquila or Sulmona, filled with clothes, furniture, pottery, eatables, farm implements, and plastic goods of every kind, also hundreds of the splendid copper pans and water-pots of Aquila, had been unloaded and their contents displayed on trestle tables, some beneath canvas awnings. In the shade of a tree, upon a butcher's table, lay that mediaeval presence at every Italian fair, *porchetta*, a roast pig complete with head, stuffed with rosemary and other herbs, and sold in slices between thick wedges of bread.

The unassisted voices of the cheapjacks are no longer heard at country fairs; instead, loud-speakers mounted on motor vans relay their patter in hideously magnified form, each shouting voice competing in a babel of sound whose combined effect destroys whatever sales effect was intended. The crowd was dressed in modern clothes. The men wore dark suits or grey trousers, and tweed jackets; the women were in suits or nylon dresses, though a number of those timeless old women in black, their heads in shawls, were present with their grandchildren, camped out on steps and handing out salami and bread from capacious plastic bags. While I was admiring a group that Rembrandt might have sketched, the old faces seamed by sixty or more years of labour and poverty, yet dignified by prayer and faith, I noticed my first *serparo*. He was a shock-headed young man who stood with his back to me, his hands clasped behind him. It was an unexpected movement which drew my eyes to him: the writhing of a large yellow snake which was coiled round his wrists. He was holding it as someone might hold a rosary behind his back and play with the beads. In the same way his fingers caressed the snake. The narrow head of the reptile emerged from his sleeve and moved from side to side in that repellant motion which is believed to hypnotize birds or small animals. I followed the young man into the crowd, where he joined a group of three *serpari* who were engaged in draping snakes round the shoulders of several small boys. The children endured the ordeal with unsmiling fortitude and the *serpari* were equally grave, as if investing the boys with some sacred emblem; indeed the curious scene had the air of an initiation rite. A fifth *serparo*, who wore a huge blackish snake draped round his shoulders, came up and transferred the reptile to the shoulders of a boy and tried to persuade him to nip the snake firmly three inches below its head and breathe at it. He demonstrated this act, but the child would not play. The *serparo* slung the snake round his own neck and wandered off.

The road to the Sanctuary of S. Domenico was by way of a steep street crowded with visiting peasants who passed down towards the church between the outstretched hands of cripples and deformed people. Many were better dressed than those who gave them money. A fortune-teller with a green Amazon parrot perched on a scarlet cage did a brisk business. The bird would climb upon the finger of its owner and, after cocking an old and malicious eye at the client, would select with its beak a small folded slip of paper. This was, of course, divination by *sortes,* well known in ancient Greece and in Rome, though the diviner was usually a child of tender years and not an old bird of dubious innocence. However, I was unable to resist the oracle. The beak appeared to sway uncertainly for a moment over the folded slips, then with the utmost neatness the bird picked out one and dropped it into my hand. I had no time to read my fortune then, so slipped it into my pocket.

I went on down to the church, where High Mass was about to begin. The building was packed. I managed to squeeze my way in and I saw, near the centre of the church, the statue of S. Domenico, almost life-size, already mounted upon its platform, ready to be carried in procession. The statue looked to me like a good seventeenth-century carving of a bearded man with a halo, dressed in a black robe and holding in his right hand a crozier and in his left the revered mule shoe. There was constant movement round him as the devout passed before him, to touch him and convey the touch to their lips, to kneel and often to attach a thousand lire note to the image. Nearby hung a rope attached to a bell which the peasants pulled, some with their hands, some with their teeth. I had been told about this in Scanno. It was an act which was believed to immunize them from toothache. I stood wedged in the crowd, unable to move as Mass began. Suddenly I became aware of a curious creepy feeling near my legs and, looking for an explanation, found that I was standing pressed against a sack of snakes which a *serparo* was holding. There was constant muscular writhing then a sudden strong upheaval which suggested unpleasantly that the reptiles were fighting. Unable to endure this, I managed to insinuate myself foot by foot towards the doors of the church and so gained the open air. Stalls stood outside loaded with brilliant tawdries, among them hundreds of charms against the Evil Eye. The most popular was the closed fist with the two pointing fingers and a little curved object which represented an oxhorn, both made of red plastic to imitate coral. Walking up to the piazza, I bought some *porchetta* and, returning, ate it with the help of an astonished ginger kitten seated on the steps of an old, deserted building near the church. While I waited, the village band, wearing peaked caps with gold braid, drifted down to the church in ones and twos; then came a charming addition to the ceremony. Five young girls in regional dress, one fair and the others dark, descended the street between the old houses followed by two young women dressed in well-pressed coats and skirts of salmon-pink linen and bearing upon their heads draped baskets containing the huge circular loaves of bread common in country villages and towns, evidently a memory of some festival of Ceres. Gradually all the *serpari* assembled outside the church with their snakes. There were perhaps fifteen or twenty of them.

The church bell began to ring. The town band formed up and broke into a lively march tune. Suddenly, framed against the arch of the church door, we saw the statue of S. Domenico come slanting into the sunlight. Instantly twenty or thirty snakes were tossed up to the saint by the *serpari*. Many of the reptiles wrapped their coils round the statue and remained fixed there, some even climbing up to his halo, a sight that appeared to shock the spectators on the balconies, while screams from the crowd indicated that snakes which had missed the target were trying to escape. These were pursued by the *serpari*, caught by their tails and again swung through the air. By the time S. Domenico was ascending the street to the piazza he was wearing a thick muffler of coiled serpents that concealed his mouth, while tails and heads wavered and flickered all round him. The priestesses of Ceres with their bread led the way; then came a priest carrying S. Domenico's tooth in a silver reliquary. There was certainly an air of pagan frenzy about the ceremony and I thought that, could one have replaced the reach-me-downs with garments more suitable to the strange spectacle, this annual progress would have appeared wild and even alarming.

The saint was carried to every corner of Cocullo. When a snake dropped off a *serparo* immediately picked it up and threw it back. The ceremony over, each *serparo* collected his snakes, but how they knew which was which, I cannot say, and once again draped them over their shoulders and packed them into sacks.

I had a word with the parish priest, who insisted that I should have lunch with him. I had already eaten *porchetta* and bread and cheese, and would gladly have fasted until the following day, but he was so polite and so insistent that I felt it might be ill-mannered to refuse. However, I thought that a frugal repast in the priest's house would be easy to manage. Little did I know what was in store for me. His reverence led the way through the crowds to one of the better houses in the village where, in a large cool room upon the second floor, a long table had been set for what was obviously an annual feast. An elderly, twinkling monsignore, and two priests who had celebrated the High Mass, were already present, looking ravenous. I was introduced to the devout matron who had prepared the feast, and, to my embarrassment, was placed at the head of the table. Then followed what to my repleted senses seemed the largest meal I had ever seen. Sumptuous antipasti of a variety and ingenuity one never sees in any restaurant were followed by soup, which was followed by roast chicken, which was followed by boiled chicken, which was followed by lamb, and then came puddings, custards, jellies and other sweets. The matron waited upon us, bending tenderly over the monsignore and the priests, while I did my best to deflect attention from my plate.

Fortunately, as the priests were hungry, there was no need for much conversation, but afterwards, as we drank coffee and exchanged snuff-boxes, I mentioned S. Domenico and the scene we had just witnessed. I could sense that the holy men considered me a bore as I, in their position, might also have done. Like a loyal parish priest, the *Parroco* stood up valiantly for S. Domenico and said how wonderful were the benefits he had conferred upon Cocullo. The other priests nodded in agreement and allowed their glasses to be refilled. They also agreed, though it seemed a trifle reluctantly, perhaps aware of other pagan inclinations among their flocks, that the snakes represent an annual offering to the Marsican goddess Angitia which the Church had adopted, but the subject was clearly one that did not interest them. However, to put the matter on the highest level, I suggested that perhaps Gregory the Great was responsible for the wise policy of adopting what you cannot prevent when he wrote to Mellitus, the first Bishop of London, and told him not to destroy the shrines of the Angli but to convert them into Christian altars. This seemed to invest the adoption of Angitia's serpents by S. Domenico with the highest authority; and we all allowed our glasses to be refilled.

As we parted, the *Parroco* gave me a pamphlet which he had written on the *Vita di S. Domenico Abate, Protettore di Cocullo*, in which the good man still further backed up his saint, expressing a sense of wonder and gratitude that, through him, Cocullo should have been protected against snake-bite, toothache and hydrophobia. Of this last, he had an extraordinary story. He writes that a few years ago, during the winter when Cocullo was deep in snow, the village was invaded by terrified visitors who arrived by motor and train. They were almost the total population of the village of Giuliano di Roma, including invalids and even paralytics. It appeared that they had all drunk milk from a cow which had been bitten by a rabid dog and had journeyed at once to seek the protection of S. Domenico. The Sacrament was administered to them in the church, in their cars and, to some who were unable to walk to the village, in the waiting-room at the station. 'By the Grace of God and the intercession of S. Domenico,' concludes the priest, 'and also because of the great faith of these people, nobody

suffered from the milk they had drunk.' A veterinary surgeon
later told me that it would have been astonishing had they done so.

The priest also tells the story of some huntsmen from Sora who
brought six dogs to be touched by the mule's shoe. The animals
had been fighting with rabid dogs and were almost uncontrollable
until they reached the Roccione near Cocullo, when they became
quiet and were led easily to the Sanctuary where each one was
touched by the relic. Presumably the animals suffered no ill
effects, though this is not stated.

After a journey over mountain roads I reached Sulmona in the
dark. On the perimeter of the town I found an hotel which offered
me a bedroom and private bathroom. Before I went to bed I came
across the slip of paper which had been given to me by the
oracular parrot. This is what I read: 'If you do not wish to have
trouble with people, mind your own business and think before
speaking. Persist and do not be afraid. Destiny has endowed you
with a practical genius for business and you must take advantage
of it. Persevere and you will prevail. Don't be so wrapped up in
yourself and so reserved. Beware of a friend whom you have
helped in the past. He is ungrateful and malicious and threatens to
ruin you.'

A cynical bird!

§ 10

Ovid, Sulmona's most famous son, is commemorated by a
statue in the main piazza. The poet, wearing a toga, gazes down
pensively upon the modern inhabitants, who may read upon the
plinth, 'Sulmo mihi patria est', a famous sentence whose initial
letters have been adopted as the town's motto. The searcher may
discover old and cruder versions of Ovid; one, built into a shop
front near the piazza, and another in the courtyard of S. Maria
Annunziata, perhaps the finest fourteenth century building in the
Abruzzi, which depicts him with the air of a mediaeval saint. The
main street of Sulmona is called the Corso Ovidio until it becomes

43

transformed at its extremity into the Viale Roosevelt, thus surprisingly linking the author of *The Art of Love* with the American Presidency.

Ovid's fame rather than his works are revered in his native town, and in the popular imagination much the same reputation for sorcery surrounds his memory, a relic of the Middle Ages, as that which haunted the name of Virgil in Mantua.

I thought Sulmona a pleasant town. At one end was an enormous market place and at the other the cathedral, and in between was a network of interesting old streets and houses from whose balconies women drape bedding and shout exhortations to their children. In the main street I saw a shop which sells exile. The lack of industrial employment in the Abruzzi has made the region, together with Calabria, a recruiting ground for factory labour and also for overseas emigration. Everywhere I had noticed the absence of young men in the mountain villages. It is the accepted custom for them to leave home, sometimes for ever, or perhaps to return in middle or old age to be known as 'Americani', even though they may have spent their working lives in New Zealand or Australia. The word *Emigrazione* was written large upon a banner in the shop window, which displayed an uninviting introduction to a change of country, hideous carved Maori heads with tufts of hair upon them. The chief attaction was a scale model of an airliner, which implied that the modern emigrant no longer has to endure the traditional ocean voyage in the steerage, but flies off like a migratory bird to alight in a matter of hours or days in his adopted country.

My first impression of Sulmona, as of Aquila, was of disciplined children. A walk before breakfast revealed little boys and girls in black smocks, and an older generation with books under their arms, all gravely on their way to school. I went into the cathedral to find that the custom of dropping in before school to say a prayer or a 'Hail Mary' was as well observed as at Aquila. Sulmona's saint is Pamphilus, of whom I know nothing except that he is not the celebrated Pamphilus of Caesarea but a saint of the same name who performed miracles in the Sulmona district more than twelve centuries ago. Descending into the crypt to see his burial place, I came upon a strange scene. It is a dark place upheld by many columns and, as I stood concealed behind one of these, I noticed a procession of schoolgirls, each child carrying her books or a satchel, making for the ancient marble throne of the bishop that stands to the east of the saint's tomb. Solemnly, handing her books to a friend to hold for her, each child, after seating herself in the bishop's throne, placed her hands upon two polished black stones that decorate the arms. Having done so, she immediately gave up her seat to the next girl; and so on until each child had occupied the seat.

This unusual little ceremony, which was conducted with the solemnity of a rite, lingered in my memory all day, and I asked a native of the town if he knew of it. 'Oh yes,' he replied, 'that has been going on for centuries. It brings good luck, especially at school examinations.'

Sulmona is renowned for an unusual industry, the making of *confetti*, or sugared almonds, which come in bulk from Sicily and are sugared and coloured in Sulmona and exported to every part of Italy. As no Italian wedding would be complete without *confetti*, which represent the nuts which were strewn before the bridal pair in ancient Rome, the trade is a large one. Among the leading artists in *confetti* is Signor William de Carlo, an interpreter to the Royal Air Force in the last war, who treasures a file of letters from friends in the allied forces, escaped allied prisoners and others whom he had met at that time. I watched girls in his factory near the station as they heated wires over methylated flames and pierced sugared almonds, deftly manufacturing six-petalled flowers, each petal an almond, some flowers white, some pink, and some blue, each with centres of silvered sweets.

These surprising confections resemble in appearance the sprays and baskets of artificial flowers which the Victorians placed beneath domes of glass. I suppose people must eventually eat them, though only the most severe pangs of hunger would persuade me to do so. Among the most realistic of Signor de Carlo's creations are sheaves of corn and maize made of almonds and sweets. There is something Byzantine or possibly Moorish-Byzantine in these pleasing compositions and I wondered whether, like the almonds themselves, the art of floral composition had come to the Abruzzo from Sicily. But Signor de Carlo traces the art no further back than his grandmother, who, it seems, had a reputation as an arranger of flowers in the convent where she was educated and decided to carry out the same compositions in sweetmeats. But the *confetti* industry must have been established in Sulmona long before, since Keppel Craven, who was there in the early years of the last century, mentions it.

Signor de Carlo took me to the Roman ruin which for no reason, except that it is Roman and is a ruin, is known as the Villa of Ovid. Crossing the little river Gizio on one of those warm afternoons in spring which often precedes rain, we made for the lower slopes of Monte Morrone. My companion pointed out to me, high on the mountain, a building which he said was the abbey of S. Spirito, founded in the thirteenth century by Celestine V, the hermit Pope whose tomb I had seen in Aquila. The building is now empty save for a caretaker who descends into Sulmona at intervals to buy groceries, and then returns to his hermitage.

The Celestine Order has had an unfortunate history. Its monks, who followed the rule of S. Benedict, and were known as Celestinians, were obliged to fly to Greece after the Pope's abdication to escape from the persecution of his successor, Boniface VIII. The Order perished in Germany during the Reformation and died out in France in 1766, but it lingered until a little later in Italy. It is curious how often the snake appears in the affairs of the Abruzzi. The Celestinians selected as their emblem a black serpent coiled round a white cross.

We descended a steep goat track on the slope of the mountain. The wild flowers shook with bees and the air was filled with the smell of wild thyme and other herbs which grow so lavishly in the Abruzzo mountains. Though no longer famous for the making of magic potions, they are still the basis of a liqueur made near by and known all over Italy, *Centerbe*. At a point in our descent the whole vale of Sulmona came into view, watered by the streams which Ovid remembered so lovingly during his exile by the

Black Sea. An ugly and incoherent mass of buildings with the unmistakable gauntness of a prison caught my eye.

'In the first war,' said Signor de Carlo, 'the English imprisoned German officers there and in the second war the process was reversed. The place is still a gaol. Many an allied officer escaped from that building and took to the mountains, and some have returned to Sulmona to find the families which hid and protected them.' We continued our descent between hot rocks where butterflies flickered above poppies and where green lizards froze in their crevices as we approached. We came at last to an imposing flight of seven or eight steps leading to a Roman pavement and the foundation walls of a large building. Though Ovid sprang from a well-to-do country family, the remains of his 'Villa' looked to me more like a public building than a country house.

'Some who have studied the site,' said Signor de Carlo, 'think that the building was probably a temple of Hercules. There was once a phallic sign which was in favour with women who had difficulty in starting a family, but it has been removed; at any rate, I can't find it. It used to be here on this step.'

Even should this not be Ovid's paternal villa, the scene that unfolds itself is that described by the poet in his homesickness. It is not really correct to say that he was exiled. His punishment, for an offence which is still a mystery, was known as *relegatio*, which meant compulsory residence in a distant place, but with no confiscation of property or fortune and no surrender of *civitas*. Ovid was fifty when he offended the Emperor Augustus, and he was fated to spend the last ten years of his life at Tomi (which he always called Tomis), by the Black Sea; it is now Constanta, in Rumania. Ovid detested the place and complained bitterly of the cold, indeed he continued to describe in his poems a land of perpetual winter where men's beards were frozen and even the wine was solid. Friends who have been to Constanta tell me that Ovid is still present in bronze in the main square. Years ago I arrived in Constantinople during a snowstorm and was persuaded to travel up the Bosphorus to the opening to the Black Sea, where a flurry of sleet and a wind pierced me to the spine, and told me that Ovid had not exaggerated the rigours of winter, as some scholars have suggested, in the hope that his poems might soften the hearts of those in Rome who had the power to recall him to civilization. Seated upon the steps of the supposed villa, Signor de Carlo and I wondered, as so many have done, what offence Ovid had committed, and I asked if Sulmona had any theories in addition to those so often put forward. No, his fellow townsmen know only the usual supposition: that he had seen the Empress Livia in her bath, which we both dismissed as absurd; that Augustus had punished him for the immoral influence of *The Art of Love* (which incidentally had been published almost ten years before); that the poet had been associated with the immoralities of the emperor's granddaughter, Julia, who was banished to a lonely island at much the same time; that he had been implicated in a plot against Augustus. Signor de Carlo wisely observed that when a man's actions appear mysterious, it is not a bad idea to examine his wife's hatreds. Possibly Livia had many an old score to settle with Ovid and was able to do so when the emperor in his old age was under her control.

On our way down from the Villa we came to a washing-place called the Fountain of Love. Two village women had just lifted their laundry baskets to their heads and were preparing to depart. Signor de Carlo asked why it was called the Fountain of Love, to which one replied that 'Viddio', an affectionate local name for Ovid, was in the habit of making love there to a fairy, perhaps his Egeria, or maybe the spirit of the water. The other woman, with an air of greater historical accuracy, said that Ovid had made love to the emperor's wife there and had been banished to Sicily. So after nineteen centuries the poet's sin and punishment still linger in the minds of the peasantry of his own Sulmona.

§ 11

The heat vanished in the night and the uncertain mountain weather changed to a thin drizzle, until the Abruzzo began to resemble Scotland. I set off on a Sunday morning to go south from Sulmona, clouds piling up above the mountains, rain falling now and again, and a bitter wind blowing from the last of the snow. I had heard so much of the beauties and peculiarities of a little town called Pescocostanzo that I decided to go there. A bitterly cold mist concealed the landscape, every now and then blowing aside to reveal a white mountainside tilted against the sky. When I arrived I found the place deserted, like an old town under a spell. No one was to be seen. I ascended a long flight of steps and entered, beneath a Norman arch, the church of S. Maria del Colle, where candles were burning before a number of altars; still not a person to be seen.

On the outskirts of the town I found an hotel which displayed a stuffed wildcat snarling in a window, a doubtful welcome which appeared to be borne out when I entered and found no one about and the chairs piled on the tables in the dining-room. There were sounds from the kitchen where a pleasant woman who was cooking spaghetti told me that the place was really closed, the winter sports season having ended and the summer season still to come. However, if I did not mind the cold, for the radiators were not working, I was welcome to some spaghetti. I sat near the wildcat wearing my overcoat. Here I was joined by a jolly red-faced little manager, who told me in a wonderful mixture of English that he had spent two years in Manchester and Liverpool. He produced a bottle of strong dark Sicilian wine which helped to restore my circulation while we talked about Manchester. I was grateful, but I thought how much better things were in earlier times when a cold traveller, arriving at an inn, could be instantly warmed with an armful of brushwood that would send a blazing fire roaring up the chimney; but in these days of central heating there are no fireplaces and one must just sit and freeze.

The rain fell depressingly as I continued, concealing what I felt sure was a superb view of the mountains. I came to a lively Sunday afternoon fair in the mountain town of Rianero Sannitico, where both sides of the main street were lined with copper pots and the usual stalls of clothing, food, and farm implements. A crowd of mountain people filled the street, talking and laughing, and with the rain still falling and mist shrouding the town, nothing less like one's idea of Italy could be imagined. I watched a group of farmers' wives testing the edges of sickles with their thumbs before buying them, and I selected for myself two little charms against the Evil Eye.

Peering into the mist, I descended bit by bit towards Molise and came in the later afternoon to Campobasso, a town of some thirty thousand people, where, unexpectedly and delightfully, the sun was shining. How does one account for the feeling of well-being and contentment roused sometimes by the first glimpse of a place which one has never seen before? Immediately I had un-packed in a good solid old-fashioned hotel in the centre of the town (the proprietor had welcomed me in the hall and had hoped I would like his hotel), I felt cheerful and knew that I was going to enjoy Campobasso. Almost next to the hotel was a cinema which advertised the *prima visione* of *Mary Poppins*, one of my favourite films. The possibility of seeing it in Italian was irresistible. Near by was a first-rate bookshop which was run by people who under-stand books. I began to like Campobasso more and more.

The town is grouped round a hill upon which rises an ancient castle, impressive to look at but of no interest except as a high place from which to enjoy the gentle curves of Molise, so different from the jagged outlines of the Abruzzo. A large proportion of the knives, penknives and scissors of Italy are made in the Campobasso district and many of them bear the name of the town, though most of them are manufactured a few miles away at the small town of Frosinone.

I enjoyed every moment of *Mary Poppins*, but to see it in Italian is to realize how English the film is! The audience reaction was surprising in a country where children are adored. The en-thusiasm I had expected was absent. I concluded that as most of the fun is aimed at a materialistic father who cannot see the magic that surrounds him, the Italian sense of family had been offended. You must not make fun of father!

§ 12

One of the most romantic ruins to be seen in Italy lies in a tangle of country lanes ten miles from Campobasso. It is practically unknown and its name is Saepinum. It was a Roman provincial town that managed to survive until the ninth century. I had been impressed by some photographs I had seen of it in Campobasso, but looking up the map reference I saw that it was not going to be easy to find and thought I would start early and take some sandwiches and a bottle of Montepulciano d'Abruzzo, an excellent garnet-red wine.

Driving into a remote and attractive countryside, I saw hills covered with purple clover which gave the impression of heather, and here I came upon one of the strangest of processions. About a hundred peasants, all the women in brilliant regional dress, were solemnly walking down the lane ahead of me. I thought at first that it must be a saint's day or perhaps a wedding, yet something about the bearing of these people ruled that out. Leaving the lane, they turned aside to mount a hill track where they gave an even more impressive idea of a mediaeval crowd in movement. I asked a woman who had come out of her house to watch, where they were going. To view 'Il Morto,' she replied. So they were going in their best clothes to pay their respects to a friend who had died.

I went on and came at length to Saepinum. Here is a small Pompeii, a Roman town with most of its wall upstanding, its main street and triumphal arch complete, a temple with all its marble columns erect, the foundations of hundreds of houses and a wide paved forum. Across this wonderful ruin passed from time to time herds of cows, men riding donkeys, and old women carrying scythes. They all used the wide paved main street of the Roman town. I selected a shady spot in the forum where I sat, astonished to see in modern Italy a ruin just as our ancestors of the eighteenth century saw one, as part of an agricultural landscape. I was reminded of an etching by Piranesi, a water-colour by Samuel Prout, or a drawing by van Heemskerck. Here was a perfect romantic ruin of the eighteenth century, wild flowers growing in the foundations of the houses, goats cropping grass in the streets, girls wearing men's boots clumping down a lane and suddenly appearing with a herd of cows upon the Via Triumphalis.

Seated upon a large stone in the forum, with another as a table, I unwrapped my sandwiches and opened the wine. It is a rare experience to have a ruin to oneself. No one gave me a glance as he passed except a poor hungry bitch whose ribs were distressingly visible. She crept forward bit by bit until she was bold enough to accept a sandwich. After that she would not leave me, and not only finished the crusts but also drove off with unexpected strength and fury another dog which thought it might be a good idea to join us. A man wearing a peaked cap arrived, saying that he was the superintendent of antiquities. I suggested that he should drink a glass of wine. He went off and returned with a cup. He told me that nothing ever happened here, nevertheless it was his duty to see that no damage was done to any of the ancient stones. He thought I was was an American and asked me questions about life and money in America; when I told him I was not an American he was incredulous and disappointed. He took me to a small house among the ruins where for greater safety he had gathered any carved stone, even one with a letter of the alphabet upon it; but I could see nothing of much interest.

We walked round the ruins where he pointed out, above the eastern gate, an inscription much worn by time and illegible to me, which he said referred to the annual migration of sheep in Roman times from the plain of Apulia to the mountains. He had heard professors say that the inscription was an order to the magistrates of Saepinum commanding them to protect the shepherds and their flocks as they passed through the town on their way to the *tratturi*. He told me that the paved roadway from the east gate to the west gate was regarded as a sheep walk and was used as such in Roman times, and that even today one could often see shepherds leading their sheep along the old road towards the Monti del Matese.

I should think that this association of a Roman town with the *tratturi* must be unique. So far as I know, the only Roman author who mentions the migration is Varro, who, writing about thirty years before Christ, said that his sheep wintered in Apulia and spent the summer in the mountains. Maybe Varro's sheep sometimes passed through Saepinum.

The modern custom of sending sheep to the mountains in lorries has detracted from an annual sight that must have been magnificent. As in Spain, where ancient sheepways ninety feet wide on each side of highways lead to summer pastures, the Italian *tratturi* are a series of mountain paths used only by thousands of sheep in the first weeks of summer. I have read descriptions of the migration as it was in quite recent times when the *tratturi* were covered for miles with thousands of sheep, about twelve abreast, moving in a slow wave of grey wool across the mountain tracks, each division led by its shepherd grasping his crook and attended by his white dogs. They wore spiked collars to protect them from wolves. As long as it was daylight these dogs were friendly, but the moment night fell they became savage guardians. Each shepherd, as he led his flock, was followed by an old ram called *il manso*, which means gentle, or, in shepherd language, trained; in other words a reliable old bellwether. So this ancient procession, as well known to the Romans as to us, would pass across the landscape.

I must say that I felt sympathy for the people of Saepinum whose main street, from east to west, was liable to be invaded by thousands of bleating sheep and barking dogs, and I do not understand why the town could not have been by-passed. The guardian said that he did not know but would ask the next group of professors. I lingered in this lovely spot until late in the afternoon, watching men come along the Roman road, riding mules and donkeys, hoping, but in vain, to see a flock of sheep with their shepherd. The guardian asked me to return some day when he would show me the remains of a theatre outside the walls, and, handing me two letters, asked if I would post them for him when I came to a post office.

# CHAPTER TWO

*The Gargano Peninsula – the sacred cavern of St Michael – Padre Pio –*
*A visit to S. Giovanni Rotondo – the life of a modern saint – how Padre*
*Pio received the Stigmata – his reputed miracles – his accessibility – the*
*La Guardia Hospital*

When I left the heights of the Abruzzi in the late afternoon I saw before me the northern plain of Apulia. I
saw it with pleasure and with a sense of physical
relief, for motoring in mountainous country is a strain upon the
nerves of anyone who still clings to life. The Plain of Capitanata is
a name I have never before encountered, though it may have
existed in other parts of the world which were once subjected to
Byzantine administration, since it recalls the title of the Catapan,
the official who ruled Apulia under the eastern emperors.

It is always exciting to stand upon the threshold of a land one
has read about but has never visited. Will it be disappointing? How
will it differ from one's preconceived notion of it, and which of
the books one has read will stand up best to one's own experiences?
At first glance Apulia surprised me. I had expected a desert.
Every time Horace mentioned Apulia, he referred to it as 'dry' or
'thirsty'; but I saw a well-watered plain stretching away into the
distance, golden with miles of wheat and other grain, with orchards and grazing land. It was intersected by roads as straight as
any familiar to the legions. I was soon to learn that the transformation of Apulia dates only from 1939 when the Apulian
Aqueduct, which took thirty years to construct and is the largest
in Europe, was finally completed and began to pour its life-giving
streams down the eastern slopes of the Apennines into every
corner of the once thirsty land. It was a peaceful scene. The smoke
of distant towns lay in the air. Upon the horizon was an added
brilliance which I knew to be the Adriatic Sea.

If the shape of Italy is to be compared to that of a riding-boot with its toe pointed to the west, the region of Apulia is the heel, its north-eastern portion washed by the Adriatic and its southern by the Ionian Sea. Today the region consists of five provinces: Bari, whose chief city is also the regional capital; Foggia; Brindisi; Lecce; and Taranto. These five provinces suggest varied historical backgrounds: Bari, which reveres the bones of St Nicholas, stolen by its mariners from Asia Minor in 1087; Foggia, which the Emperor Frederick II loved; Brindisi, where the Appian Way ends above the sea; Lecce, 'the Florence of Baroque Art'; and Taranto, the Tarentum of pre-Christian times, founded by Spartan exiles and so commercially successful that its beautiful silver coinage, which depicted a man riding upon a dolphin, became currency all over the region.

Apulia is also the key to the understanding of Southern Italy. The events which shaped the destiny of the South, the creation of the Kingdom of Sicily and, later, the Kingdom of Naples, had their origins in Apulia. The most important event was the Norman Conquest, which began in the opening years of the eleventh century. William of Jumièges tells the story of a Norman knight who said to his overlord, 'I am very poor and in this country (Normandy) I cannot obtain relief; I will therefore go to Apulia where I may live more honourably.' 'Who advised you thus?' asked the lord. 'My poverty,' replied his vassal. Thus to Normans who lived in that small and dynamic state fifty years before the invasion of England, the land of promise was the South of Italy. Landless young men heard stories of the money to be made there, of the land to be acquired, of honours to be achieved; it was a country where counties, dukedoms, and possibly even kingdoms, might be the reward of luck and valour. The Norman adventurers found themselves in a paradise for mercenary soldiers: a country distracted by political chaos, Lombards fighting Byzantine Greeks, both fighting Saracens, and the fortunes of war offering brilliant prizes for the opportunist. Like the *condottieri* of the Renaissance, the Normans took full advantage of the situation; but there the resemblance ends. The *condottieri* rarely shed blood could they avoid it, while the Normans sought the forefront of the fray.

The first name which springs from the mists is that of an adventurer, Rainulf, who was granted land upon which he built and fortified the town of Aversa, near Naples, in 1027. This became a market for fighting men. It was not long before the mercenaries lost interest in fighting battles for other people and decided to conquer the country for themselves. The first family to make history was that of a modest knight, Tancred de Hauteville, who lived in the English-looking countryside south of Cherbourg called the Cotentin. He told his twelve sons that as he was unable to find an inheritance for more than one, the rest must seek their fortunes elsewhere. Aversa was, of course, their choice. It was to the Normans of that time what El Dorado was to the Spaniards of the sixteenth century.

First the three eldest sons left, then others went out to join them. The two who wrote their names in the history of Italy were Robert and Roger de Hauteville. It was 1057. Another nine years in Normandy and possibly both would have followed Duke William to England and would no doubt have founded families in surroundings far removed from the exotic, half-oriental splendours in which their ways were to be cast. Together, the brothers conquered Apulia and Calabria and, crossing the Straits of Messina, subdued Sicily. In the year 1130 Roger de Hauteville's son, Roger II, was crowned King of Sicily. His daughter Constance married the Emperor Henry VI and their son became Frederick II, Holy Roman Emperor, and 'The Wonder of the World' – according to his friends.

As one descends into Apulia it is interesting to contrast the two Norman invasions. The invasion of England, a planned military operation under the reigning Duke, masked as a dynastic struggle which had the approval of the Church; the invasion of Italy, the haphazard action of a number of individual fighting men in search of fortune. The first was soon over; the conquest of Southern Italy occupied the best part of a century.

Anyone who is familiar with the Norman churches and castles of England must enter Apulia with anticipation, eager to see their Italian counterparts and to find that the White Tower in London has Italian cousins. But for a slight variation in time the Roberts and Rogers, who wore silk garments embroidered with Cufic inscriptions, who maintained harems like Saracen emirs and strolled in their orange groves beside blue seas, might have joined the Williams and Henrys across the Channel and have written their names in Debrett.

I had been travelling for only a short distance along the road to Foggia when I saw ahead of me what I took to be a walled town on the top of a hill. As I drew nearer, I realized that this must be the castle of Lucera. Its size astonished me. I counted fifteen or twenty towers set at regular intervals in gigantic walls and I thought that one would be fortunate to walk round the castle in half an hour. The silence was absolute. There was not a person in sight and I thought castles and towns must have looked like this when stricken by plague or after having been sacked.

Though it was late afternoon and I had arranged to sleep in Foggia, I thought I would like to see the main gate and to return the following day. I found, however, that the road ended in a ravine; I tried another with the same result and saw the walls of creamy yellow stone towering above me, but inaccessible. A priest who was passing with some small boys pointed out another road that eventually led me to the entrance along an avenue lined with trees. As I stood impressed by the building, a small postern in the main gate creaked and there emerged a tall old man grasping a staff, who might have been the reincarnation of some Norman robber baron. He was above the average Italian height and had the blue eyes so often seen in this part of Italy. There was something warlike, or at least aggressive, in his appearance, an impression aided perhaps by his formidable staff and by the old pair of German field boots, or so they appeared, which he wore. He was the guardian. Observing me, his eyes glistened, not with avarice but with the gleam of a hunter who spies his prey, and he immediately opened the postern and motioned me inside. I followed the direction of his staff and looked round at a sight for which I was unprepared. The walls and their towers which from far off had promised an intact survival of the Middle Ages, now held only a tangle of briars and undergrowth. At first I was disappointed. I had hoped that Lucera might have shown me the kind of castles which

Frederick II had erected all over Southern Italy, and in their day notable for their splendour and their plumbing: with the exception of Lagopesole, the castle Lucera was the largest of them all. As I walked across grass whose roots sprang from shattered marble it occurred to me that one rarely nowadays sees a ruin which would be passed as genuine by Jeremiah or Ezekiel. Desolation has been made less abominable by archaeologists who have unearthed buried columns and have put them together again, but much of the South of Italy is still unexcavated, and it is still possible to see, as at Lucera and a dozen other places, how complete is the annihilation of Time, assisted of course by Man, who has been always willing to carry off a nice slab of marble for his pigsty.

Mistaking my reflections for disappointment, the guardian leant upon his staff as on a spear and launched into a long account of the life of Frederick II, which I was not at that moment anxious to hear. I would, however, have been grateful could he have shown me an authentic portrait or bust of Frederick. With his contemporary, S. Francis, he was the most remarkable man of his century, yet with all his brilliance one of history's splendid failures. How truly he proved Voltaire's epigram that the Holy Roman Empire was neither holy, Roman, nor an empire. In appearance Frederick was not heroic. He was of moderate height and was rather plump. His hair was perhaps not the true Hohenstaufen red, but auburn. In the Holy Land the Arabs looked with surprise at his beardless chin and said that he would not bring two hundred drachmas in the slave market. Still, a Holy Roman Emperor who could argue about philosophy in Arabic was worthy of respect, and so were his dignity, his friendliness and his love of knowledge.

Lucera, the town and its castle, was one of Frederick's most surprising achievements, and one almost inconceivable in the crusading age in which he lived. It caused a great outcry in the Christian world and gave his enemies in the Lateran welcome ammunition. Finding that his island of Sicily was terrorized by bands of Saracens who descended from the mountains to raid towns and villages and to rob travellers, Frederick solved the

problem in an original way. Instead of waging a war of extermination, he rounded up the Saracens and, as if they had been some
rare species of game which he had decided to introduce elsewhere,
transplanted them to the northern plain of Apulia.

The old Roman town of Lucera, once the key of Apulia, had
fallen into ruin. The emperor decided to move the few Christian
inhabitants and to build a Moslem city, transforming the old
cathedral into a mosque, to the scandal of his contemporaries.
Here in a short space of time he transported twenty thousand
Saracens who lived in religious freedom under their emir and
sheiks. The muezzins called to prayer from minarets erected by the
most Christian Emperor. The result had been foreseen by
Frederick, who knew the Arabs well and had spent his childhood
among them in Sicily. The inhabitants of Lucera conceived a
fanatical loyalty for their protector and from them he recruited
his famous Saracen bodyguard which attended him everywhere,
even to the Crusade. We tramped across the waste, the guardian
now and then thumping his staff on the ground to indicate a hollow
space beneath. 'Here is a passage that led down into the town,' he
said, 'but it is now closed up. Old men can remember, as boys,
crawling for a long way into it.'

We came to a place where stone pavements were visible under
the grass.

'Many Saracens are buried here,' he said.

This I doubted. Why should they have been buried within the
castle walls? What the castle did contain, of which there is now no
trace, was a church, workshops, armouries, a barracks, probably the
imperial treasury and Frederick's notorious harem. The papal
propagandists made much of this, though in secluding his women
Frederick was merely following the example of his Norman forebears in Sicily and, one might add, of many Norman knights of
the period in Spain and elsewhere, who gladly adopted some of
the fashions and habits of their enemies.

Frederick's passage from castle to castle, from Palermo through
the Calabrian mountains into Apulia, must have resembled the
progress of Barnum and Bailey. The imperial elephant had been
taught to bear the standard of the Hohenstaufen; the imperial

treasure was carried upon the backs of camels and dromedaries; the covered litters of the harem were guarded by mounted archers of the Saracen guard; the emperor's hawks and hounds travelled like Princes, and so did the hunting leopards, riding on horseback behind their keepers. A similar progress was painted upon the walls of the Medici chapel in Florence by Benozzo Gozzoli, but Frederick's processions took place two and a half centuries before the Renaissance and reflected the half oriental life of the most luxurious and civilized court in Europe.

I reached Foggia in the dusk, a surprisingly large and bustling city full of cafés and restaurants and a great many paper mills, some run by the State, which seemed to be appropriate in an age of bureaucracy. I chose what appeared to be the best restaurant and ordered a pleasant dinner. Of all the regions in Italy, Apulia is the one most celebrated for shellfish. The *ragazzino* of mussels was delicious, so was the *scaloppina al Marsala,* which was followed by a selection of local sheep and goats' milk cheeses. For the first time I tasted a red Castel del Monte, a wine grown round the favourite hunting lodge of Frederick II, near Barletta, and generally acclaimed, and I think rightly, the most attractive of the many wines of Apulia.

After dinner I explored the streets, but found little to admire. The town was shattered by an earthquake in the eighteenth century, and badly bombed in the last war because it was a railway junction and an air base. Now rebuilt, it exhibits all the features of the modern Italian style in town architecture. I noticed that the pronounced gaiety and vitality of the streets ceased soon after nine o'clock as if a whistle had been blown. The cafés emptied, the cars disappeared, and soon Foggia was almost deserted. I found myself in what by lamplight appeared a strange and eerie scene. This was a small park or garden set out with flower-beds and seats from which rose some twenty bronze statues more than life-size depicting attenuated witchlike men and women, some in modern clothes and some in ancient costume. I wondered how anyone could read a newspaper, itself a gloomy and frightening experience these days, with these attenuated monsters looming over him. A policeman told me that the garden was a memorial to Foggia's most celebrated citizen, the musician Umberto Giordano, who was born in 1867 and died in 1948, and the bronze statues represented characters from his operas. I made a note to look up Giordano in the *Oxford Companion to Music* where, above the name of Dr Percy Scholes, I read that *Fedora* 'is probably the only opera that has ever brought bicycles on to the stage'.

I met little on the road to Manfredonia, which runs north-east from Foggia, except an occasional country bus and the farm carts with enormously tall wheels which are characteristic of Apulia. The Gargano Peninsula which I could see in the distance is often called the spur of the heel of Italy, though most horsemen would consider it too high up. The mountain which thrusts itself into the Adriatic Sea looks imposing as it rises three thousand feet above the flatness of the Capitanata.

Having been cold-shouldered by the spirits at every séance I have attended, I am nevertheless sensitive enough to the uncanny atmosphere of some houses and many countrysides. The sea plain of Apulia and the tall promontory to which I was now journeying struck me as a country haunted by the ghosts of Greek adventurers and merchants who centuries before the Christian age had settled among the sheltered bays and established the colonies of Magna Graecia; there were the spectres also of Romans, Byzantines, Lombards, Saracens, and, above all, of Normans, those northern bandits and freebooters who arrived penniless and ended in the silk robes of monarchs.

§ 2

Some miles from the coast I passed through a tortured stretch of country which I assumed to be the result of some ancient earthquake, but looking at my map I saw it to be the site of Grecian Sipus, and later the Roman Sipontum, which was famous before Christ for its wheat, cattle and horses. Like many other cities of the ancient world, it survived all its enemies save the anopheles mosquito. By the Middle Ages the town had become a malarial marsh and the inhabitants were moved by Manfred, the handsome but unfortunate illegitimate son and successor of Frederick II, to his new port of Manfredonia. It is said that the town was razed to the ground in order to force the people to move, and it is characteristic of the South of Italy that the landscape should have remained in that condition for seven centuries. The only building left standing in what must have been a large city is one church, which stands back from the road in a small grove of umbrella pines. An old man at work on the road told me that it was the sanctuary of the famous S. Maria di Sipontum and that once a year a fair is held under the trees, when pilgrims from all parts come to visit the Madonna.

The church, square in shape and Byzantine Romanesque in style, is a noble survivor of the dead and vanished town, and I admired the richly carved porch with its round arch and its columns resting upon the backs of lions, like the Lombard churches of the north. The interior was not attractive and I could see no sign of the famous Madonna. A small building attached to the church appeared to be occupied and when I knocked at the door and asked where the Madonna could be seen, an old woman took a key and without a word descended a long flight of steps into a crypt.

The only light came from a score of candles guttering on an altar in front of a curtained shrine. The walls were covered from floor to roof with the most extraordinary collection of ex-votos it would be possible to find anywhere. Striking match after match, I saw, before each flicker died, legs, arms, hands, breasts, stomachs, all modelled in plaster or wax, some of them horribly coloured and all of them grimy. There were crutches, iron boots, surgical leg-irons and trusses. When my matches gave out I fell back on a cigarette lighter. So I examined the amazing art gallery of water-colours showing men, women and children escaping from sudden death owing to the intercession of the Virgin of Sipontum, who was generally shown enclosed in a cloud in an upper corner of these pictures. So far as I know there is no book devoted to the ex-voto, although the subject is one that lends itself to illustration. Any one of such sanctuaries as that of S. Maria in Sipontum offers more than a wealth of dramatic material: escape from railway trains, from motor cars, from ships at sea, from vehicles poised upon the edge of ravines and held there by the restraining influence of the Madonna. I do not know whether such narrow escapes bring with them the gift of amateur illustration or whether in most peasant communities there is someone able and willing to paint such pictures for his friends.

When the lighter gave out the old woman brought me a candle from the altar by whose light I saw suits of male and female clothing, old hats grey with dust, walking-sticks, umbrellas, and a wedding dress made of what had once been white satin, now torn, motheaten, limp and dirty, with a pathetic wreath of imitation orange blossom hanging above it from a rusty nail. I wondered what sense of gratitude, what human grief, perplexity or what tragedy, had prompted such a gift to the Mother of God.

A shabby curtain concealed the Madonna. The old woman pulled a string, revealing in the yellow glow of the candles a large Byzantine Madonna, her face blackened by time, holding upon her knee a dark, little crop-haired Roman child, which looked like one of the Roman or Greek portraits sometimes seen on mummy cases of the Ptolemaic period. The ikon completed the atmosphere of incredible age and decay, giving the dark crypt an air of mystery. It was at the same time difficult not to feel compassion for those who had presented to the Mother of God such grotesque expressions of suffering.

As I went on to Manfredonia I came to an exquisite sight which disintegrated upon closer acquaintance into a windy little port of recent date, the town having been sacked and burnt down by the Turks in 1620. The invaders, however, were unable to make any impression upon the castle on the edge of the sea, which, though modified in later times, still remains one of those squat, square castles with rounded towers at the corners constructed before the days of firearms. It is well situated above the sea while fishing-boats with saffron sails come slipping into the harbour. I crossed the moat on a rickety bridge and found that the castle was closed. Few visitors ever come to Manfredonia and the town cannot afford the luxury of a gatekeeper. However, a notice on the gate said that the key could be obtained upon application to the town hall. I visualized the procedure: the long explanations at the *municipio* and the frantic messengers sent out to discover the town clerk: then the despair, the regrets, and the apologies because the man with the key had taken it with him into Foggia!

I decided not to visit the castle. Also, I could peep through a crack on one of the planks of the gate and see beyond a wilderness not unlike that of Lucera.

The day may come when tourist gold will flow into Manfredonia, when archaeologists will tidy up the old castle and there will be a man wearing a peaked cap at the gate to tell stories of good King Manfred and wicked Charles of Anjou, whom nobody in Apulia really likes; but at the moment this massive fortress is as Fate and Time have left it.

The road went inland from the Adriatic and in a mile or so began to wind into the mountains where twisted olive trees grew in stony ground and clumps of red poppies sprang from the soil. I was reminded of Judea. When I stopped and looked back at the sea I could hear the cicadas trilling in the morning's warmth.

The Gargano Peninsula is one of those places which appear to have been reserved by geography and who knows what else to be a place of supernatural happenings. It contains two shrines, one of immense antiquity, the other a modern one. The first is the sanctuary of St Michael the Archangel, on Monte S. Angelo – the forerunner of all the St Michael's Mounts in the Western world – and the second in the Capuchin monastery where the stigmatist, Padre Pio, whom many believe to be a saint and a worker of miracles, has lived for many years.

I went first to Monte S. Angelo, which is associated with the Norman Conquest of Southern Italy. Remote as the town is today, it was once on the main road of mediaeval pilgrimage. Ships from Venice and other ports on the Adriatic often called at the now vanished Sipontum, whence a climb up to Monte S. Angelo was a matter of only an hour or so. The story of this shrine reminded me of the legends I had heard on the Spanish side of the Pyrenees. It is said that in A.D. 490 a man who had lost a fine bull eventually found it standing at the entrance to a grotto on top of the mountain. Unable to entice the animal away, the man lost his temper and flung a dart, or shot an arrow, at the bull, which, instead of hitting it, turned round and hit him. Startled by such supernatural animosity, he sought the advice of St. Laurence, Bishop of Sipontum.

Now occurred one of those acts of supersedence so frequently encouraged by the early Church. The policy of replacing an old god with a new saint rarely failed, especially if some attributes of the old divinity could be discerned in the new one, and with incense, candles and holy water the convert was made to think that the church was not so different from the temple. The student of such matters will not be surprised to know that the grotto upon Mount Garganus had long been noted as the shrine of a pagan oracle famous for its dream cures. The visitor would take with him the skin of a black ram in which he wrapped himself, hoping that the oracle would cure him while he slept. This was a typical pagan shrine upon which the Archangel Michael was in the habit of alighting.

His cult began on the Bosphorus and in Asia Minor, it is said with the Emperor Constantine the Great, who visited a shrine at Sosthenium noted for dream cures, in which there was a statue of a winged deity. While the emperor slept a winged man appeared to him who declared himself to be the Archangel Michael. When the Emperor awakened, he built a church to the saint and abolished the pagan god, and that was the first of four churches in or near Constantinople dedicated to the Archangel. The sanctuaries of St Michael were usually shrines of healing and were always associated with water, either a holy well or a spring.

History was therefore repeating itself when the Bishop of Sipontum hurried to the grotto to investigate the mysterious matter of the lost bull. While he prayed, he saw a winged man wearing a scarlet cloak who announced himself to be St Michael, the first of the seven archangels, the Captain of the Hosts of Heaven, the Recording Angel and the Guardian of the Powers of Hell, to give him only a few of his titles and attributes, who declared that he had descended upon the mountain-top to wrest the holy grotto from its former oracle and to consecrate a Christian altar there. He commanded the Bishop to see that the grotto was dedicated to himself and all the angels. The trembling Bishop entered the gloomy cavern, which he found blazing with light, and in a corner he saw an altar newly consecrated by the Archangel himself and vested in purple in the Byzantine manner. So the cult of St Michael crossed from Byzantium to Byzantine Apulia, and the sanctuary on Monte S. Angelo became one of the chief pilgrimage sites in the Christian world.

From Monte Garganus the Archangel made several important flights. During the plague of A.D. 590 in Rome, he was seen by Pope Gregory the Great to alight upon the summit of Hadrian's Tomb in the act of sheathing his sword, a sign, said the Pope, that the plague had ended. His next flight, in A.D. 708, was to a hill-top in Normandy, where a healing well of water was found, and this shrine became famous as Mont-St-Michel. In England St Michael's Mount in Cornwall was placed under the jurisdiction of the Benedictines of Normandy at the bidding of Edward the Confessor.

No people felt a deeper reverence for St Michael than the Normans, who saw him as a warrior saint always at war with evil, one whose sword, like their own, was rarely sheathed. In paying him honour, and in asking his blessing for their enterprises, no matter how sanguinary, they felt that they were appealing to a supernatural being who was, at heart, a Norman. It was natural that those warriors, in whose devotion maybe there stirred some earlier memories of dragon-slaying gods, should have visited the parent sanctuary where the great Archangel had appeared in the West for the first time.

With some of this passing through my mind, I ascended the mountain road to the pilgrimage town. The country continued to look bleak and cheerless, some of it the stony land of the parable, some the good land which bore its olives and its almonds. A bend in the road brought into view the town of Monte S. Angelo lying upon a ridge and outlined against the sky. It is rarely possible to hope in these days that the outskirts of the average Italian town will charm one, since most have been invaded by hideous concrete buildings whose balconies are draped with bedding and washing and in whose shadow children play upon yet unmade roads. This was my first impression of Monte S. Angelo. Then I came to a narrow main street in the centre of which is the underground cathedral, approached by eighty-six steps (some purists say eighty-seven). It is a curious old town and centuries ago must have been a place of cave dwellers. Many of the houses are still built-up caves, and even in the main street the troglodytic character of the town is maintained by steps which lead to cave shops and grotto taverns.

The church of the Archangel is approached across a noble Gothic courtyard which is lined by souvenir stalls. I think this must be one of the few places where one can buy a genuine pilgrim's staff – a strangely Dionysiac object – with a pine-cone at the tip to show that it came from Monte S. Angelo, though as far as I could see, there is now not a single pine tree. I inspected a collection of cheap *bondieuserie* with the emphasis upon statuettes of the Archangel standing in a martial attitude, with poised spear or drawn sword. Some were of plaster, some, less pleasantly, of plastic, and some of tin. There were pictures of the saint, plain and coloured. There were rosaries, scarves, baskets, little holy water stoups, and every kind of inexpensive object intended to satisfy the understandable longing to take home some fragment of sanctity. I had heard that a speciality of the sanctuary, which would certainly have tempted me, were little horses made of honey-cake and horses full of cheese: but I could see none.

A double archway, pointed Gothic in style, led to a long flight of steps. Above one of the arches were the words in Latin, 'This is an awesome place; it is the House of God and the Gate of Heaven.' Awesome it certainly is, and no gloomier approach to the Gate of Heaven could be imagined, as one descends in semi-darkness beneath Gothic vaulting as if to a dungeon. The steps end in a small atrium open to the sky, with a railed gallery above it. A number of old peasants were encircling this, whispering prayers and crossing themselves as they touched the railings.

A few paces away were the doors of the church, which are among the most beautiful antiquities in Italy. At the time when

William the Conqueror was consolidating his conquest of England, the head of the Amalfitan community in Constantinople, a rich merchant prince named Pantaleone, decided to give to the sanctuary of St Michael a pair of silver damascened doors. And these are the doors which still face one at the approach to the sacred grotto. The two leaves are divided into twenty-four bronze panels, a marvel of Byzantine metal casting, and each panel depicts a scriptural scene, ending with the apparition of St Michael to the Bishop of Sipontum. The figures, the faces, and the folds of their garments, are still outlined in silver, which is mostly intact: the silver that was used nearly fifteen centuries ago by the Byzantine smiths. The doors carry an inscription giving the date 1076, and asking the visitor to pray for the soul of Pantaleone, the donor. An interesting exhortation was added to the base of the doors from the makers to the priests, asking them to see that the doors were cleaned at least once a year so that they might always shine brightly. They have, alas, long ceased to shine, but they have acquired the beautiful patina of an old coin.

As people enter the church one can distinguish the stranger from the local people, the peasantry of Southern Italy from visitors from more sophisticated regions. The stranger passes straight into the church, but the peasants take hold of the bronze rings on the doors, which fall from the mouths of lions, and bang them noisily, then some kiss their own hands where they have touched the bronze, before entering the church. Passing inside, I saw a warm glow of candles burning before the high altar some way off, under the slanting rock of the cavern. The cave, which is enormous, cannot have changed much in appearance during the course of the past centuries: it is still the rough and chilly grotto in which those who came to consult the spirit of Calchas slept upon their black ramskins. Conversion to Christianity has not changed the uncompromising roof or the walls of rough rock which drip perpetually with water until the floor beneath is a slimy filth of mud. Water also gathers in the inequality of the floor, but this is disregarded by the more pious of the pilgrims, who kneel down anywhere regardless of mud and water.

In a dark corner near one of the side altars I came upon the strange and distressing sight of two peasants hobbling along on their knees. I had last seen this act of contrition in a church in Spain. Though it is no longer encouraged, it is still common practice in Southern Italy during religious festivals, but the extreme humiliation of licking the church pavement until the tongue is raw is no longer allowed. I looked at the two figures with interest since this act is rarely seen these days, except, of course, on the Scala Sancta in Rome, where it takes its original form, that of ascending steps. (More than one of the Caesars ascended to the Capitol in this way.) Behind the high altar, which occupies the site of the first altar consecrated by the Archangel more than fourteen hundred years ago, is the well of healing water customary in the sanctuaries of St Michael. A silver bucket is dipped and the water is given to the pilgrim in – alas – plastic cups.

Near this altar is the famous statue of the Archangel which is reproduced all over Monte S. Angelo and whose pictures are carried far and wide through the South of Italy. The original statue, which must have been a fine one, was melted down during one of the many attacks on the shrine, and the present seventeenth century figure, attributed to Sansavino, and even more ludicrously, to Michelangelo, shows not the warlike Archangel but an indifferent work which might have been carved from marzipan. In the gloom I made out nearby a really interesting object, a bishop's chair of marble and resting upon two lions. Upon one side was carved the Archangel slaying the dragon, while the back of the chair was a typical Arabic design of interlaced circles and other geometrical patterns. The great antiquity claimed for this cannot, however, be believed; it looked to me like a product of Norman Sicily, a gift perhaps of one of the first Norman kings.

An event which it was not difficult to reconstruct in this mysterious cavern was the arrival there in the year 1016 of a group of about forty Norman knights, who were on their way home from the Holy Land. It seems probable that they were the same knights who, landing at Salerno, found that the town was besieged by Saracens and, arming themselves, led an attack on the infidel of such fury that the Saracens fled to their ships and vanished. This so impressed the lord of Salerno that he begged the strangers to remain and fight for him, promising them rich rewards. Anxious to return home, however, they declined, departing with presents of rare fruits, silks, and other objects likely to entice their friends at home to take their valour to Italy. Much the same offer was repeated at Monte S. Angelo. The Normans were approached by an exiled nobleman of Bari, a Lombard, who asked them to join with him in expelling the Byzantines. They returned the same answer: that they would mention the enterprise to their friends in Normandy; and that they did so is proved by history. Shortly after the knights had returned home, Norman mercenaries began emigrating to Apulia, and so began the Norman invasion and conquest of Southern Italy.

When the Normans made themselves kings of Sicily, the Gargano Peninsula became part of the dowry of the queens of Sicily, and as such it was once the property of two English princesses, Joan, daughter of Henry II, who married William II of Sicily, and Isabella, daughter of King John, who became the third consort of the emperor Frederick II. It is delightful to think of those two English princesses visiting the famous shrine, as they must have done, though for Joan the Peninsula became a cause for anxiety. When William II died, young and intestate, his throne was usurped by Tancred, who locked up his widow and stole her dowry lands. He could not have selected a less fortunate moment for villainy since Joan's brother, Richard Coeur de Lion, was approaching down the west coast of Italy with an army on his way to the Crusade. Tancred was forced to deliver Joan to her brother together with an immense sum in gold for the lordship of Monte S. Angelo. It is said that Richard and Joan soon squandered this sum during the Crusade.

I thought it improbable that a large sum in gold would be forthcoming anywhere today in Monte S. Angelo. Unlike some pilgrimage shrines, it has not become rich. A pleasant absence of salesmanship may in part explain this. It also perhaps explains why I could not find an hotel or a restaurant. Appealing to a passer-by, I was directed to a doorway off the main street which led by way of a flight of ancient stairs into a grotto *trattoria*. Tables covered with spotless cloths were set at various levels beneath a rough rock ceiling and upon each stood a carafe of red wine. The only other tables were occupied by farmers and the local *signori*. Sitting next to me was a commercial traveller from Bari. He was selling plastic buckets and kitchenware and looked as miserable as only a young Italian male can look whose will has been thwarted. His usual area, he said, was Brindisi and Taranto, but a companion's sickness had condemned him to travel the Gargano Peninsula, which he detested. He gloomily wound the spaghetti round his fork and sighed. 'It is a barbarous region,' he said. Even the enchanting young maid who waited upon us, wearing a tartan skirt and her hair shot with auburn lights, did not remove his melancholy.

I was given a sturdy and honest soup which, probably because of the kilt, I thought of as an Italian version of Scotch broth; then came the best roast kid I have eaten since I was in Greece years ago, where it was always called *agneau de lait*. There followed a pallid and rubbery cheese made of ewes' milk which I would not make any effort to find again, though it went well enough with the strong rough wine and the rock walls and ceiling of the cavern.

I walked round the town and looked at a twelfth century bell-tower and a castle erected originally by the Normans, I think by Robert de Hauteville, the Guiscard or Wise One; then I came on a large herd of goats sheltering beside the road in the shade of some trees. While I was thinking what a wonderful picture they made, some of them silhouetted against the sunny slopes of the hill opposite and poised upon a landscape scattered with boulders, I noticed that one of the goats was watching me with an expression in which hostility was equally mixed with curiosity. Looking closer, I saw that the creature was a young man who was hiding among the goats. With a pair of horns, he might well have escaped detection. Pleased to meet a goatherd and such a Panlike one, I said a few words of greeting, but the poor fellow, startled perhaps to find himself addressed in anything but goat language, darted a wild look at me and leapt down among the boulders and out of sight. There was a quick tossing of bearded heads, a click of hooves on the stones, a tinkle of bells, and the roadside was empty.

## § 3

Later in the afternoon I went on to S. Giovanni Rotondo, which is only fourteen miles from Monte S. Angelo and slightly lower down the mountain. I wanted to visit the town which has grown up literally in the steps of Padre Pio, whom millions of Catholics all over the world believe to be a saint. I knew of him only what I had read in a casual way: that he was of peasant stock and that he is now aged more than eighty; that some fifty years ago he had received the Stigmata – the wounds of crucifixion – on hands, feet and side; that his wounds still bleed; that he is said to perform miracles and read thoughts; and that he can be in two places at once, a faculty known as bilocation, or ubiquity.*

I remembered reading also that the Church, with its well known attitude of suspended judgement upon saints and its dislike of mass hysteria, has forbidden Padre Pio to preach or write; but, owing to the fact that he has built the finest hospital in the South of Italy, and one of the most modern in Europe, with funds given to him by rich and poor, he has been absolved from his vow of poverty in order that he may administer his foundation.

This was all I knew as I drove into S. Giovanni Rotondo that afternoon and saw the old village huddled round the circular church of St John (it was once a temple of Janus), from which a long modern road, lined on each side by hotels, boarding-houses, and villas, all of them recently built, terminated in the Capuchin monastery in which Padre Pio has lived for fifty years. At right angles to it stands the enormous six-storey hospital against the mighty flank of Monte Calvo.

I looked round the town before I went to an hotel. I found the place bristling with souvenir shops full of books about Padre

* While this book was on its way to the printer Padre Pio died on Sunday, September 22, 1968. A few days before, seated in a wheel chair, he had celebrated the 50th anniversary of his Stigmata. More than 50,000 people attended his funeral at S. Giovanni Rotondo on September 24.

Pio, and of postcards which depict the man of God in the act of celebrating Mass, with the photographic emphasis upon his bleeding hands. I gazed at close-up prints on glossy paper, for which there is an enormous sale, that show the palm of each hand covered with what looks like fur, but are scars which never heal. To anyone who has read the life of St Francis and St Catherine of Siena, the possibility of seeing a living person bearing the Stigmata upon his body cannot fail to excite interest and to raise a number of unusual questions.

In the meantime I noticed that S. Giovanni Rotondo lives only too evidently in the aura of sanctity. There was a pensione called Ave Maria, a restaurant named San Pietro, and another called Villa Pia, advertised as 'near Padre Pio's monastery', which may be geographically right, but not factually correct, Padre Pio being only one of a dozen or so Capuchin friars in residence there. I eventually chose a good hotel called the Santa Maria delle Grazie, which offered private bathrooms with its bedrooms. It even had an American bar. This hotel with its pleasant lounge and large restaurant (and admirable wine list) was filled with those who had not yet given everything to the poor.

I asked for tea, which was served without that lift of the eyebrow which still, in remote parts of Italy, suggests that one has demanded ipecacuanha. I picked up an American magazine which was lying on a table nearby and though it was three years old, it was full of interest, and devoted to religious travel. A full-page advertisement said, 'Italy is beautiful ... When you plan to see Padre Pio, take an Ave Maria Tour and see it all.' The title of one article was, 'Can this Man work Miracles?', and of another, 'I saw them clean his wounds'. I was slightly shocked, wondering where in these days can one escape lack of reticence. Yet, on the other hand, this was perhaps an uncharitable thought! Surely this gusto for sanctity is not a new thing; the Wife of Bath would probably have been a regular subscriber to this magazine.

Perhaps because all the saints whose shrines I have visited were dead, as the Church prefers them to be, I assumed that Padre Pio would be difficult to see, even if he were visible at all. I heard with surprise from a member of the hotel staff that, on the contrary, he could hardly be more accessible. Every visitor to the town rises at five o'clock in the morning to attend the Padre's Mass at five-thirty, which is the great event of the day. His confessional box is booked up for months ahead for women, and weeks ahead for men, and he attends Benediction in the church every evening at five-thirty. It was then nearly five o'clock and I hurried off to the church.

When Padre Pio arrived at the monastery after the First World War, it was a small establishment with a humble little church, like hundreds of others in remote mountain villages in Italy. The monastery is still small and unchanged, but to accommodate the crowds which now come here the church has been rebuilt as a large basilica in the modern style. There is an immense parking place in front of it, often filled with cars and coaches, and even on quiet days with frequent omnibuses which run a regular service from the railway station at Foggia. Passing inside, I found the church full, with crowds standing in the aisles and round the altar. It is a gaunt building with a gallery running round it, but of no architectural distinction. I thought it had the air of a secular building, perhaps a post office, which had been hastily converted to more spiritual purposes.

Suddenly the whispers of the crowd were stilled and the congregation rose silently to its feet as a door opened in the north gallery and two black-bearded friars, wearing the Capuchin habit with the brown, pointed hood lying back on their shoulders, entered supporting a third, an immensely old man who walked with difficulty. Padre Pio is now grey-haired and has a white beard; his cheeks are sunk and his face bears the signs of a life of prayer and pain. Yet his is an ordinary face, typical of many an old bearded friar whom one has seen so often in Italian churches and streets. It was awe-inspiring to look at him and to remember not only some of the extraordinary stories which are told about his spiritual gifts, but to think that a few paces outside, at the foot of the mountain, stands a hospital with a thousand beds which a man vowed to poverty has been able to give to the poor. The two friars helped the padre to a seat in the front row of the gallery overlooking the altar, and then withdrew. Padre Pio covered his eyes with his hands to pray; and I saw that each hand was covered with a brown woollen mitten that protected the pierced palm but left the fingers free.

The attention of the congregation could be felt as well as seen. People were unable to keep their eyes from the brown figure in the gallery and the hands that bore the wounds of crucifixion. When the rite of Benediction came to an end I noticed that a group of men had begun to assemble near a side door which led into the sacristy. The moment the priest left the altar there was a rush for this door in which I joined. Eventually I found myself in a fine hall, a surprising improvement on the church, from which marble steps led to an upper storey. The men raced up this staircase where their purpose soon became clear. Padre Pio would pass that way from the gallery to his cell. I was told that this audience takes place every morning and evening. No woman is allowed to set foot in the monastery, but all male pilgrims and visitors who are sufficiently able-bodied to join in the scrum are welcome to see the holy man at close quarters.

We had not long to wait. As at a papal audience, every man dropped to his knees as Padre Pio came, leaning on the shoulders of the two friars. His progress was painfully slow. The faithful crossed themselves. Some of the kneeling men attempted to speak to him, but this was discouraged by the friars.

His appearance was not unusual, though his features have been refined and sharpened by a life of meditation, austerity and pain. At the same time his eyes seemed to me capable of that shrewd peasant look which one sees in the fields and market places of Italy, and I could imagine that even now, as an octogenarian, he is well able to rebuke a sinner in unmeasured words. Personally, I always enjoy the acid humour of saints and, having seen Padre Pio at close quarters I could credit the story told of his reply to a visitor who asked if his wounds hurt. 'Do you think,' he replied, 'that the Lord gave them to me as a decoration?' Typical of a village priest was his reply to a widow with a large family who asked if she should remarry. 'Up to the present,' Padre Pio is reported to have said, 'you have cried with one eye, but if you marry again you will cry with both eyes.' I watched him cross the strip of carpet slowly, step by step. He had been up since five o'clock that morning, had celebrated Mass, and had spent hours in the confessional. He was obviously weary and anxious to reach the quiet of his frugal cell.

I returned to the hotel surprised that within an hour of arriving at this town I had not only seen its saintly inhabitant but also had been near enough to touch him.

§ 4

The story of Padre Pio's life follows a pattern well known to the biographer of Italian saints. His father was a peasant named Orazio Forgione of Pietralcina, which is the hilly country north of Benevento. In order to support his large family he went to the United States and worked as a labourer in New York. Padre Pio was born at Pietralcina in 1887 and was baptized as Francesco Forgione. He was a delicate child and at the age of five his hero was St Francis of Assisi. When he was fifteen he went to a school of Capuchin fathers and a year later became a novice known as Brother Pio. His health did not improve and he was diagnosed as a consumptive. In spite of his fragility, he seems to have welcomed penances and austerities, and once when unable to eat lived for three weeks upon nothing but the Sacraments, which recalls the experiences of St. Catherine of Siena. He was ordained in Benevento Cathedral in 1910, aged twenty-three years, and was stationed at Foggia. His contemporaries at this time thought of him as abnormally emotional and physically infectious. In her book *Padre Pio*, Miss Nesta de Robeck quotes a friend as saying, 'We were all struck with his waxen face and the hoarseness of his voice; his eyes were unduly bright, and the insidious illness from which he was suffering made him constantly cough and flush. We saw him in church but were all afraid of infection, and we told the sacristan to keep the alb, vestments, chalice, and purificators used by Padre Pio in a cupboard apart from the others. Indeed we insisted on this. . . . While praying Padre Pio always wept silently but so abundantly that his tears wetted the floor of the choir. We other youths laughed at him so he spread a large handkerchief in front of him where he knelt in prayer: when he had finished he picked it up so wet that it needed wringing out.'

Padre Pio's Mass sometimes lasted for hours. At the *Memento* he became so absorbed in prayer that he was unable to continue, sometimes for an hour. People complained that they could not spend the time while he said Mass, and it became necessary for his parish priest to station himself near and ask the young priest to emerge from his ecstasy, or agony, and continue. When he was twenty-eight and was spending a holiday at home in Pietralcina, he made himself a little arbour of branches at the end of the garden where he prayed and meditated. During the commemoration of the Stigmata of St Francis, he did not return to the house at the usual time. His mother, going out to look for him, saw him returning waving his hands in a strange way. 'Are you playing the guitar, Francesco?' she called out laughingly. He replied that he felt a curious stinging pain in his hands. That was three years before the Stigmata became visible on his body.

When Italy entered the war against Germany in 1915, Padre Pio was called up for military service. He was placed in the medical corps and served as an orderly in a military hospital in Naples. Because of his poor health, he was given a year's sick leave and was eventually discharged as a sufferer from pulmonary tuberculosis. He was sent to the village of S. Giovanni Rotondo in the hope that the mountain air would be better for him than that of the plain of Foggia.

Here Padre Pio settled into the quiet life of a remote monastery, devoting himself to prayer and contemplation. In September, 1918, when he was thirty-one years of age, the community had just celebrated the Feast of the Stigmata, and the young priest had gone to the choir to meditate. The monks suddenly heard a loud cry and, running to the choir, they found Padre Pio lying unconscious and saw that the palms were bleeding. When he was taken to his cell, it was seen that his feet were bleeding and that he had also an open wound in his side. All the marks of the Stigmata, except that of the Crown of Thorns, were visible. The Father Provincial of the Capuchins at Foggia had the wounds medically examined and photographed, and the records were sent to the Vatican. One of the most extraordinary features during the many medical examinations was that the doctors agreed that the lungs of the man who had been discharged from the army as a consumptive bore no trace at all of tuberculosis.

Since the thirteenth century there have been about three hundred cases of Stigmata, the most famous being that of St Francis. Some of them have been due to religious hysteria, and the Church does not accept Stigmata in itself as a sign of saintliness, though many saints have been marked in that way. On the other hand, millions of believers all over the world think that this is a sign made by God upon the bodies of His chosen elect, and accordingly Padre Pio is treated by millions of Catholics as if he were already a saint. In order, if possible, to place a curb on this no doubt anticipatory attitude, for the Church has never and will never permit canonization by acclamation, and it has firmly silenced Padre Pio except in the confessional.

Half a century has passed since the Stigmata became visible upon the body of Padre Pio, and during that time many competent observers have claimed several saintly attributes for him. Among these is that strange phenomenon, 'the odour of sanctity', which is a scent of roses, violets, some say of incense, with which it is said the Padre is able to announce his spiritual presence, even in distant places. Doctors have testified to the fact that bandages from his wounds have sometimes filled a room with scent. It is also said that he has the gift of healing, and a great number of cures have been mentioned by the Rev. Charles Mortimer Carty in his book *Padre Pio, the Stigmatist*. A third mysterious attribute claimed for him is ubiquity, or bilocation as it is sometimes called, which, as I have said, is the ability to be in two places at once, which is a puzzling phenomenon. Though Padre Pio never leaves S. Giovanni Rotondo, he has been seen in Rome five times, and by distinguished churchmen. One of these appearances was mentioned to Pope Pius XI, who called upon Don Orione, noted for his sanctity, to investigate the story. 'I have seen him myself,' replied Don Orione. 'If you tell me that, then I believe it,' the Pope is said to have replied.

Father Carty prints an interesting conversation between Padre Pio and his friend Dr Sanguinetti.

'Padre Pio,' said the Doctor, 'when God sends a saint, for instance like St Anthony, to another place by bilocation, is that person aware of it?'

'Yes,' replied Padre Pio. 'One moment he is here and the next moment he is where God wants him.'

'But is he really in two places at once?' asked the Doctor. 'How is that possible?'

'By a prolongation of personality,' replied the Padre.

'This observation,' comments Father Carty, 'obvious to Padre Pio, may be a problem which we leave to philosophers and theologians to explain.'

A miracle, however, which the most sceptical of observers will surely be willing to accept, is the magnificent hospital which an unworldly monk who has not left the Gargano Peninsula for fifty years has been able to give to the poor. It is called 'The Home for the Relief of Suffering', and it has the sub-title, 'The Fiorello La Guardia Hospital.' To me this is the great miracle of S. Giovanni Rotondo. It is related by Padre Pio's biographers that during the winter of 1940 the holy man was discussing the sorrows of mankind in his cell with three friends, when he said that he would like to build a hospital. Fumbling in his habit, he produced a small gold coin which someone had given him for his charities. He threw it on the table as the first contribution. Father Carty, describing this occasion, writes, 'In every sick man there is Jesus in Person who is suffering, in every poor man is Jesus Himself who is languishing, in every sick and poor man Jesus is doubly visible.' One wonders whether the writer was aware when he wrote those words that he was voicing the ideas of a saint who had lived in the the monastery at S. Giovanni Rotondo nearly five hundred years ago. One wonders too why this saint is never mentioned in the town where he found God. He was St Camillus of Lellis, who was born in 1550 and who died in 1614, and who belongs to that select group of saints whose conscience redeemed them from a life of vice and self-indulgence. St Camillus is the patron saint of the infirm and surely his spirit must have been near when Padre Pio discussed with his friends the possibility of ? hospital for S. Giovanni Rotondo.

St. Camillus was the son of a Neapolitan officer whose mother died while he was an infant. Brought up without love, guidance, or background, he became a wild and dissolute young man; he joined the army and was stationed first at Venice and later at Naples, where he added gambling to his other vices and at last gambled away even his sword. When discharged from the army, he wandered about trying to earn a living as a casual labourer. He must have been in a bad way when, having climbed the mule tracks of the Gargano Peninsula, he knocked at the door of the Capuchin monastery at Giovanni Rotondo and asked for work. Something about him appealed to the Father Guardian, who eventually converted him. When Camillus asked to join the Order he was given a specially long and severe novitiate, but he passed through and became a monk.

He suffered so severely from ulcerated legs that it was decided to send him to a hospital in Rome, where he was cured. But while he suffered and lived with other sufferers he found his life's mission. He remained at the hospital after his discharge in order to help the doctors and nurses and when a new head of the hospital was appointed he was chosen. No disease repelled him; in every sufferer he saw Christ Crucified, and with the object of extending his ministrations he founded the Servants of the Sick, a religious order whose members spent their lives visiting those in pain and soothing the last hours of the dying. St Camillus is generally shown in art with an angel by his side because of a legend that whenever he entered a hospital ward an angel walked with him.

It is appropriate, if nothing more, that Padre Pio and his friends should have discussed the new hospital in the monastery where St Camillus had been a novice. With Divine Providence as their guide, the founders gathered at first pitifully small contributions to their enterprise, but these grew as the years passed until one day an Englishwoman came to S. Giovanni Rotondo. She was Miss Barbara Ward, of *The Economist* (now Lady (Robert) Jackson), who, during a subsequent lecture tour in the United States, secured a gift of two hundred and fifty million lire from the funds of U.N.R.R.A. The chief director of U.N.R.R.A., who had just died, was Fiorello La Guardia, Mayor of New York, and by common consent his name was given to the hospital.

Looking at it today and remembering that no campaign for funds was ever launched, it seems miraculous that such a building, with its operating theatres, its surgical units, its bright, cheerful wards, and a department of radiology which is said to be among the best in the world, should have been created in sixteen years. It is a strange and unique story. When Padre Pio has been lifted to the altars of the Church, his gift to Christ's poor and suffering will continue his own gift of healing. It is easy to see the beginning of another Lourdes in this remote mountain town.

I was awakened at half-past four in the morning by noises, voices, and the opening and closing of doors in the hotel. The great moment was approaching round which the life of S. Giovanni Rotondo revolves: the morning Mass of Padre Pio. I dressed and hurried up to the church. The parking place contained a number of cars and coaches. Lights were burning in the hospital, and there was a glow from the roof indicating one of the unusual features of this institution. Serving hundreds of inaccessible mountain villages in the Apennines, many of which even today are approachable only by mule tracks, and in winter not at all, the main ambulance entrance is upon the roof, where helicopters bring in many of the patients.

The lights were also shining through the row of narrow windows in the west front of the church. A cold wind came from the mountains, but the light was growing every minute and soon the sun would rise. I found the church full and many people were standing in the aisles. Groups were reciting the Rosary as they waited for Mass to begin; some sang hymns, but most of the members of the congregation knelt and prayed. I stood among a group of people near the altar where, as we waited, I noticed that some people were writing on the wall messages addressed to Padre Pio, asking him to pray for some person or for some purpose. I read afterwards in one of the local books that two friars with a bucket of whitewash descend periodically into the church and obliterate the graffiti.

A blind man would have known the moment of Padre Pio's appearance because of the silence and the atmosphere of emotion that filled the church. He came vested for Mass, attended by a friar who helped him to walk. Every eye was fixed upon him. Though St Francis was not a priest and never said Mass, I thought that had he done so the expressions of his congregation might have resembled those I saw around me in the church of S. Maria delle Grazie. I was reminded of those mediaeval panels in Siena which show S. Bernadino preaching to devout crowds. Clothes have changed with the centuries but the attitude of devotion has not, and this kneeling crowd with every face turned towards the priest reminded me of that panel by Sano di Pietro which shows the women on one side separated from the kneeling men on the other, both groups absorbed and awed in the presence of sanctity.

The church is furnished with loud speakers but these were not in use, and as Padre Pio never lifted his voice above a whisper the Mass was a silent one. As it progressed, I noticed how often Padre Pio wiped the tears from his eyes with linen cloths placed on the altar for him. I noticed too that he is not able to close his hands because of his wounded palms, and he has difficulty in picking up small objects. I saw that at certain moments in the Mass, in particular during the Consecration, his hands were cupped, the palms held upwards in a rather unnatural way, and this, I was told afterwards, was because his wounds bleed freely during Mass and he is anxious to prevent the blood from falling upon the altar.

The average time of a Latin low Mass is about twenty minutes, though Padre Pio's Mass took nearly three times as long, but the time passed imperceptibly and I was probably the only person in the whole church who glanced at his watch, and this not for any reasons of impatience but merely to time it. I really believe the congregation would have welcomed the two hour Mass which distressed even religious persons during the Padre's youth, so great was their absorption in contemplating the presence of one whom they have already canonized in their hearts. When the old man faced the congregation and with lifted hand whispered 'Pax vobiscum,' we saw the fresh blood upon the dark wound.

I learnt something of Padre Pio's daily life from a member of the community. Though forbidden to write, he has seven secretaries who answer his large polyglot correspondence. Every day the village post-office delivers about six hundred letters and forty to fifty telegrams and cables, addressed to him from all parts of the world. He lives in conditions of utmost austerity in a friar's cell which is no different from that of other members of the community. Because of his age and the Stigmata, he requires the service of two friars who dress his wounds and accompany him when he leaves his cell for the church or the confessional.

There have been many medical reports on the wounds which can be seen publicly on his hands only during Mass; at all other times they are hidden by mittens. This is not only the easiest way to keep the dressings in place but he has been forbidden by his superiors to show the Stigmata to anyone. Even during Mass he tries to hide the palms of his hands in the sleeves of his alb. The wounds on his hands and feet correspond with each other: the wound on the top surface corresponds with one on the lower. They never heal and the wound in the left side is said to lose a cupful of blood every twenty-four hours. He is unable to wear sandals and wears shoes which are specially made for him in Switzerland, a gift of Swiss Catholics.

After the morning Mass Padre Pio returns to the sacristy to disrobe and assume his habit; then he goes to his confessional box where he hears the confessions of women for two hours. Each woman is given a numbered ticket, but the Padre is more accessible to men, consequently the male list is not so long. Men are confessed in the afternoon, after which Padre Pio rests and reads. His one meal of the day is taken at noon. The Padre is not a vegetarian, but he prefers vegetables and fish to meat; neither is he a teetotaller and drinks wine and also beer. But as Father Carty has noted, his average intake of food represents only three to four hundred calories a day, which is not sufficient to make up for the daily loss of blood. During an illness he ate nothing for eight days and drank only water, but at the end of the time he had gained a little weight. Altogether the holy man is, medically speaking, an unsolved problem.

My informant had had personal contact with one of the people said to have been miraculously cured by Padre Pio. This was Gemma Di Giorgi from Ribera, in Sicily, who had been born blind, with no pupils in her eyes. Doctors gave the opinion that nothing could be done for her.

'Padre Pio said to her, "Do you wish to see? Then you shall see"; and passed his hands over her eyes. Suddenly she gave a loud shout and said she could see. I was not there at the time but I met Gemma later after she had entered a convent, and I can assure you that, though she could now see, she still has no visible pupils to her eyes.'

I was told that there are some people whom Padre Pio will not touch, just as there are some he will not absolve in the confessional. He is said to be able to read the most secret thoughts. When a man once entered the sacristy the Padre shouted, 'Get away, you murderer!'; and it came out eventually, when the man had repented and confessed, that he had been thinking of doing away with his wife.

We were talking in a corridor in the monastery and saw Padre Pio approaching between two friars.

'Kneel down when he passes,' said my acquaintance, 'and I will introduce you.'

I did so and the saintly monk, either dazed by listening to the sins of women for hours or else perplexed to encounter someone who had nothing to ask him, gazed at me for a moment from blue eyes that had shed so many tears, then, rapping me sharply on the head with a mittened hand, he blessed me and passed onward to his cell.

§ 5

One cannot fail to meet those in S. Giovanni Rotondo who arrived years ago on a day trip and have made their lives there. Some admittedly came out of curiosity and some even to scoff, as the theologians went to St Catherine of Siena, but, like them, remained to pray. Others were searching for spiritual health and security.

IA (*above*) Castel del Monte, a typical Abruzzo town
IB (*below*) Moat and gateway of the Castle at Aquila

2A (*above, left*) Ovid's statue, Sulmona. B (*right*) Making flower baskets of sugared almonds, Sulmona

2C (*below*) Boys encouraged to handle snakes at Cocullo. (Anxiety of boy on left indicates that he holds the head)

3 Statue of S. Domenico covered with living snakes carried through Cocullo, in the Abruzzo, during the annual snake ceremony

4A (*above*) Peasant riding past the Roman ruins of Saepinum
4B (*below*) The ancient church of S. Maria in Sipontum

5A (*above*) The underground church of S. Michael, Monte S. Angelo, Gargano Peninsula

5B (*below, left*) Byzantine doors inlaid with silver, S. Michael's Church, Gargano Peninsula. C (*right*) Ikon of the miraculous Virgin of Sipontum

6A (*above*) Padre Pio's house for the relief of suffering

6B (*centre*) Padre Pio, showing signs of stigmata in palm of his hand

6C (*below*) The new façade of the church of the Capuchin Monastery, S. Giovanni Rotondo, from the terrace of the Hospital

7A (*above*) Bari from the air, Old City to left

7B (*below, left*) One of the main streets of modern Bari. C (*right*) Castle of Bari

8A (*above, left*) A pilgrim. B (*right*) Statue of S. Nicholas being carried to the sea during his annual festival at Bari

8C (*below*) The saint's statue mounted in the stern of a decorated fishing boat spends the day at sea

The most celebrated of such converts is Miss Mary McAlpine Pyle, now in her seventies, who is a familiar figure in a dress devised by herself, a hoodless modification of the Capuchin habit. Her spiritual relationship with Padre Pio is sometimes compared to that which existed between St Clare and St Francis.

Miss Pyle is an American who was on holiday in Capri during the nineteen-twenties when she first heard of Padre Pio. She went to see him with a friend, and afterwards could not settle down to her normal life but returned to live in S. Giovanni Rotondo. She bought land on which she built a house which is now familiar to English and American visitors, who are always welcome there. Unfortunately Miss Pyle was unwell when I was in the town so that I never met her.

She has devoted herself to the erection of a monastery and a church at Pietralcina, Padre Pio's birthplace, and during the last war when, as an American, she was interned, she managed to arrange to be sent to this village where she became close friends with Padre Pio's parents, who have since died. I was told that she has also bought the simple house where Padre Pio was born which some day, it is believed, will be transformed into a chapel.

While I was paying my bill at the hotel the receptionist, a pleasant young woman, said, in reply to some remark I had made about the town:

'I came here fifteen years ago from South America and have never left the place. I was interested in religions. I had read a lot about various religions. I had tried Yoga and Buddhism but I was all mixed up and discontented. . . .'

I smiled to think that she was repeating the search so well described by St Augustine.

'Then,' she said, 'I saw Padre Pio and I was converted. It was like going through a door from darkness into the light. And I was happy for the first time in my life. It is wonderful to be able to live here.'

She put a stamp on my bill, receipted it, gave it to me with a happy smile, and rang a bell for the porter; and I said goodbye.

§ 6

I went on to Sannicandro Garganico along the mountain road, with a glimpse now and then of the distant Adriatic glittering in the morning sun. The road rose and fell, now through bare rocky country of dazzling limestone then through olive groves where vast, twisted giants lifted their venerable arms, and appeared more geological than botanical.

I thought how rare it is in these days to travel through a lonely countryside, indeed the only cars I met were an occasional local bus or a lorry and, rarely, and only on the outskirts of a village, a small Fiat.

I shall often think of the road to Sannicandro, as that of the suicidal lizards. These creatures, when in miniature among the few charming reptiles, selected the last moment of safety before crossing the road, and always, I noticed, from right to left. When a hen dies in traffic its end is generally due to indecision, but the lizard is the exact opposite. If he wishes to cross the road he does so in a straight line and nothing will deflect him. The hen changes her mind ten times, but the lizard, selecting the penultimate moment, streaks across the road under one's wheels; and all one can do is to hope that this joust with death has not been fatal to him.

Sannicandro was a hungry-looking mountain village from which I hurried on down to the sea at Cagnano upon the northern shores of the Peninsula. Here, upon the banks of a large sheet of blue water called the Lake of Varano, is a small town which is separated from the sea by the merest strip of land. I turned aside from the main road to buy some matches in this town and found two French travellers in the café, who asked what the road was like to S. Giovanni Rotondo. They wore blue boiler suits with hob-nailed boots and carried what at first I thought were pilgrims' staffs, but were really alpenstocks. I saw a small car standing outside the café, loaded with coils of rope and other climbing gear. I was surprised that anyone should come to the Gargano Peninsula to climb the gentle limestone undulations when not far away they could attempt the tall serrated Apennines.

They were, however, not mountain climbers; indeed one might almost call them anti-mountaineers, and I looked with interest at the first speleologists I had met. To me the exploration of caves, even when the stalagmites are floodlit, holds no attraction at all, and when obliged to do so – I recall a frightening underworld in the Pyrenees – I cannot get out too quickly.

I realized that the more muscular and capable-looking of the two cave explorers was a woman. They told me that they were devoted speleologists and had been investigating caves in the north of Italy with the Gruppo Speleologico Piemontese, and were looking forward to the Gargano Peninsula as an unexplored underland. I should never have known, had they not told me, that the Peninsula is honeycombed with caves similar to the grottoes of Monte S. Angelo, but, of course, more impressive and most of them unknown. They had never heard of Padre Pio but knew everything about a huge cavern, for which they were bound, a few miles from S. Giovanni, called the Grava di Campolata. The woman told me that it had been partially explored for the first time in 1961 and was still a dangerous place, with unmeasured drops into total darkness and perhaps to silent black lakes. I went on, thinking how remarkable it is that in an age when the air above and the earth below are filled with peril, some people must go looking for it under the earth. Still, I told myself, if you are determined to do this, it is not a bad idea to take with you a buxom and capable Persephone.

The country now began to show signs of intensive market gardening. Acres of cabbages and lettuces alternated with sloping hillsides of olive trees and hedges of yellow-flowering cactus. I hardly saw a person in the fields and met only an occasional cart or wagon all the way to the little seaport of Rodi, whose picturesque beauty can scarcely be exaggerated. Houses rose in terraces, some whitewashed, some blue, some pink; cobbled lanes, a yard or two in width wound up in steps beneath Arabic-looking archways; and the whole place rang with the shouting and singing of children and the admonitions of their cheerful parents. There were miles of sand upon which the waves of the shallow Adriatic broke sluggishly, bright green shading to deepest blue.

Rodi has not acquired the sophistication and the touch of madness that has made Capri so attractive; it is still unexploited and, as far as one can tell, unspoilt. I liked it enormously. I liked the old women in the fish market as they presided over octopus and squid; I liked the children who played, shrieking, round the town; and I liked the baker's boy who emerged clown-white with flour from some underground room, and, shedding around him the delicious smell of new bread, crossed the piazza with a basket upon his arm full of the gigantic circular loaves that are made in Apulia. And the little piazza with its cluster of old buildings might have been a scene rejected from some film company as too picturesque to be credible.

From the heights of Rodi you can see, on a clear day, some small rocky islets far out at sea. These are the Tremiti Islands on the largest of which, named S. Domino, Julia, the granddaughter of Augustus, died after having spent twenty years in exile there. She was banished, like her mother before her, for adultery. Once when Augustus was asked to forgive the first Julia, his daughter, he flew into a rage before a public assembly and shouted, 'If you ever bring up this matter again, may the gods curse you with daughters as lecherous as mine, and with wives as adulterous!'

Rodi has long since forgotten Julia, though it still remembers Santa Rosa, a fishergirl who prophesied and performed miraculous cures about twenty-five years ago. The climax occurred when she prophesied that upon a certain date there would be a great storm in which she would die, after which the war would come to an end. Her celebrity was such that upon the appointed day such enormous crowds gathered at Rodi that police were rushed from Foggia to control them. There was indeed a violent storm. During a particularly vivid flash of lightning some said they had seen the soul of Santa Rosa ascending to heaven. The occasion was so full of *emozione* that when a café table overturned with a loud bang the *carabinieri* opened fire. But, alas, when all was over Santa Rosa was still earthbound and the war was still in progress; but, as the loyal people of Rodi say, anyone can make mistakes.

Few parts of Italy can really be called unknown, but in comparison with the more popular regions of Italy, the Gargano

Peninsula is still unexplored, and I think it will remain in that happy isolation for some time to come. I discovered that the delightful Rodi has only one hotel of the fourth class with eleven beds, and though I was tempted to linger there I had to hurry on to Bari to attend the annual festival of St Nicholas.

Beyond Rodi I saw the southern edge of the great Foresta Umbra, which is the last vestige of that primeval forest which once covered Apulia. It looked much like the New Forest round Brockenhurst on a hot summer's day, the huge oaks and beech trees stretching away in a silence broken only by that rarest of Italian country sounds, the song of birds. This was the type of forest country which the Normans conquered, in Italy as in England, and it bears no resemblance at all to the bald outlines of Apulia today. In such fastnesses lurked the game which was hunted with hawk and hound by Frederick II and gave cover, it seems, until the more recent and almost insane exploits of Ferdinand IV of Naples, whose appetite for dead boars and stags was unappeasable. I came to another pretty little town called Peschici, a complete contrast to Rodi, mounted upon a cliff above the blue water; and some miles farther on I came to a tiny port named Vieste where a pleasant *trattoria* caught my eye. There were only about six tables and there was no menu. Instead, I was invited to enter the kitchen and see what they had to offer. Here I was shown fish and shellfish which had just been caught and were still in buckets of salt water. I was advised to choose some enormous prawns, each one the size of a small lobster. They were delicious roasted with no sauce or refinement of any kind except a lemon. The wine was the same as the potent red wine I had first tasted at Monte S. Angelo and the bill came to about five shillings.

I was entertained by a party of four workmen at a table opposite, the only other people there, who were dressed in jeans and singlets, and were lightly covered with stone dust. They began their lunch with spaghetti, followed by prawns, though some chose veal instead, and they all called for cherries. They had two bottles of wine, which they had brought with them, and a bottle of mineral water. They talked, laughed and joked all through the meal, though I could not understand much of what they said. I was amused to contrast this rather sophisticated meal with the luncheon of a similar group of English bricklayers.

When I was wandering about the little harbour I was approached by a man wearing a blue jersey who looked like an ancient Phoenician. He had a thin, sharp, Semitic cast of face with calculating dark eyes capable of profound melancholy. He wanted to take me to a grotto, one, he said, of unforgettable beauty and whose colour made the 'Blue Grotto' of Capri appear to be in monochrome. It was called the Grotta Campana. I was inclined to see this until I found that it involved an hour's journey with my Phoenician in his boat. I asked if there were other grottoes of the same kind. He said the coast was perforated everywhere with them. He mentioned the Grotta S. Nicola, the Grotta dell' Abate, the Grotta dell' Acqua, and many others. When I told him I had no time to see these wonders, he shrugged and sighed; and his eyes moved over me sadly, conveying the impression that I had missed one of life's great opportunities.

# CHAPTER THREE

*The Feast of St Nicholas at Bari – the robbing of a tomb – the old City of Bari – a saint goes out to sea – St Francis at Bari – the saint and the harlot – shell-fish*

## § 1

As I approached Bari I passed several coaches filled with pilgrims on their way, as I was, to the annual feast of St Nicholas. At one place, while held up at a level crossing, I had a good opportunity to study them. The occupants were nearly all women clothed in black. They sat stiffly and solemnly, holding packages and bags, black shawls upon their shoulders, black kerchiefs binding their grey hair, and while they waited for the bus to continue they sang litanies.

I concluded that this is the new manner of pilgrimage which disregards whatever spiritual virtue existed in physical hardship. The long mediaeval processions, two by two, trailing across a bleak landscape led by a cross-bearer, described as recently as the nineteen-twenties by Estella Canziani, may still exist, but not in the parts of the south served by good roads and 'bus companies. Nevertheless the old customs are observed; the pilgrims are still led by a cross. I saw that it was strapped to the radiator.

Darkness was falling as I reached Bari, which is the largest city, except Naples, in the south of Italy. Like most of the ancient sea-ports of the Adriatic, the old town exists side by side with a new town which is often larger and always a striking contrast in appearance. Old Bari clusters picturesquely round the cathedral and the church of St Nicholas, and the ancient harbour, which was one of the departure ports for the Crusades; while new Bari has the unusual distinction of having been inaugurated by Murat, during his brief career as King of Naples. It has grown into a thriving modern city on the grid-iron plan, its wide avenues planted with palm trees and lined with impressive buildings, brilliant shops, one-way streets, and the usual traffic problems.

I was surprised by the size and the vitality of Bari. The hotel delighted me; it was modern and full of welcoming smiles and it turned out to be one of the best hotels in Italy. I found myself in an air-conditioned bedroom with a bathroom attached, a wireless inset into the wall, a telephone near the bed, and a reading light of precisely the right kind and in the proper position.

The porter, arriving with my bags, bestowed upon me a radiant smile. He asked if the air-conditioner were to my liking and if I had any clothes to be pressed. Then he drew back the curtains and, pointing to a slender floodlit candle in the darkness, said it was the campanile of the cathedral. He told me that he was married and had four children. He had been a prisoner of war – in India! As he smiled again, I thought how far I was from the tourist routes where the nightly arrival of packaged tours and a succession of one night guests, beloved as they may be by hotel managements, have banished the smile from the face of the Italian servant. No people have a greater sense of human dignity than the Italians, and to find that life consists no longer of a series of generally pleasant human contacts but in carrying a hundred suitcases upstairs every night and carrying them downstairs every morning, week after week and month after month during the season, helping to expedite a succession of apparently crazy people who have no thought of anything but to keep on the move, is lowering to the Italian spirit. The South in general has not yet experienced this, but it is on the way.

I found that the hotel stood upon the perimeter of the old town, which was only a few hundred yards distant, and I decided to take a walk there after dinner. In a few minutes I entered a different world. It happened to be a singularly noisy night in New Bari, with loud speakers casting the voices of nasal giants into the darkness as some civic occasion was being celebrated in the open air; the traffic, too, seemed to be abnormally noisy and ill-tempered that night, being obliged to take unaccustomed side streets, the main avenue having been railed off: but all this was forgotten the moment I was enclosed by the silence of the Old City. The massive stone walls insulated the modern world and its agitation. Most of the streets were narrow and oriental in appearance; others, the main streets of the Old Town, were well lit and crowded with people. The moonlight, spilling itself over white archways and ancient doorways, led into courtyards where outside steps rose to houses which had been lived in for centuries.

I was soon hopelessly lost and found that I had left in the hotel the small pocket compass which I usually carry for such occasions. Unwilling to betray my foreignness by speaking to any of the figures who brushed past me in the narrow lanes, I wandered on, turning now left, now right, attracted by a moonlit courtyard or by the sound of high-pitched voices singing songs with the Arab semi-tones which you hear all over the south, or by some ancient building, massive as a fortress, which looked as though it must have numbered crusaders among its lodgers. I began to wonder if chance would lead me out of this maze or at what point I should be obliged to ask for help.

Emerging from an alley way, I found myself in a wide and empty piazza where, like a stately ship, a splendid Norman church rose in the moonlight. Floodlights picked out a tower which I recognized as the campanile that the porter had told me was the bell-tower of the cathedral. This beautiful building, with a rose window above the west front, reminded me of some of the Norman churches in England, but with a difference. Where, for example, in England would one find the side columns of a window resting upon the backs of two elephants? Still, I thought, the men who had built this basilica had spoken the same language as those who had built Durham and Ely, and it occurred to me that possibly one reason why one feels at home in Apulia is that every town contains buildings which correspond to the Norman buildings of English towns and villages.

Walking on and passing beneath a tall archway, I came to another piazza much like the first, but even more impressive. Again, a massive Norman church rose floodlit into the night. This was the focus of all the ceremonies and celebrations of the next three days, the church of St Nicholas. A wide sweep of steps ascended to three splendid doorways; above them was another rose window. As I was admiring this building a group of pilgrims appeared in the empty square, walking with tall sticks, each one topped by a fir cone, the kind I had seen at Monte S. Angelo.

Reaching the centre of the piazza the pilgrims turned towards the church and knelt in the roadway, placing their staves beside them on the cobbles. They were all old women, with the exception of two or three men, villagers maybe from some small place in the Murge or the Capitanata. They lifted their voices in a hoarse and rasping hymn in which I could recognize only the words 'San Nicola.' A door opened in the Dominican Priory opposite and there came from the shadows a Dominican friar who held a bunch of keys. He ascended the steps of the church and let himself in by a side door; and the kneeling pilgrims continued their hymn to the saint.

I began to think that perhaps it was time for me to tear myself from the mediaeval world and find my way back to the hotel. I had to ask a passer-by who, with great kindness, insisted on taking me round one corner, and then round another, and putting me on the right road.


For nearly a thousand years the people of Bari have devoted three days in May, the 7th to the 9th, to celebrate the arrival there in the year 1087 of the bones of St Nicholas of Myra, who is, of course, 'Father Christmas.' The relics were stolen from a tomb in Asia Minor (or 'rescued' as the spirit of the time preferred to put it), by a band of seamen from Bari, homeward bound after having delivered Apulian wheat to Antioch. Through all the trials and perils of Bari's history, the latest of which included an Allied landing in the last war, followed by German air raids and the explosion of an American munitions ship in the harbour, the sacred relics have reposed safely in their silver casket in the crypt of the Church of S. Nicola. They float in a liquid called 'the Manna of S. Nicola', whose miraculous reputation has helped to make the shrine one of the most popular in the south of Italy.

I looked forward to attending the festival when I was told that during the celebrations the statue of St Nicholas is carried to the harbour and sent out in a fishing boat to spend the day at sea, in the belief that the patron saint of sailors would enjoy a day on the water. In Italy and also in Greece saints are sometimes carried to the sea once a year, and are even bathed in it, but actually to witness the great saint of the ocean, who in Greece at least superseded Poseidon, embark upon a voyage was one of those strange appointments with the past which never fail to delight me.

In addition to this role as the protector of sailors and fishermen, St Nicholas is also the patron saint of children, robbers, wolves, Russia, and of pawnbrokers. Some who have studied the subject believe that the pawnbroker's sign represents not the Medici *palle* but three bags of gold which the good saint cast into a widower's house to provide his three daughters with dowries. His transformation into Father Christmas, or Santa Klaus, is another aspect of this versatile saint.

If a popularity count of saints were held, St Nicholas would probably be near the top. There are more than four hundred churches dedicated to him in England alone, and the number of ancient family names derived from him includes Nicols, Nicolson, Nicholson, (the *h* crept in as early as the twelfth century), Nixon, and less obvious, Cole, Colley, Collis, Collett and Collins; and in France the female names of Nicolette and Colette.

Three contemporary observers have described the theft of the relics. Among them was John the Archdeacon, whose account, which was in circulation in the following year, 1088, is a fine piece of mediaeval reporting in which I think the practised ear is able to discern the echo of interviews with the chief actors in the drama. The title is rather long: *Translatio S. Nicolai episcopi ex Myra Lyciae urbe ad Apuliae oppidum Barim vel Barim, scripta ab Johanne archidiacono Barensi jubente Ursone Barensi et Canusino archiepiscopo, circa annum Domini 1088, apud Surium die nono Maii.*

The writer says that when the seamen of Bari had unloaded their wheat in Antioch, they encountered a Venetian crew who confided that they had provided themselves with hammers and crowbars with the intention, when on their homeward voyage, of acquiring the relics of St Nicholas at Myra. Without saying a word, the Baresi swiftly left Antioch with their own hammers and crowbars.

Such operations were the strangest conceivable mixture of piety and dishonesty. The cult of relics had entered the Church from the East, and though some of the finest minds had condemned the exhumation of bodies, repugnant alike to Roman and Jew in earlier ages, and had deplored the trade in bogus relics which was thriving as early as the time of St Augustine, nothing could stop the popular demand for saintly patrons and miraculous cures. The Venetians were the leading collectors. It was a commonplace that their ships' captains were expected to return from eastern voyages with some previous relic, either bought or stolen, until the lagoon had been surrounded by a protective cordon. Their greatest feat was the theft of St Mark's remains from Alexandria in A.D. 828, where, as Egypt had become a Moslem country, the saint himself in a dream expressed his willingness to be 'rescued' and taken to a Christian land. Much the same situation faced the Baresi at Myra, now a ruined site on the south coast of Turkey. In 1087 it had recently been captured by the Infidel. As in Alexandria the Christians of Myra were allowed freedom of worship and to tend and guard their shrine. So in both instances the seamen of Venice and Bari robbed churches and made off with the treasured possessions of fellow Christians.

When the men of Bari arrived at Myra, they went reverently to the shrine of St Nicholas to pray and were given by the Greek monks a little phial of the sacred liquid, the 'manna' that exuded from the bones of the saint, the first mention of this fluid. Having located the tomb, the tactics of the Baresi were the same as those of the Venetians in Alexandria two and a half centuries earlier. They offered to buy the remains for gold. The Venetians had found the Egyptian monks willing to do a deal, but the Greeks at Myra were indignant. 'We wish to bear off this holy body,' said the men of Bari, 'and transport it to our own country. We are come here in three ships commissioned by the pope of Rome to effect this. If you will consent to our doing it, we will give you a hundred pieces of gold from each ship.'

This shocking lie had no effect on the monks, indeed the morality of the Greeks was of a higher order than that of the Latins. 'Who is there so audacious,' asked the Greeks, 'as to venture to be either the buyer or seller in such a traffic?' Then, finding that the Italians were determined to break open the tomb, they said, in effect. 'There it is. See if you dare to commit an act so odious to God?' This frightened the Baresi. Two priests whom they had brought with them were praying in the church, 'but in such a state of alarm that their voices faltered in the service they had commenced.'

At length the bolder spirits decided to act, and, taking hammers broke into the tomb; they discovered beneath the brickwork what they called a 'marble urn', which was probably a sarcophagus. As soon as they smashed the marble, they became aware of the sacred liquid, the 'manna di San Nicola'. Also, like the Venetians when they broke into St Mark's tomb, they smelt a heavenly odour, perhaps the 'odour of sanctity'. John the Archdeacon says that 'it intoxicated all who were present with its delicious fragrance'. Meanwhile a young man named Matthew, who seems to have been the leader, thrust in his hand and found the sarcophagus half full of the sacred fluid. 'He then put in his right arm and, feeling the invaluable treasure which it was the object of his most ardent wishes to secure, began fearlessly to extract it without loss of time. At last in searching for the head, he plunged bodily into the full urn, and groping about with his hands and feet while endeavouring to find it, he came out with his whole person and his garments dripping with the sacred liquid.'

The devout thieves then made off with their booty. Unlike the Venetians, they did not leave another body in the tomb to deceive the local inhabitants, but hurried to their ships. The Venetians, in order to discourage a search on the part of the Moslems, had concealed the remains of St Mark in a barrel of salt pork, but the Baresi did not consider such a precaution to be necessary. 'They embarked full of joy, and wrapping the relics in an additional covering of new white cloth, they enclosed them in a wooden vessel such as sailors use for a wine-cask.'

The inhabitants of Myra flocked to the shore filled with rage and grief, 'tearing their hair and beards, and, wailing for the loss of their pastor and patron, and joining with accord in a mournful chant:

> '*Ah wretched day! Ah foul disgrace,*
> *Ah sad dishonour to our race!*
> *The gift of God, the glorious prize*
> *Has vanished from our longing eyes*
> *Not lost upon the battle-field*
> *By thronging numbers forced to yield,*
> *But ravished by a skulking crew,*
> *(Alas the deed was done by few).*
> *We wail our country's treasure gone*
> *Too easily by pirates won.*

The pious burglary was successful. No Venetian rivals attempted to interrupt the voyage so that the crews were able to land their precious cargo at Bari among rejoicing crowds in May, 1087. (Incidentally, this year was notable in Anglo-Norman history. In September, William the Conqueror died at Rouen.) The desire of the Archbishop of Bari to inter the relics in the cathedral was, for some reason, unpopular. The chest containing them was eventually loaded upon a wagon whose oxen stopped on a spot near the seashore, where the church of St Nicholas was soon built. That is why the porch pillars of this church rest upon the backs, not of the customary lions, but of two indeterminate beasts which represent oxen. They have lost their horns, which were once of bronze, but the sockets into which they fitted are visible in the stone. It would not be a bad idea to restore these horns and so re-establish the identity of the two odd-looking creatures, two porch ornaments which are unique in Italy.

Every morning before breakfast I walked across to the Old City and went to Mass either at the Cathedral or the church of S. Nicola. The extraordinary old streets seemed to me even more interesting by daylight than at night. I cannot recall another inhabited mediaeval city in Europe as large as Old Bari, and for this I suppose one has to thank Murat's plan to leave it intact and to build a new rectangular city next to it. As you pass into the mediaeval town the noises are all of human origin: men selling their wares, people learning musical instruments, women shouting to each other from balcony to balcony, children crying, and always a bell ringing somewhere. Most of the streets of Old Bari are too narrow for motor cars; the pedlar goes round with a barrow from door to door. The women seem always to be drawing water from wells or from fountains, and it was my impression that the inhabitants of Old Bari enjoyed the cheerful, crowded life of the streets and the ancient houses, and would resist any attempt to move them into the modern city.

Few would probably notice what struck me as perhaps the most authentic mediaevalism in Old Bari: the appalling mass of rubbish and refuse, cardboard, paper, rotten fruit, fish and vegetables, that had been dumped in the streets or flung through the windows. At an early hour this is swept up and carried away with the speed and efficiency of a military exercise by dustmen called *netturbini*, from *nettare*, to clean, and *urbe*, city. I had never come across this word before. In most parts of Italy a street cleaner is called a *spazzino*. The *netturbini*, unable to drive their vans into the heart of the old city, advance upon it in the early morning with handcarts. I watched them as they performed the functions of the mediaeval saint, who was expected to keep his city free from plague. By eight o'clock the streets were practically spotless and ready for the day's deluge.

Beneath the ancient archways came children with their school satchels, wearing the blue overalls and floppy ties inflicted upon the Italian young, all of them looking healthy and clean, a tribute to life in mediaeval surroundings or to the survival of the fittest. The small shops opened; many were fish stalls on which the strange and variously coloured denizens of the Adriatic were set out in rows. Through a hundred doorways one saw women busy with the first chore of the day, the preparation of home-made pasta. Characteristic of Bari is the small circular pasta called *recchietelle*, known in other parts of Italy as 'little ears' (*orecchietti*). Having made them, the women arrange them on wire tables and place them out in the open air to dry.

The pilgrims transform the character of the old city for three days as they wander through the narrow lanes in groups and processions, grasping their staves and speaking the rustic dialects of Southern Italy. A native of Bari, whose speech would bewilder a Roman or a Florentine, is puzzled in his turn by the dialect of a fellow countryman from the mountain villages of Calabria. Until the First World War shiploads of pilgrims would come from Russia, since St Nicholas is their patron saint, and before the last war they came also from the Balkans. Now hundreds of Italianized Albanians are to be met in Bari from the Albanian villages of the South, many of which were colonized centuries ago by refugees.

I could tell at a glance those pilgrims who had arrived by coach, for they carried only hand luggage. But the pilgrims who had come the hard traditional way, on foot across the mountains, were roughly clad and were hung about with all kinds of things, drinking-cups, satchels, rings of bread, sometimes speared on their staves, and always a blanket in a neat roll slung across the shoulders and resting in the small of the back. Some pilgrims carried staves tipped with bright feathers, and others, as I have already noted, had staves from Monte S. Angelo with pine cones on top. To each staff was tied, often with coloured ribbons, not the hazel branch of the mediaeval pilgrim, but the umbrella which is the constant companion of the southern Italian peasant.

Many of the pilgrims came from poverty-stricken villages of the South. There were few young men among them, for these had migrated in search of work. The women were mostly dressed in bunchy black skirts, some wore black knitted shawls across their shoulders, and all wore handkerchiefs over their heads, tied beneath the chin or at the nape of the neck. I came upon a group of them seated in a circle on the pavement. They might have been Bedouin. Their faces wore expressions of settled resignation and melancholy. Forming a circle round this group were others, similarly dressed, leaning upon their staves, old before their time, thin lips drawn across toothless gums, faces grey with fatigue and etched with lines of hardship and poverty.

Inside the church Mass had just ended. The basilica was crowded. As the pilgrims entered, they dropped upon their knees and, helping themselves along with their staves, slowly and painfully began to hobble forward up the nave. One party was led by a girl of about ten wearing her first communion dress. She walked forward carrying a crucifix and behind hobbled her elders, as if led by a little angel, stopping now and again to wipe the tears from their eyes. I noticed that several young and better dressed women wearing nylon stockings did not hesitate to kneel and hobble with the others. Their stockings must have been in shreds.

The joyful aspect of Christianity did not appear to touch these people. They looked as if they would have preferred to join the weeping Maries at the foot of the Cross rather than be among those who witnessed the Resurrection. What some of the old peasants must have endured who suffered from arthritis and rheumatism can be imagined, but possibly they concentrated on the agony of the saints and were aware of the blessings of penitential hardships. If now and again one or two were forced to stand upright for a few steps, they soon dropped down again. This strange procession pressed forward through the crowds rather like an assembly of crippled dwarfs. I had never before witnessed such a mass demonstration of humility.

The relics of St Nicholas are in the beautiful crypt of the basilica, which was built in 1087. Here the pilgrims felt themselves to be in the sacred presence. Tears flowed freely as they hobbled forward leaning on their staves, their bundles on their backs, the ancient vaults rising above them upheld by numerous columns with Roman or Byzantine capitals. Their eyes sought the silver altar beneath which lies the casket in which the bones of St Nicholas are said to float in the *sacra manna*. Here and there in awed and tremulous tones a litany would be intoned, but I could again understand only the reiterated name of 'San Nicola'; it was one of the lauds, or hymns of praise, which have been sung for centuries in the presence of the saint. To my dismay, one of the old women lay flat upon the pavement and crawled forward licking the stones. Her daughters, or perhaps her granddaughters, whispered to her and tried to dissuade her, but she was in the presence of God's elect and neither heard nor heeded them. I was deeply moved. I thought I should never again see what a mediaeval pilgrimage was like. Though these pilgrims bore no resemblance to the sophisticated tourists of *The Canterbury Tales*, such awed and expiatory gatherings must have been a familiar sight centuries ago at all the great shrines of Europe.

One of the few books in English about Apulia is a slender volume of travel by Janet Ross, published in 1889. The writer had stood in the church of St Nicholas eighty years ago and had seen pilgrims crawling up the nave and down to the crypt, as I had seen them, but she also saw a ceremony which I did not see. She wrote:

'A priest, thrusting half of his body into the hole above the tomb, ladles out the sacred 'manna', which is given in a small silver bucket to the devout to drink, and is supposed to cure all ills. I was accompanied to the church by a gentleman of Bari who knew the Archbishop well, so a priest came up and offered to get me some of the holy manna; in an undertone my friend advised me to decline, he said it was extremely nauseous, like bad brown sugar and water. As prayers are necessary before the silver door in the altar can be opened, which permits the priest to reach the tomb, we alleged want of time and promised to return next day.'

The source of the 'manna' is no longer as accessible, though the liquid itself is everywhere. I was told that there is not a house or an institution in the province of Bari, or a fishing smack in any of the ports, which does not somewhere have a little phial of the sacred fluid. It is sold to pilgrims in attractive little bottles, the shape of ordinary medicine bottles, bearing on one side the head of St. Nicholas in raised relief and, upon the other, the words 'Basilica di S. Nicola, Bari. S. Manna'. Each little bottle is securely sealed with lead. The 'manna' is colourless, odourless and, to me, tasted like ordinary water.

I was given permission to go down into the crypt with a Dominican friar after the basilica was closed, so that I had an opportunity to look into every corner of that important building. The friar told me that it was a legend of Bari that the First Crusade was preached in the crypt in the year of its opening, 1089, six years before Urban II officially proclaimed a crusade to the French nobility at Clermont in 1095.

'It is said that Peter the Hermit preached here before Pope Urban,' he said.

I asked what foundation there was for this story but he was unable to tell me. Months afterwards I came across Bari's so-called 'legend' clearly set down in some detail in the crusading history of William of Tyre, who was almost a contemporary authority. This writer says that Peter, having visited Jerusalem as a pilgrim and having been shocked by the persecution of the Christians and the condition of the holy sites under the Moslems, took ship to Bari, carrying with him a letter from the Patriarch of Jerusalem to the Pope, begging for help. When he landed at Bari, Peter found that the Pope was in the neighbourhood and therefore it was unnecessary for him to go to Rome to present the Patriarch's letter. As the Pope is known to have visited Bari twice, in 1089 and in 1098, and as the second date is too late and does not fit in with Peter's movements, it is probable that the first public appeal to Christian men to rally in defence of the holy places was heard at the opening of this crypt.

Peter the Hermit was in appearance evidently a nondescript little man who, as Anna Comnena, who had seen him, says, was nick-named *cucupiettore*, or Little Peter; and there are other indications that he was not heroic either in appearance or conduct. 'He was a man of short stature,' wrote Steven Runciman, 'swarthy and with a long, lean face, horribly like the donkey that he always rode and which was revered almost as much as himself. He went barefoot: and his clothes were filthy. He ate neither bread nor meat, but fish and he drank wine. Despite his lowly appearance he had the power to move men.'

It is believed that he was born near Amiens about 1053, the son of Reginald d'Ermite, and must have been in his forties when he had the appalling experience of leading a mob of ignorant peasants, which some scholars have estimated to have been 15,000 to 20,000 strong, to the relief of the Holy Land where, of course, most of them perished on the way. Peter then linked up with the knights of the First Crusade, though he played no prominent part in events.

He vanished after the First Crusade to appear years later in old age as the founder of a priory near Liège, on the right bank of the Meuse, near the town of Huy. When he died there in 1115, he asked, for reasons of humility, not to be buried in the church but outside in the graveyard. Though this was done, his bones were reverently taken up in the next century and re-interred inside the church, beneath a marble monument. This was described by a traveller as recently as 1761, but soon afterwards a French revolutionary mob smashed open the tomb and scattered the hermit's bones.

§ 4

Seated among the elect upon the municipal rostrum, I waited for the Pageant of St Nicholas to begin. It was now dark. Facing us across a piazza, which had been cleared of crowds, rose the noble west front of the Church of St Nicholas. Floodlights illuminated every stone and sent the pigeons exploding from their homes in rounded Norman windows and arcades, then as suddenly returned the Church to darkness. The waiting was relieved by the last minute anxieties, the gesticulations, and the dramatic shouting which precede most Italian functions. Men in grey suits strode importantly about speaking into microphones as they tested the loud speakers, electricians appeared in unexpected places (once, like escaping thieves, white-faced upon the very roof of the church), switching on and off the batteries of golden light and making penultimate adjustments with the distrust which technicians everywhere bestow upon their equipment. Into a scene floodlit for a minute appeared the usual raffish dog with the air of a returned traveller who is startled by the regrettable changes that have occurred during his absence. Then strolling over to an ancient railing, he courteously lifted a leg in acceptance of the situation and glanced round, as if hoping to be asked to take part in whatever was to come. A *Maresciallo dei Carabinieri* brought a white glove to his Napoleonic hat as the mayor's lady and her daughters were admitted to the rostrum; an usher, suddenly finding himself face to face with the Archbishop, dropped on one knee and kissed his ring before showing him to his seat, and a ship's siren sent a note of searing melancholy into the night, turning one's thoughts to Myra and the holy burglary which we were about to celebrate.

The west front of the church, now brilliantly illuminated, was a splendid sight. When the doors were opened, I was seated in such a fortunate position that I could look straight up the nave to the apse at the east end, and to a striking feature of these Apulian churches, the ciborium. This is a stone canopy above the altar, resting on four marble columns and roofed with an arcade of miniature columns, sometimes in two storeys. There seems to have been a revival of this ancient feature in the eleventh century. The ciborium of St Nicholas recalls those of S. Clemente, S. Agata dei Goti, and S. Giorgio in Velabro, in Rome, though I thought it more graceful than any of them. The priest officiating at an altar which stands beneath a ciborium generally faces the congregation, as the Pope does when he says Mass in St Peter's.

While we waited, we were entertained by solemn music which died away as a powerful voice, charged with emotion, told the story of the arrival of the saint in Bari. We could hear the sound of crowds in the distance which announced the approach of the procession. Drummers in mediaeval costume entered the piazza, followed by trumpeters. A group of *sbandieratori* now entered the square and waved their coloured flags, tossing them into the air, passing them between their legs and shooting them high into the floodlights, catching them as they descended. At last, escorted by men holding flambeaux and drawn by others dressed as sailors, came the caravel, a decorative craft of ancient design upon which stood a large framed picture of St Nicholas. As the ship entered the piazza, choirs broke into the Halleluja Chorus and the Prior of the Dominicans, followed by his friars, went to receive the picture of the saint. The mariners in hooded tunics, looking rather like Robin Hood and his men, tenderly lifted down the picture and handed it to two Dominicans. The friars bearing *flabelli* of ostrich feathers fell in beside the portrait and, with the Prior leading, slowly ascended the steps into the church as the bells of the Old City rang out.

On the way back to the hotel I was jostled in the crowds by Norman archers, by men bearing flags and banners, and by bands of youths with shaggy mops of hair carrying axes or flaming torches. A noisy fair was in progress along the waterfront. It offered a variety of useful objects. You could buy a charm against the Evil Eye, a baby's rattle of imitation coral, a pair of boots, a picture of St Nicholas, a steaming bowl of spaghetti, nylon stockings, hats, overcoats, and, of course, a slice of *porchetta*, all within a space of a few yards, and all displayed in brilliant electric light and advertised by that terror of Italian fairs, four or five men out-shouting one another in loud-speaker vans. The Spaniards are commonly reputed to thrive on noise and to be stimulated by it, but I think the Italians probably enjoy it even more.

A change too had come over the pilgrims. The sombre old women of the morning were now singing away to accordions and clapping their hands, old eyes sparkling in lined faces. There was one notably merry group. A man played a mouth organ while others formed a ring and danced with snapping of fingers, a kind of jig which I thought might possibly be a tarantella. The song was a quick cheerful one but died away into Arabic halftones and quavers. No one could tell me where these people came from, or what they were singing. Someone suggested they were from Naples, someone else said that they were Calabrians.

The hotel, when I reached it, seemed to be a million miles from these scenes and happenings. Businessmen were grasping their brief cases, which are a commercial status symbol in Italy, and asking about telephone calls from Milan.

§ 5

The life-size statue of St Nicholas was carved and painted by a capable artist in the seventeenth century. It depicts a benign, bearded bishop, haloed, and grasping a crozier, while in the other hand he holds a book upon which are balanced three golden balls, a reference to the three bags of gold with which the saint, perhaps to the puzzlement of the psychologist, is said to have saved three maidens from a life of sin. This is the statue which is carried through Bari once a year and sent to sea for the day in a fishing boat.

The day after the pageant I went down early to the Molo di

S. Nicola to select a good place from which to see the embarkation. I was so early that the breakwater contained only a few fishermen and a group of *carabinieri* in full dress uniforms, holding their hats beneath their arms as they smoked cigarettes and joked. It was a perfect morning. Beyond the old harbour stretched the turquoise blue of the Adriatic, and, looking towards the old city, I saw that it shared to the full the dazzling whiteness which is characteristic of these Adriatic towns. With their flat-roofed houses, their narrow lanes, the buildings rising in box-like tiers with domes and slender towers above them, and sometimes even a palm tree, they reminded me of the seaports of North Africa.

I asked a policeman why an Italian warship was anchored in the bay. He told me that sailors as well as fishermen form a guard of honour for St Nicholas, which I thought fit and proper since he is the patron of both. The long wait was beguiled for me by watching a fisherman catch a huge octopus among the rocks of the breakwater; his struggles when the creature wound a tentacle round his leg reminded me of the Laocoon. The contest was watched also by a school of angelic little girls wearing their first communion dresses. Each child held a missal bound in white and from each wrist depended a tiny, neat handkerchief. The two sisters in charge of them were equally interested in the octopus, and their combined expressions, the exclamations, the small hands in lace mittens held to mouths, were delightful to watch. The *carabinieri* strolled over and jokingly offered a sword to Laocoon. The mole began to fill with the élite of Bari. Distant bells rang. St Nicholas was on his way.

I had taken up my position next to a small railed-in enclosure a few paces from the decorated barge which, moored to a jetty, was ready to carry the saint to a fishing boat. The officers of the garrison, the naval officer in command of the destroyer, the mayor, the councillors, advocates, doctors, their wives and families, were received and led to their places. I wondered why the railed enclosure, which was my anchorage, should have remained vacant, and I was soon to see it become the scene of one of those last minute transformations which I think so typical of Italian ceremonies. While we could hear the bands drawing nearer, a small van drove through the assembled dignitaries from which emerged three unhurried workmen. They unloaded a massive gold and red baroque throne, two gilt footstools and a disreputable-looking old kitchen table on its last legs. These incongruous companions were placed side by side within the enclosure and in a few minutes the men, with embroidery and lace, had transformed the old table into an altar upon which they placed four massive candlesticks. They spread a rich carpet upon the flagstones and erected a scarlet background to the altar. With the same casual air of leisure, they drove away. Almost at the same moment the Archbishop arrived and was conducted in state to the golden throne in the ornate enclosure, which only a few moments before had looked like a cattle-pen.

As the head of the procession reached the breakwater, thousands of pilgrims grasping their pine-tipped staves lined up on each side singing lauds to St Nicholas. Under the influence of strong emotion many were inspired to make speeches. A microphone was handed to them and we heard, booming over the loudspeakers in strong dialect, a torrent of praise and piety. There was nothing of the tongue-tied rustic about these Italian peasants; some, having got the microphone, were anxious to keep it as long as possible and gave it up only after a struggle. I do not know whether these eloquent praises were carefully composed during the long tramp to Bari, or whether they were, as I fancy, extemporaneous and inspired by the emotion of the moment. In any event, they proved how securely eloquence is embedded in the Italian character.

The saint, borne high above the crowds upon his palanquin, turned and entered the narrow causeway. We could see the sun shining on his halo. He advanced, trembling slightly and appearing to nod to one side or another in the uncanny, rather threatening way of carried images. Upon each side of him walked Dominicans and men in white surplices bearing aloft on gilt poles tight bouquets of red and white carnations, the heraldic colours of Bari. These colours were seen again in the eighteenth century costume of two municipal beadles who advanced, one carrying the banner of the Province, the other the Banner of Bari – palewise white and red. They wore white cutaway coats, red knee-breeches and white stockings.

As the procession halted a few yards away, the Archbishop, wearing a golden mitre and a gold cope, went forward to greet the saint and to conduct him to the jetty. The statue was smoothly and efficiently transferred to the barge, the Archbishop and the notables took their places round it and, to the sounds of pilgrims chanting, the banging of rockets, which exploded in a sunlit sky, and the noise of ships' sirens, St Nicholas set out across the old harbour towards the fishing boat. This had been newly painted and a shrine erected in the stern. The saint was lifted from the barge to the shrine where he was to remain until darkness. Immediately, a flotilla of rowing boats weighed down to the gunwales set off to visit him; and these continued all day. Those on shore saw the saint, crozier in hand, dramatically facing Bari as if in the act of blessing the city. Old memories had been awakened and people of all classes crowded to the harbour or set off in boats to visit their patron. And how Italian it was that during the most emotional moments of this appointment with the past, an aeroplane should have been allowed to pass and repass over-head advertising lager beer.

The landing of the saint at night was even more dramatic than his embarkation. He arrived to a bombardment of fireworks. The sky was filled with falling stars. He was carried through the Old City, now brilliantly illuminated with triumphal arches of electric light; and to shouts of welcome St Nicholas of Myra passed through the streets of his adopted town.

§ 6

Every Sunday while I was at Bari I looked forward to visiting the shell-fish stalls on the breakwater. There were twenty to thirty of them, set up by fishermen, and as I never saw them during the week I concluded it was a way to turn an honest penny while the fishing fleet was in harbour. The display of shell-fish was impressive, in particular superb oysters at six shillings a dozen; and one could either take them away or eat them in one of the tents furnished with tables and chairs which stood behind the stalls.

When I entered one of these and ordered a dozen oysters, the fisherman placed a bucket on the table from which he withdrew the oysters and, deftly opening them with one thrust and twist of the knife, handed them one by one for me to eat from the shell, which gourmets consider the best way to eat an oyster. While he did so, he told me that the oysters came not from the Adriatic but from the Ionian Sea, from the famous beds of Taranto.

Equally good were the clams, the mussels and the sea urchins. According to Apicius, the Romans cooked the sea urchin in a variety of ways, but I have only eaten it uncooked and as it comes from the sea. The minute eatable segments of saffron-coloured roe have always tasted to me, upon the rare occasions when I have eaten them, like dehydrated ozone, indeed I know no other shell-fish which brings with it such a powerful whiff of the ocean. More adventurous for the English gourmet was a rocklike shell-fish called *tartufi di mare*, sea truffles, which, having been sated already with oysters and clams, I regret to say I never tasted. Elizabeth David, to whom all gourmets genuflect, says of them that they are 'usually eaten raw – and very good too.' Neither did I taste *datteri di mare*, sea-dates, which resemble a date stone in appearance, but I did venture to eat *cannolicchi*, the razor-fish, a three-inch long vermicular shell-fish that lives in a beautiful deli-cate pencil-like grey shell, but is still disconcertingly alive when eaten.

Marvellous are the crabs, crayfish, prawns, ink-fish, octopus and cuttle-fish, which lie banked on these stalls, and never have I found shell-fish so varied or so cheap. On Sunday mornings at breakfast I was in the habit of asking the waiter to bring me some slices of buttered bread for my tour of the shell-fish stalls, since nothing as sophisticated as even a fork is provided. It was a pleasing way to have lunch, slowly travelling from stall to stall, selecting a few sea urchins here and a few oysters or mussels there, though I beg the reader, who may find himself in Bari on such a luscious morning, not on any account to emulate my conduct without first taking the most reliable local advice. Such moments, however, were an unforgettable memory of Bari to me. A few yards away the dark Adriatic slowly lapped the break-water and there came from near at hand a slapping sound which was made by fishermen banging dead octopuses upon the rocks to make them tender.

Continuity of effort over many centuries is always impressive, and I have sometimes reflected that two activities which have managed to survive empires are street markets and fish stalls. When Horace travelled the length of the Via Appia with his rich friend, Maecenas, starting from Rome and ending at Brundusium (Brindisi), they passed through Bari – which was then Barium – and may even have stayed there. Describing the journey, Horace could think of no better description of Bari than 'fish-famous Barium'. As I strolled among the shell-fish stalls on Sunday, I thought that Horace and Maecenas may have done the same thing and have seen similar collections of molluscs caught by much the same kind of small, dark, weather-beaten men.

§ 7

Some editions of the *Little Flowers of St Francis* omit the episode of the saint and the harlot, the editors, no doubt, considering the subject to be unedifying. The story is that in 1219, during the Fifth Crusade, when St Francis was in the Holy Land, he stayed at an inn where a young woman suggested that they should go to bed together. 'I am willing,' said the saint, who followed the girl to a bedroom in which an enormous fire was burning. He undressed and, lying in front of the blaze, invited the girl to do the same. But while St Francis remained there cheerfully, neither scorched nor burned by the unbearable heat, the girl became frightened and, it is said, repented of her sinful intentions.

What a foolish story it is. Why should it have been incorporated among the *Little Flowers*? It is not subtle enough to be an allegory, neither has it any of the qualities that make a good story, or point a moral. It is merely an incident quite out of character, yet for that reason interesting. It is in this manner that a true story becomes garbled and twisted, and consequently I have often wondered what was the real truth about St Francis and the girl. I never expected to find the answer in Bari; indeed I did not know that St Francis was ever in that town.

One morning I went to visit the castle on the edge of the Old City, an immense fortification with a moat all round it, now a garden. It was first built by the Normans, then enlarged by Frederick II and brought up to date in subsequent periods. In the old days the walls were washed by the waves but now a wide *corso* separates it from the sea. I paid my fee at a gatehouse and walked up a gentle incline with ancient walls on the left, evidently a relic of the earlier castle. An inscription attached to these walls caught my eye. I read that the Castle of Bari was the place in which St Francis was tempted by a young woman.

I found that everyone in Bari knew the legend that St Francis arrived there from the Holy Land in 1220. Bari was then one of the seaports used by the Crusaders. At the time Frederick II, then twenty-six, was holding court in the Castle of Bari and was surrounded by his usual fantastic entourage of Saracens, astrologers, scholars, dancing girls, hawks, leopards and, of course, the famous elephant. The story is that Frederick, curious to test the virtue of the saint who had wedded Lady Poverty and had preached so often of chastity, invited him to the castle. His plan was to introduce a beautiful girl into the saint's bedroom with instructions to seduce the holy man, while he, Frederick, had already prepared a peep-hole from which to watch the proceedings. St Francis, who was then thirty-eight years of age, repelled the temptress with, so the story goes, red-hot coals from a brazier, and the story concludes that Frederick was so delighted that he sat up for the rest of the night in conversation with the saint.

This story has the ring of truth and it is typical of the crafty way Frederick II set about testing people, as he was so fond of doing. In much the same way he tried out his mathematician, the almost

legendary Michael Scott, by asking him to measure the distance
from the top of a tower to the heavens, then, having ordered
workmen to lower the tower secretly, he asked Scott to check his
measurement. When he found that the second measurement was
slightly higher than the first, he was as delighted with Scott as he
was with St Francis.

The saint died six years after the supposed meeting with the
Emperor, and who should be sent to Assisi to design the church
there, which still holds the remains of St Francis, but the imperial
architect, Jacobo the German. He settled down and married in
Italy (his name contracted to Lapo), earning in due course the by
no means unique distinction of an inaccurate biography from the
pen of Vasari. How interesting too is the friendship which sprang
up after the death of St Francis between Brother Elias and the
Emperor, the worldly Franciscan who has been called the man
who made Lady Poverty rich. One wishes that a record existed
of their conversations, which must have turned often on the 'little
poor man of Assisi'.

The Castle of Bari is unusual among the castles of Apulia in
having been the seat of a Renaissance court. This was the court of
Bona, Queen of Poland, and the last Duchess of Bari, who died
there in 1558 and was buried in the basilica of St Nicholas. Her
tomb is in the apse of that building, immediately behind, and in
incongruous juxtaposition with the ciborium. Bona is seen with a
sweet expression, kneeling upon her black marble sarcophagus,
guarded by two unlikely saints who stand in nearby niches, St
Casimir and St Stanislaus. Bona takes the mind back to Milan and
the great days of Ludovico Il Moro and his charming young wife,
Beatrice d'Este. Bona's mother was Isabella of Aragon, Duchess of
Milan, and wife of the weak and sickly sixth Duke, Gian Galeazzo
Sforza. It has never been proved that his uncle Ludovico poisoned
him in order to become the seventh Duke, but whatever happened
the displaced Isabella rapidly achieved the reputation of being the
most miserable and ill-used widow on earth. She signed her
letters at this period 'Isabella of Aragon, unique in misfortune.'
But the misfortune of a haughty Renaissance duchess might not be
that which an ordinary person would recognize as such. If she

believed, as she evidently did, that her husband had died of poison, she saw him avenged when the French captured Milan and took Ludovico away to life-long imprisonment. Instead of finding herself reinstated as Duchess of Milan, as regent for her elder son, both her sons were taken to France for political reasons, while she left Lombardy with her two young daughters and went to Bari. She was the Duchess of Bari and the Baresi welcomed her with open arms.

She now devoted herself entirely to the education of her daughter, Bona, who was a graceful, beautiful and highly intelligent child. She introduced, as far as she was able, the intellectual atmosphere of the Milanese court as she had known it, so that artists, musicians, and writers were always welcome to the old castle of Bari. At the age of fifteen Bona was married to the fifty-one year old King of Poland, Sigismund I, a hale Hercules of a man who, like many giants, was apparently mild and kindly. Details of Bona's farewell party have been preserved in a journal kept by Giuliano Passero, who described a feast that continued for nine hours. Bona presided, wearing a gown of blue Venetian satin covered with bees in beaten gold, and upon her head glittered a cap covered with jewels and sewn with pearls.

The elderly bridegroom was delighted with his young wife, and it is perhaps remarkable that such unions often turned out well. Schoolgirls, as we should think of them now, often proved able to control and even to dominate fierce and feared old men. Something like that happened in Poland. Sigismund and Bona reigned for thirty years, when the King died, at the age of eighty-one. At first Bona had been greatly liked, but as she grew up she became detested because of her avarice and her ability to enrich herself at the expense of the State: she was also said to be a mischievous and meddlesome influence in politics and state affairs. Probably she was given a freer hand than a younger husband would have allowed her and as Sigismund grew older, while he still presented a massive front to the world, he became apathetic and lost interest, unable to face the new world and the new men who now surrounded him. Bona bore him one son, who succeeded him, and four daughters, but her reputation was such that when her son's wife, Barbara Radziwill, died three days after the coronation, it was assumed that her mother-in-law had poisoned her.

It is also perhaps natural that Bona, who, in addition to her rank as Dowager Queen of Poland, was also the Duchess of Bari, should have decided to return to Italy. She kept her court in the old castle of Bari which once again became the scene of brilliant and intellectual gatherings as it had been in the days of her girl-hood. This echo of the great court of Milan as it was under the last Sforzas lasted for ten years, when the Queen-Duchess died at the age of sixty-five.

Such is the story behind the funeral monument of a Queen of Poland whose presence may puzzle the visitor when he comes to it in the apse of the Church of St Nicholas.

§ 8

One of the delights of Bari is a museum stacked to the ceilings with black and red figured pottery of the sixth and fifth centuries before Christ. I was taken there by an archaeologist who was absurdly apologetic about the building, an imitation Renaissance palace which I thought delightful and reminiscent of the Vatican Library. He evidently considered it old-fashioned and unworthy of Bari, explaining that soon a modern museum was to be built where everything would be seen in the best possible light.

But this old museum was good enough for me. It was my first sight of Magna Graecia and the light was brilliant enough, coming down the centuries from the ages when Athens and Sparta were young and Rome had not yet been born. The vases, the armour, the children's toys, the jointed dolls, the graceful little painted statuettes had been found in the cemeteries or on the sites of those seacoast towns of Southern Italy and Sicily which were colonized by settlers from the states of ancient Greece.

My companion explained that much of the painted pottery had been made locally centuries before Christ, though some of it had been imported. He said that as I went south I would see many of the ancient shapes still being made by modern potters. The enormous hoards of Greek pottery in the museums of South

Italy are unknown except to a few experts, and the work of classifying and cataloguing the vases and the paintings has scarcely begun.

The people who lived in the Greek coast towns so long ago were as fond of the charming little painted terracotta statuettes called Tanagra figures as their ancestors in Greece. These figures show men and women in natural poses, women dancing or playing at knuckle bones, or standing draped in the cloaks fashionable at the time; and they show men, often caricatured, sometimes as comic or tragic actors.

I was interested to see Greek armour that has been perfectly preserved in the soil of Apulia. The bronze breastplate modelled on the human torso was used in Magna Graecia, and passed from Greece to Rome. I noticed that some of the helmets had nose-guards which were similar to those used by the Normans and, after another long interval of time, by Cromwell's Ironsides. I saw a superb collection of the silver coinage of Magna Graecia, some of the most beautiful coins ever minted, but I always came back to the corridors stacked with vases and to rooms full of them where the artist had drawn pictures of gods and heroes and of ordinary men and women as he saw them bustling about the rich commercial seaports two thousand years ago.

# CHAPTER FOUR

*The Norman cathedrals of Apulia – the story of the Hauteville family –
the Norman kings of Sicily – the Normans in England and in Italy –
Marriage embassies – the battlefield of Cannae – the 'Disfida' of
Barletta – the bronze emperor – Frederick II, the 'wonder of the world' –
his castle of del Monte – his book on birds and falconry – his funeral
pomp*

## § I

The coastline of Apulia is one of the most romantic that I
have ever seen. The local limestone with which all the
ancient buildings are constructed has been bleached by
centuries of sunlight to the whiteness of chalk. For fifty miles
upon each side of Bari lies a succession of small seaports and fishing
towns, each one with its massive castle, Norman in origin, sometimes renovated by Hohenstaufen or Angevin, a cathedral, also
Norman, and a warren of streets some of them so oriental in
appearance that one might be in Morocco. But it is the dazzling
light which remains in my memory. That and, of course, the blue-
green of the Adriatic shading to the colour which Homer called
'wine-dark'.

Nowhere in Europe are so many Norman cathedrals to be found
so close together, and should the pedant rebuke me for calling
them Norman and not Apulian-Romanesque, I can only say that
the dark and solemn naves, with their rounded arches, the
carved, massive doorways, the delicate arcading and a hundred
other details, are essentially Norman. It is difficult to say which is
the most beautiful or the most interesting of these Norman
cathedrals, but their accessibility within walking distance one
from the other makes it a simple matter to re-visit and compare
them. Ten miles from Bari is the cathedral of Giovinazzo, which
was built in 1283; two miles farther on is lovely Molfetta, where

a white cathedral with three domes and two bell-towers is reflected in rock pools; eight miles on is Bisceglie with its twelfth century cathedral; then another five miles and one comes to the cathedral of Trani (1096) with its superb bronze doors and, also, like Molfetta, upon the edge of the sea. Another ten miles brings one to the coast town of Barletta, with a cathedral that dates from 1139. And one is still only thirty-five miles from Bari.

To leave the coast at Barletta and to return to Bari by inland roads is to arrive, after eight miles, at the site of the battle of Cannae; another eight and one sees the cathedral of Canosa and the tomb of the crusader Bohemund, who captured Antioch in 1098; another twelve miles and one is in Andria, in whose cathedral was buried the English wife of Frederick II; then to Ruvo with its Norman cathedral, and twelve miles farther on to the exquisite cathedral of Bitonto, which was built in 1200; and so back to Bari.

I cannot think of any other small area that holds so much of interest for the historian and particularly for the architect. These Apulian cathedrals and minor churches are a relatively unknown chapter in the history of Norman architecture and scarcely anything has been written about them. They remain in delightful obscurity, the timeless activities of small harbours going on all round them and weekly markets being held in their shadows. They are the most beautiful surviving memory of the Norman conquest of Southern Italy.

Only in England and the South of Italy, I suppose, is a Norman conquest an essential part of the history curriculum: but young Italians and English children read of two different types of conquest. In England, a feudal army under its Duke landed and possessed the country after one battle; in Italy, on the other hand, a number of individual adventurers from Normandy sold their swords to the highest bidder and gradually, over a long period of time, mastered their employers and eventually controlled the whole country.

The Normans resemble those people for whom one feels – dislike is too strong a word – an instinctive aversion. Among their vices were avarice and cruelty, and among their virtues were physical courage of the highest order, to which must be added discipline and a loyalty to the head of the house. In contrast, the Anglo-Saxons, in spite of their melancholy, were a likeable, poetic and rural people, while the Lombards, the Byzantines and the Saracens whom the Normans confronted in Italy were the product of a higher civilization. At their best the Normans were fearless soldiers, bold statesmen and good administrators and one must be fair to them; but why cannot one like them?

I think probably the answer is that they were revoltingly cruel. Perhaps the shiver which clings to the word dungeon may date from the invasion of England, when sinister accounts were told of the fate of those carried off to hill-top castles by the conquerors, never to be seen again. The English-born monk, Odericus Vitalis, who compiled his chronicle in the twelfth century, mentions *en passant* a knight called William Fitz-Girole who accepted a friendly invitation to a wedding and, while there, was 'without any cause or accusation cruelly deprived of his eyes and his genitals, and the tops of his ears cut off.' And there was the Norman who, enraged by his wife, asked her to put on her wedding dress and then burnt her to death at the stake. The same man was in the habit of humiliating his sons by making them crawl on all fours, saddled and bridled. These were not the acts of a few madmen or sadists: quite a grisly catalogue of Norman cruelty could be compiled. In time of war they would burn down a whole countryside, destroy the crops and the cattle, as witness the 'harrying of the North' in England, and the famines caused by Norman armies in Calabria.

The story of the Norman conquest of Southern Italy has been well told by Gibbon, and this has, apparently, discouraged subsequent English writers with the exception of John Julius Norwich, whose recent book *The Normans in the South* is the first in English to be entirely devoted to the subject; and it was well worth writing. Lord Norwich has painlessly disentangled the mass of contemporary evidence and given life to a number of hitherto shadowy and enigmatic characters; and his book should be read by anyone who wishes to travel intelligently south of Rome. The chief characters in the conquest were a family which I have already mentioned, the Hautevilles. The father, Tancred de Hauteville, was a modest knight who held a fief of ten men-at-arms at Hauteville-la-Guichard, about eight miles from Coutances, in that pleasant peninsula south of Cherbourg whose western coastline looks out towards Jersey. Hauteville had twelve sons and several daughters by two marriages. The five sons of his first marriage were William (known as Iron-Arm), Drogo, Humphrey, Geoffrey and Serlo; by his second wife were seven sons, Robert (known as 'Guiscard, the Wise or Crafty'), Mauger, William, Aubrey, Tancred, Humbert, and the youngest, and fated to be the most spectacular, Roger. The little castle in which this stormy brood were brought up was soon too small to hold them and, as Vitalis says, who wrote during the lifetime of the later Hautevilles, the father gave his estate to his fourth son, Geoffrey, and told the others 'that they must gain their livelihood by their courage and by their talents beyond the bounds of their native land.'

Had the Hautevilles been of age in 1066 instead of 1036, no doubt they would have applied their courage and talents to the invasion of England and have found their way into Debrett, but in 1036 William the Conqueror was only nine years of age. Ambitious young Normans were talking of seeking their fortunes in Spain, fighting the Moors, or in the rather more complicated warfare of the South of Italy. The Normans were famous in Italy as bold fighters, and for ten years the town of Aversa had been a Norman city and a market-place for Norman mercenaries. It was accordingly to Aversa that the three eldest Hautevilles departed about the year 1036, in search of fortune.

No one who saw the first three Hauteville brothers ride away from home could have imagined what distinction awaited them and how fate, usually so capricious, was consistently to shower not only upon them, but on the younger members of the Hauteville brood, ducal and, ultimately, regal crowns.

Drogo and Humphrey, arriving at Aversa in about 1035, found themselves in the centre of a political situation which offered greater rewards to a mercenary soldier than at any other period until the Renaissance. The Norman prestige as a fighting man stood so high that the emigrants were wanted by the

Lombards, by the Byzantines, and by various local grandees; and this, the perfect climate for *condottieri,* gave plenty of scope for those crafty manoeuvres at which the Normans were so adept. They cannot all have been such paladins as many contemporary records suggest, and possibly the Norman conquest of Southern Italy was not as arduous a military operation as might be imagined. Though the landscape was tough, and so were the Saracens, one well-trained Norman cavalryman was probably able to take on several Byzantines or Lombards. The Norman military base at Aversa, north of Naples, had been ceded to the Norman Rainulf about twenty years before the arrival of the Hautevilles, but Rainulf was still alive and must have welcomed three such powerful recruits. The Normans were not a tall race, but all the ancient authorities stress the height of the Hautevilles; indeed one has the impression of a family of giants. This may have been flattery since small men like to be called tall, though Anna Comnena, who had no cause to flatter, noted the height of Robert 'Guiscard'.

The first expedition in which the three brothers distinguished themselves was a Byzantine attack upon the Saracens in Sicily. During this campaign William earned the *soprannome* by which he was afterwards known, *Fer-de-Bras,* Iron-Arm, after riding out alone and slaying a celebrated Saracen warrior. Within ten years of their arrival in Italy the brothers were famous and wealthy. When Rainulf died, William of the Iron-Arm succeeded to the command, while Drogo was Count of Apulia and Humphrey became Count of Lavello. No one knows the circumstance of William's death, which occurred in 1046, after which Drogo succeeded him.

One may imagine the stories that circulated in Normandy and how many restless and ambitious young men now turned their thoughts to Italy. In particular, the Hauteville family must have been proud of the brothers, and one wonders what correspondence passed between Aversa and Hauteville-la-Guichard, but, alas, we shall never know. It is, however, a sad fact that brotherly love is not an unfailing condition in large families as in the world at large; indeed brotherly hate can take on a singularly violent character, nourished by smouldering memories of childish resentments, jealousies and injustices. There may have been something of this in the relationship of this family since the established brothers did not often welcome the arrival of their juniors. When the eldest son of the second marriage, Robert, later to be called Guiscard, and the most ferocious of the brood, arrived in Italy, William had just died and Drogo was in command. He not only refused to help his young half-brother, but sent him to a malarial part of Calabria to guard certain mountain passes. This displeased Robert. It was not what he had come to Italy for, yet he was penniless and his brother refused to help. He therefore did what came naturally to any Norman of the time: he selected a mountain fastness and became a robber baron. From his castle at S. Marco Argentano he commanded a band of ruffians who held up travellers, burnt down farms, monasteries and churches, destroyed crops, drove away cattle, and generally became the terror of the district. His ruse was to start burning corn, vines, a house, or a church or a monastery, but agree to put out the fire when a stipulated amount of gold had been handed over. The chronicles are full of his tricks, which included even a mock funeral (the coffin filled with swords and the mourners suddenly leaping to the attack), though one is surprised that anyone in Calabria could have been taken in by that ancient subterfuge. Amatus, the chronicler of Monte Cassino, made a catalogue of Robert's misdeeds, putting down the number of oxen, brood mares and porkers which he stole, and noting that he did not even spare the peasants, making them pay a ransom of bread and wine. In view of the scope of his depredations, it is surprising that Robert remained so poor and grew so thin. During a visit to Apulia, perhaps with the object of trying to extract some money from Drogo, he met a kinsman named Girard who – says the chronicler – was the first to call him Guiscard. 'O Guiscard,' said Girard, 'why do you thus wander hither and thither? Behold now, marry my aunt, the sister of my father, and I will be your knight, and will go with you to conquer Calabria, and I will bring two hundred riders.' Robert took this advice and married the aunt, whose name was Alberada and whose claim to fame is that she became the mother of the great crusader, Bohemund of Antioch. She must have been an unusually young aunt since there is documentary proof that she was still living seventy years later.

Robert Guiscard's position continued to improve. One day in the year 1051, while Drogo was on his way to Mass, a man named Risus stepped from behind a door and stabbed him to death. Though he had been heartless to his young half-brother, Drogo was probably the most amiable of the three elder Hautevilles. Humphrey, who succeeded him, was not so pleasant: he possessed a vein of Norman sadism. In order to 'relieve his grief' – as the old writer put it – he had the arms and legs of his brother's assassin cut off and then buried the torso alive.

Drogo's death was part of a conspiracy, supported possibly by the Byzantines, but clearly a sign that the native population was exasperated by the avarice and the cruelty of the Normans. Robert Guiscard was not the only robber chief: there were hundreds of them. The disciplined commands under such chiefs as Humphrey were relatively respectable; it was the private operator, the knight with a gang of rascals infesting every corner of the country, who made life intolerable. In 1053 the saintly Leo IX, in response to pitiful appeals, wishing to uproot the Normans, marched south with a large but undisciplined army, stiffened by some trained German infantry. The Normans were alarmed by this, so far the greatest threat to their power, and they were also disturbed to think of drawing their swords upon God's vicar. Nevertheless, in time of danger they closed the ranks, and Robert Guiscard came hurrying up from Calabria with every man he could muster to help his half-brother.

The papal army crossed the Fortore river at the northern entrance to the Capitanata and camped outside a town called Civita, which no longer exists, though what appear to be its ruins lie near a farm road about thirty miles north-west of Foggia. The Normans sent a respectful embassy to the Pope, confessing their faults and promising reforms, but the German infantry, who were blond giants, mocked the smaller Normans and jibed at them as little men who fought on horses. When Humphrey and Robert saw a fight to be inevitable, they thought the sooner it began the better, particularly as they knew that the Pope was expecting

Byzantine reinforcements. The battle which followed was a massacre. The Norman cavalry ploughed through the papal army while Leo IX watched its destruction from the ramparts of Civita. Only the German infantry stood up to the Normans and died fighting to the last man. The town of Civita, fearing Norman vengeance, handed the Pope over to Humphrey and Robert. Then a strange scene was witnessed. The triumphant Normans, faced by the proud, sad figure of the Pontiff, fell upon their knees and begged forgiveness and conducted him under a guard of honour to his own city of Benevento, 'providing him continually with bread and wine.' Leo IX reached Rome the following year, where he died within a few weeks.

The battle changed the status of the Normans and brought Robert Guiscard to the front; it also had a notable repercussion in Normandy. For three years William the Conqueror had been writhing under a ban placed by Leo IX upon his proposed marriage with Matilda of Flanders, possibly because of blood relationship. Immediately William heard that the Pope had been captured he defied the ban and married Matilda in the minster at Eu.

In four years time Humphrey, upon his death-bed, appointed his half-brother Robert Guiscard to be his heir and the guardian of his young son, who then vanished from history, though it was never suggested that his uncle had anything to do with his dis-appearance. The Guiscard was now upon the road to fame and fortune. No longer a brigand but leader of the Normans, defender of the Papacy, and soon to be Duke of Apulia and Calabria, he was the greatest power in the south of Italy. Thinking that he deserved a nobler and more spectacular duchess than his wife Alberada, he discovered a fatal flaw in their association, a frequent divorce trick of the Middle Ages: they were too closely related. He parted from her with rich gifts and Alberada took with her the Guiscard's only son, Bohemund, then a small boy. Robert then married Sichelgaita, sister of the Lombard Prince of Salerno. If he had wished for a spectacular mate, he could not have done better. Like many women of the time, she liked to wear masculine dress and even had a suit of armour tailored to her figure. Anna Comnena was perhaps quoting someone who had seen Sichelgaita in her war-paint when she wrote that she was a fearsome sight. Though the vision of an operatic Brunhilde may rise in the imagination, Sichelgaita was much more formidable. Having been brought up in Salerno, whose medical school was long famous, she is said to have been an enthusiastic amateur poisoner, but who can say what truth there may have been in this; every sudden mediaeval death was attributed to poison. Odericus Vitalis, who must often have heard travelling monks and churchmen dining out on stories of the escapades of the South Italian lords, has preserved a story of the Duchess's later life. She was, he says, filled with hatred for her step-son Bohemund, and had one of her potions administered to him. When he was almost on the point of death his father, the Guiscard, suddenly realizing what had happened, called for a copy of the Gospels and a sword. 'Listen to me, Sichelgaita,' he said, 'I swear by this holy gospel that if my son Bohemund dies of the malady under which he labours I will plunge this sword into your bosom.' Sichelgaita, the story concludes, retired to her laboratory, and Bohemund began to recover, though, as Vitalis notes, he looked pallid for the rest of his life.

Whatever the gossip, Robert Guiscard and Sichelgaita appear to have been well suited. From the day of their marriage, and until Robert Guiscard died twenty-seven years later, they were rarely parted. She appears in the chronicles travelling about with her husband to various threatened points of his dominion; she is seen riding beside him in triumph, often spear in hand; and she tended him upon his death-bed.

At the time when Count Humphrey died, and just before Robert Guiscard was made Duke of Apulia, more Hautevilles began to arrive, and among them was one who was fated to place even the Guiscard in the shade. He was the youngest, the last child of the second marriage, Roger. He was then about twenty-six years of age and his famous brother was forty-two. Precisely the same relationship began to develop between them that had once existed between Robert Guiscard and Drogo. The older man put every possible difficulty in the way of the younger. They often quarrelled openly. On one occasion Roger drew his sword on the Guiscard, who threatened him with a dungeon. They besieged each other in towns and castles, but when real danger came they lined up together. Such was the beginning of a great partnership.

With Roger one meets for the first time a likeable Hauteville, a cheerful, irreverent young man who, so one fancies, enjoyed baiting his powerful, and perhaps pompous, ducal elder and leading him many a dance over the mountains of Calabria. How pleasant it is also, in this long record of blood, torture and conquest, to come upon a charming love story. It appears that before he left Normandy Roger fell in love with a young woman called Judith, who was a near relative of the Conqueror, though perhaps above the aspirations of a humble, unfledged Hauteville. However, Judith arrived in Italy with her guardian, who was apparently flying from the rage of the Conqueror. Roger immediately married her and took her to his castle at Mileto, on the north-west coast of Calabria. Vitalis writes a malicious account of this affair. He says that Judith was a nun at St Evroult who, becoming weary of her quiet life, broke her vows and went to Italy, where she married Roger Hauteville, who had no idea that she had taken the veil. He also makes the monstrous statement that Judith remained barren because she had incurred the displeasure of her heavenly Spouse!

As far as one knows, Roger and Judith were happy; at least we know that she wept when he left her at Mileto and went off on one of his Sicilian adventures. On a subsequent occasion he took her with him. They crossed the Straits of Messina and captured Troina, the highest town in Sicily. Here they were besieged in the citadel for months in the depths of winter, and Roger, remembering the incident in later life, said that he and Judith had only one mantle which they wore in turn, trying to keep warm. Like a good Norman wife, Judith took her turn as orderly officer and went round the sentries on the ramparts. They lived on horseflesh and anything that they could steal on sorties after dark.

In his later years Robert Guiscard devoted himself to the conquest of Bari, the last Byzantine stronghold in Italy, leaving to Roger the conquest of Sicily. Of all the foes encountered by the Normans, the Saracens were the most formidable; their organization, too, was efficient. How interesting it is, for example, to read that they went into battle with baskets of homing pigeons (the birds were fed on corn and honey) to send back news to headquarters. And how typically Norman it was of Roger, having captured enemy pigeons after a victory, that he should have dipped paper in Saracen blood and sent the birds back with their grim message. Bari fell in 1071 after a gallant siege that lasted for three years; in the following year Palermo fell, and the victory march through the streets of the Sicilian town was led by Robert Guiscard, with Sichelgaita by his side. So thirty-six years after the first members of this warlike brood had arrived in Italy they had expelled the Byzantines and were about to subdue the Saracens. The second act of their astonishing epic then began.

Robert Guiscard's ambition now took its boldest flight. He was in his sixties and still strong and violent. Why should he not attack Constantinople, dethrone the Emperor Alexius I, and place upon his own head the diadem of Byzantium? He transported an army and a fleet across the Adriatic in the year 1081. The advance guard was commanded by Bohemund, his son by his first wife; he followed with Sichelgaita. Compared with this adventure, had it been successful, the Duke of Normandy's invasion of England would have appeared a minor affair. The Guiscard had scarcely established his army in what is now Albania when trouble descended upon Rome and upon Robert's overlord, Pope Gregory VII. Four years had passed since this Pope had excommunicated the Emperor Henry IV and had forced him to climb the mountains (legend says in the snow) to the Castle of Canossa above Modena, where the Pope then was, to beg forgiveness. This was granted but only after the Emperor had been kept waiting like a penitent for three days. Burning to avenge this humiliation, Henry now marched on Rome to dethrone Gregory, who sent out a call for help to his Norman vassal.

The appeal did not reach the Guiscard until the following year, 1082. But immediately he received it, although such a demand could scarcely have been made at a more difficult moment for him, he instantly answered it. Swearing upon the soul of his father that he would neither wash nor shave until he was on his way to Italy to help Gregory, he left his army in charge of Bohemund and hurried across the Adriatic. In southern Italy he gathered the terrible host of Normans, Calabrians and Saracens who sacked Rome. They arrived in May, 1084, to find that the Emperor's army had fled but that the Pope was still a prisoner in the Castel S. Angelo. The Guiscard rescued Gregory, then allowed his army to put Rome to the sword and to fire. As Lanciani wrote, 'the unhappy city became the scene of horrors, in comparison with which the sack of the Vandals seems merciful.'

The Norman army marched south, leaving Rome, in places, twelve feet deep in ashes. They took with them, for his own safety, Pope Gregory VII, who was lodged in the Guiscard's palace at Salerno while his rescuer crossed the Adriatic to rejoin his army in the Balkans. In the following year, 1085, the Pope died, saying, 'I have loved righteousness and hated iniquity, therefore I die in exile.' The visitor to Salerno, coming to his tomb in the cathedral, may wonder, perhaps, how the greatest of the mediaeval popes came to be buried so far from Rome.

That year also saw the death of Robert Guiscard, who survived the Pope by less than two months. Anna Comnena, the sister of Alexius I, wrote in her wonderful contemporary history that the Guiscard died of a fever, aged seventy, and that Sichelgaita was at his bedside. Some historians have said that he died at Durazzo, but Anna Comnena says that he died on the Greek island of Cephalonia, which is more likely. In the days when I knew Greece, a small ship that smelt of goats and olive oil would leave the Piraeus every week, I think on a Thursday, and, in the course of its meanderings, it touched at the northern tip of Cephalonia, where the people would swear, as if it had happened yesterday, that Robert Guiscard had died there and, in proof, would point to the name of their little port, which is Phiscardo.

Sichelgaita had seen to it that her stepson Bohemund, who had inherited something of the Hauteville quality, did not succeed to the dukedom, which passed to her own indifferent offspring, Roger, known as 'Borsa' (a purse), from his habit of counting out his money. He ruled discreetly for twenty-six years, leaving the dukedom to a young son who died without an heir.

The heroic stage of the Norman Conquest of Southern Italy was over; now began the period of statecraft and kingship. The interest centres upon Roger, aged fifty-four, and the youngest of the family. He had set his heart, not on Byzantium, but on Sicily, where he founded a dynasty whose blood was to run in the veins of the Hohenstaufens and in many of the royal families of Europe. His son, Roger II, was crowned King of Sicily in 1139, and became one of the most celebrated monarchs in Europe. His exotic court at Palermo was noted for its culture and its luxury, and for the toleration extended to Arab, Greek and Jew. Sicily became the leading sea power in the Mediterranean, and how interesting it would be to say that the descendants of the Vikings had taken to ships again; but that was not so. The Sicilian sailors were Arabs or Greeks from those regions of Calabria which had been colonized by Greek seafarers centuries before Christ. The word 'admiral' entered the vocabulary about this time from Sicily. It is derived from the Arabic *emir* or *amir* (commander) and *amir-al* (commander of) was thus easily Anglicized as 'admiral'.

At this time English influence was strong in Sicily. The Archbishop of Palermo was an Englishman named Walter Offamil. The King, William II, had married Joan, daughter of Henry II of England and sister of Richard, Coeur de Lion. A traveller of the time described William as surrounded by eunuchs and women, wearing silken robes embroidered with Cufic inscriptions and speaking Arabic. When no heir was forthcoming, the kingdom was settled upon William's aunt, Constance, a woman of thirty who had retired to a convent of Basilican nuns. She was forced out of obscurity to the centre of the stage. Married to the Emperor Henry VI, she became the mother of the greatest potentate of the thirteenth century, the Emperor Frederick II, known as *Stupor Mundi*, the Wonder of the World.

So in only a hundred and sixty years the Hautevilles, arriving in Italy as penniless adventurers, had conquered the southern half of the peninsula; and now Norman blood ran in the greatest of the Hohenstaufens. This is surely the greatest success story of the Middle Ages.

§ 3

Though I went up and down the coast in the hot spring days, I could not decide for some time which of the little towns I liked best. They all bore a strong family likeness: they were all blindingly white; they all clustered on the rim of the bluest of seas, some upon sand, others, like Polignano a Mare, upon rocks; they all had busy fishing harbours and above each one rose a cathedral, sometimes of Norman date, sometimes of Hohenstaufen. Eventually I narrowed down the choice to Molfetta and Trani, with many a backward glance at Giovinazzo.

Molfetta is one of the busiest of the smaller fishing towns. The port is an elevated paved piazza upon which stands the old cathedral. Hundreds of painted boats, each one named after a saint, deposit in the shade of that noble building all the curiosities of the Adriatic Sea. Many of the boats are ordinary rowing-boats fitted with two huge globular acetylene lamps for night fishing. One of the fishermen told me that he had just returned from the coast of Yugoslavia where he had caught the largest octopus of his career. I asked how one catches an octopus. He went to his boat and returned with a trident rather longer in the haft than the one used by Neptune, but the same type, and a weapon which has been employed on this coast since antiquity.

The view from the harbour is superb. Even now I wonder whether it is not finer than that at Trani! Large blocks of stone have been tumbled into the sea at the end of the jetty to break the force of winter gales, and these have formed rock pools in which small boys bathe and catch crabs and shrimps in the seaweed, while in the background, as dazzling as if carved in chalk, rise the twin towers of the cathedral, seen against the winding warrens of the old town and reflected in the small rock pools. The church was consecrated about 1150, a time when Roger II was still alive. Kings and knights who had been on the Second

Crusade were disembarking at the Apulian ports. Only the year before the unfortunate Louis VII of France, returning home sickened by his failure as a crusader, was still further humiliated to be captured by Greek pirates. He was rescued by a Sicilian admiral, who having audaciously sailed up the Golden Horn shot arrows tipped with silver into the imperial gardens before sailing home and depositing the rescued King with Roger II at Palermo.

I always went to Trani, ten miles farther along the coast, full of pleasurable anticipation. Slightly smaller than Molfetta, like all the Adriatic coast towns, it leads a dual life, that of an ancient fishing-port with a modern extension devoted to minor industries which have been introduced within the last twenty-five years. At Trani, however, one of the industries is an old one: it is a centre for the South Italian wine trade. The cathedral stands upon the most seaward point of the old harbour, rising against a background of sky and sea at the end of a huge and dignified piazza whose walls are washed by the Adriatic. It is unusual in these days to find so large an empty space in a town, and I was glad to have seen the elegant architecture of this lovely church rising from an acre of stone pavement uncluttered by a foreground of coaches and motor cars.

On the opposite arm of the harbour there is a pleasant park where children play in the shade of ilex and palm trees while gardeners direct their hoses upon beds of yellow and red cannas. Here I saw a floral clock, a feature of one of the flower beds, where the hands were moved by some clockwork or electrical contrivance buried in the soil. I prefer a sundial, but I thought the very existence of this clock intact in a public place haunted by so many small boys a tribute to the civilized behaviour of young Italy.

It is curious to notice how much the southern Italians love to have their fortunes told, even by mechanical oracles. There was a machine in the park which, in return for a coin, gave one a message every bit as ambiguous as those delivered by the Pythia. It was a commonplace Sibyl, rather like a weighing machine in appearance. In return for my coin, it told me to have nothing to do with a dark woman, that I should be going to America, and it ended with 'you will soon be confronted with an unusual situaation.' This prophecy was almost immediately fulfilled. Standing next to the machine were two men in friendly conversation, one with his back to me. As I stood reading my fortune, I glanced up and saw him place his hands behind his back and make the sign against the Evil Eye. This, to me, was indeed an unusual situation: I had never seen anyone make this sign seriously. He stood there talking with the first and fourth fingers of his right hand pointing to the earth. I moved round to have a good look at his companion, but I could see nothing in his face to suggest evil, indeed he looked rather a pleasant individual. If anyone had asked me, I should have said that the other man was the suspect. But the Evil Eye is a strange thing and even your best friend will not tell you if you have it. Pope Pius IX was said to have it, and I have read that sometimes those who knelt to receive his blessing made the sign of the horns as they did so.

The neat little port of Trani, which is semi-circular in shape, recalls the Cala of Palermo. With the lovely cathedral rising seaward in isolation in a place where you might expect to see a lighthouse, the scene creates the impression of a trim model in the window of a travel agency. The story of the cathedral is more than lightly touched with fantasy. There are three churches, one on top of the other, and this attractive sandwich of devotion began in Roman times with a tomb or catacomb which the Christians of that day associated with a saint called St Leucius. In the sixth century a fine cathedral was built and dedicated to the Blessed Virgin without destroying the Roman church below: this is now the crypt of the present building which was the cathedral of Trani for nearly four centuries. Then, at the height of the crusading fervour, when the best and the worst of Europe were passing through these Adriatic ports on their way to the Holy Land, a young Greek pilgrim arrived in Trani carrying a heavy cross and singing *Kyrie Eleison*. This young man, whose name was Nicola, had an extraordinary effect upon his contemporaries, since his death in 1094 was followed five years later by his canonization by Urban II. In the meantime the people of Trani, adopting S. Nicola Pellegrino as their patron and abandoning their first patron, St Leucius, decided to erect above the old cathedral a new one to be paid for by *aere minuto*, or small subscriptions, which probably explains why it took so long to complete. The building of the present church began in the year of the pilgrim's death, 1094, but the work was not completed for about a century. The result is that you can see a beautiful Norman church standing above its Byzantine predecessor, and, lower still, a tiny Roman catacomb.

The finest exterior feature of Trani cathedral is a pair of bronze doors about sixteen feet high and ten feet wide, which are one of the wonders of Southern Italy and have been in position since 1179. William II, the Good, and his English Queen, were reigning in Apulia at that time, and in England, William Rufus, had not yet been shot in the New Forest. Every afternoon and until sunset for nine hundred years the bronze doors have been warmed by the sun until now they are as green as a field of Irish clover. They may not be as elegant as the Byzantine doors which I had seen in the cave church at Monte S. Angelo, with their silver inlay, and they are cruder, more massive, but the figures which stand out in high relief from thirty-two panels are less conventional and more life-like. What a pity we know little of the maker of these doors except his name, Barisanus of Trani, and that he also made the doors of Ravello cathedral and the side doors of Monreale at Palermo. It would be interesting to know where he learnt to make such massive castings and whether he, or someone else, designed the thirty-two panels, which show saints, seated and standing, and on horseback, as well as other scenes and subjects. The model for his St George, lance in hand, was certainly some Norman baron, and St Eustace (riding out to hunt with his favourite hounds) must have been a familiar sight in the peaceful days of good King William. The heavy bronze framework of the doors is a mass of intricate decoration and medallions, each one containing an animal, a bird, and one, in particular, which pleased me, a centaur galloping straight from the pagan world, shooting an arrow backwards.

The cathedral is as dark as a Spanish church; the light comes filtering through thin plates of alabaster as in some of the churches at Ravenna. This golden wash falls upon twin columns of granite and alabaster which stand two by two down the nave, supporting

round Norman arches and a clerestory above, which has groups of
three smaller arches with marble columns, some plain, others fluted.
In the impressive church below, a forest of ancient columns rises
close together and steps lead into the dark and ancient cathedral of
S. Maria. Beneath the altar of the crypt I saw the bones of S. Nicola
Pelligrino, neatly tied with red ribbon in a glass-sided reliquary.

In the lower church I came upon the first Madonna Dolorata I
had seen in the South of Italy. She stood in a glass case, a life-sized
figure with a grief-stricken waxen face, clothed in a black velvet
sixteenth century dress like a Shakespearean heroine, Olivia perhaps. A veil was draped over her head, a neatly folded lace handkerchief was attached to her wrist, and the brass handle of a dagger
protruded from the region of her heart.


Each seaport of Apulia has its own little lido a mile or two away
where a narrow strip of sand and a few dozen beach umbrellas
await the summer visitor. Some one had given me the name of a
new hotel with a good cook in one of these *lidi*, and when I found
it, I thought I would lunch there. The dining-room was filled with
large, grim-looking men all of the same type and obviously
foreigners from some other part of Italy. They did not seem to
know each other or wish to do so. They might have been members
of some convention of undertakers or private detectives. The waiter
told me they were dealers from Lombardy who had come to buy
the Trani wine for blending. I was given a *moscato* to try which
certainly had tremendous flavour and body. I was told that without a touch of Trani wine the wines of the north would not be
worth drinking, but that was probably local pride. But I must say
that southern wines make those of the north seem thin.


§ 4

The biggest planned robbery of the world was the Sack of
Constantinople in 1203, when the men of the Fourth Crusade
scattered across Europe the treasures of centuries. Every visitor to
Venice has admired the four bronze horses above the entrance of

St Mark's, which were a part of the Venetian plunder, and by sheer accident the town of Barletta acquired a massive piece of the loot when a galley sank off the coast, consigning to the waves a colossal bronze statue of a Roman emperor. For some reason I thought that this statue had been erected near the cathedral at Barletta, but I could not find it, neither did the people I asked seem intelligent about it until an elderly man, brighter than the rest, said, 'Oh, it's Aré you want!', which is the local name for the giant, evidently a contraction of 'Ereclio', Heraclius. He led me to the centre of the town, where, in front of the church of S. Sepolcro, stands the largest Roman bronze statue in existence. Those who have measured him say he is sixteen feet high, but to me he looked taller. He wears the armour of a Roman general and holds an orb in one hand and a cross in the other. No one knows whether he represents Heraclius or Valentinian, the two most popular guesses. He is a heavy and unattractive figure, seen to the utmost disadvantage, for he was designed to stand upon a column or a tall building and so from pavement level he appears clumsy and out of proportion. My acquaintance told me that the statue had been lying on the sea-shore for two hundred years before it was set up in the town, and during that time the Dominicans from Manfredonia had hacked off a hand and a wrist, at anyrate they took sufficient metal to cast a bell for their church.

Though Aré is popular with the people of Barletta, he comes second to the *Disfida*, the Challenge of Barletta. This is something you hear about whenever anyone discusses past events in Apulia; it is one of those stories of Italian history which every child knows. The *Disfida* has also provided material, and continues to do so, for articles, short stories, poems, and the titles of newspapers. We came to a building in the old part of the town where steps led down to a vaulted cellar which was decorated with heraldic shields and lighted with flambeaux. My guide called this the *cantina*, which, he explained, had been an inn in 1503, when the French were besieging Barletta. The town was at the time defended by a mixed garrison of Italians and Spaniards under Gonsalvo da Cordova. One day an angry and scornful French captain named La Motte was captured, and here in the *cantina* the

Frenchman began to decry Italian valour, saying that he would beat any number of Italians with an equal number of Frenchmen. His challenge was taken. Soon afterwards thirteen French and thirteen Italian knights met in combat outside Barletta on the 13th February, and the Italians unsaddled their opponents and were declared the winners. A stone tablet with an inscription was erected on the spot, but in 1805, during the Napoleonic wars, French soldiers pulled it down: but it was proudly set up again after Waterloo. It is still to be found beside the road, mid-way between Andria and Corato.

The old town of Barletta wears an air of past consequence. I was shown a small church in which I was told the Crusaders prayed before embarking for the Holy Land. There is a legend that 'Riccardo Cuor di Leone', our Richard Lionheart, contributed to the building of Barletta Cathedral, and that an inscription records this. I spent some time looking for it and eventually found the figure of a man in a boat carved on one of the left-hand columns of the nave, with an inscription too worn and too high up to be deciphered. The verger assured me that the man in the boat represented 'Riccardo' embarking for the crusade; but Richard did not embark at Barletta and, so far as I know, was never in the town.

I acquired a rare object, a local guide-book which was about forty years out of date, having been published in 1926. I also found some ancient postcards of the same period which showed the harbours of these Apulian towns full of Arabic-looking dhows, quite large ships with an upright mainmast cut across by the enormous sickle curve of a lateen (Latin) sail, which was once the typical sail of the Mediterranean. These, alas, have nearly all vanished, so far as my observation goes, and one would be more likely to find a speedboat in the harbours of Apulia than one of the old Latin rigs.

The guide-book reminded me that the Emperor Frederick II summoned all the barons of his kingdom to Barletta in 1228, upon the eve of his departure on crusade, and declared his son Henry to be heir to the Empire and of the Kingdom of Naples and Sicily. It is not Frederick, however, but the most attractive of his children, the illegitimate Manfred, whose memory haunts Barletta. It was this charming young man's favourite town, and it has been recorded that he loved to wander about its streets at night, accompanied by two Sicilian musicians, singing old country songs.

§ 5

Turning from the main road, I entered a land of olive and almond trees. Occasionally I met farm carts with wheels the height of a tall man, which are characteristic of Apulia; sometimes they were coloured red, and now and again the horse would be wearing a head collar decorated with brass and a string of blue beads as a protection against the Evil Eye. I noticed that only the finest horses wore this protection; presumably the Eye of Envy never alights upon a lean and undesirable animal. The farms looked prosperous, the cattle sleek, and the southern poverty was not visible, at any rate upon the surface.

I came to a lane whose indication post read, '*Canne della Battaglia*' – the battlefield of Cannae. In 216 B.C. upon this homely plain was fought the battle of Cannae, when one of the craftiest of generals, the Carthaginian Hannibal, encircled a large Roman army with his smaller force and destroyed it so completely that to this day the word 'Cannae' is synonymous with defeat. I looked with interest at the battlefield as I had recently read a lively reconstruction of modern history called *August 1914* in which the author, Barbara W. Tuchman, explains how the strategy of Hannibal inspired the German *blitzkrieg* of 1914. It is strange to link Hannibal with the monocled, wasp-waisted Prussian, Count Albert von Schlieffen, who was Chief of the German General Staff from 1891 until his retirement in 1913; but then, as Miss Tuchman explains, 'dead battles, like dead generals, hold the military mind in their dead grip.' Count Schlieffen was hypnotized by Cannae, and even after his retirement he continued to write about it and, dying at the age of eighty in 1913, he muttered, 'It must come to a fight. Only make the right wing strong.' A year later the 'Schlieffen Plan' was put into operation when the German armies moved through Belgium to encircle France as Hannibal had encircled the legions: but this war of swift movement envisaged by Count Schlieffen developed into the prolonged stagnation of the trenches. Hannibal's achievement was not repeated until 1967, when Israel inflicted a modern Cannae upon Egypt and Jordan, annihilating their armies in a few days.

I came to a small museum beside the road, quite a modern building, and wondered whether I should find some earnest military students inside, but the place seemed at first to be empty. Then I heard laughter from a refreshment room where a young man, leaning against an ice chest, was buying his young woman an ice-cream with a cherry on top called 'The Kiss of Love.' They were not interested in military strategy, and why should they have been? I watched them depart on a Vespa which was parked outside, the girl modestly seated side-saddle at the back.

There is little to see in the museum except broken pottery: I had hoped for bronze swords and helmets. Perhaps the most interesting object is a good wall plan which shows how Hannibal drew the Roman generals into his trap and how efficiently he closed it when the moment had arrived to do so. It is a mistake to think that ancient warfare was just a matter of two armies drawn up opposite each other, meeting with a mighty clash in which the stronger army was victorious, for, as Schlieffen himself said, though arms may change, strategy remains the same, and the ancient commanders knew all the tricks of the trade and many that have been forgotten. A work that is not read much, even by classical scholars, is a collection of military anecdotes called *Strategems*, collected by a Roman of the imperial period, Sextus Julius Frontinus, who for a time was Governor of Britain, and in later life became head of the Roman Water Board. He preserved several anecdotes of Hannibal, most of them, I think, taken either from Polybius or Livy. Only an extraordinary general could have conceived the idea of conquering a city by first giving its army the common cold, perhaps the first instance of germ warfare. This, says Frontinus, was Hannibal's object when he decoyed the army of a town he was besieging across a river in winter then, rushing his own men back to camp, he lit fires and dried them and had them massaged with oil. Assuming that his foes would not have had such care and attention, he waited for colds to develop and then, early on a chilly morning, captured the town. Typical of the way his mind worked was his action when his elephant corps refused to cross a wide river. He ordered a mahout to wound one of the animals behind the ear, then to swim across the river as if in flight. The wounded elephant pursued the man in rage, and his companions followed him without trouble.

The men of 216 B.C. asked the question: why did Hannibal not march on undefended Rome after the battle of Cannae, just as many wondered why Hitler did not attempt to invade England after Dunkirk. Perhaps sea power was the answer in both cases. Though Hannibal had destroyed the largest army Rome had ever put into the field, the Roman fleet was still intact. One of the strange things about Cannae is that it never seems to have occurred to Count von Schlieffen that, in spite of that battle, Rome eventually defeated Hannibal.

## § 6

A few miles farther on I arrived in Canosa di Puglia during that sacred moment of the Italian afternoon when the population is horizontal. There was scarcely a sound in the siesta. The main piazza was deserted; the shops were shut; the churches were locked. No moment is more maddening to the traveller, who has often come a long way to see the sights of Italy, when he finds that four hours of his precious time are lost every day by what, in spring and early autumn, seem to him like a piece of wilful Italian self-indulgence. I stood looking down upon the old cathedral, which lies in a hollow representing the pavement level of Canosa in Norman times.

I noticed a lad of about twelve who was lying full length upon a wall, but saw that he was only pretending to be asleep and was watching me. I asked him if there were any chance of seeing the cathedral. He replied that the *parroco* was asleep, and that the man with the keys was also asleep, but at four o'clock. . . . While he was talking I produced a five hundred lire note; and he was off the wall in a flash and soon back with the keys.

The millionaire who is said to have bought an hotel because he could not get something in the grill-room can hardly have enjoyed the power of money more than someone who, like myself, has managed to bribe his way into an Italian church during the siesta.

We entered a cool, dark place smelling of stale incense, which, though it may not have been the finest of Apulia's cluster of cathedrals, was, I thought, among the most solemn on that quiet afternoon. It is said that the cathedral was built by Bohemund and that he was buried here in IIII by his mother, Alberada. Why, I wonder, should the early historians mention his mother and not his wife, who was Constance, daughter of Philip I of France; and why should Bohemund, Prince of Otranto, have been buried in Canosa di Puglia and not in his own capital?

Like Molfetta, this cathedral proclaims a Byzantine tradition in its domes, five of them to Molfetta's three. But here, as in the other churches of Southern Italy, it is the sturdy Norman nave that holds one's attention, and the great columns, mostly discovered in classical ruins and fitted with capitals hardly two of which match, in the gloom of this Norman forest at Canosa. In the deeper darkness of the apse, I came upon one of those episcopal thrones which are a feature of Apulian cathedrals. Unlike the marble throne at Bari which rests upon human figures, this is carried by two elephants. I wondered if perhaps the elephant of Frederick II, which accompanied his frequent progresses, was perhaps commemorated in these unusual decorations.

Bohemund has rested for eight and a half centuries in the courtyard of this church in a tomb chapel built against the south wall. I tried to remember the tomb of another leader of the First Crusade, but could recall only that of Duke Robert of Normandy, in Gloucester. The door of Bohemund's tomb is a fine example of early bronze-casting. The left-hand leaf is cast solidly in one massive sheet; the right-hand leaf is formed of four plates fitted into their frame so beautifully that a finger-nail can scarcely tell where they have been joined. The door is the colour of verdigris. Two panels on the right-hand leaf bear incised figures which were once outlined in silver in the Byzantine manner; the left-hand leaf is decorated with raised arabesques in large medallions, and there is also an inscription in Latin which is still legible, extolling the bravery of Bohemund and giving the bronze-caster's name as Roger of Melfi. When we unlocked the doors, they gave out a humming vibration which rose to something like a musical note, a sound which recalled the 'singing doors' of the Lateran Baptistry. The interior was cold and stark. Two columns upheld arches and beneath them, lit only by the light from five small windows in the dome above, was a bare tombstone in the pavement with one word upon it:

Boamundus.

Nine aspidistras in flower-pots stood about the stone, a strange tribute, I thought, to the memory of a warrior. The one word on the tombstone was pathetic in its inference that everyone would know who Bohemund was, which was once true, but now his name means nothing save to a few scholars and to the people of Canosa. And what a fantastic name it is. He was baptised Mark, but his father, Robert Guiscard, became so enthralled by the exploits of a giant called Bohemund that he insisted on giving this uncouth name to his infant son. In appearance, Bohemund was like his father, abnormally tall and blue-eyed. Anna Comnena, who disliked him because of his designs on her brother's throne, was nevertheless aware of his charm and good looks and paid reluctant tribute to them in her history. He was, however, a disgruntled giant. As I have mentioned, he was an infant of four when his mother Alberada was discarded by Robert Guiscard, who then married Sichelgaita. His stepmother feared Bohemund all her life and saw to it that her own indifferent son, Roger Borsa, should inherit the dukedom and the Guiscard's wealth. Resentfully, but with Hauteville energy, Bohemund began to make his own name and fortune and, as luck would have it, the First Crusade was being preached.

In the kindly processes of time the Crusaders have been credited with a nobility of purpose which only a few of them possessed; and Bohemund was not among these. He cared more about winning a kingdom for himself than in freeing the holy places, and to such men the Crusade was a golden opportunity. It enabled them to enlist and command armies which otherwise they could never have hoped to lead; and with such power in his hands Bohemund became the first Prince of Antioch. It is a little difficult, in view of his undisguised materialism, to understand the awe in which his contemporaries held him, a tribute perhaps to his fearlessness. When he arrived in Italy to find money, one contemporary author said that people flocked to gaze at him 'as if they were going to see Christ himself'. When, still seeking money, he arrived at the court of Philip I of France, his charm and fame triumphed as usual and the battle-worn veteran of fifty-three was given the French King's daughter, Constance, as his bride.

In four years time, while he was fitting out yet another warlike expedition, Bohemund died of some disease in his native Apulia, and we learn that it was his mother, Alberada, who buried him and supervised the building of his unique mausoleum. He is more interesting as a personality than his father. While the Guiscard was feared, his son was genuinely liked and admired. His ups and downs, the stormy struggle of his life, the spur of disinheritance which drove him out in search of fame and fortune, make him a more romantic figure than his always successful parent. In the course of eight and a half centuries the dust of emperors and kings has been scattered on the wind, but Bohemund sleeps on. At intervals someone enters his tomb and sponges the leaves of the nine aspidistras which are the world's last tribute to his splendour. And I am not so sure that the aspidistra is, after all, such a poor tribute to a warrior. The Greek *aspidion*, from which this plant takes its name, means a shield.

Another fifteen miles brought me to the bustling town of Andria, which was just resuming life after the siesta. The air rang with the characteristic sound of the machine-gun rattle as iron shutters were run up from shop windows all over the town. Andria looked undistinguished, and one might pass through it never dreaming of its great antiquity, since it was already ancient when the Normans captured it in 1046, one of their first footholds in the South. The town prides itself upon its association with Frederick

II, who loved to stay there, so the Andrians will tell you, more than in any other town in Puglia. Among the imperial fads was the composition of Latin slogans for his towns which he inscribed upon arches and walls, some bitter, some sweet. His adjective for this town was 'faithful Andria', and the inhabitants still treasure the description. Frederick's second wife, Yolanda, died in child-birth at Andria, aged sixteen, and is buried there. She was probably the most pathetic of his three wives, all of whom were the victims of political unions. Though she had no dowry, her empty title of hereditary Queen of Jerusalem had attractions at the time for Frederick. She was fourteen when she was brought from the Holy Land to marry the Emperor, who was thirty-one and was said to have deserted her immediately for a charming and sophis-ticated young woman of twenty in her entourage. Poor Yolanda presumably spent her two years reign in tearful luxury. Her child Conrad survived.

Hidden away in Andria are several fine old churches and a superb ducal palace. The cathedral, which has suffered much altera-tion from time to time, is as old, or older, than the town. The custodian led me through the Norman nave down into a crypt which we explored, candles in hand. Our shadows were cast upon stone arches and venerable columns with carved capitals, which sprouted without pediments straight from the ground like toad-stools, as if we were travellers in a nineteenth century aquatint.

'You are American?' asked the custodian.

'No, I am not,' I replied. 'I am English.'

'Ah', he said, 'come, I will show you something.'

He lifted his candle and illuminated an inscription upon the wall, which I translated:

Here lie the mortal remains of
Yolanda de Brienne
1228
and Isabella of England
1241
The august consorts of Frederick II, King of
Puglia and Sicily.

143

I asked if any bones remained; for answer the custodian lifted a slab of pavement sufficiently for me to cast the light of my candle inside, though I could see nothing but stones, dust, and a length of lead piping. 'There is a chest!' said the custodian. 'Did you not see it?' But I restrained him from lifting the stone again.

So here lie all that is left of two empresses, both of whom died young and in childbirth. I have mentioned Yolanda's unhappy two years of marriage. Isabella's reign of six years was not entirely miserable, indeed it is probable that Frederick, whom nobody could claim to have been a perfect husband, even managed to make his beautiful English wife happy. The convention that all princesses are lovely seems to have been true in the case of Isabella, daughter of our slandered King John of England. Her father had been dead for some years, and her brother Henry III was King, when she was sought in marriage by the Emperor Frederick II in 1235. She was then twenty-one years of age. Her brother sent her off to her wedding in a splendour which dazzled Europe. Even her cooking-pots were of silver, noted Roger of Wendover. When passing through Cologne, she delighted those who crowded the balconies by casting off the veil which covered her to ride bare-headed through the streets. Frederick was charmed with her and must have compared her with his two former wives, the first of whom was his senior by ten years and the second his junior by seventeen. Among the gifts which the Emperor sent back to Henry III were three leopards, an allusion to the Royal Arms of England. If they were the pampered hand-reared hunting leopards which were taught to sit on the cruppers of horses and were accustomed to human companionship, one feels sorry for them since their fate was to be sent to the Tower of London. In time they were joined by a polar bear and an elephant, so forming the nucleus of the Royal Menagerie whose nineteenth century occupants were moved to Regents Park, to become the London Zoo.

Isabella is notable for having given us a glimpse inside the imperial harem in Sicily. In 1241 her brother, Richard of Cornwall, arrived from the Holy Land and was made much of by his brother-in-law, who – says Matthew Paris – 'ordered him to be gently and mildly treated, with blood-letting, baths, and divers medicinal fomentations, to restore his strength after the dangers of the sea.' But his sister was not visible and Richard was impatient to see her. His request was not granted for some days, when he was invited to attend an entertainment in her apartments. He found her surrounded by costly toys and musical instruments and, one imagines, by eunuchs and Saracen guards. After enjoying a long conversation with her, he was entertained by jugglers and dancing-girls. Two in particular caught his attention. As the curtains parted, they advanced to four glass globes that had been set on the polished floor, and each girl, selecting two of them, stepped on them and began to dance. 'They walked backwards and forwards, clapping their hands, moving at pleasure on these revolving globes', wrote Matthew Paris, 'gesticulating with their arms, singing various tunes, and twisting their bodies according to the tune, beating cymbals and castanents together with their hands, and putting their bodies into various amusing postures, affording with the other jugglers an admirable spectacle to the lookers-on.' This scene, so well described, but rather outside the ordinary experience of a monk, is almost certainly one of many contributions made by Richard of Cornwall to Matthew Paris's *Chronica Majora*.

## § 7

Soon after I had left Andria I saw, not more than ten miles away, the most prominent landmark in Apulia, the Castel del Monte. I had seen it crowning the hill-top from every part of the province, an apparently circular tower, but I had never been so close before.

As I rounded the hill, the castle became invisible, then as I reached the top I saw with surprise that it was not circular, as I had supposed, but octagonal, and it was not small: it was enormous. This great castle shouldering the sky, its yellow limestone walls warmed by the evening sun, was impressive. There was an air of habitation about it, and of watchfulness, as it looked down over the Murge (which is the name given to the Apulian foothills) towards the coastal cities of the plain.

The castle was closed for the day, but I noticed some slight distance away a tavern or refreshment room, where I thought I might possibly find a man with the key; but he was not there. I sat down with a glass of red Castel del Monte wine, while the proprietor, pointing towards a group of vines, said that the wine had been produced there. It reminded me of the fragrant, flinty red wines drawn from a wineskin in the taverns of La Mancha, and made from grapes grown in much the same hot, sunny landscape.

I think it is a fairly accurate generalization that in Italy the wine gets better the farther south one goes; it is certainly less adulterated and stronger than the more familiar wines of north and central Italy. Most wine drinkers would probably give the prize to Castel del Monte, which may be red, white, or rosé, though I think highly of an almost deep red wine called simply Barletta. There is also a dry, straw-coloured wine, not unlike Chablis, called Torre Giulia, which is a good wine to order with shellfish, and a delicious, heroic, orange-red wine of the kind described as 'generous' by connoisseurs, called Torre Quarto. There is a great amount of strong, sweet dessert wine in Apulia: there is Moscato di Trani, which has a bouquet rather like roses; there is Mistella, which is another fragrant sweet wine; and Moscato delle Murge, which is aromatic and looks like a glass of melted amber. Anyone who likes a sweet, rich wine should try Zagarese, which is dark red.

Before leaving, I walked round the castle, which was built, and some believe designed, by Frederick II, and completed about 1240, during the last ten years of his life. No one knows why he selected the design of an octagon, whose general effect is that of a colossal crown. It has been suggested that he wished to represent in architecture the eight-sided crown of the Holy Roman Empire; others have said that perhaps he took as his model the octagonal plan of the Mosque of Omar, in Jerusalem, which it is known he studied and admired when he was in the Holy Land. The crown-like character of the castle is emphasized by the eight octagonal towers standing at the angles; the windows are few and are high up on the walls, and there is only one entrance, a beautiful classical gateway of marble.

· · · · ·

Returning the next morning, with the sun high in the sky, I found it so agreeable to sit upon the castle mound and contemplate Apulia and the Adriatic, that I postponed my entrance to the castle. This seaward view towards the ring of little cathedral towns lying upon a plain planted with olive trees, almonds and cherry trees, was a contrast to the view to the south over the rolling hills towards the bleak country of *Christ Stopped at Eboli,* where upon mountains only thirty miles away as the crow flies were those remote villages, such as Grassano and Gagliano with their pagan backgrounds, so well described by Carlo Levi. Farther to the south-west the dramatic feature of the hill country is the enormous blue eruption of Mount Vulture, thirty to forty miles away, just south of the old Norman stronghold of Melfi, an extinct volcano whose crater, today a forest, was explored in boyhood by Horace from his nearby home at Venusium, now called Venosa.

In the days of Frederick II, the well-planted plain and the bare foothills were a dense forest in which an incredible amount of game was to be hunted even until the fifteenth century. It is said that Frederick I of Aragon, once setting out at daybreak from Barletta to surprise his enemies, received such alarming reports from his scouts of a vast cloud of dust raised by enemy cavalry that he ordered a return to camp 'but when the sun arose,' wrote Pontanus, 'this formidable host was discovered to be a herd of stags.'

I watched sparrow-hawks gliding above the castle on the wind currents, travelling with scarcely a wing beat, and they, of course, turned my thoughts again to Frederick II. I like to imagine that he had written part of his book on falconry in the castle, as indeed he probably did. The book was completed before 1248 and now, more than seven centuries later, new editions still appear. The latest English translation, by A. Wood and F. M. Fyfe, *The Art of Falconry, being the De Arte Venandi cum Avibus of Frederick II of Hohenstaufen,* appeared in 1956. There is a legend that Frederick's favourite child, the illegitimate Manfred, to whom the work was dedicated, persuaded his father to write it, and after the Emperor's death Manfred brought out a new edition. One of the sorrows of bibliophiles is that among the world's lost books is the Emperor's own two volume copy, beautifully illustrated with pictures of birds, some said to have been drawn by Frederick himself, and enriched with silver and gold. It was heard of last in 1265 but has since vanished without trace.

The *De Arte Venandi* was not the first book on falconry (Alfred the Great is believed to have written one, and also Edward the Confessor), but it was the first scientific book on ornithology and hunting with birds written during the Middle Ages. Frederick wrote only about the things which he had himself observed and tested. If he did not know the answer, he admitted his ignorance. He did not relate everything to holy writ as the book attributed to the Confessor did: he set down in clear words the life experience of one who placed falconry among the arts rather than the pastimes, one who cared nothing for the size of the kill but only for the thread of understanding between man and bird: the skill which enabled a man to extend his will into the sky and to draw back his emissary from the clouds. Frederick was the first bird-watcher; he it was who also established the nesting habits of the cuckoo when, finding a strange egg in a nest, he removed it and had it hatched; and he also exploded the absurd mediaeval legend of the 'barnacle geese', which were said to breed from certain limpets found on ships' timbers. He sent to the north for good specimens and proved by experiment that the story was a fable. It is astonishing that a man as busy as Frederick, in perpetual conflict with the Papacy and harassed by the thousand problems of his wide empire, should have had the time to sit down and write this scholarly book on falcons.

It is in six parts, though few, if any, complete copies exist. After a general survey of birds and species, nesting and breeding habits, migration, the bird skeleton and flight, he describes the different types of falcons and how to train them. His own mews contained birds from all parts of the world. He advised a falconer always to sing to his birds at feeding time, and to sing always the same song, so that the falcons would associate it with food. He should also lavish affection upon them, and, after washing his hands thoroughly, stroke and pet them. To calm them, he should spray them with

9A (*above*) The crypt of S. Nicholas, Bari, which was consecrated in 1089 A.D.

9B (*below, left*) The Ciborium of the Cathedral, Bari. C (*right*) The episcopal throne (1089), S. Nicholas, Bari

10 The Cathedral of Trani (1169–1250)

11A (*left*) Norman gateway, Ruvo Cathedral
B (*below*) Norman gallery, Bitonto Cathedral

12A (*above*) Tomb of Bohemund in the courtyard of the cathedral, Canosa di Puglia

12B (*below, left*) Elephant throne, Canosa di Puglia. C (*right*) Pulpit, Bitonto Cathedral

13A (*above*) Frederick II's Castel del Monte from the air

13B (*below, left*) Distant view of Castel del Monte. C (*right*) Giant statue of Roman Emperor, Barletta

14A (*above*) A street of 'Trulli' at Alberobello

14B (*below*) End of the Via Appia at Brindisi

15 The baroque glories of Lecce. A (*above, left*) The Cathedral. B (*right*) Detail, Santa Croce

15C (*below, left*) Church of S. Chiara. D (*right*) Roman theatre under main piazza of Lecce

16 A (*above*) The Castle of Otranto

16B (*below, left*) Old print showing S. Joseph of Copertino in flight. C (*right*) King Arthur, from the twelfth century mosaic pavement of Otranto Cathedral

water from his mouth but not until he had washed his mouth out three times. When a falcon was becoming used to new quarters, the Emperor prescribed, as a good meal, a chicken's leg or eggs carefully cooked in milk. He emphasized that a falconer must be the devoted servant of his birds, and should be ready to visit them in the middle of the night to see that all was well with them. The last part of the book is technical and is still of great interest to the few who pursue the most aristocratic of sports. Among the objects which Frederick introduced from the East was the hood, which is said to have been unknown in Europe until then, though it seems strange that his Sicilian Arabs should never have heard of it.

To enter the Castel del Monte is to find oneself in a mathematical formula: the building is an exercise in octagons carried out on two storeys. One enters an octagonal courtyard whose centre until recent times was occupied by an eight-sided fountain or bath. The eight rooms of the ground floor octagon are repeated almost exactly on the floor above. The eight octagonal towers contain spiral staircases, bathrooms and lavatories with water laid on in lead pipes from a cistern upon the roof, surely one of the earliest existing examples of mediaeval plumbing. With few exceptions, all the rooms in the castle are the same size and shape and all were sheeted in the finest of marbles, with floors of mosaic. A peculiarity of the design is that nearly all the sixteen rooms have inter-communicating doors. A spiral stair, which is reached by way of a ladder and a trapdoor in the room below, is called the *Scala del Falconiere* – the Falconer's Staircase – which leads to the roof where, it is believed, the Emperor kept his falcons; and in that way locked them away from the rest of the castle and from unauthorized admirers. Perhaps the idea of the castle was to provide the birds with an artificial eyrie.

For whom was the castle built? What guests did Frederick intend to entertain there in the suites of inter-communicating rooms? And where were the kitchens, the stables and the servants' quarters? I assume that these had perhaps been of perishable material and have vanished long ago. To me, the building is a mystery. From the outside it looks like a Norman keep, its octagonal towers lit by arrow-slits; inside, it has the luxury and elegance of a Renaissance palace and might have been built by the Medici. In spite of this, however, it is a gloomy place and I could not imagine looking forward with much pleasure to a week-end there. Any building with high walls and hardly any windows, and only one entrance, must suggest a prison, and charming as Frederick II could be no doubt as a host, I should think that some of his guests at the Castel del Monte, especially those with uneasy consciences, must have felt it trying to have so little privacy, to know that their rooms opened out one into the other, and that they could not leave the castle except by the one gate immediately below the master's quarters.

I was glad to come out into the open air and watch the hawks circling above.

§ 8

The best way to see a country is on foot, the next best is either on horseback or on a bicycle, according to the type of country; then comes the motor car and lastly the railway train. Apulia is perfect bicycling country: the towns with their lovely cathedrals are so close together that a cyclist could see a great deal in a week. Also, at the moment the main roads are comparatively uncrowded and the side roads are deserted.

A few miles from Bari are two towns, Ruvo and Bitonto, which are so close together that they can hear each other's church bells. Ruvo is an immensely old place. Centuries before the birth of Christ, it was the site of a Greek colony of potters. Not only did they make a great variety of pottery but they also imported from Greece urns, vases, plates, and drinking-cups. About a century or more ago ancient cemeteries were discovered from which thousands of beautiful examples of local and Attic pottery were recovered. About two thousand of these are to be seen at the Jatta Museum, which is one of the largest and finest private collections of the kind in the world. It is necessary to write and make an appointment to see it.

Ruvo was especially interesting to me because it is mentioned in one of the most celebrated of Horatian satires, which describes so pleasantly and with humour Roman travel in the last century before Christ, when the poet, accompanied part of the way by his friend Virgil, journeyed with their millionaire patron, Maecenas, from Rome to Brundusium (Brindisi) along the Appian Way. They arrived at Ruvo tired out, having travelled over roads made slippery and pitted by rain. It would seem that travelling with a Roman millionaire was not the luxurious safari one might have imagined, with delicious picnics in pavilions at frequent intervals, since Horace complained of unpleasant situations and, in one stopping-place, of undrinkable water. Possibly Maecenas was one of those millionaires who liked to set his friends a good example in frugality, certainly there was no hint of that luxury one reads about such as the sleeping-car (*carruca dormitoria*) which Martial said cost as much as a farm.

The cathedral in Ruvo is one of the finest in the province of Bari and, like that at Canosa, it lies in a hollow which represents the street level at the end of the twelfth century. The main door was one of the richest I had seen, a round arch surrounded by several bands of intricate lacelike carving. In the Lombard fashion, flanking pillars rested upon the backs of two lions and all sorts of strange creatures protruded like gargoyles from the walls above, including two menacing griffins which held human heads between their paws. Inside, a dignified Norman nave led to a noble ciborium.

In the main street of modern Ruvo I noticed, in a market, *braseros* precisely the same in appearance to those in Spain which burn crushed olive stones and grudgingly emit a faint warmth which serves only to emphasize the severity of a Mediterranean winter.

I went on to Bitonto, whose arms are two rampant lions facing each other beneath an olive tree. It is an Apulian agricultural town with a history that goes back like that of Ruvo to pre-Christian times. And then to the site of a Roman town called Butuntum, of which nothing has survived save its name and a few coins. When I saw Bitonto cathedral, I thought it the finest of them all, and for a moment my loyalty to Trani wavered. As an expression of Apulian

Romanesque, Bitonto cathedral is probably architecturally more notable than any of its companions. It stands in a wide open space and one's eye immediately seeks out its special feature, which is an open gallery high up on one of the walls, no two columns alike, and each Byzantine capital different, supporting a series of round arches. Inside, the church is richly carved and reminded me in some way of S. Nicola at Bari. The nave and triforium might belong to any Norman church in France or England, but not the Byzantine capitals or the two elaborately decorated pulpits, upon one of which is a strange, primitive group believed by some to represent Frederick II with Isabella of England and two of his sons; but there is no attempt at portraiture.

Standing in the piazza outside and admiring that glorious little open gallery, I remembered that at the end of December, 1250, the chronicler Spinelli came to Bitonto to see the funeral procession of Frederick, which paused there on its way to Taranto, where a ship was waiting to take the body to Palermo. He saw the bier hung with crimson velvet carried into the piazza, escorted by the Emperor's Saracen bodyguard all in tears. The great barons of the realm followed on horseback, wearing black cloaks over their armour, while heralds blew their trumpets and proclaimed the death of Frederick and the accession of his son Conrad. So the remains of the great Emperor – Anti-Christ to some, the 'Wonder of the World' to others – passed on its way to Sicily, where they still lie in a porphyry urn resting upon lions. When the tomb was opened in the last century, it was seen that Frederick had been buried in richly embroidered garments of silk, bearing Cufic characters worked in gold thread. A crusader's cross had been sewn to his red mantle; his silken boots were spurred; his sword was by his side; a purse was at his belt, and a golden ring containing a large emerald was upon the middle finger of his right hand.

Remembering something of this in the empty piazza, I became aware of a stir of movement behind me and, turning, I saw a funeral approaching at less than a walking-pace. Two bony horses drew forward across the flag-stones the customary elaborate Italian hearse, but it was an aged one which had recently been given a coat of glossy black paint but, instead of rejuvenating it, this made it seem even older and more rickety. Attached to this vehicle by ribbons of white satin, six little girls walked, wearing their first communion dresses. As the pathetic procession drew nearer I could see that the coffin was not more than four feet long. The children walked slowly in their soft white kid shoes, holding the satin streamers, the last link that bound them to their companion; and the sunlight of a late Italian afternoon lit this sad little picture for a moment before the procession moved into the shadow of the church.

# CHAPTER FIVE

*The coast of Apulia – where William the Conqueror's eldest son found his wife – the country of the Trulli – Brindisi – the baroque charm of Lecce – the 'heel' of Italy – the Castle of Otranto – Italy's Land's End – the town of Gallipoli – the Flying Monk of Copertino – the tarantula spider – peasants who dance until they drop – the mystery of Tarantism*

§ 1

With the Adriatic sparkling on my left and the sun in my eyes, I left Bari early one morning and took the coast road to Brindisi. Every mile or so I came to a little bay or a cove not yet dignified by the word 'lido' or 'marina', where on Sunday the Baresi go in family parties to bathe in warm blue water and to picnic. High on the rocks the ancient towns, rising in terraces, flat-roofed, snow-white and Islamic in appearance, or else curved in a crescent upon the shore, bear names well known in history but are content now to cherish their fishing fleets and to accept with gratitude whatever new industries the *Cassa del Mezzogiorno* considers to be good for them.

There was a crowd round the harbour of Mola di Bari where all the fishing-boats were dressed with bunting. A policeman, who politely apologized for the lack of parking space, told me that the town was celebrating the annual Festival of the Octopuses. In honour of the event the fishermen had assembled in the market a collection of Adriatic fish in banks of silver, red, grey, and pink, as vivid in colour as any harvest festival. Upon the far point of the jetty a priest in a green cope was blessing the boats and returning thanks to God for one of His strangest creations.

Coming to a fishing village called, appropriately, Cozze, which is the Italian word for mussels, I saw a signpost which pointed in the direction of a town named Conversano, no great distance away. It was the stronghold in Norman times of Geoffrey of Conversano whose daughter, Sibylla, married Robert of Normandy, the eldest son of William the Conqueror. I thought it would be interesting to see if anything remains in Conversano to link the town with the family of a young woman who might have been, indeed, one might say, should have been, Queen of England.

I came to a clean and tidy old town upon a hill, which commanded a marvellous view over the olive, peach and cherry trees to Bari and the sea. A man upon his knees in the cathedral, washing the steps to the high altar, was only too willing to leave this task and to pull a cord which withdrew a satin cover from the most important object in Conversano, the Madonna of the Fountain. She is a Byzantine ikon, a painting of indeterminate age, which, so the man told me, had been brought to Conversano centuries ago and was the oldest Madonna in Apulia. I must have looked incredulous, for he went to the sacristy and returned with a little book in which the ages of the various Virgins of Apulia were set out. First came the Madonna of Conversano, which is said to have been brought by Bishop Simplicio on his return from a mission in Africa in the year A.D. 487; then came the following in order of venerability: the Virgin of the Seven Veils at Foggia (A.D. 500); the Madonna of St Luke at Bari (A.D. 733); the Virgin of Constantinople at Acquaviva (A.D. 750); S. Maria di Siponto, which I had seen in the dark crypt there (A.D. 900); and the Madonna of the Sterpeto at Barletta (A.D. 1000). He told me that the Madonna of Conversano had arrived by ship at the village of Cozze, which I had seen on my way up to Conversano. In memory of this, she is taken in procession every year, during the month of May, round the countryside and down to the sea.

As I walked about Conversano, I found it to be one of the chief centres of cherry cultivation in Apulia. The big wheeled carts of the province, loaded with cherries, were drawing up outside semi-basements where the fruit was unloaded. I entered one and watched the fruit being weighed and the growers paid in cash. The cherries were then sorted and graded by girls and packed for export to towns and factories. I heard the names of *Donnalella, Tosta, Francia,* and *Ferrovia,* which were among the most popular local varieties, and, asking if I might buy half a kilo, I was given about twelve pounds and was charged only two shillings. They were beautiful cherries, large, crisp and sweet and not unlike the Whitehearts I have eaten in Kentish orchards.

The Castle of Conversano is a massive, meandering building with a Norman core and additions from every succeeding century. It has a long record of continuous habitation, and today, lacking a lordly family, it has been divided into flats. I could see that there is now nothing to remind one of that day in the year 1100 when a distinguished guest arrived on his way home from the First Crusade. He was the eldest, the most inept and the most likeable of the sons of William the Conqueror, Robert of Normandy. William disliked his eldest son and not only bullied him and shouted at him, but worse, made fun of his appearance – he was short and fat – calling him 'Robin Curthose' and 'Gamberon', words which politely approximated to 'Shorty'. Robert retaliated by leading revolts against his parent which poisoned the Conqueror's later life, a double dose of poison, in fact, since Robert was his mother's favourite and she helped him behind her husband's back, thus creating that mother-son situation which few men, even conquerors, have been able to fight.

Robert was no fool, but a gay and charming spendthrift, emotionally unstable and, like many another happy-go-lucky character, apt to astonish his friends by competence and bravery in battle. He came to Conversano fresh from his triumphs in the Holy Land, an attractive, middle-aged man, a misfit maybe, and quixotic, and one who had seen a younger brother ascend the throne of England while he went off on a holy war. His host, Geoffrey of Conversano, no doubt thinking him a good investment, gave him not only his daughter, Sibylla, as wife (for Robert, though several times a father, had never married), but also lent him a large sum of money. It was Robert's intention to claim the throne of England as the eldest son, but it was typical of him that although his brother Rufus was killed in the New Forest while he was in Italy, Robert, instead of returning home to seize the throne, continued to drift about and so gave time for another younger brother, Henry I, to establish himself as King.

Of Sibylla nothing is known except that a contemporary observer said that she was radiantly beautiful and that she was more capable of managing Robert's affairs than he was: but she had little opportunity to do so. Three years after her marriage she died in Normandy, some said of poison administered by an ambitious widow who fancied Robert's chance of kingship, but more likely of bad nursing after a difficult confinement. She left an infant son, William, 'The Clito', or Prince, who might have changed the course of English history, and who for twenty years was the centre of intrigue.

Robert was one of those people who invariably do the wrong thing, or the right thing at the wrong time, and his luck was always so consistently bad that contemporary chroniclers had to find a reason for it: this was that he had piqued God by refusing the Crown of Jerusalem, and that the Deity had decided to punish him 'everywhere thwarting him,' (said William of Malmesbury), 'and turning all his enjoyments into bitterness.' When in his fifties, Robert was captured by his younger brother, Henry I, and placed in lifelong captivity, first, possibly, in the Tower of London, then in Bristol, and, finally, in Cardiff Castle, where eventually he died at the age of eighty. It has been said that during his captivity of twenty-eight years he learnt to speak Welsh and wrote a poem in Welsh which was inspired by a green oak tree that he could see from his window. There are six three-line verses and the poem is quite up to modern Eisteddfod standards. Unfortunately every trace of the origin of this poem having been lost, the only text is that which was preserved in the last century by the Welsh bard Edward Williams, known as 'Iolo Morganweg', whose enthusiasm as a collector was matched by his ability to turn out a nice period verse. Welsh scholars, frightened of being taken in, shy away from 'Iolo Morganweg' like nervous horses. Still, one can say that if the feckless Robert was able to learn Welsh (and after all he had twenty-eight years in which to do so), and were he capable of writing verse in that exacting medium, this is probably just the kind of poem he might conceivably have written.

At least it is interesting, though I have never seen it mentioned in connection with the poem, that his jailer should have been his bastard nephew, the natural son of his brother Henry I, Robert, Earl of Gloucester, the first of England's literary noblemen and patrons. He held the honour of Gloucester as well as the lordship of Glamorgan with the castle of Cardiff. He was a friend of writers and poets and he gave information about current events to William of Malmesbury, who acknowledged his debt in dedicating his English chronicle to the Earl. It may be extravagant to imagine the learned earl and his captive studying bardic matters together, but at least the character of Robert, Earl of Gloucester, gives the lie to later stories of Duke Robert's sad and painful imprisonment; indeed, as William of Malmesbury writes, Robert's life was as pleasant as any captivity can be, with plenty of amusement and plenty of food. It was either William or some other contemporary who mentioned that the captive Duke, and, as some believed, the rightful King of England, had several knights to wait upon him.

If the Conqueror's eldest son still had any hope of ascending the throne, or believed that his son, 'The Clito', might do so, these must have been encouraged in 1120, in the fourteenth year of his captivity, when the 'White Ship' went down, drowning Prince William and his brother Richard, sons of Henry I and the heirs to the throne. This made Robert, aged sixty-six, and his son, aged nineteen, the only direct, lawful descendants of William the Conqueror: but the bad luck which haunted Robert was relentless. Eight years after the wreck of the 'White Ship' he dreamt that his right arm had been pierced with a lance and, awakening, said to his jailers, 'Alas, my son is dead.' This proved to be true. It soon became known that in the course of an unimportant skirmish in Flanders, 'The Clito' had received a hand wound which turned septic, with fatal results. So in the twenty-seventh year of his age died the only son of Sibylla of Conversano and Robert Curthose, and the only surviving legitimate grandson of the Conqueror.

I thought that probably not a living soul in Conversano knew that one of the most provoking 'ifs' in English history had originated there; but I was wrong. I was introduced to the local historian, who knew a great deal about the ramifications of the family.

'It is well known,' he said, 'that the daughter of Geoffrey married the King of England.'

What irony! I made no attempt to put him right, and was to find out later, and in another place, that in the south of Italy those few who care about such things often believe that Robert had ascended the English throne.

I regained the Via Appia and, after travelling for a few miles, came to the ruins of a Roman town on the left of the road and within a hundred yards of the sea. The line of roads and the foundations of buildings covered several acres before vanishing into a hillside. Lizards froze until the last moment as one approached, then flashed into a crevice of the warm rock; poppies were growing in the main street. This was the town of Egnatia, whose only claim to fame is a line or two in a poem by Horace. It was the last place before Brundusium where he stopped during his journey with Maecenas. And it was here that the poet made fun of the local miracle (a phenomenon mentioned solemnly by Pliny), which was an altar that consumed incense without any trace of fire. It is odd that Horace should have been so scornful, since a similar altar heated by an underground furnace was among the inventions of Hero of Alexandria. It may be, of course, that Horace knew this and refused to be impressed.

§ 2

As one travels towards Brindisi unusual and attractive features of the landscape, dotted about vineyards and olive groves, are circular stone buildings whose cone-shaped roofs are made of limestone slates beautifully packed together without mortar, like the dry-stone walls of Cumberland. These buildings are called *trulli*. Their origin, and also the origin of the name, are unknown.

The first *trullo* one sees is probably a tool-shed in which workers in a vineyard keep their ladders and wheelbarrows, but as you go deeper into the *trulli* country you see groups of circular dwellings, each one with its cone-shaped roof of packed limestone, a peculiar sight that gives the impression that native villages have migrated from Africa.

The *trullo* achieves its metropolis in the town of Alberobello, where there are about two thousand of these buildings. There are regular streets of them where you can speak to the friendly inhabitants, who will gladly invite you to step inside to see their houses. Most of the buildings are circular, but the more important are rectangular, though even these retain the conical roof. A *trullo* may begin as one room, then as a family grows, or a man becomes prosperous, another *trullo* is added and sometimes you may see as many as five or six clustered and linked together, but each with its characteristic roof. The most sophisticated is a two-storey *trullo* which is known as a *trullo sovrano*.

Alberobello is naturally haunted by artists and photographers. I was told of a Canadian and his family who arrived to find out if this most bizarre of Italian towns really existed, or whether he had imagined it when he saw it first by moonlight during the Allied invasion of Italy. I could sympathize with him. The place has a strange, dreamlike quality which makes one doubt the evidence of one's eyes.

All the *trulli* which I entered were clean and cool. Some were rather crowded with household possessions and many had alcove beds. The walls are sometimes five feet thick and the windows were the size of a sheet of writing-paper, admitting only a faint glow. In some large *trulli* there were separate bedrooms almost entirely occupied by the family bed. In one of the *trulli* the owner invited me to drink a glass of wine with him. He raised a stone slab in the floor and, to my surprise, I saw there his wine-cellar, which was a concrete tank full of wine. He let down a rubber tube into it and siphoned the wine into a jug. It was dark, red and strong, and rather sweet, like most of the best wine in the South; indeed it was so strong that a small quantity was sufficient. He told me that some of the finest wine of Apulia is made in the *trulli* country and that most of it is eagerly bought up for blending by the wine merchants. Here also I tasted a cake made of almonds, raisins and candied fruit, called *pan pepata*, or spiced bread, which seemed to me to have an Arab origin, or rather, as the Arabs never invented anything, a Byzantine one. After bidding my host goodbye, I was soon on my way to Brindisi.

§ 3

Tired of tramping all over Brindisi, I looked round to find somewhere to eat. I was standing upon the most celebrated spot in the city: the summit of the beautiful flight of steps from which rises the tall Roman column that marks the termination of the Via Appia. The column commands the port today as it did centuries ago. The harbour is one of Nature's supreme achievements. The sea flows in through a narrow entrance and forms two wide protected arms, or bays, to left and right of the town where ships may anchor in safety even should a gale be blowing.

It was a warm day. Sky and sea were gentian blue. I descended the steps and walked along the western arm of the harbour in the direction of a castle built by Frederick II and added to in a massive way by its later occupants. Here I came to a modest *trattoria* whose tables were set out in the open, almost on the edge of the harbour wall, and shaded by a pergola of dry palm branches. The proprietor was a burly individual dressed in a fisherman's jersey. He recommended his *cozze alla marinara,* but by that time I had eaten so many *cozze* that I showed some resistance, which caused the man to shout to a boy who was crossing the quay, bucket in hand, to come to us. The bucket was filled with perfect mussels, all large and uniform in size, and still in salt water straight from the Adriatic. I gave in.

It was pleasant to sit there with a glass of white wine and look out from the shade of the palm awning to the hot, white world beyond, where a yacht was coming in through the channel, where children were splashing in clear green water near a patch of sand and a ferry was crossing from the bank opposite upon which stood a piece of Fascist architecture, an example of bad manners in stone and brick. This was an out-of-scale ship's rudder, a monstrous gaunt tower of much the same height, I should say, as Nelson's Column, which, conceived as a memorial to mariners in the nineteen-thirties, looks, like so much official architecture of that period, as though it had been designed by someone wearing a uniform too tight for him and anxious to impress his superiors.

I was told that a lift runs to the top and that the view is sublime, as it should be, for you look down upon Brindisi embraced by two arms of the sea, a sight which suggested to the ancient Messapians a stag's head with its antlers; and to the east you would see the outer harbour protected from the full fury of wind and ocean by the island of S. Andrea and the smaller Petague islets. When the *cozze* eventually arrived, they were, as the proprietor had suggested, worth waiting for. A touch of the exotic was given to the *trattoria* by an African, his wife, and their child, an infant of about three, who gazed about with enormous eyes and looked as if it had just come from a toy shop. It will be admitted by some that only parents are able to see exquisite beauty in a pink infant, whereas black ones, like kittens and puppies, are never again as attractive as long as they live. The father placed this charming little black Sambo upright on the table and let it put its fingers in his mouth. These were the first Africans I had seen in the south of Italy, and I wondered what odd chance had brought them to Brindisi. I found it impossible to place them. They sat isolated in their Africanism, while the roof of palm fronds above them suggested that they had been surprised in an affectionate domestic moment in their native land.

My first thought was that possibly they were stranded without much money, or perhaps none at all, since they had ordered only a bottle of orangeade, with a straw in the neck which the man and woman shared in turn. That sometimes excessive sympathy for the simple African which still flows, it seems, from Harriet Beecher Stowe, made me uneasy, and I wondered if I could help in any way. Then to my surprise the waiter covered their table with antipasti and huge mounds of spaghetti. I expected them to set to like famished people, but, instead, they tasted a mouthful here and there and pushed their plates away. Some meat dish followed and received the same petulant treatment. A bowl of oranges, cherries and bananas was not even touched.

I went out and walked up and down the quay, where the first thing that caught my attention was an English car of a distinguished make, but somehow different in appearance so that I thought it must be a new model. It was piled with luggage almost to the roof. While I was looking at it, a deep, velvet-lined voice, rather like the voice of 'Ole Man River,' said, with a pleased chuckle, at my elbow:

'You like my car?'

The African had followed me out of the *trattoria*.

'I had it specially designed with a left-hand drive,' he said, 'and balloon tyres, for my own country.'

I congratulated him. (And this was the man who, so I had thought, might have been in need of aid!) His English was fluent and upper-class, but still African. He opened a wallet in which I could not help seeing more money than most people would care to carry about, and as he fumbled for a visiting-card, I wondered whether he was the king of some African state or perhaps the Minister of Finance. But no; his card bore his name and his address in Africa, and in a corner I read the words, 'Locust Control'.

I said with a smile that he was rather off the locust route, a remark which seemed to disturb him. When he asked abruptly for the return of his card I thought that I must have offended him. But no: he took the card and gave me another, but instead of 'Locust Control' I read the words 'Public Administration'. He told me that he had just taken a six months course in local government at Manchester University and was crossing in the car ferry to see Greece on his way home to Africa. He then made a remark which I shall never forget.

'Greece rates as an under-developed country,' he said.

Brindisi is haunted by ancient memories just as its name is haunted by the older form of Brundusium. It was the chief port of Rome for Greece and the East, and the old link appears to be as firm as ever. In the Corso Garibaldi I read the following on shop signs, within a few yards of each other: *ΒΑΕΙΛΗΕ Ο ΡΟΔΙΤΗΕ ESTIATOPION, ΕΛΛΗΝΙΚΗ ΓΩΝΙΑ.*

The sea connection with Greece is as strong as it was in the days of the Caesars. From March until October two air-conditioned car ferries are in circulation between Brindisi, Corfu and Patras; one of them can carry more than seven hundred passengers and more than a hundred motor cars, while the second is slightly larger. How interested the Roman engineers would have been in this car ferry! I watched one of them, the *Egnatia*, unload her passengers and vehicles, remembering that nineteen years before Christ a sick man, who had been travelling in Greece, was landed in much the same place and, after lingering for a few days, died. He was the poet Virgil, and he was only fifty-one years of age.

The name of the ferry, *Egnatia*, recalled the old crusading route from the Adriatic ports to Dyrrhachium, which is now Durrës, in Albania, where the Crusaders met the Via Egnatia, which led them to Constantinople. Robert of Normandy selected Brindisi as his port of departure, but spent such a long time enjoying himself that many of his followers lost their enthusiasm and deserted. At last, in the spring, he embarked his troops, but the first galley sank before it had cleared the outer harbour, with a loss of about four hundred lives, many horses, mules, and chests of money. Happily it was reported that the dead bodies which were washed up at Brindisi were all miraculously marked with a cross upon the shoulder-blades, which helped to calm those who were thinking of giving up the Crusade.

I found two attractive links with the Crusaders, the charming round church of St. John, founded by the Templars, and a wonderful old fountain where, local tradition says, the Crusaders watered their horses before they embarked. The water falls through masks in a long wall of masonry which terminates at each end in a domed structure like a Moslem shrine.

Books written even forty or fifty years ago described Brindisi as a squalid, dying town, and I was unprepared for the vigorous, bustling city of today. I was told that its prosperity is due to the gigantic petrol and chemical works established there recently, which are among the largest in Italy, and also, I think, in some degree to the popularity of Greece as a tourist country. As I moved south into the heel of Italy, towards the town of Lecce, I remembered the lovely harbour of Brindisi, which is not unlike a lakeside. I remembered the snatches of Greek heard in the streets and the African who had patronized the 'undeveloped' land of Homer and Plato. I recalled the tall marble column (there were once two) that marked the end of the Appian Way; and I thought that the flight of steps which leads to the column is one of the most majestic in Italy, fit to be compared with those of the Piazza di Spagna and the Quirinal Palace in Rome.

## § 4

As I approached Lecce, I felt for the first time that the full heat of summer had come. The June sun beat cruelly upon the stony earth. Vineyards and fields of tobacco succeeded one another upon the fiery landscape, and not a living thing stirred save lizards with palpitating throats upon stone walls; and from vineyard and olive grove sounded the ceaseless chirrup of the cicada, the pulse of the hot afternoon. Lecce was enfolded in the hush of the siesta. A sleepy hall porter in a large old-fashioned hotel gave me the keys of a room with a bathroom, and I moved gratefully across the darkened hall.

The cold tap produced a stream of peat-brown water. I filled the bath, past caring whether it was rust or not, and lay in the cool water, feeling my body temperature gradually go down. Later, I sat enjoying the darkness of the shuttered room. One of the many advantages of an old-fashioned hotel is that everything is on an ample scale; the bed is large, the room is high, the bath has not been designed for a dwarf, neither is the bath towel a miserable yard of linen but a robe of imperial proportions.

Cooler and dressed again, I prowled round the hotel and discovered in a corridor a fascinating series of English coaching prints, depicting not the four-in-hand but the first 'steam carriages' to run in England between 1830 and 1840. I think this must be a

little known chapter in locomotion since the odd-looking jugger-
nauts which puffed at four miles an hour along English roads
were an extraordinary experiment in mechanical traction which
ended as suddenly as it had begun when the companies which
financed it became bankrupt. There was Mr William Church's
curious coach of 1832 that went from London to Birmingham;
there was Mr Walter Hancock's oddly named 'Autopsy' of 1833;
also a steam carriage of the same year – a two-tone model in yellow and brown – in which five men wearing stove-pipe hats were
rigidly seated with one intrepid female, as well as other equally
interesting and ill-fated prophecies of a distant future. I wondered
how these unusual glimpses of old England had come to Lecce.

The sun, though near to setting, was still hot and golden when
I took my first look at a town which is called 'the Athens of Apulia'
and 'the Florence of Baroque', two well-meaning compliments
which, however, do not mean very much. During a period of
extraordinary commercial activity at the end of the seventeenth
century and the beginning of the eighteenth, Lecce was rebuilt in
the fashionable style of the period, the once despised and now much
prized rococo or baroque. It seemed to me that history is repeating
itself in the main piazza, but with dismal results. Lecce is indeed a
decorative survival of the seventeenth century, and I felt that
instead of dodging the cars one should be riding through its
streets with a plume in one's hat and followed by Sancho Panza
on a mule. I sensed something Spanish in the atmosphere of Lecce,
in the gravity and dignity of its people, in the formality of their
manners and in the elaborate architecture of their background,
which reminded me of Spanish baroque in those regions where the
stone cuts like butter and hardens like steel. Lecce's baroque is not
spectacular, but is a style based on the classical, and having
explored the cathedral, the bishop's palace, several churches, some
streets with lovely carved stone balconies, the noble Porta Rusce,
and several ornate palaces, I thought that the exotic overcoat of
carving superimposed upon classical façades had more in common
with the late Roman temples of Syria, for example, Baalbec, than
with the Jesuitical extravaganzas of Rome.

The greatest fantasy in Lecce, however, is not the imaginative

work of Giuseppe Zimbalo and Cesare Penna, but a vast hole
in the central piazza in which crouches half a Roman amphitheatre of the best period, probably that of Hadrian. Upon a tall
column nearby (the twin of Brindisi's column which fell down
and was then acquired by Lecce), stands the patron saint, S.
Orontius, vested as a bishop with uplifted hand, but whether in
blessing or in dismay at the classical revelation at his feet, who can
say?

It must indeed have been a shock to Lecce at the beginning of
this century when, in the heart of the town, this extraordinary
intrusion from an earlier period was revealed. The amphitheatre
fascinated me. It is a fine relic: you can walk about it and ascend
to the semi-circle of seats just as an audience used to do eighteen
centuries ago. Young Leccians now chase each other about the
vaults and arches as no doubt young Romans used to do on days
when there was no show. The sky above was filled with screaming
swifts that dived and soared, filling the air with a shrill clamour
that dominated the evening sounds and might have been the
applause of a distant audience.

For a town of its size Lecce is well provided with bars and cafés.
I sat at one near the amphitheatre and thought how amazing it is
that though little is known of Lupiae, which was the Roman Lecce,
in modern times an amphitheatre suddenly comes into the sunlight large enough to seat twenty-five thousand people. A man
came up and in a gentle and polite manner sold me a small bag of
fresh almonds; which I found to be tasteless.

The shops were unusually elegant, and one of the local industries
was unexpectedly the making of papier-maché objects and ornaments. Like most southern towns, Lecce is on the lookout for new
industries. Already she has a State tobacco factory and a market
which shows that her wealth is agricultural and vigorous. A picturesque assembly of farmers and peasants gather in the shadow of
a fine castle built by Charles V, thus again stressing maybe an
affinity with Spain. There is a learned academy, the Salentine
Academy of Letters and Arts; there is also a Dante Society, a
Centre of Salentine Studies, and even a Rotary Club and a Lions
Club. It is only fair to add that there are eleven large garages and

five petrol stations. Of all the towns I had seen in southern Italy, Lecce, I thought, was the one most likely to appeal to that almost extinct character, the well-off, intelligent English traveller.

I was awakened in the middle of the night by a subconscious message. I was being attacked by something which I fear more than serpents or vampires: I was being devoured by mosquitoes. I snapped on the light. It was the melancholy hour of two o'clock. Upon the walls waited my enemies, not mosquitoes, but a formidable species of gnat. I attacked them with a rolled newspaper, and in doing so discovered upon the wall squalid evidence that former occupants of the room had waged similar battles. Outside the window was what, owing to a peculiarity of the architecture, though my room was only on the second floor, appeared to be a roof garden where dozens of pot plants, geraniums and oleanders were flowering (such a pleasant sight, I had thought), and these I suspected, offered an ambush for my enemies. I closed the windows and the temperature of the room rose unpleasantly. Sleep was no longer possible, so the small hours passed in guerrilla warfare and eventually came the blessed, unbelievable dawn. Such was the penalty I paid for disregarding one of the first rules of travel; whenever you hear swifts screaming over a town, go instantly and provide yourself with a flitgun.

The museum of Lecce, which is obliged to share the Governor's delightful palace, would be better off in less exalted quarters. Still, from the crowded mass of urns and vases, from inscriptions in Latin and Greek and wistful marble faces, one carries away a few clear memories. I recall, as something I should like to see every day, a small, biscuit-thin cup made by some Attic potter maybe five hundred years before Christ, decorated – black on red – with wicked satyrs and startled, long-necked fauns; there was also a larger vase with a charming picture of Polynices in the act of bribing Eriphyle with the famous necklace of Aphrodite. He holds it up temptingly so that it falls extended by its own weight, displaying each magic stone, and she turns, desperately anxious to clasp it round her neck and thus to restore her fading youth.

I was interested to see that the museum bore the name of its founder, Duke Sigismundo Castromediano, who had a fleeting and unusual contact with England in the eighteen-fifties. Readers of G. M. Trevelyan's famous account of the Risorgimento may recall that the Duke was one of three noblemen who were savagely sentenced by the Neapolitan Government for their liberal opinions. Gladstone, who happened to be in Naples, not only attended the trial but visited Neapolitan prisons and so accumulated material for his attack upon the Bourbon monarchy which did so much to damage it in the eyes of Europe. It was natural that when the Duke of Castromediano managed to escape and find his way to London, one of his first acts was to seek out his hero, Gladstone. By one of those strange chances, the visitor happened to call at the very moment when the statesman was reading an account of prison life written by the Duke and printed in an Irish newspaper!

This is related by Janet Ross in her book *The Land of Manfred*. During a visit to Lecce in 1888 the Duke showed her over his museum, saying that 'nothing gave him so much pleasure as to see an Englishwoman'. She was greatly impressed by his tall, spare aristocratic figure and his shock of hair which had turned white in prison. He described the horror of life in frightful dungeons, shackled by the leg to the lowest type of criminal. Sometimes, he said, when grubbing in the soil of the prison floor they would turn up human bones. The Duke died almost penniless in the smallest room of his castle at Cavallino, outside Lecce; upon his coffin were placed the chain of a galley-slave and the red jacket worn by Neapolitan convicts. These, he used to say, were his decorations. His two books, which were published in Lecce, *Memorie* in 1885, and *Carceri e Galere politiche* in 1895, are classics of the fight for Italian unity.

I wondered if this link with England might explain in some way the prints in the hotel corridor and the partiality for England surely a pleasant relic of the last century, which I seemed to detect among the inhabitants of this elegant city.

§ 5

As I plunged into the sunlight on my way south to the coast at Otranto, I realized that this was not the heat of summer: it was the *sirocco*, that dry and hateful wind which stirs up the liver and makes people short-tempered and argumentative. It blows from the steppes and the sandy wastes of North Africa, where it is equally loathed as the *khamsin*.

The province of Lecce includes what is known as the heel of Italy, but is called more properly the Salentine Peninsula. One side is washed by the Adriatic, the other by the Ionian Sea, and there is hardly a place more distant than fifteen miles from one sea or the other. It is one of those parts of Italy where old ways and traditions are believed to linger from the pagan world and many a guidebook claims that some of the villagers speak Greek, a relic, it is believed, of remote Magna Graecia, though it is more likely that they are the descendants of Greek-speaking Albanians who emigrated to the south of Italy centuries ago.

I passed through small towns and villages separated from each other by a few miles of stony earth on which vines were growing, while olive trees of immense girth shimmered in the heat. I soon came to the coast at Otranto. I saw an ancient castle standing upon the edge of a deep green sea, its circular bastions perfect. Nearby a warren of old streets struggled up a hill upon which I could see the roof line of a large cathedral. A short distance away a few holiday bungalows and a pleasant hotel stood almost in the gentle waves that curled over every now and then with a sound that resembled the laziest of sighs. Opposite was a restaurant which had been built over the sea, like a pier.

Otranto is distinguished among the innumerable castellated towns and cities of Italy as having inspired perhaps the most attractive title in the history of the English novel. Horace Walpole's *The Castle of Otranto*, which has been called the ancestor of the 'thriller', was, more importantly, one of the first literary signs of a change in taste that was to lead to Walter Scott and Barry's Gothic Houses of Parliament. So perfect is the title that any writer may be forgiven the suspicion that it came first and the book afterwards; but that was not so. Walpole described how, after a vivid dream, he wrote at white-hot speed for nearly two months, a feat which must always arouse the envy of slower practitioners, and then, having finished his novel, cast about for a title. He had never been to Otranto and did not even know that it had a castle, as he confessed to Lady Craven when she sent him a drawing of the building. 'When the story was finished,' he wrote, 'I looked into the map of the Kingdom of Naples for a well-sounding name, and that of Otranto was very sonorous.' So *The Castle of Otranto* was one of literature's happiest chances, even though the euphony may be due very largely to the usual English pronunciation of Otranto. In Italy the accent is on the 'O', not the 'trant'.

I walked up to the castle, which is now a school. The scholars enter beneath a grand coat-of-arms of the Emperor Charles V carved above the main gate, and, crossing a paved yard, reach their classrooms, once, I suppose, the quarters of the garrison. I found that steps ascend behind these buildings to a fine stretch of sentry walk which commands an impressive view of this lovely emerald and indigo sea and the white coastline. It was here that I saw the distant mountains of Albania on the opposite shores of the Adriatic, vague outlines pencilled against the sky and tipped with snow or cloud.

I sought out the restaurant which was built over the sea and selected a table which might have been set in the prow of a ship. It was a triumph, I reflected, to have walked round the ramparts of the Castle of Otranto, a feat which, had it been performed two centuries ago, would have justified a neat little note to Strawberry Hill. How beautiful are the colours in the south of Italy. I could see, as through several layers of green glass, the purple weeds swaying in the water; a girl who wore a red bikini paddled across in a yellow *sandolino*, her shadow following her along the sea bed.

The menu offered *pesce spada*, swordfish, the *xiphias gladius* of the ancient world, a fish which has been caught round the southern shores of Italy since the days of Ancient Greece, and no doubt long before. The waiter told me that it was not often to be found at Otranto, and that this was the last one they would see that season, though he thought they were still catching them in the Straits of

Messina. The fish arrived, resembling a white salmon steak, grilled on both sides and covered with an aromatic sauce in which there was olive oil, lemon, and origano, that attractive herb which is the sweet marjoram of the English herbal. I thought the fish would have tasted like tunny, but it was more like turbot in flavour, and I resolved to eat it whenever I could.

While in the old town I was shown some of the largest cannon balls I have ever seen, indeed I think they must have been flung by catapults. They were relics of Otranto's undying nightmare, the terrible *sacco*. Two old men described this event to me as if it had happened last week, and not in the year 1480, when Otranto was a busy port with a population of twenty-two thousand. They said that in August, 1480, a powerful Turkish fleet, which had been driven from Rhodes, decided to bombard Otranto. The Turks then landed and, after massacring the inhabitants, ran up the Turkish flag and took over the town. The capture of Otranto sent an apprehensive shiver through Europe; many feared that the banners of Islam might soon fly above St Peter's and even Nôtre Dame. However, Mohammed II died in the following year and during the struggle between his heirs for the succession, Otranto was evacuated: but it has never recovered from the *sacco*, either materially or spiritually.

'If you wish to see how we remember the eight hundred martyrs,' I was told, 'go to the duomo.'

The cathedral is the greatest surprise in Otranto. It is a basilica whose nave columns came from a Greek temple, and the church cannot have changed much since it was consecrated in 1088 when, so I was told, Bohemund was present.

'Bohemund the Crusader?' I asked.

'Yes; the son of Robert Guiscard. This town was his fief.'

The word my informant used was *feudo*, and I thought that only in the South of Italy could anyone use this basic Norman word. It is like the survival in Ireland of the word 'demesne.'

Alone among all the cathedrals of Italy, the cathedral of Otranto has an intact Norman tesselated pavement that stretches from the west door to the altar and is continued in the apse. I felt that I might have been walking on the Bayeux tapestry. A priest told me that it was the work of a monk or a priest called Pantaleone and was completed in 1166, the year when William I of Sicily died. Artistically, the pavement is decorative but crude; it is also a strange glimpse into the mind of a man who was born in the Norman-Arab-Byzantine world of southern Italy. The design begins at the west end of the nave and the two aisles with three 'trees of life' in whose branches are to be found a colourful company of men, women and animals. Adam and Eve are being expelled from Eden, Noah is building the Ark, and we can recognize Cain and Abel; but the secular scenes are even more interesting. Students of the Arthurian Cycle may perhaps be surprised to know that Pantaleone was familiar with it and has decorated the pavement with a mounted 'Rex Arturus', clean-shaven and Norman in appearance. The mythical monsters and zodiacal signs framed in medallions might have been copied from Byzantine textiles.

The priest took me to a side chapel which was lined with tall wall-cases enclosed by double doors. He opened one and revealed, behind glass and neatly arranged on shelves, several hundred human skulls. He opened a second and a third.

'The eight hundred martyrs of Otranto,' he said. 'Beneath the altar is the stone of execution.'

He was interested in the history of Otranto and reminded me that, as the nearest point in Italy to Greece, it was famed in Roman times as the shortest sea passage between the two countries, a route that was favoured by Cicero.

'The ancient name was Hydruntum,' he continued, 'and you may think it a curious example of conservatism that to this day the few thousand people who live here refer to themselves, and like others to do so, as Idruntuni. Did you know that after a lapse of centuries a regular sea ferry has been running between Otranto and Greece since 1964? The voyage takes only three hours. Everyone will tell you that the shortest sea passage to Greece is from Brindisi, but it is not so.'

I told him that I thought Otranto one of the most beautiful little towns I had seen, and that I should like to return one day and spend a month there. This seemed to please him. He gave me as a parting gift a coloured reproduction of a picture by a painter in some past epoch showing the population of Otranto lined up naked, ready for execution, while in the foreground headless bodies weltered in pools of blood and three cherubs circled overhead bearing crowns of martyrdom. It was a curious memorial of a place which I shall always think of as peaceful and serene.

§ 6

For twenty miles or so the road ran along the edge of the cliffs to the extreme point of the heel of Italy, called Finibus Terrae. The translucent sea moved below upon deserted beaches and ran into lonely, rocky coves, and sometimes, in places where the land thrust itself out into the water, I could hear the sea booming in caverns. The earth was Devonshire red and if only there had been apples instead of olives, I might have imagined myself travelling through the West Country during a phenomenal heat wave. I descended to isolated fishing villages clustered upon rocks, the houses lime-washed blue and pink, a small jetty sheltering a few fishing-boats, and then up again out of the valley to the main road above the sea.

Half way to the Cape I came to a spa owned by the State called *Santa Cesarea Terme*, where hot sulphur water is pumped from grottoes, one of them beneath the sea. The houses, with their flat roofs, lay in tiers upon the hillside, blindingly white, their look of Morocco assisted by a large Arabic-looking palace. It seemed to me an admirable place to take one's arthritis. Unfortunately the source was closed so that I was unable to drink the sulphur water or see the medicinal mud, but I did encounter a fantastic legend. Happening to ask who Santa Cesarea was, I was told this story. There was, at some unspecified period, a man called Aloysius, who lived nearby and was devoted to his wife. When she died suddenly his grief was overwhelming. His only daughter was the image of his dead wife, and, in his grief, he decided to marry her. The horrified girl planned to run away from home. She told her father one night that she was going to have a bath, and tying two pigeons together by the feet, she left them to splash in the water and escaped into the night. In the morning her father, setting off in search of her, found her wandering lost upon the seashore, but as he approached a dense sea-mist concealed her from view, and in this mist Aloysius became lost and was drowned. In the meantime Cesarea fled along the shore until a rock moved like a door and she saw a heavenly radiance streaming from a cave. As she entered, the rock closed behind her and she was received into heaven. It is said that even today fishermen who are off this coast on the eve of Ascension Day see the rock open and heavenly light stream out. Such is the saga of a coastline famous for its caverns, and a Mass is said every year in a church near the cave.

The road rose and fell towards the heel of Italy, the Cape of S. Maria di Leuca, or S. Maria di Finibus Terrae – Our Lady of Land's End. I noticed that for a few miles nearly every house was limewashed in a peculiar shade of purple, the exact colour which I had noticed surviving in the folds of drapery on many of the Greek terracottas in Bari Museum. I had never before seen houses in this colour, and they did not look attractive. I was soon running down to the south-eastern extremity of Italy, the Cape of S. Maria di Leuca, which takes its name (Greek, *akra leuca*) from the white limestone cliffs that rise to about two hundred feet above the meeting of the Adriatic and the Ionian Seas. It was once familiar to every sailor on his way to and from Sicily, and to the cities of Magna Graecia, as the Iapygium Promontorium, upon whose highest point was the ancient equivalent of a lighthouse, a Temple of Minerva. Now the headland, beautifully landscaped with terraces descending to the water, carries a tall column with a statue of the Virgin upon the summit of the cliff, and nearby, where the Temple once stood, is the church of S. Maria de Finibus Terrae. The oddities of conversion are just as frequent in the inanimate as in the animate world: the altar is said to have come from the temple of the goddess.

Having travelled south since I left Bari, I now turned north-west, round Finibus Terrae, where the coast is washed by the wine-dark Ionian Sea. But what a disappointment it was! The Gulf of Taranto lacked the sparkle and colour of the seascape I had left, or perhaps it was the low, treeless coastline with its bony limestone protuberances and its sad-looking fishing villages that depressed me. Or it may have been the *sirocco*, which seemed to be even more potent on the Ionian coast of the peninsula than on the Adriatic side. However, I looked forward to seeing Gallipoli (Kallipolis, 'the beautiful city') which, like its namesake on the Dardanelles, was founded centuries before Christ. At the entrance to the old town I met a man who was walking in the middle of the road, holding a large processional cross. He was concealed by the robes of a Confraternity and he picked his way carefully, gazing through two slits in the cowl which covered his head. Behind that sinister, mediaeval figure walked four or five elderly nuns, followed by a rickety hearse drawn by a bony horse, then came a priest and an altar boy with a thurible. In the background the warren of old Gallipoli lifted its white houses in the setting sun and the encircling sea was a heavenly blue.

The South Italian habit, which began first at Bari under Murat, of building a new town next to the old one, has changed the character of the country beyond the recognition of such travellers as Ramage (1828), and Edward Lear (1847), though it was already operating by the time Norman Douglas visited the South in the early years of this century. Since then the process has been accelerated by Government policy and grants. It seems to have become an accepted principle that every old town in the South must have a brand new companion. In nearly every case the new towns are not only ugly, but depressing examples of mediocrity; but they offer one great boon which the old cities never knew: they have at least one clean hotel with running water in the bedrooms.

If anyone wishes to experience the mediaeval conditions described by early travellers, he might do worse than begin in Gallipoli. The *Guida d'Italia del Touring Club Italiano* does not list one hotel in the whole of the old city, and only one in the new. There is scarcely a tree in the old town, which resembles a crowded island in the Venetian lagoon, but no Venetian lagoon was ever quite as blue as the sea that surrounds Gallipoli, neither is any Venetian island so white and African, nor has Venice anything like the massive Angevin fortress with its circular bastions in whose immense wall nestles a little cinema which, when darkness falls, is outlined by electric light.

The pride of Gallipoli is a Greek fountain almost eaten away by Time. It is the architectural type of fountain known as a nymphæum, and was popular in Hellenistic times. The sculptured figures of men and women illustrate some Greek myth, and I suspect that puritan hammers have assisted the years in an attempt which has not been entirely successful, to tone down certain details of an Olympian revel: but the beauty of Gallipoli, evident enough by day, transcends reality by moonlight. It resembles some enchanted, timeless city of silence, surrounded by a dark, murmuring sea. The Greeks must have seen it like this – *kalli-polis*, the beautiful city.

§ 7

On my way to Taranto I stopped at the little town of Copertino which, as readers of Norman Douglas's *Old Calabria* will remember, was the birthplace of Joseph, the flying saint. I stopped to watch some girls drawing water from the town fountain in waterpots of Greek shape; facing the fountain was a pleasant statue of St Joseph in his Franciscan habit, with outstretched arms, perhaps about to take off on one of his flights.

He was born in 1603. His father, a carpenter, died before his birth, leaving his mother without means, and the future saint was born in a stable. Quite early in life, it seems, Joseph was subject to levitation of a particularly baroque and effective kind. He could rise in the air and fly about either inside the church or in the open air. Most of us, particularly in childhood, remember dreams of being airborne in this way, a memory, the psychologists say, of arboreal adventures in a simian past: but Joseph could actually make such flights while awake, unless the people who testified that they had witnessed them were unreliable.

I found Copertino a curiously quiet and deserted little town and could not imagine why the Italian guide-book should call it *simpatica cittadina,* which was not my impression. I found the church of St Joseph, which was erected in 1754, about ninety years after the death of the saint and several years before he was canonized, while a few steps away I saw a humble little white-washed building, shabby and windowless, which bears an inscription over the open door, *Casa Paterna*. I went inside and had to wait for some time before I could see anything. The only light came from a few candle butts guttering on a rough piece of wood. There is a notice which says that in 1603 St Joseph was born there, and preserved in a glass case is a brown garment which I took to be his habit. It is unusual in Italy to see a saint's birthplace in its original condition. No doubt lack of money explains why it has not been piously transformed by precious marbles.

A priest in the church unlocked a desk in the sacristy and sold me a life of St Joseph, by P. Bonaventura M. Popolizio.

'No, the saint is not buried here', he replied to my question. 'He is buried in the cathedral at Osimo, near Loreto, where he died: but we have his heart. Look; it is here, beneath the altar. It was brought back in 1953.'

Norman Douglas's chief authority for the life and flights of St Joseph was the biography written in 1853 by Giuseppe Ignazio Montanari, a work which is quoted in the volume which I bought in the church, issued almost a century later. Neither author makes any attempt to slur over the fact that Joseph was what would be called nowadays retarded, or mentally defective, a condition which may be defined in more kindly terms as childlike. It was when the saint fell into an ecstatic trance induced by the liturgy, or by contemplation, that, uttering a sound which is described as a 'loud cry' or 'oh!', and sometimes as 'a sound like thunder', he would soar into the air and move about with a firm sense of direction, often to pay his devotions to some inaccessible image or portrait of the Madonna. One has the impression that his flights could be alarming and irritating. On many occasions he was sharply commanded to return to earth by his superiors, as if he were an over-exuberant pet bird.

Had these flights been confined to obscure churches in remote villages, it might have been said that his defiance of the law of gravity – his typically baroque buoyancy – had perhaps been exaggerated, but he flew in Rome, Naples, and other cities in front of cultivated and distinguished gatherings, including one pontiff, Urban VIII. The astonishment he caused has been well attested; at least one member of a distinguished audience is said to have fainted from fright as Joseph passed overhead.

Sometimes he took a friend with him on his flights. When a number of nuns were taking the veil, he was so carried away by the beauty of the ceremony and of the hymn *Veni, sponsa Christi* that, running to the Father Preacher and taking him by the hand, he flew up to the ceiling with him; upon another occasion he ran to the Confessor of the convent and, hand in hand, they rose from the ground, turning round and round in a *violento ballo*. The most remarkable of his passenger flights took place at Assisi when, having uttered his usual cry of 'Oh!', he seized a certain Chevalier Baldassare by the hair and drew him up into the air, to the intense admiration of the spectators. When they touched down again the Chevalier confessed that he had been cured of a severe nervous complaint.

In 1645 the Grand Admiral of Castile, who was the new Spanish ambassador to the Holy See, having heard of Joseph's saintliness, made a special journey to see him at Assisi, accompanied by his wife. He had a long conversation with the saint in his cell and remarked to his wife, 'I have just met another St Francis.' She begged the Father Guardian to ask the saint to step down into the church so that she might see him also, and a messenger was sent for him. The moment Joseph entered the church he fixed his eyes upon a statue of the Virgin high above the altar, and, uttering a piercing cry, took flight and, passing over the heads of those present, embraced the statue. The Admiral's wife fainted.

Contemporaries saw in Joseph a striking resemblance to St Francis. Like his great predecessor, he had the beguiling habit of referring to his body as 'Brother Ass', and of claiming relationship with the animal and vegetable creation: but there was no St Clare in his life until 1650, when he met Princess Maria, Infanta of Savoy, a deeply religious woman and a Franciscan tertiary. Their meeting is said to have been that of twin souls, indeed she went to live at Perugia to be near him. Among his other exalted friends were Prince Casimir, who became King of Poland, and kept up a correspondence with him for years; Prince Leopold of Tuscany;

and Frederick, Duke of Brunswick, who was converted after having witnessed one of the saint's flights. Towards the end of his life St Joseph's fame became so great that he had to be locked away to save him from the attentions of his admirers and the importunity of the curious. Though he had become infirm, he was able to take a short flight the day before he died. While upon his death bed he was heard to whisper, 'The little ass begins to climb the mountain; the little ass can go no farther, and is about to leave his skin behind.' He was sixty years of age. He was buried in the cathedral at Osimo and a hundred and four years later he was canonized.

## § 8

I passed through many Salentine towns, some so small that an Englishman would think of them as villages, but they are not: there is no village green, for, even though it may be minute and dusty, there is that germ of Latin urbanism, a piazza. The small farmer and the labourer leave the town in the morning to work in the vineyards and the olive groves, returning in the evening. It is easy to detect a Greek face in this part of Italy, though it may be a romantic delusion. The landscape is heavy with time, the Ionian Sea curls over in the little rocky bays with immemorial murmurs, and in the silence of the olive trees and the stir and movement of the towns it is possible to feel that the past is deceptively near.

On the way to Taranto I stopped in a small town to look at a church, and on my way back to the car I heard the sound of music. It was a quick kind of jig tune played on a fiddle, a guitar, a drum, and, I think, a tambourine. Looking round for the source of this sound, I saw a crowd standing in a side street. Glancing over the heads of the spectators, I saw a countrywoman dancing alone with a curiously entranced expression on her face, her eyes closed. She held a red cotton handkerchief in her hand which she waved as she undulated round the circle with more grace than I should have expected. I was surprised by the gravity of the crowd. There was not a smile. There was something strange about this. I wondered whether the dancer was mad, or perhaps – unusual as this would be – drunk. Glancing round at the set faces, I did not like to ask any questions, and, not wishing to intrude upon what was obviously a rather painful scene, I turned away. I shall always regret having done so.

Some days later, I recollected the dancer and happened to mention her to a friend in Taranto. 'Do you not realize what you have seen? The woman had been "taken" by a tarantula spider and she was dancing, and might dance for days until completely exhausted, to expel the poison. I have only seen this twice myself and I have lived in the Salentino all my life. It is a matter of luck. Sometimes you will come across the *tarantolati* in village streets, at cross-roads, but generally in the houses, and though most people imagine that the tarantella ceased to be danced for serious reasons long ago, it is still danced by hundreds of peasants in the region of Lecce who believe themselves to have been poisoned by the spider.'

'When you say the woman was "taken" by the tarantula, what do you mean?'

'Simply that she was bitten. We call it *pizzica* (a pinch), and people who believe themselves to have been bitten are the *Pizzicati*. Women are particularly exposed to tarantula bites because they work in the harvest fields after the corn has been cut, when these spiders are common.'

'But I have read that the tarantula is not poisonous, or that it is no more dangerous than a bee-sting.'

My friend lifted his shoulders.

'Perhaps,' he conceded. 'This has been going on for centuries. Who can say what is at the back of it?'

§ 9

Having seen a *tarantolata* in action, I returned to the town in the hope of finding another dancer, but I had no luck. I was told that the woman having danced at intervals all that night and the next day, and in the process having exhausted herself and the musicians, fell asleep to awaken in a normal state of mind. Her family treated the affair casually, as if she had merely recovered from a nasty cold.

They were polite and charming to me, thanking me for my solicitude.

I was so surprised to think that this malady, or delusion, which I had always associated with ancient magic or the mediaeval dance mania, should still exist, that I sought out several people who were familiar with this phenomenon, among them two doctors, and they kindly told me all they knew. The literature on Tarantism is considerable, and began in the sixteenth century; the symptoms are unvarying, as are the remedies; and the odd happenings today in the Salentine Peninsula are the same those described so fully in the seventeenth century by the Italian doctor, Epifanio Ferdinando.

There is considerable mental confusion among the *tarantolati*, some of whom attribute their maladies to the bite of a scorpion or some other venomous creature, though the chief causes of the disorder are the spiders which are to be found in the Italian stubble fields in summer. One is a hairy creature with a body about three-quarters of an inch long, quick in movement, called *Lycosa tarantula*, which despite its forbidding appearance is said to be harmless. It takes its name from the city of Taranto where it is said to have been most frequently found, though several acquaintances there told me that they had never seen one. The second is a smaller spider, slow in movement, *Latrodectus tredecim guttatus*, whose poison can inflict two days of pain, fear, vomiting and hallucination: but no doctor to whom I spoke believed that the poison could lie dormant for twelve months and cause a second attack on the anniversary of the first, as so many of those bitten by the *latrodectus* insist. One might think that such an ancient malady, with its unusual antidote of music and dance, might have been shrouded in some secrecy, but that is not so. Often the sufferers themselves will freely discuss their symptoms and every peasant in the Salentine Peninsula will tell you that the only cure for a bite is to dance until the poison has been sweated out, and should the symptoms recur, the only thing to do is to dance again. The afflicted are acutely sensitive to colour. They will not fully respond to the music until they have been given a ribbon or a handkerchief of the colour that appeals to them. A woman who was bitten described her feelings to Giuseppe Gigli: 'I was cutting corn on a farm,' she said. 'It was so hot that it was difficult to breathe and before noon we ceased work and lay down in the shadow of a wall. After eating a mouthful of bread, I closed my eyes and tried to sleep, when, suddenly, I felt a pain in my hand, but I saw nothing! I knew at once: I had been bitten by a tarantula. I began to cry. This is a terrible misfortune for poor people: it is a long disease which makes it impossible to work.

'I went home and the evil pursued me. I knew that the only thing was to dance. The pain in my hand never ceased. I felt a deep melancholy of the soul. Everything seemed to be black: people dressed in black, things painted black, black houses. The thought of death haunted me. If I died, I would leave a poor man with four children, the youngest only two years of age. I was compelled to stand and walk about my house, up and down. I found it difficult to breathe; it was as if an iron hand were squeezing my heart and my breasts.

'They began to make preparations for the dance. I felt better and put myself on the bed. But half an hour later I sprang up, unable to rest. They went to call the musicians. They spread out in front of me ten or twelve handkerchiefs of different colours. I began to dance, but who can say how much I suffered! The colours did not soothe my agony. This meant that none of those colours corresponded to the colour of my tarantula. Suddenly, I screamed! I had seen a young man dressed in black! I felt better. He represented the colour I needed because evidently my tarantula was black. I looked fixedly at this colour. After three days of continuous dancing, I was well.'

The long history of tarantism is full of stories which illustrate the importance of colour to the afflicted, and their despair until the colour that matches their tarantula is produced, though the idea that the spiders are of different colours is, of course, pure imagination. A seventeenth century writer mentions a Capuchin friar in Taranto who had been bitten, and whose feats of dancing roused such interest that Cardinal Caetano went to see him. The moment the friar caught sight of his visitor's red robes he leapt towards him with strange gestures and would have embraced him had he not been restrained. He refused to dance or to pay any attention to the music, which until then had delighted him, but collapsed into a mood of sadness that ended in a swoon. When the cardinal detached and offered the friar his red cape, the man instantly leapt to his feet and began dancing madly with it, pressing it to his face and head.

Just as it is necessary for the cure of the *tarantolati* to find which colour is important to them, so they have the same firm preferences for the music. There are about thirty tarantellas, all of them well known and some dating from the seventeenth century. One of the most ancient is called *panno rosso* (red cloth), and another, in slower time, is *panno verde* (green cloth). Three musical instruments are essential, a violin, a guitar, and a tambourine; sometimes a flute or an accordion may be added. The players require a large repertoire, since, I was told, it is sometimes necessary to play the opening bars of ten or twelve tunes before the right one is discovered.

There appears to have been a good deal of sympathetic hysteria in tarantism in past centuries when many who had never been bitten, either excited by the antics of the genuine *tarantolati*, or perhaps just for the fun of the thing, joined in. Bands of wandering musicians would roam the south of Italy to play at these dances, and so notorious was it that women were more frequently infected than men that these summer exorcisms were known as *il carnevaletto delle donne,* the Little Carnival of the Women.

One of the most quoted stories is that of a rich man near Taranto who did not believe in tarantism and put the whole thing down to female hysteria, threatening at the same time to punish any woman in his household who developed symptoms of the malady. As fate would have it, he himself was bitten by a tarantula and after suffering intense pain and fever leapt out of bed and began to dance. Music was brought to him and his leaps and capering became more frenzied than ever, until he rushed from his house into the street, shouting, 'Hanno ragion' le femmine! Hanno ragion' le femmine!' – 'The women are right! The women are right!' Another unwilling victim and sceptic was Baptist Quinzato, Bishop of Foligno, who, allowing himself to be bitten by a tarantula as a joke, became so ill and restless that he could obtain no relief except by dancing.

The most important book on tarantism to appear for years was published in 1961, *La terra del rimorso* – 'The Land of Remorse', by Ernesto de Martino, Professor of the History of Religions in Rome. The Professor had the idea of subjecting tarantism to modern treatment, recruiting for the purpose a learned team which included a psychiatrist, a psychologist, an anthropologist, and a musician. This he led to the Salentine Peninsula and into the province of Lecce. In June, 1959, the team identified thirty-five people who believed themselves to be suffering from the bite of the spider; of these, nineteen were closely observed in their own homes.

Though the investigators did not discover anything in the actual symptoms that has not been described by seventeenth century investigators, they observed the weird manifestation from a number of new and erudite angles. They discovered that one place exists in the Salentine Peninsula in which it is believed no case of tarantism could ever occur. This is the town of Galatina, one of the larger centres of the wine trade with a population of more than twenty thousand. Among its churches is one dedicated to St Peter and St Paul, by virtue of which, as a *feudo*, or fief, of the Apostle, according to general belief, the town is free from snakes, reptiles of all kinds, spiders and venomous creatures. The reason? Because St Paul suffered no harm from the viper that fastened itself on his hand in Malta (as described in Acts, 28–iii.); and the Apostle is believed, not only in the Salentine Peninsula but through the Deep South generally, to be the protector against venomous bites. The phrase used by the peasants to describe the town is *'feudo di Galatina'* – 'the fief of Galatina' – another use of the word which, as I had already found at Otranto, has survived in common speech from the days of the Hautevilles and the Norman kings of Sicily.

Professor de Martino and his colleagues noted that the annual recurrence of tarantism takes place in June when the *tarantolati* become restless and melancholy and begin to feel the poison exerting its dreaded power over them, until it is necessary for them to dance. The team studied one woman who having danced for days began to bark like a dog, and, having been in a kind of trance, suddenly became normal, nodded to the musicians to tell them to stop, and went to bed exhausted, and cured. Such people then visit the 'fief of Galatina' to give thanks to the Apostle on June 29th, the Feast Day of St Peter and St Paul. It is customary for them to go clothed in white. The professor was able to watch, while concealed in a gallery of the church, the astonishing and crazy proceedings from which the clergy had tactfully absented themselves. One man flung himself on his back as he entered the church and, uttering loud cries, proceeded in this position to impel himself towards the altar in a series of spasmodic movements. When he reached the altar he climbed up on it and touched the picture of St Paul that hangs over it. One woman lay full length on the altar while another stood over her. It must have been difficult to discover whether the *tarantolati* were expressing gratitude for their cure or whether they were offering the Apostle whatever venom still remained in their systems.

The book will surprise those who believe, as most do, that tarantism no longer exists, and that the tarantella is played only as a dance tune to amuse tourists. One of the book's most fascinating features are the first photographs to be taken of the dance cycle of the *tarantolati*. They strip the last shred of gaiety and liveliness from the word tarantella, and show poor haunted-looking peasant women, shoeless and wearing thick black woollen stockings, sadly revolving in squalid little whitewashed rooms while unsmiling musicians in open shirts and singlets perform their ancient exorcism. They show the dancers at the beginning of their dance and, days after, at the end, as they collapse into the arms of their friends. Most extraordinary are the pictures taken in the church of St Paul. This is obviously the end and dregs of tarantism. Yet there still clings to it a mystery. No intelligent person can really believe that these people have been poisoned by a spider, but it is probable that the image of the spider is used by them unconsciously to unlock and release ancient pagan impulses which, strange as it may seem, perhaps link these Apulian peasants with something as distant as the frenzy of the Corybantes and the even stranger Cabeiri.

This nervous disorder, blamed on a more or less harmless spider, may be also the last vestige of the mass manias which were common in the Middle Ages. There were many of them. Some aspects of the Crusades were of this kind, for example, the child pilgrimages during which thousands of boys and girls marched off to the Holy Land, all of them to die or to be sold into slavery. There were the Flagellants, both before and after the Black Death, who wandered all over Europe whipping themselves for the sins of the world, and attracting thousands of recruits from the places through which they passed. They became such a menace that towns would shut their gates at the sound of their approach, and some, like Milan, erected scaffolds as a warning to them.

The Flagellants were followed by the Dance Plague, which is more to the purpose, which swept over Europe, beginning in Germany, after the Black Death. To the sound of drums and bag-pipes, people left home in their thousands and danced about the country hand in hand, suffering from convulsive movements, skipping and leaping, until they fell down senseless. Many died, while others fell into rivers in their delirium or otherwise destroyed themselves. Like the last of the *tarantolati* in the south of Italy today, the dancers believed themselves to be suffering from a painful malady which could be cured only by the most violent exertion. In Liége and Utrecht and other northern cities, the dancers flocked out with flowers in their hair and their waists bound with lengths of cloth in the hope that when they fell senseless someone would thrust a stick into the cloth and bind it as tightly as possible, a constriction which it was believed brought relief until the next attack. In Metz the streets on one occasion were filled with more than a thousand jigging, jumping, shrieking dancers. Peasants left their fields, artisans their workshops, women their houses, to join in the revel, and soon the rich city became a scene of the utmost disorder. A curious fact about the mania was the belief that the afflicted might be cured in the chapels of St Vitus, near Zabern and Rotestein; and there is no doubt that such cures did occur. The great physician, Paracelsus, who studied the problem in the sixteenth century, said that some who had no

other course than to dance until they were dead were cured if they
went to St Vitus.

And who was St Vitus? He was a southern Italian, born in Sicily
and martyred under Diocletian in A.D. 303. There are many
southern Italian churches dedicated to him, though there is
nothing in his legend to connect him with dancing. The story
that as he bared his neck to the executioner he asked God to give
him power to cure all those afflicted with the dancing mania, and
that a heavenly voice replied, 'Vitus, thy prayer is accepted', was
a late invention of the Middle Ages. It was, of course, an attempt of
the Church to curb the appalling hysteria which actually de-
populated villages and created chaos in towns. As with the
*tarantolati*, music was so attractive to the dancers that magistrates,
in order to lead them away from their towns, sometimes kept
musicians in readiness to decoy them into the countryside.

Those who visited the chapel of St Vitus were, after a religious
ceremony, led to the altar where the dancing demons were exorcized, and though many were completely cured, some, it is said,
continued to twitch for the rest of their lives. The name St Vitus'
Dance has survived to this day, and is applied to a muscular disorder which has nothing to do with the contagious mass dancing
of the Middle Ages.

The English have always been interested in the tarantella, during
the seventeenth century in the genuine dance and during the
eighteenth century in the lively Neapolitan measure into which
menservants and chambermaids flung themselves at the slightest
prospect of a tip. One of the earliest English references to the
tarantula that I have found is that of George Sandys, who,
returning from the Near East in 1611, landed on the coast of
Calabria, where, he wrote, 'there are great store of Tarantulas.'

'They lurke in sinkes, and privies,' he continued, 'and abroad in
the slimy filth between furrowes; for which cause the country
people do reape in bootes. The sting is deadly, and the contrary
operations thereof most miraculous. For some so stung are still
oppressed with a leaden sleepe: others are vexed with continual

waking, some fling up and downe, and others are extreamely lazy. He swears, a second vomits, a third runnes mad. Some weepe continually, and some laugh continually, and that is the most usual. Insomuch that it is an ordinary saying to a man that is extraordinary merrie, that he has been stung by a Tarantula. Hereupon not a few have thought, that there are as many kindes of Tarantulas, as severall affections in the infected. ... The merry, the mad, and otherwise actively disposed are cured by musicke; at least it is the cause, in that it incites them to dance indefatigably: for by labour and sweate the poyson is expelled. And musicke also, by a certain high excellencie, hath been found by experience to stirre in the sad and drowsie so strange an alacritie that they have wearied the spectators with continued dancing. In the meane time the paine hath asswaged, the infection having been driven from the heart, and the mind released of her sufferance. If the musicke intermit, the maladie renewes, but againe continued, and it vanisheth.'

Sandys then mentions that character so familiar in the story of tarantism, a bishop clothed in red.

'A Bishop of this countrey,' he writes, 'passing in the high way and clothed in red: one bit by a Tarantula hooting thereat, fell a dancing about him. The offended Bishop commanded that he should be kept backe, and made haste away. But the people did instantly intreate him to have compassion of the poore distressed wretch, who would forthwith die, unless he stood still and suffered him to continue in that exercise. So shame and importunitie enforced him to stay, until, by dancing certaine houres together, the afflicted person became perfectly cured.' Sandys did not understand that the 'hooting' was not derision but admiration, and that the villagers begged the Bishop to remain in order that the red colour of his robes might soothe the *tarantolato*.

Pepys in his Diary for February 4th, 1661–1662, mentions a 'Mr Templer', a great traveller, who, speaking of the tarantula, said that during the harvest in Italy 'there are fidlers go up and down the fields everywhere, in expectation of being hired by those that are stung.' An English traveller who was fascinated by tarantism was the philosopher George Berkeley, Bishop of

Cloyne, who was in southern Italy in 1717–1718, and it is a pity that he did not see more since he would have been an ideal recorder. In Bari, however, he witnessed a rare manifestation when a dancer grasped a sword and made menacing gestures towards him with it. In days when swords were common the *tarantolati*, women as well as men, often danced with a sword and sometimes slashed themselves like priests of Cybele. Everywhere that Berkeley went he asked for spiders, but few were produced. He heard much nonsense about the tarantula, such as the story told to him by the Prior of the Theatrines at Barletta that one could be poisoned from eating fruit that had been bitten by the spider. This story shows how the tarantula was feared.

From the eighteenth century onwards travellers who rarely penetrated farther south than Naples knew the tarantella only as a quick country dance, which Ramage thought 'not unlike an old rather vulgar Scotch dance, called the Pillow, which has been banished since quadrilles became fashionable.' A notable performance was witnessed in London on the night of April 15th, 1801, the day the news of Nelson's victory at Copenhagen reached England. Wraxall says that at about ten o'clock that night he decided to call on Sir William Hamilton, who was then living at what was 23 Piccadilly, opposite the Green Park. He found a small company of friends to whom Emma Hamilton sang songs at the harpsichord. Then she decided to dance the tarantella.

'Sir William began it with her, and maintained the conflict, for such it might well be esteemed, during some minutes. When unable longer to continue it, the Duke de Noia succeeded to his place, but he, too, though nearly forty years younger than Sir William soon gave in from extenuation. Lady Hamilton then sent for her own maidservant, who being likewise presently exhausted, after a short time another female attendant, a Copt, perfectly black, whom Lord Nelson had presented her on his return from Egypt, relieved her companion.'

Lady Hamilton was then forty; Sir William was seventy-one.

# CHAPTER SIX

*The ancient port of Taranto – an Irish patron saint – the nerve-racking sirocco – superb oysters – the shellfish 'farms' – Plato's visit to Taranto – relics of Magna Graecia – the pottery town of Grottaglie – Rudolph Valentino's birthplace – the site of Metapontum – Matera and its cave houses – the Carlo Levi country and Eboli.*

## § 1

Among Taranto's claims to fame, according to Lenormant in *La Grande-Grèce*, was the importation into Europe for the first time of *cattus domesticus*, or the household puss. She is supposed to have come from Egypt or Crete. Should this be so, one treads upon holy ground and, gazing at the strand upon which philosophers, including Plato, poets, merchants and conquerors have landed, one wonders upon what particular spot first stepped ashore, no doubt with tail indignantly twitching, the creature which has graciously consented to share the fireside with us. To have assisted at the embarkation would be sufficient fame for a lifetime, to have helped to pour the first saucer of milk or perhaps cream, would have been almost too great a privilege. But we must not look too closely into this legend since it would be unkind to find a flaw in it, and so cheat the noble city of Taranto of such distinction. And how appropriate it is that S. Cataldo (better known as the Irishman, St. Cathal), should be the patron saint. (Incidentally, the accent is on the first syllable of Taranto.)

The city was noted in antiquity for its geographical position; it was remarkable also for its cultivation of shellfish, which remains its most spectacular activity. Though southern investments and developments have endowed Taranto with a giant steelworks and other industries, one recalls as typical only the fish market and men rowing ashore with festoons of blue-black mussels and buckets filled with oysters and clams.

For continuity of effort, this activity must be surely among the most ancient upon earth. Taranto – the Greek Taras – was founded seven hundred years before Christ, which is more than two thousand six hundred years ago: the world has changed, nations and cities have dawned, flourished and vanished, but the fishermen of Taras – of Tarentum – of Taranto – seem immortal, and they look, with their brick-brown faces, their Greek noses and crustacean eyebrows, much as they must always have done.

The origin of Taras was different from that of the other Greek cities of southern Italy. The Greeks founded colonies overseas, often at the bidding of the Delphic Oracle, for a number of reasons: because the population had outgrown the agricultural capacity of the parent city, because the colonists wished to trade overseas, and because they were adventurous; but, generally speaking, they left because a poor rocky country could not support all its people. The Tarentines, however, left home because they were disparaged as bastards, though the word used was more pleasant, *Parthenioi*. These young men had been born in Sparta during a nineteen-year-long war when the army was away from home. Resenting their status, they decided to leave Sparta and form a colony of their own where they would be politically independent and could make their own fortune. This they did. Taras became the most famous and the richest city of Magna Graecia, and at the height of her fame could place an army of thirty thousand infantry in the field, to say nothing of the famous Tarantine cavalry.

There it stood on that airless, hot evening, the westering sun full upon it, just as I had imagined it would be, a slender island covered with white houses, blocking the entrance to the blue lagoon beyond, where the still water lay for sixteen miles, reflecting the southern sky. Two bridges, one at each end, connected the island with the land on either side. The lagoon was shared by fishermen and warships, as if we were still living in the days of Magna Graecia and before anyone had heard of Rome.

Alas, I looked upon this in pain and melancholy, believing that I must have caught a chill. Irritated with myself for feeling ill at this high moment in my journey, I cruised miserably all over the new and rectangular Taranto unable to decide on an hotel. At last,

because the parking space was good, I chose one of those apart-
ment hotels which offer only bed and breakfast, though it was the
grandest example of its kind I had ever seen. It had been recently
opened and was typical of the changing face of southern Italy. I
stepped from the lift into dim, cool corridors sheeted with marble.
I thought, so sombre was my mood, that it was attractively
funereal. I walked to my room as if towards the tomb chamber of
the Great Pyramid. One entire wall was plate-glass which offered
a view below of a pleasant public garden where old men were
seated under trees while children chased each other on the gravel.
The room was mercifully air-conditioned. The bathroom was an
example of the Italian passion for *far figura*, the art of cutting a
dash or making a good show. Its origins lay in Hollywood and in
those films where actresses recline in foam baths. Chromium taps
protruded from black marble walls. Everything was magnificent,
except that the washbasin plug did not work: it was too modern.
The waste pipe was closed by a tap that moved something below
in the pipe and had probably been dislocated by a child of nature
who had never before seen such a sophisticated bathroom. Nor-
mally I would have been amused, but saddened by pain, I sharply
rebuked the management over one of two telephones; this
produced a young man in blue jeans with spanners protruding
from every pocket. Like all plumbers, he wore the distraught air
of one enslaved by a force beyond his control, and, after tapping
gently, he told me that nothing could be done. Before he went
away the chambermaid came in and listened to the discussion. She
was a sturdy peasant girl, if ever there was one, short, dark,
capable, and, so far as I could judge, without a single feature that
Praxiteles could have used. She took me as if I had been a child of
six into the bathroom and, speaking rapidly in Tarantese, not one
word of which I understood, demonstrated that it was the simplest
thing in the world to plug the outlet of the costly basin with a wet
sponge. I was grateful to her for having reduced this particular bit
of *far figura* to its proper proportions.

I then went to a chemist. In Italy the chemist, with Latin logic,
sells medicines. He does not sell cameras, watches, bath salts,
beauty preparations, cigarette lighters, pencils, lipsticks or razors.

This means that the average *farmacia* is still dignified by some memory, no matter how remote, of Aesculapius; indeed some have later associations and look as if they had only just removed the stuffed alligator. This shop was a good one, dark and smelling of spicy drugs. An elderly man of learned appearance detached himself from the shadows and to him I confided the severity of my indisposition.

"*Signore*," he said. "It is only the *sirocco*. When it is over you will recover immediately."

"But when will it be over?"

The apothecary lifted his shoulders and sighed.

"Who can say? One day, two days – no more."

He prescribed a lip salve, a gargle jet-black in colour that smelt as if it might have been compounded by one of the Medici, and a bottle of aspirin.

§ 2

I remember with pleasure the day when the *sirocco* departed. Walking in the public gardens in the morning, I was pleasantly aware that the world looked and felt as it used to do. An oppressive anxiety had been lifted from the human spirit and people were already laughing and smiling once again.

I was now able to enter the new National Museum with added zest, where even during the days of depression I had been greatly attracted by a number of women who had lived in Taras several centuries before Christ. I believe the museum owns the largest collection of Greek terracottas in the world: I was told that there are nearly fifty thousand of them, and more are often found when new blocks of flats and suburban roads are constructed. The resurrection of Greek Taras in the last eighty years is, in its way, as sensational as the discovery of Pompeii and Herculaneum. All the delightful objects in the museum have been found in the cemeteries of Taras, which were first revealed when Taranto was made a naval base and the new city was built. It is curious that no one appears to have suspected the existence of this buried treasure. When the English traveller Swinburne surveyed the scene at the end of the eighteenth century, he wrote, 'Never was a place more completely swept off the face of the earth.'

Of all the minor arts which have survived from the past, I think Tanagra figures are among the most endearing. They are about a foot high, or less, finely modelled in baked clay, and sometimes they bear faint traces of colour. They generally depict women with the folds of their draperies well defined, sometimes they wear little flat or cone-shaped hats, and occasionally there are two figures gossiping together, or they may be seated. These women hold a fan, a mirror or a ball. Now and again a dancer is to be seen standing upon one leg. Two girls dancing side by side were discovered at Taranto, evidently professional performers, so too, was the African dancing girl discovered there, and perhaps also the delightful dancer who has paused with uplifted leg to adjust her slipper. But the usual Tanagra figure is a woman admiring herself in a mirror, inspecting her hair style or drawing her *himation* about her, hat perched charmingly upon her head, ready to go out.

These little figures appeal because they are a true reflection of ordinary life twenty centuries ago. Such candid glimpses of human beings are infinitely more lifelike than the posed figures of Sèvres and Meissen porcelain. Many of us who have explored ancient sites and have roamed through museums have wondered from time to time what it would be like to encounter a man who had lived in a distant century and what points of contact one would discover with him. The Tanagra women suggest that they, at least, would have been entirely comprehensible; indeed some of them, as they draw their draperies about them, look as if they were standing on the steps of a theatre at night, waiting for a taxi.

Such an introduction to the metropolis of Magna Graecia could not be more pleasant, neither can I think of any morning better spent than passing from case to case admiring the objects, the vases the jewellery, the coins and the sculpture which the people of this city once handled and treasured. Some writers have compared the opulent enterprising cities of Magna Graecia with the United States; should this be a fair comparison, Taras must have been the New York of the fourth century B.C. 'The Greek cities in the west were prosperous, *nouveaux riches*; their temples were that little bit bigger than those at home; their art that little bit more ornate,' wrote John Boardman. 'Artists and philosophers could readily be tempted from Greece by commissions or lecture tours, and their work did not always suffer.'

In that bright and prosperous world the once despised *Parthenioi* soon became millionaire ship builders, cattle breeders, wool magnates, and made fortunes as mill owners, dyers, and potters. Their docks and warehouses were filled with the beautiful commerce of the time, and, to show how rich and important they were, the largest statue in the world, except the Colossus of Rhodes, a bronze Jupiter, shone above the acropolis. The wide roads, the temples, the market places, lay mile upon mile; the shores of the lagoon invited villas and swimming pools, orchards, gardens; and the bee-hives produced a superb honey that was compared with that of Hymettus.

The Greeks said that once the dog of Hercules, finding a shellfish on the seashore, crushed it in his mouth and remained for ever after with purple jaws. The shell was the murex, a mollusc which was the source of the purple dye so highly prized in ancient times. The dye works of Taras were famous and until a century ago a hill of murex shells was pointed out as one of the curiosities of Taranto, but with the building of the new city this unique pile has vanished. The dye of the murex is found in a small gland that secretes a fluid, at first colourless, which, when exposed to the air, changes to a reddish-purple. One of the sights of Taras which many a traveller must have watched in ancient times was that of the dye workers extracting the colour sacs and tossing the discarded shells to be dumped on the hill.

The wool of Taras was as fine and as highly prized as the purple into which it was dipped. It was said that the sheep wore overcoats of skin to protect their precious fleeces. Another fabric made in Taras was a gossamer tissue, in great favour with dancing-girls, which was formed by spinning the silky filaments by which a shell-fish still called *lana pesce* (wool fish) attaches itself to the rocks. This was, as may be imagined, a costly material and could be bought in its natural brown colour or dyed purple. It is, of course,

no longer made, but someone told me that he remembers when
ties and gloves were sometimes made of it as a curiosity, and he
thought he had seen a tie recently in a shop; but though I searched
the haberdashers of Taranto, and those shops in which the young
men go for purposes of *far figura*, I could not find one.

The museum contains rooms full of objects which existed in the
great period of the history of Taras, about 409 B.C., when the city
was at the height of her fame and fortune. Her affairs were then
conducted by a man who has come down over the centuries
without a single blemish, which is rare. Not only was he apparently a perfect husband and father, he was also the Admirable
Crichton of Magna Graecia, philosopher, mathematician, astrono-
mer, inventor, statesman, and victorious general. Were he ever
guilty of a mistake, it has not been remembered; if he ever
sinned, the fault has been lost in his virtues. We are told that
he devoted as much attention to the comfort, happiness and
education of his slaves as to those of his own family. Among
his inventions was a wooden dove that flew about a room and
was one of the wonders of antiquity. It is to the credit of
Taras that she continued to elect Archytas to power year after
year.

One of his friends was Plato, who was in Taras more than once
on his way to and from Sicily, when summoned there, rather as if
he were a psychiatrist, to see if the character of Dionysius II
would respond to treatment. Like most psychiatrists, and even
ordinary well-meaning friends, the philosopher roused the enmity
of the patient; it was said that Plato was rescued from danger only
by the intervention of the all powerful Archytas. Among the few
surviving memories of Plato in Sicily is a massive snub which he
administered to the tyrant. 'No doubt, Plato,' Dionysius is reported by Plutarch to have said, 'when you are at home among the
philosophers, your companions, you will complain of me, and
reckon up a great many of my faults.' Plato replied with a smile,
'The Academy will never, I trust, be at such a loss for subjects to
discuss as to seek one in you.' Rather a cruel snub, since there is
something appealing about the tyrant's admission of his short-
comings, a proof of humility which a later age might have found

promising. It is, however, pleasant to think of Plato upon the crowded quays of Taras greeted by his friend Archytas. One likes to think of the two great men flying the wooden dove. But there is no record of this, indeed the only mention of Taras in the whole of Plato's works is the remark of a character in one of the Dialogues who says that he arrived there on a public holiday and found the whole city drunk.

How Taras became Tarentum is interesting. This happened in 272 B.C., though for a long time the growth of Rome had been resented by the rich Greek city of the South. Taras declared what is known today as a 'cold war' on Rome: behind the diplomatic scene she sided with the enemies of Rome, she played the part of Big Brother, promising financial and military aid (which was not always forthcoming) to those in conflict with Rome; but she herself was careful to remain uncommitted. One day in the year 302 B.C. the theatre of Taras, which offered a fine view of the sea, was filled with an audience whose applause changed to cries of rage and dismay as ten Roman warships were seen in the gulf approaching the walls of the city. Such a breach of a treaty with Rome, which forbade the passage of Roman warships beyond the Lacinian promontory a long way south, was immediately avenged as crews, hastily manning the Greek triremes, gave battle to the invaders. The audience, a moment before watching perhaps one of the burlesque farces which the Greeks loved, now saw a real drama as their ships sank four of the Roman galleys, drowning the commander and capturing a Roman ship, which was towed triumphantly into the harbour. This was followed by a nine year war with Rome, which ended with the subjection of Taras; and from the year 272 B.C. the name of the city was Tarentum. The city retained its Greek laws and customs, but a Roman garrison was stationed in the citadel.

There was always a powerful anti-Roman party in Tarentum, and it took action during the Second Punic War. Livy's account of the betrayal of the city to the Carthaginians, and later its betrayal, but by an entirely different type of collusion, to the Romans, is fascinating. Also, I have never read anything which gives a better idea of the size and strength of Tarentum.

Hannibal, the foxiest of generals, when camped three days march from Tarentum, was only too willing to receive the leaders of the anti-Roman party, which he did secretly and at night. With their help he set one of his typical traps. The leader of the Greeks was a young man named Philomenus, a keen hunter. He was told to go out hunting each night until his departure and return would pass unnoticed. This he did so often, passing out after dark with his hounds and returning before morning with game (sometimes with Carthaginian cattle which Hannibal had provided for him), and always with a present for the guard. Soon the Roman sentries automatically opened the gate at the sound of his whistle.

The victim having been lulled, the moment came to spring the trap. One night with Philomenus as guide, whose load of game included a gigantic wild boar, Hannibal approached the sleeping city while his army, lightly-armed, also moved up in silence. At the sound of the whistle the Romans opened the postern as usual, and while the guards were admiring the wild boar they were cut down. Like a commando operation, the plan depended on split timing. Other conspirators at the same moment slew the guards at the east gate, and soon the Carthaginian army was making silently and speedily for the forum. The alarm was raised too late. The Roman garrison retreated to the citadel which is now the old city of Taranto, a place of such strength that Hannibal was never able to dislodge them. The citadel, also commanded the exit from the lagoon in which the Greek fleet was bottled up. This did not worry Hannibal. 'Many problems naturally difficult are solved by a little brainwork,' Livy reports him as saying. 'Look: your town is situated on open ground; you have broad and level streets running in all directions. I can quite easily have your ships transported on wagons by the road which runs from the harbour through the centre of the town and down to the sea.' To make the operation easier, the main street was repaved and in a few days time, we are told, the warships, drawn on rollers and carts, were carried from the lagoon and launched in the sea.

Three years later the Roman commander, Fabius, recaptured Tarentum by craft. It was the old trick of finding the weak link in a chain which was as well known thousands of years ago as it is in these days of defecting scientists. It happened that the captain of an enemy detachment had fallen in love with the sister of a Roman soldier. She wrote to her brother in the citadel describing her admirer as a man of wealth and position. The soldier thought, as Livy puts it, that 'through his sister's influence the lovesick captain might be induced to do pretty well anything they wanted.' Placing the matter before his commander, who thought the plan worth trying, the Roman received instructions to enter Tarentum in the guise of a deserter, and to make friends with the captain through his sister. The details of the plot are not known, but through the defection of the unfortunate captain the gates were opened one night and the Romans poured in. The city was pillaged, the statue of Hercules was sent to Rome, and thirty thousand Tarentines were sold into slavery.

Shorn of its power and grandeur, Tarentum seems to have enjoyed a happy old age and to have shared in the Augustan peace. It was still Greek and elegant, not yet abandoned to the barbarian tribes and the mosquito; still beautiful to look at and famous for its scented honey and its sheep, which, as Horace noted, wore overcoats to preserve the fineness of their wool. The poet selected Tarentum as the place, with its exquisite springtime and its mild winters, to which he would be happy to retire were his beloved Tibur – now Tivoli – to be denied to him.

As I have said, it is a wonderful experience to explore the museum where so many traces of Tarentum's past are to be seen. Some of the objects suggest how strange and alien certain aspects of life must have been, while others, particularly a love for animals, seem a bond which links us with those distant people. What affectionate observation went to the modelling and drawing of frisking dolphins, of long-necked fauns, of highly bred horses, of supercilious cranes and smug, contented ducks. Only a people devoted to animals could have modelled with such humour the little vase in the shape of a hedgehog and the jug in the form of a donkey with panniers. But no cats: in view of the legend, how strange!

§ 3

The old city of Taranto is on a thin spit of land washed by the sea upon one side and by a salt water lagoon on the other. There are only three parallel main streets intersected by a warren of lanes and alleys so that anyone, unless he gets lost, can cross at any point from the lagoon to the open sea in a few minutes. The place is a confusion of yellowish old buildings which in certain lights, and from a distance, can look as romantic as one's idea of Camelot.

Such is the site of the once splendid acropolis of Taras, not a commanding rock, but a lido not much above sea level. That must have been why the Tarentines erected the colossal statue of Jupiter whose crown would have heliographed to steersmen when miles away that their ships were approaching the famous city. One of the best places to stand and watch everyday life in Taranto is near the swing bridge connecting the new town with the old on the east, spanning a channel that was not cut until the fifteenth century. The machinery for the bridge is concealed in one of the circular towers of the Angevin castle which was built at the same time. This channel is used by the warships of the Italian Navy, which pass into the lagoon, usually in the evening or after dark, and steam to the dockyard beyond, where the war galleys of Taras once anchored. The scene was familiar in the First World War to British troops on their way to eastern theatres; in the last war the British Navy, having bombed Taranto and the Italian fleet, sailed into the lagoon in 1943 and landed troops there. Winston Churchill noted in *The Second World War*, 'I have in my home the Union Jack, the gift of General Alexander, that was hoisted at Taranto, and was the first Allied flag to be flown in Europe since our expulsion from France.'

Some of my happiest moments were those spent wandering about the Città Vecchia watching the fishermen and wondering what jokes they were making in their special brand of the Tarentine dialect. Some listeners have mistaken this for Greek, but it is not, though I suspect that many a Greek word may be embedded in it. The fishing quarter does not face the sea, but the lagoon. The crowded quaysides, combined with the busy coming and going of boats, lends to the line of old houses in the background, their balconies draped with carpets or bedding, the air of a shabby Venice. It is curious that fishermen should turn their backs to the sea, but then the fishermen of Taranto have always been on terms with Poseidon, who seems to have reversed some of his laws in their favour. Unlike other fishermen, they do not disappear for days to scour the ocean: they sleep in their beds most nights and catch the rich harvest which the tides sweep into the lagoon every day, at the same time cultivating the oyster beds in the lagoon and the curious mussel nurseries, which are marked out by poles from which depend thick blue-black ropes of the shell-fish. In fact their activities resemble farming more than fishing.

When in Bari I thought that never again should I see or eat so many shell-fish, but I now realised that Bari was merely a side-show. The true metropolis of ichthyophagy is Taranto, so much so in fact that I began to fancy facial resemblances to crustacea in those about me, while a flabby handshake suggested a dead octopus and a lack-lustre eye was only too easily identifiable. The fish market of Taranto is a museum of the southern sea: I was told that there are nearly a hundred different varieties of fish and shellfish to be seen there, and I think I must have seen them all.

The oysters of Taranto, famous for centuries, were preferred by many Roman epicures to all others, though when Britain was invaded the Colchesters, which were rushed to the kitchens of Rome packed in snow, ran them closely in popularity. I thought the Taranto oysters equal in every way to the large Colchesters of years ago when it was possible to afford to buy oysters. I ate a dozen in the fish market at Taranto at the back of a fish stall. They were picked one by one from a bucket by a deck hand, opened and offered to me on the shell. After some difficulty, a lemon was found. My friends told me that the price, ten shillings a dozen, was extortionate, but then the fishermen could see I was a foreign millionaire! This, I think, was a little unjust. I did not find the fish merchants at all extortionate; on the contrary when I stopped at shops or stalls in the new city to ask the name of an unfamiliar shell-fish, I was nearly always invited to step inside and sample one or two. If I praised them, the smiles, the compliments, the invitation to try just one or two more followed me down the street. The learned say that no trace of Greek blood survives here, but I felt that Taranto was largely inhabited by characters from Aristophanes. It must be something in the genius of the place.

The cathedral of the Irishman S. Cataldo lies in the most crowded part of the old city. Having been described by Norman Douglas as 'a jovial nightmare in stone,' I was prepared for something really exotic in the baroque, but since Douglas wrote, the plaster has been removed and the church is now revealed as a solemn eleventh century basilica with a nave of classical marble columns with Byzantine capitals and all the features which one associates with an Apulian cathedral of Norman date.

I knew nothing of S. Cataldo and the verger said only that the saint was a great worker of miracles who came to Taranto in the seventh century from a place called Rachau in Ireland. He did not tell me, as I was to find out later, that St. Cataldus, or St. Cathay, landed at Taranto on his return from the Holy Land, and, finding the city steeped in the most appalling wickedness, decided that it was his duty to stay there. It is said that he had a brother, S. Donatus, probably a Latin version of Donagh, who became the patron saint of Lecce and, as I have said, surveys that town from the summit of a column.

I watched with pleasure a class of tiny girls which was being conducted in a side chapel by a little elderly nun who was teaching them to chant the multiplication tables. The sun slanted in from an oval window that might have come from Durham or Ely, and the rounded arch beneath which they sat at their desks rose to a painted ceiling. The quiet scene, so far removed from the shouting of the quayside and the dusty games of the streets outside, was symbolic of the Church's function through history. I thought there seemed a tendency to trade on the Church's compassion as many of the pupils held up their hands and received permission, with a kindly gleam of spectacles, to leave the room.

The saint's tomb is visible through a grid in a dark *confessio*, approached by a double flight of steps. I descended and gazed through iron bars into the crypt, where impenetrable shadows concealed a sarcophagus which is said to contain Irish bones.

I walked down to the fish market after dark to one of the little restaurants there. The front door opened onto the quays. I sat at a table a few yards from the fishing boats, which moved just sufficiently to prove that they were not on dry land. The moon, in its second quarter, shed a green wash of light over the vast stillness of the lagoon. Far off to the right a warship was blinking a message by lamp. The *zuppa di pesce* was the best I had tasted in Italy. It had a great number of the ninety odd varieties in it. I was recommended to follow this with *triglie*, a red mullet cooked in a special way. I ordered this, though I have never cared much for this particular fish or been able to understand why it appealed so much to the Romans, who often paraded fine specimens of it at dinner parties before they were cooked. My fish came wrapped in the tinfoil in which it had been baked. It was fresher than the usual red mullet and it tasted of the sea; but I still thought it a dull fish.

I walked back through the old city, enjoying vistas through open windows of crowded hearty life, rather Hogarthian but without the gin; radios sounded from balconies and from dark alleys, and I looked into a café where men were seated in the dark, silent as if in church, watching a football match on television. When I climbed the slight rise to the swing bridge, I found that half of it had swung over to the new city and the other half to the old. The channel leading into the dockyard was open. I waited there with a crowd of motorists and men on scooters while the moon poured down upon a scene operatic in its extravagance. The Angevin castle lay in a green light, its circular bastions touched by a lazy sea; there were green and red lights, then suddenly, one after the other, huge grey shapes filled the channel as three destroyers came in from the sea, and, with no more noise than a swish of water, vanished towards the lagoon. The two portions of the bridge then returned into position, and a petty officer with a number of naval ratings ran forward and made everything fast. The cars started up and we surged across into new Taranto.

§ 4

Though there is no reason why romantic young men should deny themselves the squalid experiences described by travellers to the South, even such recent ones as Norman Douglas, it is not really necessary to sleep in flea and bug-ridden inns. Unless a motorist punctures the spare tyre as well, it has been my experience that it is always possible to reach a tolerable hotel by nightfall.

Becoming attached to my room with its studio window and its Hollywood bathroom, I made a number of forays into the surrounding country, returning to the comfort of Taranto at night. One of these outings was to Grottaglie, about fourteen miles away, a small town that lies in a hilly landscape riddled with caves. They say that groups of cave dwellers came together long ago and, deserting their grottoes, formed Grottaglie. It is a pottery town. Delightful replicas of amphorae, large and small, which I had noticed in use at public fountains, as well as dozens of old Greek shapes to be found in any hardware shop or kitchen, also many decorative, and some ghastly, painted vases, come from the workshops and kilns of Grottaglie. It may be that this industry is a continuation of the famous potteries of Taras, whose products were exported to many parts of Italy. The clay pot must have been used in the way a tin is used in modern civilisation. Hundreds of products were sold in pots: wine, grain, honey, olives, oil, salted fish and suchlike, were transported and sold in amphorae. The potters I met in Grottaglie believed that they were indeed the direct descendants of the ancient potters, though there is nothing to support their belief. They use a fine local clay, and it seemed to me that their most popular shapes were similar to those manufactured centuries ago. I thought the town a good reflection of what the potters' quarter – the *cerameicus* – must have looked like in any of the cities of Magna Graecia. There were a number of masters, each with his own *officina*, or workshop, his own staff and apprentices, his own trade secrets and methods. In these disruptive days it seemed to me admirable to see so many boys and young men happy to follow in their fathers' footsteps.

Everywhere I looked I saw thousands of pots standing in rows upon the flat house-tops, in yards, upon the floors of sheds, and even in caves. There would be a regiment of amphorae, then one of jugs or plates, all lined up in the sunlight, each one with its own shadow. To climb up to one of the higher workshops, as I did, and to look down on Grottaglie, was to wonder how room could be found for one more jar, yet all the time men in gym shoes, two by two, like stretcher-bearers, walked catlike between the rows with new recruits. I took away with me the memory of a sight that can never become less magical: a potter's hands, grey with slime, coaxing a shape as if conjuring it from the air; and I also remember a young lad seated in a dark shed, paint brush in hand, adding a Greek figure to a vase.

I went into the hills one day about twenty miles north-east of Taranto into a tortured countryside honeycombed with caves; in some there are dark abandoned chapels, in others faded frescoes from Byzantine days. A shepherd to whom I spoke, either misunderstanding me or not accustomed to strangers, turned and without a word vanished with his sheep among the rocks. A girl tying vines told me that in the old days Greek hermits used to live in the grottoes. It was a weird, haunted landscape.

As I mounted the hill towards Castellaneta, I paused in surprise before an unexpected sight on the side of the road. It was the figure, the size of life, of a Bedouin sheik in his robes, executed in coloured porcelain, the prevailing colour being a glossy blue. Steps led to the monument, upon which I read, 'To Rudolph Valentino.' So here, in the heart of the pottery district, the first great film lover has been commemorated in an unusual medium by the people of his native town. He was born there in the year 1895 and went as a dancer to the United States in 1913, when he was eighteen.

I drove into the town which stands upon a hill with an appalling gorge on one side and on the other a splendid view over the coastal plain and the sea, in the direction of Metapontum. The place seemed singularly quiet. No one was about. Even the café was empty. It was called the 'Bar Rudi', and I noticed that the barber's shop was called '*Basette* (whiskers) *di Valentino*.' So he was not forgotten.

In the *farmacia* I eventually found a few elders and members of the intelligentsia who, when they were satisfied that my motives were merely those of curiosity, offered to show me the house in which Valentino was born; it was almost opposite the statue and is now occupied by a dentist. Valentino's father had been the veterinary surgeon for the district. No, I was told, so far as they knew there were no longer any members of the family in the neighbourhood. One old man recollected that he had been at school with Rudolph, but he had nothing to remember. Someone recalled that the great lover had arrived in a large motor car at the height of his fame but had not stayed long, and had gone on to have lunch in Taranto; and that, so far as they knew, was his only contact with his native town after he had become famous. But I knew they were proud of him not as an actor, but simply because of the immense impression he had made upon women.

I was glad to have seen Castellaneta, and went away recollecting that one of the penalties of being in love with a girl in the nineteen-twenties was the ordeal of having to see Rudolph Valentino. I have shadowy recollections of a gaunt, side-whiskered figure mouthing passion while the piano increased its tempo and a languishing form fell sobbing into his arms. Oddly enough, it was rather embarrassing in those days. For the first time the English virgin came face to face in public with the devastating Latin lover; and Valentino's fame appears to have been thrust upon him. He became a film actor by force of circumstance, for his career as a dancer was interrupted in San Francisco when the musical comedy company in which he was travelling was stranded there. He applied to a studio for a job and was given a humble one. The problem of a stage name did not worry him: he had an unrivalled selection. He was Rudolph Alfonso Raphael Peter Philip William de Valentino d'Antonguolla. One must give him credit for choosing the winning number. His name was made by his acting in *The Four Horsemen of the Apocalypse*, and his fame became world-wide with a film which most people called 'The Sheek', though some, who had perhaps served with Allenby in Palestine, called 'The Shake'. Nothing could now stop him; the women of the world went mad about him.

One of the first film press agents, a lively cynic called Harry Reichenback, persuaded Valentino, during a lull in his triumphs, to grow a beard. Immediately, as Reichenback had foreseen, there was a shrill international demand for its disappearance and the beard was ceremonially sacrificed by a representative of the Master Barbers of America; but the famous *bisette* remained. Reichenback's many stunts – a word now taken over by the film industry from the airmen of the First World War – became notorious – he referred to them pleasantly as 'phantom fame'.

It is amusing to reflect that a critic as eminent as Elinor Glyn thought that the great lover's technique was rather tame. In his biography of his grandmother, Anthony Glyn says that when Elinor Glyn went to Hollywood in the nineteen-twenties, she thought Valentino's love-making amateurish. 'Do you know,' she would murmur in later years, 'he had never even thought of kissing the palm, rather than the back, of a woman's hand until I made him do it.' The truth is that Valentino was a success with women only on the screen. 'No man had greater attraction for women than Valentino', wrote Charles Chaplin. 'No man was more deceived by them.'

Valentino's death in 1926 from septic endocarditis at the age of thirty-five, and the hysteria it touched off all over the world, are probably more clearly remembered now than his life. The police had to disperse crowds outside the hospital; during the lying-in-state hundreds of women fainted, plate-glass windows were smashed, a depressed actress committed suicide, saying that Valentino's death was 'the last straw'; and a doctor attributed his death to an overdose of ultra-violet rays due to studio lighting, plus the Californian sun, a verdict which alarmed Hollywood. Though Valentino had been married twice, the actress Pola Negri, though not one of the wives, was prostrated with grief. She was present at the funeral, attended by a doctor and a nurse, and later that night, when Elinor Glyn went to see her, she was wearing 'the blackest of widow's weeds'. Even today, more than forty years after, women in black, their faces covered with mourning veils, make a pilgrimage on August 23 to the grave of the great lover.

I did not ask the people at Castellaneta whether any of them had ever paid homage to the glossy effigy of their idol.

§ 5

There is often nothing to see at all except an expanse of scrub or sandhills, with blue mountains in the distance, and at one's feet a torrent bed full of stones winding its way across the desolation to the sea. Yet such places bear high-sounding names which live only in a few stray references from Greek and Roman writers. This is Magna Graecia; this is a country for scholars. Only those who remember the part played in the history of mankind by cities now ruined or vanished are able to imagine the lonely landscape as it once was, covered with streets, houses, palaces, temples and market places, and to visualize the fleets and navies of the ancient world busy in docks and harbours.

Thinking of the fame of Metapontum, I travelled the twenty miles or so from Taranto along the western curve of the gulf and came to a lonely region in which I was soon lost. Newly made roads led to the sea and ended in tiny lidos, consisting of one hotel with a restaurant, a few holiday bungalows and a beach. These places have grown up with the motor car and cater for week-end visitors from the nearest towns. Castellaneta has two bathing-places, twelve miles away, one called St. Castellaneta Marina and the other Marina di Castellaneta. How astonished Ramage would have been (and how delighted Norman Douglas) to have come across such places on a Saturday afternoon or Sunday when Nausicaa and her maidens may be seen beneath beach umbrellas almost in a state of nudity 'after bathing and rubbing themselves with olive oil' in true Homeric style.

I came to the dry bed of a river in which even the merest trickle had ceased, where I stopped a man with a mule. He told me that the name of the river was Bradano, and I knew then that I was not

lost since Metapontum had stood near a river called Bradanus. I
came to a railway station and read upon its indication board the
word 'Metaponto', a strange, thought-provoking sign. The wheat
millionaires and the barley kings had vanished, the shipping
magnates, whose galleys had exported the golden harvests of
Metapontum, were no more, but the name of the city lived on in
that somnolent little railway station. I asked a man who was load-
ing sacks into a truck where the ruins of Metapontum were. He
pointed inland and said that if I went on for a few kilometres I
would come to the *Tavole Paladine* – the Table of the Knights –
which I knew had been for centuries the local name for the ruins of
the Doric temple. Remembering King Arthur on the pavement of
Otranto cathedral, I asked if the Table were the Round Table of
King Arthur's paladins, but the man shook his head and shrugged.
In a few minutes I came to the plain which had made the fortune
of Metapontum centuries before Christ. Here had once waved the
wide cornlands whose memory still exists upon the reverse side of
Metapontum's beautiful gold coinage, which shows an ear of
wheat.

With pleasure I came to what at first I thought was a small
restaurant set back among flowerbeds, then, realizing that no such
place would be likely to exist in this deserted spot, I was equally
delighted to see that it was a museum. The curator, who welcomed
me with a warmth which suggested that I was the only visitor he
had greeted for some time, told me that the museum had been
open only since 1961. There is little to see in it, though every scrap
of pottery or corroded bronze is lovingly displayed as if it were
unique. The great Doric temple is a hundred yards away, standing
upon a carpet of daisies and poppies, the only upstanding relic of
Metapontum, a Greek Stonehenge visible for miles. There are
fifteen columns, badly eroded by time and, as far as I could see,
there was not a sign of life on this once crowded plain. One of the
guardians strolled across from the museum to keep me company.
I remarked that the *Tavole Paladine* bore little resemblance to a
table, and he agreed: and it may be that the table is invisible, since
he told me that the peasants claim that each column was once the
seat of a Saracen emir. 'In that case,' I said, 'the paladins must have

been Saracens and not Christian knights.' He inhaled deeply and lifted and dropped his arms in the national gesture which nearly always accompanies the words '*Chi lo sa*'. Who knows indeed!

'And what is the name of this temple?' I asked.

'We call it the Temple of Pythagoras,' he replied.

It was useless to ask why they should do so, or how old the name is, yet how tempting it is to think that the name may have come down from distant centuries, for when Pythagoras died some ancient writers say that the people of Metapontum built a temple to Hera upon the site of his house and redesigned the approaches to it, calling it the Academy. Two and a half centuries after Metapontum had been deserted, it was visited by Roman tourists, among them Cicero, who said that he refused to go to his lodgings until he had seen the house where Pythagoras had lived and had breathed his last. Surely this suggests that the house of Pythagoras, or a building that was pointed out to tourists as the house, had been preserved in the temple of Hera, or else that tradition is at fault and the temple was never built on the site of the house. Pythagoras died in 497 B.C. and Cicero was in Metapontum before 43 B.C. A house which was then four and a half centuries old could scarcely have existed intact through all the perils of Metapontum's later history unless it had been protected by the temple walls; in which case it must have been in a tolerable state of preservation.

The only other relic of Metapontum is a temple of Apollo which, said the guardian, lay about two miles away. What a city it must have been! Following his directions, I drove along dusty roads with acres of tobacco plantations on either side. I saw some wheat here and there which reminded me pleasantly of the vanished city and of the tides of life which had ceased to flow there two hundred years before Christ. Roman tourists who visited Metapontum were told several fanciful legends about its origin, and one was that the founder was Epeios, the hero who had made the Trojan Horse. In proof of this, the visitors were taken to a temple and shown the hammers, the axes and other carpenter's tools used by Epeios. Another tourist attraction was mentioned by Herodotus, who lived in later life, and died in 432 B.C., about fifty miles away at Thurii. This was a statue of that mysterious magician

Aristeos, who was said to have risen from the dead and to have been able to reinhabit his body at will and to appear whenever he chose to do so. Following one of his disconcerting appearances at Metapontum, his statue was erected in a market-place, surrounded by bay trees, which may have been made of bronze.

Wealth came to Metapontum with its grain exports, and fame with the philosopher Pythagoras, who sought refuge there during a political revolution in his own city of Croton. Even if he wrote anything, not a word has survived, though his teaching is well known. He taught serenity and self-discipline; he was a vegetarian, though for some unknown reason he forbade his followers to eat beans; he believed in the therapeutic value of music; he taught that vice is a sickness of the soul and that virtue is rewarded by translation into some higher form of being after death. Though his teaching was not intended to be political, he believed that human affairs should be conducted by a disciplined, élite aristocracy. To be a Pythagorean was rather like membership of an exclusive club, or perhaps it might be compared to mediaeval knighthood or even to Freemasonry. There was an initiation ceremony and there were signs whereby the initiated could identify each other. He believed also in the transmigration of souls and that reincarnation was a process of purification. Shakespeare twice mentioned this doctrine. 'What is the opinion of Pythagoras concerning wild fowl?' asks the Fool in *Twelfth Night*. 'That the soul of our grandam might haply inhabit a bird,' replied Malvolio. Evidently Shakespeare found the Pythagorean theories attractive, since Gratiano says in *The Merchant of Venice*:

> *Thou almost makest me waver in my faith*
> *To hold opinion with Pythagoras,*
> *That souls of animals infuse themselves*
> *Into the trunks of men.*

Like many other Greek cities in the South of Italy, Metapontum was ruined by the Second Punic War. Either from fear or hatred of Rome, the city preferred Hannibal, and after the recapture of Tarentum by the Romans in 207 B.C., Hannibal made it his head-quarters and introduced a Carthaginian garrison. One day the sentries picked up an object which had been flung down outside the walls. It was the severed head of Hannibal's brother, Hasdrubal, which had been preserved in wax or oil by the Romans and transported from the west coast of Calabria. That was how the news reached Hannibal that the Carthaginian army, commanded by his brother, had been defeated; and from that moment his luck began to turn.

He decided to leave Metapontum. It was only two years since Tarentum had been retaken by the Romans and its population sold into slavery or massacred. To save the Metapontines from the same fate, Hannibal removed the entire population of the city and they became what we now call 'displaced persons'. What happened to them, and there must have been hundreds of thousands, is unknown. But from that moment in 207 B.C. the city of Metapontum, with its golden prairies and its fleet of grain transports, disappeared from history.

Cicero, who was among the tourists who visited the site in later times, described Metapontum as if it were still a town, so that a few people must have returned to live there. But it was a dying town, and no doubt malaria delivered the final blow. In another century and a half Pausanias said it was a ruin. 'I do not know what was the occasion of the destruction of Metapontum,' he wrote, 'but in my time nothing was left of it save the theatre and the circuit wall.'

I went on between the tobacco fields looking for the temple of Apollo, but there was not a single signpost to help the traveller. I was soon hopelessly lost. I could see no one to ask until I came across a man who was spraying some vines with sulphur. He sent me off in an entirely different direction, but still I could see nothing resembling a temple. In the end I returned to the museum, where the curator courteously offered to accompany me.

We set off along side roads across the plain and, leaving the car on the edge of a field, walked to a mass of fallen masonry. Hugh blocks of grey stone lay piled in confusion in pools of stagnant water. The moment we appeared there were a thousand simultaneous plops as elegant little green frogs dived for safety. Here was the site of the temple of Apollo. This, said the curator, was once the centre of Metapontum. Waving his arm towards a field of tobacco, he said that the agora – the market-place – stood there and round about were temples and public buildings. A little more than a century ago, he said, the temple had been excavated by the Duc de Luynes, whose discoveries may be seen in the Bibliothèque Nationale in Paris. About twenty superb terracotta water-spouts in the form of lions' heads were found, still coloured, the teeth white, the gums and the inside of the mouth dark red, the tongues bright red. I could see a similar spout from this temple, he said, in the museum at Naples.

Metapontum has never been scientifically excavated. Who knows what may still lie beneath the tobacco? When we returned to the museum the curator went to his office and gave me a farewell gift. It was a replica, so well done that at first sight it appeared to be genuine, of the beautiful gold coin of Metapontum which shows the head of Leukippos, one of the legendary founders of the city, a bearded Greek wearing a helmet, and upon the other an ear of corn. The originals were in circulation in 350 B.C.

With this talisman in my pocket, I went happily across the plain towards the hills.

§ 6

I had now left Apulia and was travelling in the region of Basilicata, whose earlier name was Lucania. The *basilikós*, from whom the word Basilicata is derived, was the Byzantine representative of the Eastern Emperor. It is not a large region and stretches across the width of Italy under the 'instep', with a small coastline on both the Ionian and the Tyrrhenian Seas. There are only two provinces, Potenza, with the regional capital of that name, and Matera, with its rather strange provincial capital which I had read about and where I hoped to sleep that night.

I had noticed that the oleander becomes a notable feature of the landscape from Taranto onward, not growing wild in clumps, but cultivated as a standard, and sometimes even as a bushy tree.

There was quite a display of them in the public garden at Taranto, and I remembered an avenue of oleanders leading into Castellaneta. It is not a shrub I like, though once, in a moment of misguided fervour, I grew a whole hedge of them, white and pink. The milky sap is poisonous, and I have read somewhere that troops when serving in Africa in the last war were poisoned by roasting meat on skewers of oleander wood, a story which was also familiar to Wellington's army during the Peninsular War.

Norman Douglas told his friend Orioli that you could have malaria without oleanders, but never oleanders without malaria, a statement which Orioli questioned, though maybe Douglas was thinking of the marsh oleander. Classical scholars are extremely canny about malaria and its influence on cities of the ancient world. They say there is not sufficient evidence to justify the belief that the end of Magna Graecia and other districts was chiefly due to malaria, or whether the spread of malaria was due to depopulation. It hardly seems to matter. Surely what happened in these cities was a fall in prosperity which meant a decline in public works, lack of drainage, the silting up of harbours and consequently the increase of the anopheles. Until recent times it was the custom of many southern Italian peasants living on malarial land to take the train at night to sleep in the nearest hill town. Perhaps something of the same kind happened in Magna Graecia.

Oleanders certainly blazed the trail through the valley of the Bradano, then the road mounted into hill country. After a few miles I saw a city on a hill-top, outlined against the sky: this was Matera. I cannot recall anything written in English about this curious place. It was not, as far as I know, visited by any of the early travellers, and neither Gissing nor Norman Douglas ever went there. The fullest account, in an English translation, is that in Carlo Levi's *Christ Stopped at Eboli*; and a fearsome description it is. Readers of that powerful book will remember that when the author was exiled in the nineteen-thirties for his anti-Fascist opinions, his sister, a doctor in Turin, received permission to visit him in a remote hill town south of Matera. Arriving at Matera by train, she was appalled by what she saw. In the nineteen-thirties half of the population of forty thousand lived in terraced cave dwellings on either side of a ravine. 'They were like a schoolboy's idea of Dante's Inferno,' she said, describing it to her brother.

'The houses were open on account of the heat,' she continued, 'and as I went by I could see into the caves, whose only light came in through the front doors. Some of them had no entrance but a trapdoor and ladder. In these dark holes with walls cut out of the earth I saw a few pieces of miserable furniture, beds, and some ragged clothes hanging up to dry. On the floor lay dogs, sheep, goats and pigs. Most families have just one cave to live in and there they sleep all together; men, women, children and animals. This is how twenty thousand people live.

'Of children I saw an infinite number. They appeared from everywhere, in the dust and heat, amid the flies, stark naked or clothed in rags; I have never in my life seen such a picture of poverty. . . . The women when they saw me look in the doors, asked me to come in, and in the dark, smelly caves where they lived I saw children lying on the floor under torn blankets with their teeth chattering from fever. Others, reduced to skin and bone by dysentery, could hardly drag themselves about.'

She was followed by children who were shouting something, but she did not understand their dialect. She thought they were asking for pennies to buy sweets, but eventually made out their cry, which was '*Signorina dammi 'u chini!*' 'Signorina, give me some quinine'

There was, of course, nowhere to stay in Matera until a Jolly Hotel opened there a few years ago.

At first sight Matera appeared to me a normal Italian town with its Piazza Vittorio Veneto, its Via Roma, and its outskirts covered with hideous blocks of flats; then, having reached the cathedral, there opened at my feet a stupendous vista of troglodytic slums which for picturesque squalor cannot be matched in the whole of Italy. This was the place which upset the Dottoressa Levi in the nineteen-thirties, but since that time nearly twenty thousand people have been moved into the new housing estates. Both sides of the ravine are covered with abandoned cave-houses; one side is called the Sasso Caveoso, the other is the Sasso Barisano. I have never seen anything like them. Unlike most cities, which are ashamed of their slums, Matera, aware of their unique picturesqueness, has devised little railed-in look-out places at certain vantage points where you can get the best views of the Sassi. There is even a Strada Panoramica dei Sassi which skirts the whole area and, as a local guide-book says, in a rare moment of under-statement, 'offers the tourist a strange experience.'

While I was looking down into this architectural fantasy a man attached himself to me, speaking a strange language which at first I thought was the local dialect, but then discovered that it was his attempt at English. He told me that he had been an interpreter with the British Army during the last war. I have noticed that many Italians have worked themselves into the tourist network on the strength of saying 'yes' and 'no'. However, he was a pleasant fellow and we went down together into the Sassi. The place is even more incredible when you are wandering about in it than it appears from one of the look-outs. It is an unbelievable Pompeii. My acquaintance told me that some believe that the first inhabitants of Matera were Greek fugitives who came from cities like Metapontum during the Second Punic War; and he mentioned in support of that extravagant theory the number of words of Greek origin in the local dialect. It is curious how popular tradition often goes back to vanished Magna Graecia rather than to the more recent Byzantine period.

It is misleading to describe the Sassi as cave-dwellings. They are houses built above caves, at all angles, all sizes, all periods and of many styles. They rise in terraces and there is no attempt to make roads; there are only passages and steps leading up or down. It is scarcely conceivable that any plan should exist of the Sassi, which resemble the work of termites rather than of man. I asked why some of the caves had been blocked up with cement: it was to prevent the *Sassini* from finding their way back to their insanitary old homes from the rectitude of the new flats. I did not see any of the naked, malarial children, but I did see, and gave some marzipan sweets to, some well-dressed little girls at one of the street fountains.

The sunlight slanting into one of the still inhabited caves

revealed a bent old woman busy with a wooden tub full of washing. Seeing that I was interested, she smiled and invited me to step inside. It was a roomy cavern. The doors, which might have come from some old church, were at least fifteen feet high, thick and panelled. A bed many times the size of an ordinary double bed occupied a corner; above it were shrines, including a picture of Matera's Madonna della Bruna, and nearby a coloured postcard of the late President Kennedy. One of her four sons, she explained, was working for a road construction firm in Pittsburgh. Her husband had been born in the cave, she said, and she had come there as a young bride more than fifty years ago, and had had her five sons and six daughters in the vast bed in which, eventually, all the family had slept together. Happy days. She looked up at us, her old lined face filled with anxiety, believing we were from the municipality, pleading with us to let her go on living in the cave and not in some flat in the new town. While she chattered to my acquaintance in dialect, I noticed a donkey tethered to a ring; a number of hens were running about everywhere. It may have been unhygienic, but I thought it a tranquil scene.

We visited abandoned cave-churches whose walls were frescoed with faded saints, stiff Byzantine figures with uplifted fingers and staring eyes: in one little church the *ikonostasis*, concealing the holy of holies, was cut from the solid rock. These Greek churches cast a revealing light, I thought, on the early years of the Sassi. When in the Sasso Barisano, we descended steps in semi-darkness and tried to make out mediaeval coats-of-arms carved above the gates of grim, abandoned palaces. Upon the hill again, we entered the cathedral, which was built in 1268. Its carved doorways are encircled by recessed bands of stone lacework, but inside, save for the Byzantine columns of the nave, everything had been smothered in baroque stucco. Here we saw the presiding genius of Matera, the Madonna della Bruna, who is not brown at all but pink and cream and dressed in a long white gown. Once a year, my acquaintance told me, the Madonna, guarded by a mounted escort, is placed upon a triumphal car drawn by mules and, after encircling the town, returns to the cathedral. The moment she vanishes into the church, the crowd hurls itself upon the triumphal car and tears it to pieces, some with kicks, some with knives; and each person keeps a fragment as an amulet to see him safely through the next twelve months.

The restaurant which my acquaintance recommended was a long tunnel-like place which reminded me of a wartime Nissen hut, but it was one of the best, and certainly one of the cheapest, Italian restaurants I have encountered; and I wish there were more like it. Don Eugenio, which is near enough, and a Spanish title is general in the South, never refused an invitation to dinner and rarely ceased to pour out a constant stream of self-pity. Should there be anything divine in discontent, which I have always doubted, he must have been the most god-like of men. His one desire was to escape from Italy into golden America. Like so many other Italians, he believed that he had only to land in a foreign country for fortune to overwhelm him with favours, and, like nearly all Italians whom one sees idling about in cafés, there was an invisible wife and several children in the background. What his job was, I never knew, save that it had something to do with engineering. He told me that half the male population of Matera is in foreign countries or in the industrial north of Italy. There was also a lot of migrant labour and these men returned after the harvest.

The restaurant was hot. The ceiling fans revolved above an entirely male gathering, mostly in shirt sleeves, though a few *gente per bene* wore suits. While we ate, we watched an old American television drama about a sadistic Civil War *capitano* who was brutal to his southern captives, and even worse when his pretty wife (from South Carolina) interceded for them. How all this ended I shall never know, since a large man greeted my companion and accepted a glass of wine. One side of his face was that of a notably handsome man, the other was that of an ogre, all puckered and seamed. When he had gone, Don Eugenio told me that his friend, like many others in Matera, had worked on the Kariba Dam in Rhodesia, and he talked about nothing else except returning some day to Salisbury or Bulawayo.

'Unfortunately,' he said, 'when he had saved money he longed to see Matera again, and, in the delight at seeing familiar faces and scenes he married an old *innamorata*. He now has five children and must stay here for the rest of his life.'

Don Eugenio sighed in sympathy.

'He was badly wounded,' I said.

'That was not a war wound,' replied Don Eugenio. 'When he was a baby a wolf ran off with him, and he was found only just in time.'

§ 7

The new town of Matera is distinguished by one of the best museums in the south, the Ridola Museum, which was formed by a distinguished local man who bequeathed it to the State about fifty years ago. It is beautifully arranged in chronological sequence and is particularly strong in its prehistoric section. Some of the Greek pottery found in the district is very fine. I was interested in an unusual collection of carvings in wood and bone made by shepherds, such as walking-sticks, musical instruments, and models of animals and birds; there was also a fine assortment of objects saved from the bonfire and the rubbish heap: spinning wheels, distaffs, wooden buckets and all kinds of kitchen utensils.

One evening, having nothing to read, I pounced on a Neapolitan newspaper which someone had left in the hotel. It was only a week old. I found in it an announcement that the *Danza dei Gigli* – the Dance of the Lilies – would take place at Nola shortly. I have always wanted to see this and though it meant a change in my plans, the chance was too good to miss. Nola is a town near Naples, and I decided to go there without delay. I left early one morning and was touched to see that Don Eugenio had come to say goodbye. He pressed into my hands a cardboard box hardly larger than a matchbox. Inside was a small fragment of varnished wood. It was a piece of the triumphal car of the Madonna della Bruna.

'It will bring you luck,' he said.

· · · · ·

Though the distance between Matera and Naples is a little less than two hundred miles, the road across the mountains is trying and the journey is one not to be completed in a day, at least not by me. The morning was perfect. Cloud shadows moved across the distant plains; mountain roads gave the impression of travelling in a low-flying aeroplane, and a treeless countryside, golden with stubble in the valleys, golden with ripe wheat on the hills, lay as far as the eye could see. The beautiful gradation of colour from golden yellow to brown umber and burnt sienna was broken only to the north, where the Lake of S. Giuliano reflected the sky. There was no sign of life upon this wide landscape save where far off, catching the sun upon the shoulders and crests of mountains, a gleam of white denoted towns and villages. I met no cars upon the road, or even a muleteer seated with his panniers. The only movement was the flight of hawks, sometimes high above me, sometimes below in the valleys, gliding upon the air currents.

This was the country described by Carlo Levi. This was the scene of *Christ Stopped at Eboli*. Far to the south, impossible to see, were Gagliano and Stigliano, two of the lonely mountain villages to which the writer had been exiled in the nineteen thirties by the Fascist Government. Ahead of me was Grassano, where his exile had begun. Unlike Ovid, who was sentenced to a similar wilderness where he did little but bewail his misfortune, Carlo Levi employed his exile to get beneath the skin of the peasantry and to write the best book of its kind on the South of Italy.

I was soon ascending the road to Grassano, a straggling village whose buildings followed the line of the mountain. Unshaded electric lights were strung from poles across some of the streets. There were no shops to be seen. Women dressed in black looked at me from doorways. Children played in the dust and hens pecked in the débris; in the church a few women with black shawls over their heads were at prayer. Lying within a broken glass coffin was a figure dressed in cardboard armour as a Roman centurion, but he too had been broken and a stream of chaff and straw was oozing from his side. A woman whispered to me that he was St. Donatus and that they were organising a collection for his restoration. Which St. Donatus he represented, I do not know. There are many, including the martyr of Arezzo, also the Bishop of Fiesole, who had power over wolves. Carlo Levi wrote of this unknown part of Italy as 'a world apart . . . hedged in by custom and sorrow, cut off from History and the State, eternally patient,' a land 'without comfort or solace, where the peasant lives out his motionless civilization on barren ground in remote poverty, and in the presence of death.'

I walked to the upper part of Grassano, which was just as he described it. A pig was rooting in a pile of garbage and children were chasing a goat. There was an absence of adult life, even of the old men who usually sit on walls in the sun like aged lizards: but I did come across a member of the gentry walking with the village priest. He was clothed in a neat grey suit and wore a grey felt hat squarely upon his head. I wished them good day and enquired if they remembered Carlo Levi. This question was a mistake. I had touched an exposed nerve. Glancing at the priest, as if for approval, the man replied with indignation:

'Christ stopped at Eboli! Such wickedness!' He spread out his arms. 'Christ is *everywhere*!' he concluded. The priest's spectacles flashed approval and confirmation, and together they turned and continued their walk.

Most of the women appeared to be in late middle-age or elderly, but when I asked one the way to the local café it occurred to me that she could not have been more than thirty: but a woman of thirty who has mothered five to eight children, who has never been to a dentist or a hairdresser, who has never been totally immersed in a bath and has never known a day's holiday from the domestic treadmill, may not surprisingly appear older than she is. I remembered how much thought, Carlo Levi said, these women gave to love and passion. It was difficult to believe such witch-like characters (and witches in fact as well as in appearance) could harbour tender emotions. Nevertheless, Carlo Levi was warned the moment he arrived in Grassano by the local doctor.

'Good people, but primitive,' he said. 'Above all look out for the women. You're a young man and a handsome one. Don't take anything from a woman. Neither wine nor coffee; nothing to eat or drink. They would be sure to put a philtre or love potion in it. The women here will certainly take a fancy to you and all of them will make you such philtres. Don't accept anything from the peasant women. The mayor knows I'm right. These potions are dangerous. Unpleasant to the taste, in fact disgusting.'

It would have to be an astounding potion, I thought, to transform these poor women into Helens of Troy, but apparently it was possible, otherwise surely they would not have continued to compound them for centuries.

Worn out with mountain roads, I spent the night at Potenza in a bedroom upon the fifth floor of an admirable new hotel, the cool air coming in from a horizon of slopes and summits. The town, which is nearly three thousand feet above the sea, has been so repeatedly destroyed by earthquakes since the thirteenth century that most of it is modern. A mediaeval fragment has been granted immunity and in this, after darkness had fallen, I witnessed the finest *passeggiata* outside Spain. The young men and women of Potenza, attired in their best, passed and repassed, eyeing each other for two hours in decorum and gravity; occasionally there was giggling and a backward glance as decreed by the spirit of natural selection.

In the morning I was away early and was held up several times by roadmakers blasting rock for new roads and viaducts, all leading to the south. I went up a hill into the town of Eboli and, rather than face the ordeal of trying to penetrate streets made for mules and donkeys, I parked where I could in a tiny piazza and almost in the doorway of a wine shop. Standing arms akimbo was the strapping proprietress, who seemed to have stepped from the pages of the *Decameron*. She had a beguiling air of complicity, and when I suggested that she might give me some lunch she conspired at once. Yes, she whispered, some artichokes in oil and anchovies, then a beefsteak, which she would cook herself. Would I return in twenty minutes?

I went down to the wide market place where I found a news-agent's shop. The man thought he had a copy of *Christo si è fermato a Eboli*, and, after searching everywhere, discovered it under a pile of stuff in the window. It was interesting to have

bought this classic actually in the town where Christ Stopped. I
was appalled to learn that the bookseller had never read it. Eboli, I
discovered, has St Vitus as its patron saint. He was a Sicilian whose
shrines and headlands are frequent all the way from the tarantella
country, which, as I have said, suggests that there may be a link
between tarantella exorcism and the dancing mania of the Middle
Ages. On the way back to the wine shop I visited the church of
S. Maria della Pieta di Eboli, where I saw a striking baroque *coup
de théâtre*, an east window representing the descent from the Cross
in which life-size figures were dramatically lit from above by daylight carefully filtered in from the top of the tableau.

After lunch the merry padrona and her husband waved me off
on the road to Salerno, where I found myself plunged into the
tourists' Italy. The hotel was packed. A coach had just delivered a
consignment of the wives and mothers of the United States.
Porters stood scowling at the daily mound of suitcases. The air was
filled with questions and complaints. 'Is there any mail for Mrs
Wannamaker?'; 'Say, porter, I've been given the wrong key';
'The air conditioning is not working in room five zero six'; 'Do
you have a hairdresser in the hotel?'

I watched how skilfully a young man was managing these
difficult women with a mixture of charm and wary good humour.

I liked nothing about Salerno except the fish and vegetable
market, the museum, and the cathedral, which is superb. I went to
look at the gulf, and thought how different Salerno must have
appeared to those young British and Americans who waded
ashore in the autumn of 1943 to face the sixteenth Panzer Division.
I walked about the crowded streets wondering where the famous
medical school once had its headquarters. It existed from the Dark
Ages until the nineteenth century, when I believe Murat closed it.
One of its most illustrious patients was Robert of Normandy, the
eldest son of William the Conqueror, who went there on his way
home from the Crusades, suffering from an arrow wound that had
turned septic. Some say that the celebrated Latin poem giving
rules for health, *Regimen Sanitatis Salerni*, was dedicated to
Robert; others point out that it was too late in date, and that
'England's King', mentioned in the first line, could not have been

Robert, as he never ascended the throne: but that might even be an argument in its favour since it is generally believed in Italy that he did.

The School was already venerable when Frederick II organized it and forbade any doctor to practise without its diploma, which was issued after a course that lasted eight years, though this included surgery. The practitioner swore to denounce all foul play attempted by chemists, and to attend the poor free of charge. The scale of fees laid down permitted a doctor to charge more should his patient live outside a city's walls. The medical profession must have been very much on its toes in the thirteenth century, since the Emperor was himself a formidable amateur physician and a fanatical believer in baths and the simple life. I once saw an old print of the School of Salerno which depicted a Palladian building and next to it a physic garden in which a group of professors and students were gravely examining beds and borders of flourishing herbs.

Having climbed through narrow, noisy streets to the glorious cathedral, I felt that I had made full circle: I was back in the busy, violent world of Robert Guiscard. This church, in a sense, was his epitaph and also his monument to the Norman conquest of southern Italy. Let anyone sit on the wall outside the Gate of the Lions and try to recollect a finer vista than that of the atrium beyond. I know of none. While the Guiscard was challenging the Eastern Emperor, his architects and builders were searching the recently deserted town of Paestum for the twenty-eight marble columns which one now sees round this lovely courtyard. I know of no finer example of the entrance to an early Christian church, with its central fountain - which reminds us that it was the custom to dip the hand in water in ceremonial purification before entering the basilica, and also reminds us, in this case, that the huge granite basin originally there was taken off to Naples and is now in a public park. It would be a gracious act on the part of Naples to restore it to Salerno.

Like several of the greatest churches of the period, the main gates of the cathedral came from the bronze foundries of Constantinople, and their fifty-four panels were once inset with silver.

Beyond lies a church which does not deserve the disparagement of the guide books, which imply that it was ruined by restoration in a former century, for this is not so. It is, as it always was, one of the greatest monuments of the Norman power in Italy. The student of mediaeval Rome will link it with one of the darkest of Rome's disasters, the Norman sack of 1084. The building was complete, but had not yet been consecrated in that year. I have told how Robert Guiscard, leaving Rome feet deep in ashes, persuaded the Pope for his own safety to return with him to Salerno, where, in the following year, Gregory VII died.

Thinking of these things, I came to a side chapel whose altar was fronted with glass. In the floodlit space below lay the figure of a pope, his gloved hands folded in death. He wore a tiara of antique shape, his vestments were decorated with medallions containing birds and crosses of Byzantine origin, embroidered in gold, and upon his feet were red slippers. This was an effigy of Gregory VII. Standing next to me, gazing at the dead pope, was a good-looking young woman. I noticed that tears were pouring down her cheeks. I wondered why. It was surely strange that a pontiff who had died more than eight centuries ago should have had such an effect upon a young woman today.

Later that day, in the evening, I was seated in a café in Salerno where I saw with sorrow a young man, a tourist, making himself deliberately and horribly drunk on Italian brandy. This reminded me of perhaps the finest lines Norman Douglas ever wrote, and I made a note to look them up. Here they are. They come from his book *Alone*.

'I am not more straight-laced than many people, yet I confess it always gives me a kind of twinge to see a young man yielding to intemperance of any kind. There is something incongruous in the spectacle, if not actually repellent. Rightly or wrongly, one is apt to associate this time of life with stern resolve. A young man, it appears to me, should hold himself well in hand. Youth has so much to spare! Youth can afford to be virtuous. With such stores of life looming ahead it should be a period of ideals, of self-restraint, and self-discipline, of earnestness of purpose. How well the Greek Anthology praises "Temperance, the nurse of Youth". The divine Plato lays it down that youngsters should not touch wine at all, since it is not right to *heap fire on fire*. He adds that older men like ourselves may indulge therein as an ally against the austerity of their years – agreeing, therefore, with Theophrastus who likewise recommends it for the "natural moroseness" of age.'

In the morning I was soon speeding along the Autostrada with its tempting branches to Pompeii and Herculaneum; then came Naples, where motor traffic has long since passed exasperation point.

# CHAPTER SEVEN

*A balcony in Naples – demented traffic – Neapolitan legends – the blood of S. Januarius – the eloquence of Neapolitan gesture – Angevin and Aragonese – the Bourbons of Naples – Sir William Hamilton – Emma and Nelson – the Palace at Caserta – Capua and its Colosseum – the Phlegrean Fields – Pozzuoli – the Sybil of Cumae – the Dance of the Lilies at Nola – Ascending Vesuvius.*

## § 1

My room in Naples had a balcony high up opposite the Castel dell'Ovo. I was able to look down with Olympian perspicacity upon every detail of the rock and its dramatic fortress, and upon the little harbour in its shadow with its fringe of tourist restaurants. The see-Naples-and-die view was cut off on my left by the buildings of the Via Partenope, but I did not mind, indeed I preferred the Egg Castle, which I found to be a source of constant entertainment.

I had been in Naples only twice before for brief periods in the nineteen thirties when Vesuvius wore a white plume and sometimes glowed at night. But since 1944 the volcano has entered upon one of its periods of quiescence and the plume has gone; so too, for me, has vanished a great part of its character. It is now just another mountain. A whole generation has grown up in Naples which has never seen that marvellous question mark in the sky, and only older people know how greatly one misses the picturesque blossom of smoke and steam, perpetually rising and moving, which one's eye sought a hundred times a day as if it were a barometer or an oracle. One used to hear people refer to Vesuvius as 'he'. They would say 'He is smoking a lot to-day', or 'He is very quiet at the moment'. Now Vesuvius is 'it'.

Below me upon the Via Partenope moved four parallel lines of one-way traffic that ceased neither by day nor night. Naples, for

geographical reasons connected with the mountain round which
it sprawls, has fewer broad main roads than most cities of its size,
and consequently the traffic achieves nightmare proportions. But
that is nothing new: it is only the character of the congestion that
has changed. In the seventeenth century the jam of sedan chairs
and coaches was just as alarming to contemporaries as the motor
cars of to-day. In the eighteenth and nineteenth centuries the
Riviera di Chiaja and the Via Toledo were as difficult to cross as
the modern Via Partenope. Lady Blessington, writing of Naples
in the 1820's, mentioned an English resident, T. J. Mathias
once the Librarian at Buckingham Palace), who was so
terrified of being mown down by the coaches that he 'had often
been known to stop an hour before he could master courage to
cross the Chiaja'. As he was well known to everyone, the coachmen sometimes pulled up their horses to help him, 'but in vain',
wrote Lady Blessington, 'for he advances half way, then stops
terrified at his imaginary danger and rushes back, exclaiming
"God bless my soul!"' His dilemma is shared by the modern
visitor.

My own method is to select a pedestrian crossing, then, lifting
an arm in an abrupt Roman salute rather like an angry actor in the
part of Cassius, to step straight off the kerb and start walking. The
arm must be uplifted with resolution and maintained in that
position until the other side of the road is achieved. There must be
no weakening like that of poor Mr Mathias. At the slightest hint
of irresolution the four lines of racing motorists, less humane than
the coachmen of 1820, would gladly encircle one. The act is
really a battle of wills between oneself and the drivers; though I
am glad to say that it is not as dangerous as it looks since
all Italians drive on their brakes and are able to pull up within a
foot if obliged to do so. I have convoyed numerous people
across the Via Partenope and have never lost anyone, though
I admit that I have had crossings during the rush hours which
have justified the anguished expressions of those unwilling to
make the adventure, who have remained on the other side
watching their loved ones advancing apparently into the jaws of
death.

The first thing I would see in the morning, sometimes before sunrise, lying on a grey-blue sea, was the old Castle of the Egg, rising powerful and uncouth against a sky from which the stars had just faded. Already fishermen would be untying their boats and rowing out, some to dredge bright sea-grass upon which to display their oysters and mussels, others to go beyond the harbour and drop their lines. I used to fancy that if some Greek traveller from the early morning of the world could look at the same patch of sea he would have witnessed much the same scene: galleys instead of cargo boats coming in with the first light and men going out to fish. There cannot have been a single day for nearly two thousand years when someone has not gone out to fish from this place.

It was here that Naples began. The castle rock, once an island, was the place where in Greek legend the dead body of the siren Parthenope was washed ashore after her song had been heard by Odysseus; and how tenaciously the name, which means 'maiden face' (scarcely a description of Naples that would occur to one), has clung to the city. Virgil, and all the poets after him, have used it; the Parthenopian Republic was the name chosen for Masienello's brief régime and Via Partenope was the obvious choice for the road along the front. The boats that go to Capri belong to the Societa Partenopea, thus appropriately linking that island with the Sirens.

Though the Castel dell'Ovo has never been open to the public, I was told that the immense labyrinth is shortly to become one of the sights of Naples; indeed by the time this appears in print the traveller may already be able to buy one of those tastefully engraved little *Ministero delle Pubblica Istruzione* tickets at the entrance gate. When this happens, providing that the architects and restorers have been allowed their way, I would prophesy that this gloomy mass may become one of the wonders of Italy. Little is known of it. Even those who have taken the trouble to obtain the permission of the War Department to enter it have a confused memory of dark passages, gaunt barrack rooms, a seventh century church, fearful dungeons and, most provoking of all, marble columns that are said to have belonged to the villa which Lucullus built on the rock fifty years before Christ. His sea walls, fish ponds, his banqueting houses, his parks and his gardens stretched back from the sea across the flat land. The villa must have been kept up in style for centuries since it received its most mysterious guest in the year A.D. 475, a boy named Romulus Augustulus, the last of the Caesars. He had been elected at Ravenna but, instead of being assassinated, was forced to abdicate by a Gothic overlord who, with unexpected tenderness, and because 'of his youth, beauty and innocence', gave him a pension in gold and exiled him to the old Lucullan villa on the Bay of Naples. What he did with his life is unknown. Upon that lovely scene the last of a line of emperors which had ruled the Roman Empire for five centuries vanished from history.

The story was conceived in the Middle Ages that Virgil, who then was believed to have been a wizard, had built the castle upon an egg, which was balanced upon the sea-bed, a legend which explains the name of Castel dell'Ovo. It was actually reconstructed by William I of Sicily and added to by the Emperor Frederick II, who paid a tribute to its strength by keeping his treasures there. Under Robert the Wise the Chapel of the Saviour was painted in fresco by Giotto in 1309, though no traces of these are visible. The dungeons are as gloomy and as full of tragic stories as those of the Tower of London.

In the evening coloured lights shone upon the waters of the little harbour. Dining-tables were set along the quayside. Guitars and violins played from restaurant to restaurant while a tenor voice throbbed out *O Sole Mio* and, after a good tip, *Bella Napoli*. Stealthily, one of the harbour cats sprang from boat to boat like a squirrel in a forest, and a fisherman, untying his boat, rowed off on some errand, standing up and facing in the direction of the boat, his movement over the still water shattering the reflections of neon and electric signs into an oily whirlpool of reds, greens and golds before the pattern reformed itself again. In the background, like a mountain or a sleeping leviathan, the ancient Castel dell'Ovo obliterated a million stars. Never have diners all unwittingly eaten in the presence of so many varied ghosts.

. . . . . .

In the course of an early morning walk, I happened in passing to glance through the window of a restaurant where I saw an American breakfasting upon bacon and eggs. Dislike, to use a mild word, for the Continental breakfast which had been smouldering for many weeks now reached explosion point, and, pushing open the door, I entered the restaurant.

'American breakfast, sir?' asked the waiter.

'You can call it what you like' I said, 'as long as it is bacon and eggs, toast and marmalade.'

The restaurant was American, one of those places where members of a master race may go and read the menu in their own language and order nostalgic food. Everyone in the place, except myself, was American. There was iced water and orange juice on every table; children were tucking into cornflakes upon which cream had been poured; people were drinking not European coffee but real caw-fee. The atmosphere was a thousand miles from Italy. The pavement had suddenly become the sidewalk, the *farmacia* over the way had become the drugstore, the lift had become an elevator, biscuits had become crackers, and braces, if worn by usually belted males, had suffered a sex change and had become, most surprisingly, suspenders. One was aware of the same effect of breathing one's own supply of air which once characterized the travelling English before the social revolution.

While I enjoyed the first real breakfast for weeks, I watched the early morning sights of Naples: the crowded omnibuses festooned with passengers, the flower-sellers spraying their carnations and gladioli with water, and the airing of the prestige dogs. These were boxers, Maltese terriers, a fine bull-dog, several lapdogs and, most distinguished of all, a beautifully behaved Doberman Pinscher bitch. I noticed a middle-aged man walking along with a miniature white poodle beneath each arm. They were evidently not allowed to mix with others dogs. They wore the rather fraudulent expression of their breed, as if they knew that they had entered high society under false pretences and expected to be detected at any moment as honest working water dogs. They looked longingly at the lamp-posts and clearly resented the humiliation of being carried. The man turned into the restaurant, where he was evidently well known and expected. The waiter arranged three chairs. The man sat with a poodle on each side of him, each animal as white as snow save for a round black dot of a nose and two dark eyes. He was an American. He talked first to one dog, then to another, and during his breakfast he cut small segments of buttered toast, which they politely accepted.

Every morning while I was in Naples I went to this restaurant for breakfast, and at the same time the American arrived with a poodle beneath each arm. One morning, the restaurant being full, he asked if he might sit at my table, and the waiter arranged the three chairs. I began by praising the poodles. He accepted my praise with a slight inclination of the head, then he sighed heavily. He told me that he, his wife, his daughter and the two dogs had arrived reluctantly in Naples from the United States a week or so before, reluctantly because they would rather have been in England, but quarantine restrictions (here he nodded paternally towards the poodles) made such a visit impossible. However, they had decided to stay in Naples for a few days, then to motor to Rome and Florence before returning home. Here he sighed again. On the evening of their arrival, he continued, as they were mounting the steps of the hotel his wife collapsed suddenly with a coronary thrombosis and was taken to hospital in an ambulance. His expression conveyed to me the full horror of the crisis, for to an American there are few situations more alarming than to be at the mercy of a foreign doctor.

To his relief and astonishment the Italian doctors were first-rate. It was unbelievable but they sure were. As his wife would be unable to move for weeks, he had taken a flat for the poodles where he devoted his time to them, to washing them, to combing them, to carrying them about and seeing that they had no contact with foreign dogs, and when he was not doing this he was visiting his wife in the hospital. Of Naples he had seen nothing, neither did he wish to do so.

To his astonishment, the authorities had been more than co-operative. They had allowed him to instal an air-conditioner in his wife's room in the hospital and, more surprising still, they had, in the humane Italian way, allowed the daughter to sleep in the hospital near her mother.

'It's the darndest luck', he said, buttering a segment of toast and placing it on a pink tongue, 'and the moment my wife can travel off we go back home to the United States'.

He sighed, paid his bill, nodded, and picking up a dog beneath each arm, walked out into the street.

§ 2

'Naples has been truly described as "a paradise of devils"; but they are lively and amusing devils – insouciant and idle; good-natured and thieving; kind-hearted and lying; always laughing, except if thwarted, when they will stab their best friends without a pang. Almost everybody in Naples cheats, but they cheat in as lively and pleasant a manner as is compatible with possibilities. Nearly all the officials still peculate, and probably not more than two-thirds of the taxes ever reach the public exchequer. If the traveller is robbed, he will never secure redress, for, as in Ireland, it would be impossible to obtain evidence, or to find a jury sufficiently fearless to convict. . . . Very little, however, is needed to sustain life at Naples, and there are thousands who consider a dish of beans at mid-day to be sumptuous fare, while the horrible condiment called *Pizza* (made of dough baked with garlic, rancid bacon and strong cheese) is esteemed a feast.'

So Augustus Hare wrote in 1883. Time, of course (and perhaps less garlic), has admitted the *pizza* to international society, but for the rest there are many who would say that Hare's summing up of the Neapolitan is probably as true to-day as it was nearly a century ago. My own feeling is that no one who does not speak the Neapolitan Italian perfectly, and is not familiar with a great number of Neapolitans, has any right to form such judgements. Hare lived in Italy and knew what he was writing about, but unfortunately Naples has suffered from a number of priggish verdicts, like that of Ruskin, who described the city as 'the most loathsome nest of human caterpillars I was ever forced to stay in – a hell with all the devils imbecile in it.' How curious it is that someone who was so sensitive to stone could be so incurious about humanity.

The days I spent wandering about old Naples were exhausting but fascinating. I explored streets where, beneath festoons of washing, children ran and shouted, while a generation soon to join them was borne proudly past beneath apron and maternity gown; where from basement and cellar one's hastily averted glance was cheerfully acknowledged by people lying in bed; where individualists, rather than work in factories, preferred to hammer and saw in tiny cell-like workshops open to the street and accessible to the comment and gossip of their friends; where the matriarchs who rule this violent explosion of life shouted from balcony to balcony, and where life was lived in glorious turmoil from which loneliness, that corrosive acid of the soul, had been banished.

In a delightful book *Naples: a Palimpsest*, Peter Gunn mentions a Neapolitan who, when asked why he had returned from abroad where he was doing so well, just nodded in answer towards the noisy street. And I am well able to understand this. The sounds and smells of Naples are the true siren music of Parthenope, always urging exiles to return to the suffocating embrace of their beloved city.

It should not be forgotten that every slum dweller in Naples has a princely drawing-room only a few paces from his *basso*, as an underground cellar is called, and even though he may cook and eat in the street he is free to seek relaxation and contemplation, and to enjoy even comparative silence, in gilt halls modelled on the princely reception rooms of the seventeenth century. I refer, of course, to the churches. I gave up when I had counted a hundred and forty of these, which include three catacombs, one of which I thought was finer than anything in Rome. I visited about thirty churches at one time or another and was impressed in every one by the groups of matriarchs who had dropped in for a moment's peace and prayer, genuflecting upon arrival and departure to one of the many Christian manifestations of Hera or Venus Genetrix.

I stood in the beautiful church of S. Lorenzo, where Boccaccio, who was one of the first mediaeval links between poetry and business, first saw and instantly loved his Fiametta. Some believe that her real name was Maria, the natural daughter of Robert the Wise, King of Naples. Those instantly loved and permanently adored women of the Middle Ages were a fascinating trio – Beatrice, Laura and Fiametta. Boccaccio met his Fiametta in the year 1341, the time when another great lover arrived in Naples, Petrarch, who had come to be examined by Robert the Wise to make sure that he was worthy to accept the laurel crown offered to him by the Senate of Rome. Poet and king talked together for three days, which has been called 'the longest *viva voce* on record'.

Crossing the cloisters, where air raid damage was still being cleared up twenty odd years after the last war, I was taken by a Franciscan into the monastery in which Petrarch stayed when he came to Naples as the Pope's ambassador. Four years had passed since the poet's *viva voce* and Joan I had then succeeded her grand-father, Robert the Wise. We ascended worn steps which were those used by the poet as he mounted to his bedroom in the guest quarters. I wondered which of the gaunt old rooms he was occupying upon the night of the fearful storm of 1345 when the friars burst in carrying torches and relics, and together with Petrarch descended to the church to spend the hours until morning upon their knees, while ships sank in the bay and Naples rocked to the storm.

The most important of all the churches is, of course, the cathedral, which is dedicated to the miracle-working S. Gennaro or S. Januarius, a saint who protects the city against natural disaster and is in general its advocate in heaven. The church is built upon the site of a temple of Apollo; and those Neapolitans fortunate enough to be christened there receive baptism at a huge basalt urn decorated with Bacchanalian symbols which is said to have come from a temple of Dionysus. In this perhaps appro-priate pagan setting the head and blood of S. Januarius are kept in an ornate chapel glittering with gold, silver and precious marbles. A red brocade curtain conceals the silver doors of a safe behind the altar which can be unlocked only by several keys, which are in the keeping of different officials. Inside is the palladium of Naples, the phial containing a hard brown substance said to be the blood of S. Januarius, who was martyred in the year A.D. 305. Three times a year, upon the first Sunday in May, upon September 19 and December 16, in the course of a noisy ceremony, the Saint's blood generally liquefies, and sometimes turns red and appears, as many have said who have seen it, to 'boil'.

The reliquary is circular, and in size and shape is like a hand mirror. Clear glass back and front protects and also reveals two ancient phials inside, which contain the sacred 'blood'. I wondered how many of us, if we came across this reliquary in the window of a curiosity shop, would give it a second glance. The substance has never been chemically examined, therefore no one really knows whether it is truly blood or something else. In an appendix on this subject in his *Naples and Campania Revisited*, Edward Hutton writes that 'in 1902 a ray of light was passed through it, during the liquefaction, by Professor Sperindeo and gave the spectrum of blood'. Lacy Collison-Morley wrote in *Naples Through the Centuries*, 'The mystery of the melting of the liquid is not to be disposed of as airily as some people imagine. . . . A Professor of Chemistry at the University of Naples not long ago (1925), placed a thermometer on the altar, first without, then with, the permission of the priests, and a friend of mine, at that time a student, helped him with his experiments. The melting took place sometimes at a temperature of 18–20° Cent. (65–68° Fahr.), sometimes at 15–17° Cent (59–63° Fahr.), once at 3° Cent. (38° Fahr.). Together they tried every chemical formula and found only one that gave anything approaching satisfactory results, but it would work only at blood heat, a temperature never to be found in the church or on the altar. The liquid often continues to boil after the miracle. My friend has himself touched the silver stand and found it quite cold after the boiling. Then there is the difference of time required for the melting and the difference of the colour of the liquid, which ranges on different occasions from rich chocolate to blood red, to be explained. There is no conscious trickery by the clergy.'

There is, however, a well-known story that during the French occupation of Naples the blood refused to liquefy, with a distressing effect upon the morale of the population, upon which the

French general in command threatened to shoot the Archbishop and his Chapter if the miracle did not occur within ten minutes. It did so. Great offence was caused in the eighteenth century by the Prince of San Severo, an amateur chemist and inventor, who claimed to be able to produce the phenomenon. 'He designed a monstrance or reliquary similar to that containing the saint's blood,' writes Harold Acton in *The Bourbons of Naples*, 'with phials of the same shape filled with a mixture of gold, mercury and cinnabar, whose colour resembled coagulated blood. To make this fluid there was a supply of mercury in the hollow rim, with a valve which opened to let the mercury enter the phials when the reliquary was turned about. The Prince used to entertain his guests with such conjuring tricks.'

The frantic scenes inside the church both before and after the miracle have reminded some observers of a pagan ceremony, and as I turned from the splendour of the churches into the noisy streets again, meeting at every turn some exuberant manifestation of life, I thought of the ancient world, particularly of ancient Greece, and the characters of Aristophanes. Here I thought is the ribald laughter, the earthy wisdom, the fatalism of Attic comedy; and many of the gestures I noticed were surely to be seen in Herculaneum and Pompeii.

If you wish to see the most eloquent Neapolitan gestures you must keep your eyes open in the streets and the cafés. These are not the exaggerated arm-waving gestures of the stage Italian, indeed they are remarkable for their inconspicuous subtlety. They belong to the art of mime. They are to conversation what a piano accompaniment is to a song. It would be impossible to invent them, they must have been a silent language for centuries. I think that among the most eloquent of all gestures is the scarcely visible Neapolitan shrug. The most expressive shrugs are merely a contraction and relaxation of the shoulder muscles, yet they are able to convey incredulity, compassion, sorrow, contempt, and a whole range of feelings according to the assistance given by arms, hands and eyes, and, most important, to the intake and expulsion of breath. The shrug is, it seems to me, the basic gesture upon which so much varied eloquence depends. A north European, if asked a question that demands a negative answer, will say 'no' in his own language, but the southern Italian will not utter a word, yet he will manage to convey a devastating 'no' by slowly raising his head and gazing steadfastly at his questioner. Police magistrates are familiar with this gesture, which in a court of law is indispensable. It can mean 'yes', 'no', 'perhaps', or 'go to hell!'.

An uplifted forefinger can also be eloquent. It can convey caution, disbelief and many other feelings. Moved slowly backwards and forwards beneath the chin, it can mean 'you can count me out'; placed for a second upon the nose, the mouth or the right eyebrow it can cover a range of meanings from the need for discretion to a suspicion of madness.

Sometimes the motorist in Naples finds in his panic that he has cut in on another car, or that in some other way he has offended an adjacent driver. He will soon be aware of a pair of dark, dispassionate eyes travelling beside him, dispassionate and implacable, and the stranger may even smile, or wave his hand or say 'sorry' in an attempt to appease those accusing eyes, but with no success at all. He will then notice that the driver of the other car is casually pointing his fist at him with the first and fourth fingers extended in the well known *fare le corna* gesture. 'Good heavens,' thinks the innocent stranger, 'surely he can't think I've got the Evil Eye!' No, of course not! It is not a gesture of self-protection but one inviting calamity. It might be grouped in the catalogue of gesture with Winston Churchill's famous V sign, which has a meaning other than that obviously intended by the statesman, but the extended fist has a much wider scope, its essential meaning being, 'If you are not already wearing antlers, may your wife at this precise moment be betraying you with your best friend!' Having expressed these sentiments, the implacable eyes disappear in the traffic.

When in Naples, Dickens noticed that 'everything is done in pantomime'. He gathered some good specimens. 'A man who is quarrelling with another, yonder,' he wrote 'lays the palm of his right hand on the back of his left, and shakes the two thumbs – expressive of a donkey's ears – whereat his adversary is goaded to desperation. Two people bargaining for fish, the buyer empties an imaginary waistcoat pocket when he is told the price and walks away without a word: having thoroughly conveyed to the seller that he considers it too dear. Two people in carriages, meeting, one touches his lips, twice or thrice, holding up the five fingers of his right hand, and gives a horizontal cut in the air with the palm. The other nods briskly, and goes his way. He has been invited to a friendly dinner at half-past five o'clock, and will certainly come.'

I thought I detected several gestures which I have always thought of as Greek, such as the scooping up of imaginary gold with one hand, to indicate riches, also the use of the coat lapels: a gentle shake of a lapel and a scornful expression, meaning someone of no importance; a vigorous agitation of both lapels accompanied by puffed cheeks or the sound pup-pup-pup means someone of inconceivable wealth, or the shake of a lapel and a mournful swaying of the body which can express incredulity, the need for caution or, better still, the advisability of doing nothing at all.

§ 3

While walking through the back streets of Naples I came to the Piazza del Mercato, where a fair was in progress. It was a seedy, dusty piazza which had been bombed during the last war and had not recovered. The centre was occupied by a circular platform upon which, to the accompaniment of ear-splitting music, children were driving miniature cars and bumping into each other, so imitating their elders and perhaps rehearsing their future fate.

The piazza had been the place of execution in mediaeval Naples. It may be seen in old paintings pleasantly rural and open to the bay on one side so that people mounting the scaffold really did see Naples and die. And it was in this gloomy piazza that an event of importance occurred on an autumn day in 1268, when the Hohenstaufen dynasty was extinguished in the person of a gallant and good-looking lad of sixteen named Conradin.

His grandfather, the great Frederick II, had been dead for eighteen years. The Papacy, detesting the Hohenstaufens, had invited Charles of Anjou, the brother of the French king, Louis

IX, to go to Italy and seize the crown of Sicily, which he gladly did. He was assisted by his wife Beatrice of Provence, whose three sisters were all queens, a fact which had given her such a sense of inferiority that she willingly pawned her jewels to help her husband to make her a queen too. One of her sisters was Eleanor of Provence, Queen of England and consort of Henry III. Unfortunatelp the ambitious Beatrice lived to enjoy her queenship for scarcely a year, dying unexpectedly in Italy.

Opposing Charles of Anjou when he invaded Italy was the Emperor Frederick's illegitimate and favourite son, Manfred, one whose noble character has inspired many a ballad and romance, and whose name is still commemorated upon the map of Italy in the little port of Manfredonia which I had visited upon the Gargano Peninsula. His army was, however, no match for that of Charles of Anjou. Surrounded by his Saracen bodyguard, Manfred was cut down at the age of thirty-four in the year 1266, and the only legitimate male Hohenstaufen left at liberty was then a boy in Germany, aged fourteen, Conradin. 'He was as beautiful as Absalom and spoke good Latin', wrote a contemporary.

Having slain Manfred, the victorious Charles advanced to Naples, which he selected as his capital instead of Palermo. He had been on the throne for two years when young Conradin, against his mother's instinct, was persuaded to invade Italy and claim the crown of his ancestors from the Frenchman. The boy was defeated by Charles at a place called Tagliacozzo in the Abruzzo, which I remember seeing at the outset of my journey under cloudy skies in a stricken earthquake country of folded hills.

Conradin was sent to Naples in chains, but these were soon removed since Villani records that he was playing chess with Frederick of Austria when the Grand Protonotary of the Kingdom broke the news that he had been condemned to death together with his supporters and several Neapolitan nobles who had rallied to him. Upon the morning of the execution, Charles of Anjou was seated upon a throne that had been erected in the Campo Moricino, as the Piazza del Mercato was then called. A fanfare of trumpets announced the arrival of the condemned lords. No sooner had the Grand Protonotary read the sentence of death on

Conradin than the king's brother-in-law, Count Robert of Flanders, shouted that it was unlawful for him to condemn so great a gentleman and, drawing his sword, he attacked and killed the Grand Protonotary. This must surely be the only instance of a judge dying in sight of the gallows before the prisoner whom he had condemned.

The body of the Protonorary was removed and the execution proceeded. The first to die was the young Duke of Austria. As his head fell into the sawdust, Conradin sprang forward and shed tears as he kissed it. He then prepared to die himself. He declared that he was no traitor but one who had come to recover the kingdom of his ancestors. He flung his gloves into the crowd and after asking God to forgive his sins, he placed his handsome head upon the block crying, 'Ah, my mother, what grief I am bringing you!'

While this painful scene was in progress his mother, Elizabeth of Bavaria, was hurrying from Germany to Italy with a large sum of money in the hope of ransoming her son. She arrived too late. It is said that she gave the money to the monks of S. Maria del Carmine nearby, to enable them to rebuild their church. But Conradin was not at first buried there. A man as pious as Charles of Anjou could not permit his dead rival's excommunicated body to lie in consecrated ground. So the last of the Hohenstaufens was buried beneath the sand of the Campo Moricino. More than three and a half centuries later, in 1631, workmen digging in what by that time had become the Piazza del Mercato came upon a lead coffin bearing the letters 'R.C.C.' (*Regis Conradini Corpus*); inside was found the skeleton of a young man. His severed head lay upon his rib bones and beside him lay a sword. The bones were reverently buried in S. Maria del Carmine, where to-day the sexton will point out behind the altar the letters 'R.C.C.', which mark the spot.

I stood in the dusty piazza thinking how swiftly the mighty can fall, a trite reflection, no doubt, but one that comes unbidden to the mind in this place to anyone who has recently seen the castles and palaces up and down the land where the great Emperor, Frederick II, held his court. I remembered the tall walls of Lucera, the hawks gliding above the Castel del Monte, the great castle of Bari where Frederick once spied upon St Francis, and I wondered whether it would have pained 'the Wonder of the World' to know that his greatness would be so brief a thing or whether he would have shrugged it off with Greek irony or an Arab proberb. Who can say?

The extinction of the Hohenstaufens has left no shadow. The gloom of the piazza is caused not by the memory of a young heir executed like a criminal, an unheard of fate for a prince captured in battle, but by poverty and dirt and sad old buildings that have known better days. I watched the children bumping round in the cars, wondering where they had found the money for this amusement, and I thought too of the mystique of kingship which still sheds its enchantment upon Naples and the south. Not a stone's throw from the place where young Conradin had died I saw, scrawled upon a wall in whitewash, the words, 'Viva il Re'.

The young man was standing in the sunlight surrounded by a group of tourists. Behind him rose the elephantine Castel Nuovo and, beyond, lay the Bay. None of the tourists held a Baedeker or a Muirhead. It is now the fashion not to seek information for one's self but to be fed with it by a guide or a young university student who is trying to earn a few honest shillings during the vacation. The elderly men and women stood about like a group of school children on an outing, listening reluctantly to the teacher.

'The French', said the young man, 'were not loved in Naples and much less loved in Sicily. One day, in the year 1282, a French sergeant who had insulted a girl in Palermo was killed by the girl's young man.'

An elderly American, wearing an eccentric straw hat acquired in Capri, moved to the kerb and flung the butt of a cigar into the road. He remained standing moodily with his back to history.

'Very soon,' continued the guide, 'every Frenchman in Palermo was killed. This is called the Sicilian Vespers because the killing began as the bells were ringing for Vespers. Even foreign monks and friars were killed if they could not pronounce a word that no Frenchman could say properly.'

The tourists stirred uneasily. Some were thinking of lunch. The woman in the front row, who always asks questions, piped up.

'And what was the word?', she asked earnestly.

'The word was *ciciri*', replied the young man. All the tourists then pronounced it, laughing and saying how easy it was; and the group passed out of hearing.

Curiously enough, the young man's lecture was a continuation of my own thoughts as I left the scene of Conradin's death. The Sicilian Vespers were, of course, a reprisal, but how spontaneous or how calculated it is impossible to say. The technique of organizing crowds, working up demonstrations and arranging assassinations was as well known in the Middle Ages as it is to-day, or perhaps it would be better to say that as we slide back towards the new Dark Age this technique has been successfully revived. Some historians believe that the Sicilian Vespers were the culmination of a plot hatched by those whom the Angevin conquest of Naples and the south had ruined. The collapse of the Hohenstaufens had been so rapid that men were still alive who had been devoted friends of Frederick II and who owed their wealth and position to him. Such men, now ruined and their lands confiscated by the new administration, were anxious to see the expulsion of the French and the restoration of what remnants were left of the Hohenstaufens. And what remnants they were! With Conradin dead, there remained only illegitimate descendants, and most of these were in prison. Indeed the most accessible and the best available claimant was Manfred's daughter, Constance, who had married Peter III of Aragon.

The conspiracy accordingly moved to Barcelona. Eventually, with more spies and counter plots than any novelist could handle, and with the involvement of the Pope, the Byzantine Emperor, kings and – most important – Florentine bankers, Peter of Aragon was persuaded to invade Sicily and claim the throne on behalf of his wife. He landed successfully and was soon followed by Constance and her children. So Spain set foot in Italy; thus began the tug-of-war in Italy between Spain and France.

The situation was exasperating for all concerned, as it remains for anyone who tries to simplify it. The result was that two rival houses reigned at the same time, calling themselves the Kings and Queens of Sicily. The French Angevins ruled from Naples, the Spanish Aragonese from Sicily. The rivalry between them lasted until the fifteenth century when the Spaniards ruled both Sicily and Naples from Madrid, and appointed Viceroys. With the War of the Spanish Succession the French returned with the Bourbon dynasty.

The Castel Nuovo which formed the dramatic background to the young guide's account of the Sicilian Vespers is the Tower of London, and also the Bastille, of Naples. A strange procession of uninhibited characters, some of them obviously mad, passed across its stage for centuries, at first Angevins, then Aragonese. The visitor is attracted, or repelled perhaps, by two huge semi-circular entrance towers which hold between them a gay and spirited, and quite ridiculous contrast, in the form of a Renaissance relief which depicts the triumphant entry of Alfonso I into Naples in 1443. The two great masses of mastodonic stone or brick, instead of crushing this incongruous intruder, bear it with almost touching gentleness, as an elephant might be imagined to carry a rose. The castle is not the easiest place to see or the most rewarding. There is nothing of the ruin about it. It has been occupied for centuries and is now full of learned societies.

Its most impressive feature is the Hall of the Barons whose roof is ninety feet high. Its name perpetuates a rather typical event of the Neapolitan Middle Ages. A King of Naples, in order to show his barons that their revolt had been forgiven and forgotten, invited them to a wedding feast, but no sooner were they all happily seated round the tables than the drawbridge was lifted and the guests were taken from the dining hall to the dungeons. Somewhere in the massive building was the cell contrived there for the poor old hermit Pope, Celestine V, whose tomb I had seen in Aquila. Believing every word of the ambitious and violent crooks by whom he was surrounded, the old man was easily influenced to abdicate, greatly assisted in this by a mysterious voice heard at night, which as I have already said, was that of his successor Benedict Caetani (Boniface VIII), whispering down a speaking tube.

Unlike the Tower of London, which seems to have been exorcized, the Castel Nuovo, in spite of the learned societies, is still, I think, badly haunted. I should hate to be the secretary of any society who left any petty cash lying about in this castle since I have little doubt that ghostly Angevin or Aragonese fingers would almost certainly discover it!

It is, however, pleasant to recall the happy reign of Robert the Wise (1309–43) when Petrarch and Boccaccio visited Naples. Those bright days are still reflected in the *Decameron*, which owes more to Naples than to Florence. Two notorious queens haunt the castle, as they do the popular legends of Naples: Joan I, the granddaughter of Robert the Wise, who, after a spectacular career in the course of which she married four husbands and had innumerable lovers, was smothered with a pillow, and her namesake, Joan II, an infinitely more evil character, many of whose sins have probably been heaped upon the head of her predecessor.

Some of the Aragonese kings were not much better than the Angevins; one of them, perhaps inheriting a Moorish strain from Córdoba, loved to preserve the corpses of his enemies; another was reported to have kept a crocodile in a dungeon which from time to time was rewarded with a prisoner.

One accepts such stories with the usual grain of salt, but I must say that the gloomy old castle lends itself to them.

§ 4

One Sunday morning I took the funicular to the summit of the hill behind Naples on which stands the old fort of St Elmo. Though not a breath of wind stirred the trees and the blinds of the expensive flats were pulled down to exclude the sun, it seemed to me cooler than at sea level and the streets were mercifully quiet. One could even cross the road without hoping that one's guardian angel was on duty. Now and again, through gaps in the buildings, I looked down and saw the Bay of Naples far below, curving round to Vesuvius, as in a thousand illustrations and post-cards, with Capri in the distance, and immediately below the crowded roofs and domes of Naples and its busy port.

I came to a restaurant built up on the extreme edge of the hill, where tables were arranged on a terrace which offered an even finer view, if possible, of the Bay and the city. To a clatter of cutlery and backchat, the waiters, smoking cigarettes, were setting the tables for luncheon, their professional manners not yet assumed with their black trousers and aprons. I thought I would return later and lunch there, but I never did so. I found the S. Martino Museum so absorbing that I forgot all about lunch until four o'clock, when the museum closed, and, suddenly finding myself ravenous, entered a humble little *trattoria* where I ate my favourite Neapolitan dish, *mozzarella in carrozza*, a kind of Welsh rarebit made of buffalo cheese. I have not mentioned *mozzarella* before, and I should have done so. Hotels are too grand to put it on the menu. Should you ask for it in a fashionable restaurant, an embarrassed head waiter would react much as one might expect the Ritz to respond to a request for whelks. But *mozzarella in carrozza*, which means buffalo cheese in a carriage, is well worth finding, though it varies widely from place to place. At its best, generally in the most humble of restaurants, it can be superb. The recipes for this dish in Colette Black's *Southern Italian Cookery*, and in Elizabeth David's *Italian Food*, are more elaborate than I should have believed, but that is typical of Italian cooking in general: it is never as simple to make as to eat. As Elizabeth David says, with her infallible wisdom, '*Mozzarella* must be eaten absolutely fresh and dripping with its own buttermilk. . . . As a matter of fact genuine *mozzarella* is becoming increasingly rare, for the simple reason that every year there are fewer and fewer buffaloes in Italy. It is being replaced by *fior di latte* and *scamorza*, the same kind of cheese made with cow's milk but with much less flavour.'

The museum which enchanted me for so many hours is devoted to objects which illustrate the history and the social life of Naples down the centuries. No museum could be more beautifully housed: it occupies a mediaeval monastery, which was rebuilt in the seventeenth century and suppressed in the nineteenth. Here are to be seen pictures, costumes, proclamations, engravings, coins, maps, and a hundred other objects all with some bearing on the life of Naples. The general effect is that of the gilded baroque city of the Spanish viceroys and of the Bourbon Naples that followed. Some of the ninety odd rooms were closed; concealed in one of these, I suppose, must have been the state barge, which I should like to have seen. Ferdinand IV was fond of circling round the Bay of Naples in the cool of the evening, followed by a string orchestra in another barge. It was for such outings, but on more distant and chillier waters, that Handel composed his *Water Music*. Before marriage to Sir William Hamilton made Emma socially accept-able, the King often ordered his barge and his minstrels to approach that of the English Minister, and while he payed her compliments in the Neapolitan dialect, the musicians saluted the English beauty with melodies. After her marriage the Queen received Emma at court, pleased that the King's compliments had not turned her head, probably one of the reasons why the sister of Marie Antoinette and the daughter of a Cheshire blacksmith became such great friends. My failure to find the state barge was in some way compensated by the discovery of the state coach of Charles III, slung like a golden casket between tall, painted wheels.

The most popular sight of S. Martino, certainly with young people, is the *Presepio*, or crib, which stands illuminated behind a plate-glass window. It must be the finest, and also the largest, example ever made of the Nativity scenes which were, and in some places still are, shown in churches and private houses at Christmas time. This elaborate and remarkable work of art shows a rocky landscape covered with hundreds of beautifully carved and painted figures, each one about six inches high. Angels suspended from thin wires float above the remains of a classical temple on a hill-top where the Magi are offering their gifts to the infant Christ. Everywhere are scenes of bustling activity which recall the streets of Naples: men play guitars, women prepare food, shops expose strings of sausages; there are cowherds and shepherds, a party is sitting down to a huge meal under a trellis; and the whole scene is charming and pretty, the result, one fancies, of a loving study of Nativity scenes by the great masters. There was, I thought, a reminiscent touch of Botticelli about it. Among its greatest admirers are the children of Naples, many of whom, in their Sunday clothes, stood with their enchanted faces pressed against the glass, pointing out in whispers to each other a hundred charming details.

The belvedere of the museum is a balcony which offers the finest of all the views of Naples. This must be a marvellous sight at night but, as the museum closes at four, no one is privileged to see it except the caretakers.

I spent half an hour in the aquarium, which I came across by accident in the centre of the public park that lies between the Riviera di Chiaia and the sea. I believe it was the first of its kind when it was opened by Dr Anton Dohrn in 1874, and was one of the great sights of Naples. Until recently the building had the odd distinction of remaining open until ten at night, and sometimes until midnight. In a city where many churches, museums and art galleries close at four, or even at noon, it is strange to think that one could contemplate an octopus until midnight.

I must say I found these creatures fascinating. Dead, flaccid, deflated and in buckets, the octopus is a depressing sight all over the south of Italy, but alive and in movement, I was surprised to see that it is hideous at one moment and quite beautiful the next! Moving by some system of jet propulsion, it ceases for a time, as it rises to the surface of the tank, to be a horrid mass of probing tentacles, and as it moves upward, folding its arms to its sides, it rises like a ballet dancer, giving a brief demonstration of the poetry of movement.

§ 5

Visitors to the Prado in Madrid may remember a portrait by Goya of an old man in hunting dress who grasps a long shot-gun in one hand while, in the other, he holds a white glove. Beneath a tricorn hat, in shape a huge jam-puff, one sees a thin, quizzical face whose most notable feature is the nose. This is Charles III of the Two Sicilies, who inherited the throne of Spain when in middle age. He is a tough old character who looks rather like a gamekeeper, though possibly his cynical air of having weighed a great number of human beings and found them lacking in something, is one not common to gamekeepers. Still, that rustic air, which so many of the Italians and Spanish Bourbons possessed, is a curious trait to occur in such a blue-blooded family.

Charles was the son of the first Bourbon King of Spain, Philip V, by his second wife, Elizabeth Farnese of Parma. When her son was sixteen she sent him from Spain to rule Parma, then two years later, after a not very serious military engagement, he became King of Naples and Sicily. Charles liked Naples and Naples liked him. He married Amalia of Saxony in Naples and there his family was born. It is usual to describe such eighteenth century monarchs as 'benevolent despots', and the phrase fits well. 'Everything for the people,' was his motto, 'but nothing by them.' He was incurably paternal and loved to make minor reforms, such as forbidding people to fling their slops out of the window or to wear a certain kind of hat.

He found some relief from the appalling melancholy which afflicted the Bourbons, as the Hapsburgs before them, by shooting and building. No one can spend even a day in Naples and fail to see something built by Charles III. His architectural achievements include the San Carlo Opera House, the Palace of Capodimonte, the colossal poor-house in the Piazza Carlo III, and the Palace of Caserta. He must have expended his architectural energies in Naples for when he became King of Spain he added nothing to the buildings of that country except the palace in which General Franco lives, El Pardo, outside Madrid.

When Charles inherited Spain he was forty-three. It is typical of him that no recorded outburst of anger or sorrow at exchanging the land he loved, and the exquisite Bay of Naples, for the aridity of Madrid, ever passed his lips. He went off like a good branch manager who has been appointed to the head office. He knew that it would have to happen some day. There must, nevertheless, have been one extremely painful scene. That was the meeting of a committee of officials and doctors appointed to decide whether his eldest son, Philip, aged twelve, was fit to succeed to the throne. The finding was that the Prince was hopelessly insane and would have to be debarred from the succession.

Leaving the unfortunate heir in charge of doctors and guardians in the Palace at Naples, Charles and his Queen left for Spain with their second son, who in time became Charles IV of Spain, and was also painted, quite ruthlessly, by Goya. This left a third son, Ferdinand, who was proclaimed Ferdinand IV of Naples. It is said that the two princes discussed their inheritances. 'I am destined to rule the largest dominions in the two worlds', said Charles, aged eleven, to which Ferdinand, aged eight, is said to have replied, 'Yes; you may rule one day, but I am a king already.'

If he really did say this, it was probably his brightest recorded observation. He grew up completely uneducated. With the lunatic brother in mind, his father, before leaving for Spain, gave strict orders that Ferdinand's brain was never to be overtaxed, thus from the start he had the upper hand with his tutors. The only things he cared for were hunting and fishing and mixing with the lowest grade of his subjects, the *lazzaroni*, whose dialect he spoke all his life. They loved him for it but others found him rather trying. He married Maria Carolina of Austria, the sister of Marie Antoinette, who once described him to her brother, the Emperor Joseph: '*Er ist ein recht guter Narr*' – 'He is a right good fool.'

I was always delighted and at the same time irritated by the Piazza del Plebiscito, which has on one side the Royal Palace and the Opera House and, on the other, the church of S. Francesco di Paola, an architectural echo of the Pantheon and of Bernini's colonnade. It is depressing that the noblest architectural composition in Naples should be ruined by hundreds of motor cars parked in the great circular space in front of the palace.

Above the rows of machines, which resemble an advertisement for the annual output of the Fiat company, rides in bronze, and in a toga, Charles III, looking younger than Goya knew him, and his companion on the other side of the square, is his son and successor in Naples, Ferdinand IV. Every day, as I passed this place, which should be one of the finest sights in Naples, I asked myself, 'If nothing can be done to close cities, or portions of cities, to private motor cars, is it impossible to prevent them from invading such architectural unities as the Piazza del Plebiscito?'

I went to the Palace eager to see the stage on which so many tragic and ludicrous events had occurred, so well described by Harold Acton in the two most readable books about Italian history to be written in our time – *The Bourbons of Naples* and *The Last Bourbons of Naples*. As I walked through the succession of ante-rooms with their perfectly aligned chandeliers, with pompous riders prancing within gold frames on each side of me, I thought of the poor mad prince of Naples who was hidden away here. Palaces are well designed to conceal such tragedies. Princes must always smile and look happy, and be bronzed and fit, and of all the buildings through which crowds trail curiously, peering and wondering, palaces are perhaps the most deceptive as they are certainly the most monotonous.

Sir William Hamilton told many stories about the mad Prince Philip to Nathaniel Wraxall, who preserved them in his *Memoirs*. 'He attained to manhood,' wrote Wraxall, 'and was treated with a certain distinction, having chamberlains placed about him in constant attendance who watched him with unremitting attention, as otherwise he would have committed a thousand excesses. Care was particularly taken to keep him from having any communication with the other sex, for which he manifested the strongest propensity; but it became at last impossible to prevent him altogether from attempting to emancipate himself in this respect. He has many times eluded the vigilance of his keepers, and, on seeing ladies pass through the apartments of the palace, would attack them with the same impetuosity as Pan or the satyrs are described by Ovid when pursuing the nymphs, and with the same intentions. More than one lady of the court has been critically rescued from his embraces. On particular days of the year he was allowed to hold a sort of court or levee, when the foreign Ministers repaired to his apartments to pay their compliments to him; but his greatest amusement consisted in having his hand held up by attendants, while gloves were put on it, one larger than another, to the number of fifteen or sixteen.'

Ferdinand IV was touchingly attached to his unfortunate brother, and often visited him. Now and then Philip was dressed up and taken for a drive through Naples to show the people that the government's conduct was justified. These must have been anything but pleasant processions, since it was possible to see at a glance that the Prince was an idiot. He died at the age of thirty, it was said of smallpox.

To me, it is his hearty brother, the 'guter Narr', who really haunts the Palace of Naples, an odd character who might have been invented by Fielding or Surtees. With absentee parents and tutors who had been commanded to let him have his own way, he grew up to be an uncouth character. It would have taken an exceptional tutor in the eighteenth century to have placed a reigning king across his knees, but it might have done him some good. As it was, he grew up with grooms, fishermen and hunt servants and beggars, speaking their dialect and known to them affectionately as 'King Nosey', a reference to this Bourbon feature. His lifelong passion for hunting amounted to mania. He was metaphorically and literally soaked in the blood of wild boars, deer and other animals. Sir William Hamilton, who happened to be a good shot, immediately endeared himself to Ferdinand and was his companion on many a gory day. Hamilton said that at the end of a shoot the King would strip and put on a flannel dress in which, with a dexterity that no butcher could have exceeded, he gutted and cut up the carcasses. 'He was frequently besmeared with blood from head to foot before he had finished'.

His wife, Maria Carolina, the daughter of the Austrian Empress, Maria Louisa, was a different character: she was interested in public affairs and was consumed by a loathing for the nation that had guillotined her sister, Marie Antoinette. It was Ferdinand, Maria Carolina and their family whom Nelson smuggled out of Naples to Sicily to save the Bourbon dynasty during the brief Parthenopian Republic. As the French armies approached Naples, the Queen was convinced that the guillotine was to be set up in the capital; and she may have been right. By this time Lady Hamilton had become her devoted friend and busied herself with the problem of saving the royal family. As the only female representative near the throne of the nation that was saving Europe by its example, it may have seemed that for a moment the mantle of Britannia herself had descended upon the pretty shoulders of one so famous for dramatic draperies. The strictest secrecy was maintained for days before the flight, while treasures and money valued at more than two million sterling were transferred to Nelson's flagship, *Vanguard*. Melodramatic precautions were taken in the Palace. The royal party was to steal away by means of a secret passage that linked the Palace with one of the landing stages. The passwords were in English. 'All goes well,' meant that it was safe to embark; 'All is wrong, you may go back', meant that something unforeseen had changed the situation. Fortunately all was well and the royal party sailed for Sicily in the worst December storm that even Nelson could remember. One of the princes died in Emma Hamilton's arms during the hurricane, and the Austrian Ambassador threw a valuable snuffbox overboard because it contained a nude portrait of his mistress, considering it 'impious' to retain such an object on the edge of Eternity. Sir William Hamilton quietly loaded his pistols and was ready to commit suicide rather than to die by drowning. Fortunately the weather improved and the King remarked to Sir William, scenting the wind, 'We shall have plenty of woodcock.'

It was interesting to recall such events as I was shown over the Palace. I mentioned the secret passage to the Arsenal Quay, but the guide had never heard of it.

The exile of the Bourbon court to Palermo marks the depth of Nelson's love, or infatuation, for Lady Hamilton, and he was often noticed seated asleep behind his mistress at the gaming tables. At that time Emma was about thirty-four, Nelson was forty-one, and Sir William Hamilton was sixty-nine. Some will always suspect that the old diplomat, who had often been cynically aware of the age gap between himself and Emma, had a shrewd idea that the man he admired so much had deceived him with his wife. In any event the child Horatia, who was so secretly born in

London nine months after, under another name, was conceived in Palermo. Four years later, in England, Sir William died, with Emma holding one hand and Nelson the other: six years later Nelson died at Trafalgar with Emma's name upon his lips. Sixteen years later Emma Hamilton died in poverty in Calais, unloved uncared for and forgotten.

There is always an 'if' in history. What would have happened had Nelson survived to marry Emma Hamilton? The surgeons said that his body and his vital organs were more like those of a young lad than of a war veteran of forty-seven. There is a hint in one of his letters that he might have retired with Emma to the Sicilian estate at Bronte which Ferdinand IV gave him as a reward for saving the dynasty.

There seemed to me little to say about the Palace itself except that it appeared to possess the usual number of red and gold chairs, its proper collection of flattering portraits, its correct series of inter-communicating rooms, except this extraordinary story – surely one of the oddest of British naval manoeuvres – when an admiral in love with the British Ambassador's wife saved a dynasty.

§ 6

Though the San Carlo Opera House was closed, I was politely shown over a hushed and shrouded building. As I waited for some time at the stage door entrance, I observed the arrival of singers and musicians, perhaps for rehearsals, possibly for auditions, some trying to conceal their nervousness beneath masks of improbable gaiety, others professionally invincible; and so they passed through the swing doors, inhabitants of the mysterious world of music. I listened fascinated, as I waited, to the inner regions beyond the swing doors which echoed to scraps of song, or to a remote trumpet call as if to some lost cause, but suddenly terminated as though the trumpeter had been slain. There were far-off pipings which suggested that perhaps imprisoned shepherds were trying to communicate with, or console, one another.

I was led across the vast, empty and intimidating stage of the

San Carlo. In the centre of that bleak desert a girl wearing tights and a jumper was slowly and deliberately standing upon blue satin toes and pirouetting like a figure in a dream. She was a pretty girl and looked like a fairy lost in a furniture repository. Suddenly she darted, still on her toes, to a dusty and squalid corner where she bent forward charmingly with one hand to an ear as if listening for a message, then, as though realizing that she had come to the wrong meeting-place, she vanished in a series of little tripping steps into the shadows. A few puny lights were turned on which vaguely illuminated the auditorium with its rows of boxes and the royal box flanked by two more than life-sized palm trees, but I could perceive nothing of the magnificence which amazed the President de Brosses, so that he confessed himself 'terror stricken'. What I did think was that, of all buildings seen *en déshabille*, an opera house is probably the most distressing. Designed for light, for music, for jewelled women, such buildings, when gaunt and unlit, with a cleaner banging round with a broom and exchanging pleasantries in the vernacular with an electrician in the roof, strip the magic world of Carmen and Mimi of the last shred of romance.

My guide, suddenly walking downhill, and how steep these stages are, sent forth a tenor trill into the musty air, inviting me to do the same. I have rarely been more embarrassed. Unable to sing a note, yet unwilling to be silent upon the stage of the San Carlo, I stood forward and while a sweeper somewhere was busy with brush and pan, began 'God save', but, finding that I had selected too high a key, started again with 'God save our gracious Queen'; and so managed to awaken a few echoes and to say that I had sung on the stage of the San Carlo. Insincerity and politeness achieved a climax when my guide murmured 'bravo'.

The interior of the theatre had been destroyed by fire in 1816, but was admired and described in 1786 by an English surgeon, Samuel Sharp of Guy's Hospital, London, who, while travelling for his health, wrote some observant *Letters from Italy*. As one would expect from a surgeon, they are crisp, and sometimes cutting. 'The Pit here,' he wrote 'is very ample; it contains betwixt five and six hundred seats, with arms resembling a large elbow chair, besides an interval all through the middle, and a circuit all

round it, under the boxes. . . . The seat of each chair lifts up like
the lid of a box, and has a lock to fasten it. There are in Naples
gentlemen enough to hire for the year the first four rows next to
the orchestra; who take the key of the chair home with them,
when the Opera is finished, lifting up the seat and having it
locked. By this contrivance they are always sure of the same place
at whatever hour they please to go to the Opera; nor do they disturb the audience, as the intervals betwixt the rows are wide
enough to admit a lusty man to walk to his chair without obliging
anybody to rise.'

In the year following the fire, the theatre, reconstructed with
astonishing speed, was reopened. Perhaps the Milanese had this in
mind when they restored the bombed La Scala in record time
after the last war. Stendhal, to whom life without opera would
have been pointless, came from Rome especially to attend the re-
opening of the San Carlo. He was in ecstasies. He described the
details, the colour scheme, the boxes, and preserved a curious
memory of the opening night. A cloud of dark smoke invaded the
auditorium, which alarmed the audience so much that had royalty
not been present Stendhal thought there might have been a rush
for the doors. It was not smoke, however, but fog caused by the
drying out of the new building.

One of the peculiarities of the San Carlo during the Bourbon
period was that the ballerinas wore black drawers by royal decree,
that colour being considered less provocative than others and so
(incredible to relate) less perilous to the morals of Naples.

I went with my acquaintance across the road to the Galleria,
which will probably remain for ever the American Army's pre-
dominant memory of this city. While we drank several cups of
bitter and corrosive *espresso*, I happened to ask how often Caruso,
one of Naples' most famous sons, had sung at the San Carlo. He
told me this story.

Caruso, he said, one of a family of eighteen in a Naples slum,
was born with a golden larynx. After he had sung his way in
triumph through Italy, the moment came when he was offered an
engagement at the San Carlo. For some reason which was not
clear to me, he roused the enmity of a claque, who hissed him.

Though he finished the opera, and his engagement, he swore that never again would he sing in his native city; neither would he ever return to Naples, except to eat a plate of spaghetti. And he kept his word.

'Some men are strange,' said my acquaintance, shaking his head, and thinking maybe of some of the temperaments he had encountered across the road. Then he shook hands and walked back to the theatre.

I was detained by the shoeblacks who have established themselves at the entrance to the Galleria where, with Spanish insistence, they crack their brushes at you, call you 'duca' or 'professore' or 'capitano', according to your age and appearance, and generally bully you to have your shoes cleaned. They can look at a perfectly clean pair of shoes with such disparagement that the sensitive wearer feels he has been wading through mud. Whoever succumbs to them is waved to a baroque chair or rather throne, the kind of seat in which Titian painted Popes, decorated with brass nails and finials. Thus enthroned like some eastern monarch with a kneeling slave before him, the client is given the full Madrid treatment. Slips of cardboard are inserted to guard his socks from damage, liquid is smeared on his shoes, which are polished first with brushes, then with fabrics and, finally, with a pad. Such a man can then descend from his throne and go with God.

Other relics of the Spanish occupation to be noticed in Naples are the use of the title 'don' (unhappily on the decline), gory crucifixes, formal compliments (Luigi Barzini called Naples 'the capital of meaningless flattery'), and love of titles.

§ 7

The Hamilton period in Naples was a brief thirty-five years of enchantment during which *Vedi Napoli e poi muori* – 'See Naples and die' – was substituted for the more exciting promise of an earlier generation, *'Ecce Roma!'* A brilliant and friendly royal court ruled by an Italian version of Squire Western, together with delightful palaces which could be rented with gilt furniture and beguiling servants, made Naples an attractive city for the rich and well-born. Sir William Hamilton, British Minister, moved everywhere, urbane, cultivated and admired by all, studying volcanoes, collecting Greek pots, writing a treatise for the Royal Society, holding open house for his nation's migrants, an indispensable companion to the King during his majesty's devastating visits to the countryside. It is doubtful whether British diplomacy can find a better example of the right man in the right spot at the right moment. His varied interests were those of the dilettante of the period. One is grateful to the observer who once saw him in court dress helping a ragged workman to carry a basketful of Greek vases.

Sometimes a man on horseback would arrive with news of a world beyond the magic Bay, but this would be already two or three weeks old. No disembodied tones announced themselves to be 'The Voice of America'; no dazed, untidy traveller descended from the sky with disturbing rumours from distant places; it was thus possible for the visitor to achieve a detachment which is no longer possible anywhere; and reading the diaries and letters written in Naples from 1764 to 1799, one finds no mention of the outside world, no murmur of Bunker's Hill, no angry shouts from the Gordon Rioters, even accounts of the Bastille were not allowed to interfere with dinner parties. Nevertheless, it was the guillotine that at last concluded the Neapolitan Elysium and with the execution of the French Queen, the happy dream came to an end. Goethe, Mrs Piozzi, William Beckford, and many more, have described how enchanting it was while it lasted.

William Hamilton was the fourth son of Lord Archibald Hamilton and Lady Jane Hamilton, daughter of the Earl of Abercorn. When he was twenty-eight he married Catherine Barlow of Lawrenny Hall, Pembrokeshire, a delicate and charming young heiress who adored him. When he was thirty-four, Hamilton was appointed to Naples, where he and Catherine lived a happy life together for twenty-four years. Sorrow touched them when their only child, a daughter, died. When Dr Burney, in the course of his musical tour of Europe, visited Naples, he said that in his opinion Catherine Hamilton was the best harpsichord player there.

So to the sound of a harpsichord played in a music room with a view of Vesuvius, the first Lady Hamilton passed from history. So too might her husband, diplomat, writer, scientist, the author of the first and still the most sumptuous book on Naples and its volcano, the first scholarly collector of Greek vases, the first who saw the importance of Pompeii and Herculaneum; even he might have been remembered only by bibliophiles, had he not, when an elderly widower, taken over his nephew's beautiful young mistress, Emma Lyon or Hart.

That a young man should be anxious to transfer a beautiful young mistress to an uncle for no material gain, but merely to rid himself of her, is sufficiently unusual to suggest the eighteenth century stage; it is a theme that would have appealed to Sheridan. The reason was that Charles Greville, the nephew, had befriended the desperate Emma during a pregnancy ('What shall I dow? Good God, what shall I dow?' she had written in her characteristic spelling) and Charles had installed her with her mother in a little house at Edgware Row, then on the edge of the country. Emma fell passionately and possessively in love with her gallant benefactor and, to please him, was only too willing to learn to behave like a lady. But the time came when Greville, who was poor, was on the look out for an heiress with at least £30,000, and he realized that he did not stand a chance unless he could rid himself of the lovely, clinging Emma and her mother. What could have been more convenient than a rich, distinguished, widowed uncle who lived in Naples?

Emma Hamilton is one of the leading examples of female adaptability and of the genius which some women possess of acquiring superficial knowledge, together with speech, manners and social attitudes different from those into which they were born. Such gifts, in her case, were assisted by great beauty, by warmth of heart and by fidelity. She was the daughter of a blacksmith on the borders of Cheshire and Lancashire of whom nothing is known save his name, Henry Lyon, which he signed by making a cross. Her mother, however, who never left her side, and to whom Emma was devoted, was of different clay, Though also illiterate at the time of Emma's birth, she had the ability to rise

17 A (*above*) Old city of Taranto with Aragonese castle in foreground, the sea to left, the lagoon to right

17B (*below, left*) Street in Old City, Taranto. C (*right*) Dredging up ropes of oysters, Taranto

18A (*above*) Mussel cultivation in the lagoon, Taranto

18B (*below, left*) Greek dancers (first century B.C.) found at Taranto. C (*right*) Greek terracotta (B.C.), Taranto Museum

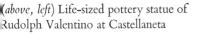
(*above, left*) Life-sized pottery statue of Rudolph Valentino at Castellaneta

(*above, right*) Pupil vase-painter at Grottaglie

(*right, centre*) Amphorae made at Grottaglie

(*below*) All that remains of Metapontum

20 The dead cave city of Matera

(*above*) Tomb of Pope Gregory VII at Salerno

(*below, left*) Eleventh century ᴄosmati pulpit, Salerno Cathedral

(*right*) Cosmati pulpit, Ravello Cathedral

22A (*above*) The celebrated view of Naples with the Castel dell' Ovo jutting out to sea on right and Vesuvius in background

22B (*below*) Cloister of the Carthusian Monastery of S. Martino, Naples, now a museum

23A (*above*) The Acropolis at Cumae

23B (*below*) The cave of the Sibyl of Cumae

24 The Diana Fountain, the Palace of Caserta, Naples

socially and to accompany her daughter on her dazzling upper flight. Known later (no one knows why) by the aristocratic name of Mrs Cadogan, mother and daughter were to form a powerful combination though the old lady never managed entirely to cast off all trace of her origin, but remained a much liked and reliable old character in a mob-cap. ('I love Mrs Cadogan,' Nelson once wrote. 'The King says my mother is an angel,' Emma was to write of Mrs Cadogan's effect upon Frederick IV.)

Greville had begun the education of Emma but the real Professor Higgins was Sir William Hamilton. When he was in London in 1784 – Emma was then nineteen – Greville's plot came to a head and it was suggested that perhaps Mrs Cadogan and her daughter might like a holiday in Italy where Emma could continue her studies under classic skies. It was just a holiday, nothing more. They travelled overland and Sir William met them in Naples. Emma was given a suite of four rooms in the Palazzo Sessa, which was Sir William's public and private residence. In those days it had a view straight out across the Bay. Here Emma took lessons in French and Italian, in singing and in other subjects, though her spelling always remained more than a little wilful. As time went on, her letters to Greville became emotional, passionate, and angry. She could never love anyone but him! Why had he deserted her? However, she continued to be suffocated with kindness and enchanted by admiration. One suspects at this point some worldly advice from a worthy old character in a mob-cap, since the time soon came when she was Sir William's mistress and confessed that now she was able to love him alone.

For six years the happy state lasted. Emma Hart became one of the sights of Naples. She was admired by all and loved by the greatest connoisseur of the time. Her beauty and her talents conquered not only the most sophisticated members of society but also simple Neapolitans who more than once compared her appearance with that of the Virgin Mary. In the year 1791, when he was more than sixty and she was nearly thirty, Hamilton took her and Mrs Cadogan to London, where he and Emma were married. She who, as his mistress, had already intrigued and captivated Naples, now, as Lady Hamilton, entered royal circles and vanquished even that forbidding queen, Maria Carolina. It seemed that Venus, but a faithful Venus wearing a wedding ring, and one who could be true only to the British Minister, had arisen anew from the exquisite waters of the Bay.


Wishing to walk through the rooms where Lady Hamilton had held her court and had performed her famous 'Attitudes', I asked the way to the Palazzo Sessa, but could find few who had ever heard of it, and these thought that it had been pulled down. At last the office of the British Consulate-General recollected that someone long ago had made the same enquiry, and eventually I was directed to the old Pizzafalcone quarter at the back of my hotel, and to the Vico Santa Maria a Capella Vecchia.

A steep street was lined with small shops and workshops where, in typical Neapolitan style, cobblers and a man mending an old chair were at work on the pavement, chatting all the time to friends and passers-by. The street terminated in an archway which led to a courtyard in which a number of cars were parked. I asked a woman if the building, whose windows and balconies rose above us, was the Palazzo Sessa, but she did not know. I could imagine a time before it had been divided into flats when carriages would drive in under the arch and after encircling the courtyard would draw up at the main entrance opposite, which still seemed to retain just the faintest touch of grandeur. The wide stone steps of dark volcanic stone were those of a house of quality, but they led now to flats and passages. The only thing to do was to ring bells and bang knockers until I found someone who could answer my question.

The second door I tried was opened cautiously, just sufficiently for me to see a room beyond piled high with old furniture, chests, tables and beds one on top of the other. The old man in charge of this treasure trove had never heard of the Palazzo Sessa and believed that I had come for a bulky object wrapped in brown paper, which he attempted to foist upon me. I then tried a more prosperous staircase and came to an imposing flat. The bell was answered by an elderly man-servant in a white jacket. When I had asked my question, he bowed gravely and said that he would consult his employer. He motioned me towards a renaissance chair, a splendid aristocratic version of the shoe-shine thrones of the Galleria, while he vanished behind a tapestry. He returned to say, yes, this was indeed the Palazzo Sessa but, alas, the marchesa, who was no longer young, was also unwell, and regretted that she could not receive me. What could have been more courteous? I felt that the diplomatic manners of the days of George III still lingered in the old building.

I found what I think may be a fragment of the old palace in a corner flat whose windows now look down upon a slum and whose view of the Bay has been obscured by tall modern buildings that now intervene between it and the sea. Once the windows must have offered an uninterrupted view of the Bay from the Castel dell'Ovo and eastward to Vesuvius. I wondered if this were a part of the celebrated room in which Lady Hamilton gave her entertainments. Assisted by a shawl or two, she adopted a number of poses which enraptured society while her adoring husband illuminated her with a lighted candle. Goethe probably gave the best account. He was invited to see the 'Attitudes' in March, 1787, three years after Emma's arrival in Naples and three years before she became the second Lady Hamilton. He wrote:

'Sir William Hamilton, who still resides here as ambassador from England, has at length, after his long love of art, and long study, discovered the most perfect of the admirers of nature and art in a beautiful young woman. She lives with him: an English woman of about twenty years old. She is very handsome, and of a beautiful figure. The old knight has had made for her a Greek costume, which becomes her extremely. Dressed in this, and letting her hair loose, and taking a couple of shawls, she exhibits every possible variety of posture, expression and look, so that at the last the spectator almost fancies it is a dream. One beholds here in perfection, in movement, in ravishing variety, all that the greatest artists have rejoiced to be able to produce. Standing, kneeling, sitting, lying down, grave or sad, playful, exulting, repentant, wanton, menacing, anxious – all mental states follow rapidly one after another. With wonderful taste she suits the folding of her veil to each expression, and with the same handkerchief makes every kind of head-dress. The old knight holds the light for her, and enters into the exhibition with his whole soul. He thinks he can discern in her a resemblance to all the most famous antiques, all the beautiful profiles on the Sicilian coins – aye, of the Apollo Belvedere itself. This much at any rate is certain – the entertainment is unique. We spent two evenings on it with thorough enjoyment.'

Perhaps from the windows of this room, I thought, when England and France were at war, six years later, those who looked out just as it was getting dark on the evening of September 12, 1793, would have seen an English warship come to anchor in the Bay. *H.M.S. Agamemnon* was carrying despatches from Lord Hood for Sir William Hamilton. Her captain, Horatio Nelson, had just finished writing a letter to his wife in England. 'My poor fellows,' he wrote, 'have not had a morsel of fresh meat or vegetables for near nineteen weeks, and in that time I have only had my foot twice on shore, at Cadiz. We are absolutely sick with fatigue . . .' In the morning Nelson in full dress uniform was rowed ashore to deliver his despatches. He and Sir William liked each other at sight, and Hamilton invited Nelson to stay in the Palazzo Sessa during his brief stay in Naples. He accepted. Sir William told Emma that she was about to meet a little man who could not be called handsome but one who, so Hamilton thought, might one day astonish the world. Writing later on to his wife, Nelson described Lady Hamilton as 'a young woman of amiable manners, and who does honour to the station to which she is raised.'

The fate of the Palazzo Sessa is interesting. During the French occupation of 1799, it was sacked by revolutionary mobs and, in the course of a bombardment of the city ordered by Nelson, a shot aimed at the St Elmo battery on the hill behind fell short and exploded there, doing great damage. The building was, of course, empty at the time, Sir William and Lady Hamilton having left for Sicily with the royal family. Fortunately, several cases of Greek vases were saved and dispatched to England in *H.M.S. Colossus,* which, to Sir William's sorrow, sank in a storm off the Scilly Isles. Happily some of the crates were saved from the wreck, but others which have never been recovered possibly even now offer a reward greater than pieces of eight to those who dive for treasure in those parts.

In later years, when the Hamiltons were settled in England, Nelson put into the Bay of Naples in the course of his duty. He wrote to Emma Hamilton that her old home had become an hotel.

§ 8

The professor was an unusual Neapolitan type: small, rotund, shaggy and merry, indeed he reminded me of an overfed Irish terrier. He was one of those fat men who cheerfully accept their weight and go bouncing happily through life full of carbohydrates and high spirits. Having met the same Sancho Panzas in Spain, I suspected that perhaps he was of Neapolitan-Spanish descent.

He took me to Caserta in a small, angry-looking red Fiat into which he was so firmly fixed that I begged him on his arrival not to detach himself to perform the usual courtesies. I thought that he drove well through Naples where I noted with satisfaction that his brakes were working. But the moment we entered the autostrada his manner and his merry quips ceased. Crouching over the wheel with a reckless swaying motion of the body, he put down his foot and with a kind of snarl passed Ferraris and Masaratis, and everything else in the way. This transformation of Faust into Mephistopheles will be familiar to anyone who has motored in Italy.

'I think it would be good to drink some beer!' he shouted above the noise of his engine.

'A splendid idea!', I shouted back, thinking that any stationary act would be welcome.

He turned off the autostrada into an unspoilt pocket of country where ox carts were climbing a hill through vineyards. We had returned to the Middle Ages in a few hundred yards from the modern Via Appia. We came to a picturesque hill town one of whose highest points was occupied by an *osteria* with a superb view of the plain below. We sat beneath a vine trellis while a girl brought us Neapolitan lager. This town, explained the professor, was Old Caserta, a place now rarely visited and almost deserted since the eighteenth century when the building of the palace of Caserta drew the population down to the plain.

We visited a beautiful mediaeval church whose nave was a collection of unmatched Byzantine columns and many a Norman arch; and outside we admired old houses nodding together across a tiny piazza, and a campanile whose lower portion was an archway. The professor told me that only about two hundred people now live there in blessed freedom from mechanical noise. The little red Fiat was the only visible motor car in the town.

He agreed that buildings, together with money, are among the few inanimate objects capable of reproducing themselves. This is especially true of cathedrals and palaces, which often have not only parents but uncles and aunts, and illegitimate cousins. For example, Versailles has fathered many a Bourbon palace, among those that come to mind being La Granja, near Segovia, in Spain, which French Philip V built to assuage his homesickness. The professor was ready to argue – for the sake of argument, I think – that the palace at Caserta was also a reflection of Versailles, but I rather doubt this. Charles III was by nature a builder but, unlike his father, he had no nostalgic longing for France. He had been born in Spain and had become King of Naples at sixteen; at twenty-one he had built the San Carlo Opera House and the following year he began the huge palace of Capodimonte, which is now full of the attractive white porcelain which he sponsored to please his wife; and Caserta, impressive even among palaces, was built when he was in his late thirties.

'But I insist that, like a true Bourbon,' said the professor, 'he was haunted, as they all were, by Versailles.'

'Or was it the Escorial?' I asked.

Descending to the plain, we came to a straggling and featureless town stretching on both sides of the colossal palace. Tourist coaches were arriving in the forecourt and were permitted to go in under the archways and drive through the gardens to the cascades. The professor told me that when Charles III decided to demolish the hunting lodge which once stood there and to build the palace, he found that all the best architects were working for the Pope in Rome. He would have liked the Neapolitan Nicholas Salvi to be his architect but he was wrestling with the final stages of the Trevi Fountain and was unable to leave Rome. Fortunately Luigi Vanvitelli was not working on St Peter's, or any other church, and was available. This famous architect was not an Italian but the son of the Dutch painter Gaspar van Wittel, not too impenetrably Italianized as Vanvitelli.

Soon came the day in 1752 when the ground plan of the vast building was outlined by lines of infantry and cavalry, with cannons mounted at the corners. From a pavilion erected in the centre of the site stepped Charles III with Maria Amalia of Saxony, and, with a silver trowel and hammer, he laid the foundation stone. The regal bricklayer presented the silver implements to Vanvitelli, who sent them as votive offerings to St Philip Neri in Rome.

An army of stone masons, reinforced by gangs of criminals and galley slaves, worked on the site for years, cutting and erecting mountains of stone and unloading from ox-wagons every variety of marble produced in Italy.

We stood looking at the terrific façade, the largest palace ever built in a small kingdom.

'What a superb piece of megalomania!' exclaimed the professor. 'How I wish I could indulge myself like that! What would I build? Perhaps a gigantic mausoleum for dead lecturers! But, seriously,' he continued, 'how infinitely preferable this expression of megalomania was to that of Hitler and Mussolini. Let us have a hundred Casertas rather than some "ism" and a world war. It is the fashion to be hard on kings and especially on the Bourbons, who were not bad, and Charles III was the best of the lot. And he squared his conscience by building an even larger palace for paupers, the *Albergo dei Poveri*, which occupies an entire side of the Piazza Carlo III in Naples. Every tourist comes to see Caserta, but no one ever goes to see its poor relation!'

We ascended a staircase such as Hollywood has never erected in its most grandiose moments; above was a lovely marble dome in which a string orchestra would play when Charles III ascended the shallow steps, and all round were marbles of green, white, black and red. The royal entry must have been an absorbing scene: Charles in his shabby old clothes, his sad, cynical face with its long nose and undercut chin reflecting the Bourbon melancholy, as he, who was only really happy with a gun and a retriever, entered the magnificence, which, by some strange psychological freak or paradox, he had created.

We progressed through the usual palatial apartments, admiring some pleasant portraits, many gilt tables and those huge uncomfortable-looking curtained beds found in all palaces, wondering, as we went from splendour to splendour, where royal families really lived in such places; whether, hidden away and not shown to visitors, are perhaps quite ordinary rooms of normal size where the king might take a nap and a queen might eat bread and honey.

Curiously enough, there happens to be a record that in later years, during the reign of Ferdinand II, a court official visited the palace at Caserta to show the king a loaf of the bread that was being baked for the poor during an epidemic. As this official tramped through the reception rooms, he noticed clothes hung up to dry in a marble hall, and, reaching the royal apartments, found the King nursing an infant while the Queen sat nearby sewing and rocking a cradle. As the official produced the loaf of bread the infant in the King's arms set up a howl and attempted to seize it. 'Do give him a slice,' said Ferdinand, 'or he will never allow us to talk.'

We continued to walk from hall, to hall sated by marble and admiring some nice pieces of French furniture perhaps imported by Murat during a Bourbon interregnum. All trace of the last war when Caserta was 'G.H.Q., C.M.F.' have been removed, at least we could discover none of them. The headquarters of the British-American command in Italy were quaintly described by General Eisenhower in his *Crusade in Europe* as 'a castle near Naples', and inaccurately by Field Marshal Lord Alexander in his memoirs as 'built about the same time as Versailles.' It was here, in April 1945, that Lord Alexander accepted the surrender of the German forces in Italy.

It was delightful to explore the park and gardens. The enormously long Dutch-looking canal suggested that Vanvitelli was, after all, van Wittel, and at the end of it in remote perspective (we were glad to be able to take the red fury there), we came upon the greatest attraction of Caserta, the cascades. A delightful life-sized group of unclothed and half-clothed maidens stands reflected in water upon artfully disposed rocks. It is a scene which no one with a camera can resist, and small wonder, since it is among the most photogenic groups of statuary in Italy. These are Diana and her maidens who were surprised while bathing by Actaeon and his hounds, and, as a punishment, the unfortunate Actaeon was transformed into a stag. The group showing Actaeon, still a man but growing antlers at an alarming rate, was particularly fine, and I admired the dog knowledge of the sculptor who had cleverly indicated the bewilderment of the hounds as they watched their master gradually changing, some of them hesitating to attack him while there remained something human about him which they were able to recognize.

'Don't you think it interesting', asked the professor, 'that though female anatomy has not changed, the female forms here are definitely period in appearance? No similar group of modern girls would look quite like these nymphs of Diana?'

But I refused to be drawn into this.


§ 9

We drove on to Capua, which is only a few miles away, where, as at Caserta, there is an old town and a new one. We went to Old Capua – Capua Vetere – where I saw with delight in the afternoon sunlight the ruins of an amphitheatre which in size and in its state of preservation rivals the Colosseum in Rome. There was not a soul there. The professor and I wandered all over the grassy giant as if we were the solitary figures in some print by Piranesi, an unusual experience these days when ladies from Bradford and Kansas City are so often to be found seated upon the most remote altars.

The circus was the largest in Italy until the Colosseum was built and as a ruin, and also as an example of back-stage complications with traces of the subterranean cages and hoists, was, I thought, more interesting than the Colosseum. Old Capua is the site of the great city, the capital of Roman Campania, which disgraced itself by making friends with Hannibal. It was not only the largest but the richest city of the south, a kind of Campanian Paris famed for its good living, which was said to recall the indulgence of Sybaris, and for the beauty and gaiety of its women. The ancient writers mention that a whole street of Capua was devoted to the sale of perfumes. Livy blamed a touch of fecklessness on 'the licence of the common people who enjoyed unlimited freedom'. The historian was evidently not an enthusiastic democrat.

Capua opened her gates to Hannibal and allowed the Carthaginian army to winter there because she believed that Hannibal would conquer Rome and that when that had happened she would become the most important city in Italy. The welcome given to the Carthaginians, and the enthusiasm with which the women of Capua greeted so many varied new boy friends, has been blamed for the fact that Hannibal never again won a victory; though that is not entirely true. It is true, however, that when the army took to the field again the desertion rate was high as soldiers fled back to the brothels and the night spots and to the arms of their sweethearts. Instead of being grateful to Capua for having caused such psychological havoc, Rome, when the tide began to turn in her favour, revenged herself savagely upon the traitor city. She slew or imprisoned the nobles and the members of the Senate, at the same time reducing the capital of Campania to the rank of the most humble provincial town. Livy tells how some of the leading citizens held banquets when, after getting drunk, they took poison.

The professor sat on a stone in the amphitheatre, smoking a cigarette and looking like a plump Italian *elfo*.

'The story of Capua and its effect on Hannibal's troops is the most human of the Punic wars,' he said, 'and, sad as it may be, as a student of human frailty I can sympathize with those poor fellows so far from home who went back there. Can you imagine the conversations that went on in Hannibal's camps during the campaign that followed, the reminiscences, the comparing of delicious experiences, the memory of good dinners and kisses? Still, Rome did not, and could not, entirely stamp out Capua. At least the perfume trade survived her fury for in quite late times Capua made perfumed buskins for the emperors. And did you know that the only surviving vestige of Capua's splendour is now the municipal notepaper, which bears the letters S.P.C. – *Senatus populusque Capuanus.* Only Rome still uses S.P.Q.R. on its municipal stationery and its manholes.'

'Is it true' I asked, 'as an Italian once told me, that Capuan women are still held in contempt for having entertained the soldiers of Hannibal?'

He exploded with laughter.

'Not held in contempt,' he said, 'but admired as our greatest practitioners in the art of love! Some like to believe that this goes back to the days of Hannibal; and maybe it does. All I can tell you is this. In the days of my youth no respectable brothel could have done without at least one Capuana.' He threw away his cigarette. He sighed. 'At the age of sixteen,' he said, 'I was the pupil of a lovely Capuana called Diana; and I like to think that history has conferred respectability upon my lessons.'

Upon our return to Naples we paused outside a village called Sant' Arpino where some ancient remains were being uncovered, I think of public baths. The professor expended much energy and dialect as he bounced about shouting in search of a friend associated with the excavations: but, as it turned out, the man had gone to Naples. The ruins are those of the ancient Oscan city of Atella, which was notorious in Roman times for impromptu farces of the utmost indecency, in which some have seen the origin of the *Commedia dell'Arte.* Among the characters originated here, they say, was Punchinello. The Oscan farces were performed in Rome but became so improper, and dealt so scurrilously with prominent persons, that they were banned in the reign of Tiberius. The professor told me that the Italian word *osceno* (obscene) is derived from the Oscan improprieties; but how true this may be I cannot say; and the *Oxford English Dictionary* is no help.

We encountered a workman, still apparently speaking Oscan, who told the professor that the present excavations began two years or so ago when a huge walnut tree had blown down revealing walls and buildings quite close to the surface.

'But the great point is this,' said the professor. 'The four villages round about, which are so poor that half the population has to go into Naples for work, saw in this discovery the possibility of tourist gold. And they have actually combined – an extraordinary feat in Italian country life – to excavate Atella in the hope that they may share a little gold mine here. They have even,' he continued, 'appealed for funds to all local men who have emigrated to America, who, of course, are believed to be rolling in money!'

It did not seem to me that the response had been overwhelming. This is a pity. I think the local people are right and that the birthplace of Punch would be a great attraction.

When almost in Naples we passed through Aversa, a bustling town of about thirty thousand inhabitants. It was a disappointment to me. This was the once famous market for Norman fighting men, the first Norman foothold in Southern Italy, the town associated with Rainulf and the Hautevilles. I had imagined it as perhaps a lonely stronghold upon a hill, with a mouldering castle and possibly a cathedral, certainly not this crowded extension of Naples where the red Fiat was almost annihilated by a lorry with its trailer.

'Still, you must not be disappointed,' said the professor. 'Fame has not deserted it. It has the largest lunatic asylum in the south of Italy.'

§ 10

One of my greatest delights in Naples was a visit to the Phlegrean Fields, to the town of Pozzuoli, to the Grotto of the Sibyl, and to Cape Misenum, a few miles west of Naples. It is one of the oldest of all classical sites, so old indeed that the modern traveller

seems to have forgotten all about it: but for centuries this fantastic and eerie region was what Pompeii and Herculaneum are to
the modern tourist.

I think the earliest English traveller who described the Phlegrean
Fields was Gervase of Tilbury, who about 1190 was one of the
many Englishmen in the service of William II of Sicily, whose
queen was Joan Plantagenet, daughter of Henry II. His book, *Otia
Imperialia*, a marvellous jumble of mediaeval fancies and beliefs,
describes a sightseeing trip to Naples, which for men of his day
was, above everything, the city of the magician, Virgil. As soon as
Gervase arrived, he began to encounter wonders. He came to the
Nola Gate, which had a bust of Virgil above each of its two
entrances. Nobody who knew Naples ever entered by the left side
because it led to bad luck. Fortunately for Gervase, a donkey
loaded with wood happened to block up the left-hand entrance, so,
without realizing it at the time, he entered by the gate of happiness.

He wrote of the bronze fly made by Virgil which was said to
have abolished flies from Naples; there was a magic market in
which meat remained fresh for six months; Virgil had also driven
snakes out of Naples; he had created a bronze trumpet aimed at
Vesuvius which kept the volcano quiet. The only one of these
fantastic legends which survives is the story of the Castel dell'Ovo
balanced on its submerged egg.

Like other early travellers, Gervase saw the sunken crater of the
volcano in the Phlegrean Fields, which seems to have remained
unchanged for centuries. At any rate, the marvels which were
shown to him are still shown today. The most fantastic of all is
that this volcanic landscape gave the Greeks their conception of
Hades and the Elysian Fields.

On the way there, as was fitting, I paid a brief visit to what for
centuries has been known as the tomb of Virgil. It is now a charming little garden planted with laurels and other shrubs and flowers
mentioned by the poet, above the main road to Posillipo where
motor cars race and lorries thunder. In this pretty spot I was
touched to see a marble bust upon a plinth supposed to be the
poet when young, with an inscription from the Latinists of the
American State of Ohio. Whether the mass of crumbling masonry

is truly the tomb of Virgil does not really matter. I returned to the noisy road with the feeling that I had stood in a place where it was fitting to remember the author of the *Georgics* and the *Aeneid*.

In twenty minutes or so I was in the Phlegrean Fields – the Fields of Fire, a name once applied to the whole region west of Naples including the islands of Procida and Ischia, because of the dormant volcanic character of the land. I drove through a gateway and having bought my ticket, a tall, gaunt Mephistophelian figure advanced and claimed me. He was one of a waiting group of guides, each one carrying a tightly rolled newspaper whose purpose was soon made clear. We set off at a brisk pace, the thin man waving his rolled newspaper at the stricken landscape, talking rapidly all the time in English. He explained that we were walking in the crater of a volcano that had sunk to sea level in some remote convulsion, but was still smoking here and there as spurts of smoke or steam and a stench of brimstone indicated. This was the famous Solfatara of Pozzuoli. Notices marked 'Dangerous' warned us not to walk in certain places; in others the ground was soft and yielding. The thin man said that here the Greeks had conceived their idea of hell.

We came to a horrid pool of bubbling mud. At one of the *fumerole* the guide revealed the purpose of the newspaper. Lighting it, he applied the flame to the crack and, with a loud cry of 'Via – *houpla!*' pointed to the clouds of smoke and steam that immediately began to puff from other cracks even fifty yards away. We came to a grotto full of hot steam. I went in and saw a naked man sitting there, his hair plastered to his head with sweat. He turned a boiled face to me and said 'Good Morning' in German.

'Who is he?', I asked the guide when I had come out.

'He is one of the Germans from the "camping",' he replied, 'who is taking a steam bath.'

It was a reassuring explanation. I should probably not have questioned it had I been told that he was a well-known inhabitant of the underworld.

I asked about the 'Grotto of the Dog', which is mentioned in every early account of Solfatara, and was glad to know that the horrible practice of asphyxiating a dog in a cavern two feet deep in poison gas is now illegal, but, surprisingly enough, it lasted until the beginning of this century. George Sandys, who was there in 1611, described how at the approach of a stranger all the dogs took to the hills, but there were evidently always some poor little victims available for the beastly experiment. This was to drag the animal into the cave where in a few moments it collapsed, apparently dead. It was then flung into a lake nearby, which is now dry, where it recovered consciousness and ran off yelping, as fast as it could go. Sometimes the revival process was left too long and the dog died. Even such a gentle person as John Evelyn described this cruel business with gusto.

I tipped Mephistopheles, who bowed from his immense height and wished me well, and, as I went off towards Pozzuoli, I caught sight of him busily rolling another newspaper.

§ 11

Upon the outskirts of Pozzuoli, which was the ancient port of Puteoli, I came to the ruins of a huge amphitheatre. It is the third largest in Italy, the Colosseum being the first in size, the amphitheatre of Capua the second. Here even more clearly than at Capua may be seen the methods used to introduce wild animals into the arena. The avenues and passages and underground chambers have been marvellously preserved.

I had always imagined that animals arrived in a Roman arena either in angry snarling droves prodded by men with torches and spears, or else that they were released singly. One sees in Puteoli how sixty animals could be released simultaneously from cages cranked up from below and fitted with trap-doors, thirty of these lying in a semi-circle on each side of the arena. It must have been the most exciting moment of the day to a blood-thirsty mob when sixty trap-doors were automatically lifted and sixty lions and tigers, and other animals obtained by the theatrical agents in Africa, glad to find themselves in the sunlight, leapt out into a landscape that was often strewn with sand and decorated with palm trees. Like its Roman counterpart, this provincial amphi-theatre was known as the Colosseum.

I went on into Pozzuoli, once Rome's chief trading port with the East, now a busy, crowded little seaport. I stood in a waterfront café and drank an *espresso* while I listened to the gossip of the young barman and a friend as they discussed a celebrated film actress who had been born in the town. Their conversation was rather like one of the dialogues of Lucian; the things people say about each other, particularly the things young men sometimes say about young women, have not changed much in the course of the centuries.

I went down to the harbour, which has been transformed by earthquakes since Roman times. A great part of it has fallen into the sea. An old man told me that when he was a boy, before alterations had changed the old harbour, he remembers swimming and diving there with other lads and seeing the Roman mole beneath the sea, with huge bronze rings still in position to which the galleys were tied. I do not know how much imagination there was in this.

It was upon the now vanished mole that St Paul landed, a prisoner who had appealed to Caesar. He arrived in the Alexandrian corn-ship, the *Castor and Pollux*, which, as readers of *Acts* will recall, carried him to Puteoli after his shipwreck on Malta. This vessel was one of a fleet which brought Egyptian wheat to Italy every spring. The ships often sailed in convoy escorted by warships, but the *Castor and Pollux* was evidently on a lone voyage. Even by modern standards, such vessels were large. Two hundred and seventy people were wrecked on Malta with St Paul, yet this ship found room for them apparently without difficulty in addition to her own crew and passengers.

In one of his letters Seneca has preserved a picturesque memory of the Egyptian corn fleet. He says that it was a rule that all ships except the corn-ships had to strike their topsails as they entered the Gulf of Naples; the Alexandrian vessels alone might come on under full sail and were visible from a great distance. Immediately they were sighted, crowds began to assemble in the harbour to welcome them.

One can imagine St Paul gazing about him at a scene many of whose details have now vanished beneath the waves, though the broad outlines remain the same. As the *Castor and Pollux* drew near the shore he would have seen the crowded harbour of Puteoli ahead; to his left the seaside villas of Baiae crowded the hills down to the edge of the water; to the right he may have noticed the small harbour of Neapolis that was to grow into Naples; and in the background, rose Vesuvius, which was not to erupt and overwhelm Pompeii for another seventeen years. Among the crowds who raced down to the harbour to greet the corn-ship were Jewish friends, converts to the Faith. . . . 'and on the second day we came to Puteoli: where we found brethren, and were entreated to tarry with them seven days.'

Clustered upon the cliffs to the south-west of Pozzuoli one sees all that is left of the famous Baiae, now called Baia; and these remains are surprisingly numerous and are still being excavated. Most of ancient Baiae lies beneath the sea, but on the high ground are a series of classical ruins, all of them called 'temples' but they are really the remains of an enormous spa.

Perhaps the French Riviera during the 1930s may have borne some resemblance to ancient Baiae, but I cannot think of any other place in the modern world as opulent and fashionable as Baiae's 'golden shore' during the Roman Empire. It was said that upon this strip of coast men who possessed provinces competed for a single acre. The villas were built upon the cliffs during the Republic, but in imperial times they were even built out over the rocks above the sea. The greatest names in Roman history had holiday villas there: Marius, Sulla, Pompey, Julius Caesar, Tiberius, Nero, Cicero, Lucullus, Hortensius – indeed the place was a *Who's Who* of Roman fame and plutocracy. It was a place where all restraint was cast aside and where the finest characters often exhibited the defects of their qualities.

As I clambered about from bath to bath, and what a number there are, some still beautifully preserved and one, a circular bath still roofed like a small Pantheon, a most picturesque and lovely ruin, others merely a row of slender columns, I remembered the agonies of the poet Propertius, who dreaded the effect of the *dolce vita* upon Cynthia. The beach life and other temptations of Baiae were believed to be fatal to female virtue. Cynthia in her bikini, and with her hair newly gold-dusted, probably justified her lover's anxiety, and she may even have written to tell him what a quiet time she was having and how bored she was, but Propertius was in torture, his love increased by his agony. 'Propertius had something in common with Marcel Proust,' writes Gilbert Highet in *Poets in a Landscape*, 'whose male characters are usually unable to experience love to the full, while they are happily in the arms of the woman they adore, but can feel it only when they are separated from them by change of place, or by the painful hallucinations of jealousy.'

A beautiful walk across the hills and through vineyards leads to the ancient city of Cumae, the oldest of all the colonies of Magna Graecia, also the mysterious home of the Cumaean Sibyl. The ancient city has, of course, long since vanished, but the Acropolis remains, a tall, romantic hill, its summit occupied by a temple, its base honeycombed with passages which lead to the eerie hall where the Sibyl delivered her prophecies. I have not seen a more romantic classical site in Italy.

This is one of the most ancient monuments in the country, though it was not possible to walk through the gallery and stand in the grotto of the Sibyl until 1932. Countless attempts to penetrate the tunnel were foiled by the debris of a stone quarry, which blocked the entrance and filled part of the tunnel itself. But in May 1932 the diggers struck the tunnel and found their way to that underground chamber so vividly described in the Sixth Book of the *Aeneid*, where the Sibyl's voice echoed in the vaults. So was found what is now one of the least known but most impressive relics of the Mediterranean world.

I left the sunlight of a hot afternoon and entered the twilight of a Cyclopean tunnel that was dimly illuminated at intervals by cuttings in the rock. The shape of this tunnel was that of a huge inverted V. The workmanship was perfect and I felt myself, as at Mycenae, or, for that matter, at Stonehenge, in the presence of an

age incredibly distant and powerful. Anyone who is even remotely
interested in the classical world who comes to Naples yet fails to
visit the Grotto of the Sibyl is missing a great experience; should
it be a matter of time, I would rather see what is left of Cumae
than Pompeii.

At the end of the tunnel I came to an ominous and sinister
chamber cut in the tufa where the Sibyl made her utterances.
Virgil must have stood here many a time. His account reads like
that of an eye-witness. The roof of the chamber is higher even
than that of the corridor and a feature of it is several large arched
niches. In many places there are holes in the rock which presumably held wooden jambs for doors so that portions of the sanctum
might be closed for some purpose connected with the Oracle. I
must say that this subterranean vault is still, so it seemed to me,
powerfully charged with religious fear.

The origin of the Sibyl is a strange one. It was rooted in the
belief of remote ages that certain old women were able to communicate with the other world. They were always old and they
were always women. The three most famous Sibyls were those of
Erythrae, of Cumae and of Delphi. They all seem to have been
what the modern spiritualist would call trance mediums. After an
elaborate ritual they prophesied with wild gestures; at Delphi the
Pythia chewed laurel leaves and inhaled fumes, which evidently
assisted her trance. Plutarch mentions the frantic grimaces of the
Sibyl. As an oracle, the Delphic Pythia probably had a greater
effect on public affairs than any other, but the Cumaean Sibyl had
an exceptional importance to Rome since it was she who sold the
Sibylline Books to Tarquin. First she offered him the whole set of
nine books, but when he questioned the price she burned three and
offered the remaining six at the same price.

Once again, Tarquin would not buy, so she burned three more
and offered the last three at the original price. Tarquin then gave
way and concluded the most extraordinary book sale ever
recorded.

What were the Sibylline Books? Probably, in the form of Greek
hexameters, they covered a variety of human problems and, like
oracular utterances everywhere, were capable of being interpreted

in a number of ways. Anyone who has had a sitting with a modern
Sibyl will be familiar with similar ambiguities. The faithful go
off to ponder, while the disbelievers consider them nonsense.
To the Roman Senate, the Sibylline Books were, in early times, a
window on the other world. They were buried in a temple for
safety and were consulted solemnly in times of emergency by
persons trained to interpret them. When the Forum was destroyed
by fire in 82 B.C., the Sibylline Books were lost. It was felt to be a
devastating calamity. A commission was sent to Asia Minor to
gather in the Greek cities there as many Sibylline utterances as
possible in the hope of sifting these and compiling a second
edition. The commission returned with what was probably the
greatest mass of nonsense that has ever been subjected to official
scrutiny (perhaps a rash supposition!), and when Augustus became
emperor, wishing to make a gesture of respect to tradition, he
appointed a committee to go through the new material and see
what could be made of it. This new collection was reverently
interred in a safe in the Temple of Apollo on the Palatine Hill,
where, it would seem, it remained until A.D. 400; but what
ultimately became of it no one can say.

Standing in the dark, mysterious vault with an occasional drop
of water descending from the roof, I could understand how
frightening it must have been to have had a 'sitting' with the
Cumaean Sibyl in the bowels of Mother Earth. Her voice was
projected, as Virgil describes, from many directions, and no doubt
the priests made the occasion as startling as possible. I could not
discover where the Sibyl sat, and whether one could see as well as
hear her. All I can say is that after an audience the believer must
have retraced his steps along the stone gallery in a disturbed state
of mind. As I did so, my steps echoing beneath the Cyclopean
roof, I was glad to be welcomed by the sunlight at the tunnel's end.

An ancient paved road like the Via Sacra in the Roman Forum
winds round the hill to the summit, where the ruins of a temple to
Apollo stand among gorse, thyme, wood sorrel and clover. Half
way up is a farm with a wall round it and an arched entrance like
that to a castle. A barefoot girl came along leading a black and
white plough ox. With the deftness of long practice, she let

down a bucket into a well and drew it up full of water. It was a sight, I thought, as old as Cumae itself.

There was not a soul upon the hill-top and no sound but the hum of insects, busy from flower to flower. This was the site of the Acropolis of Cumae, on its summit a temple to Apollo, in its depths the grotto of the oracle. I thought it one of the truly enchanted spots in Italy. Seaward I looked towards Cape Misenum, which recalls the trumpeter of Aeneas; landward I saw Lake Avernus and to the north, far off in the haze, at the extremity of miles of coastline and hill, was Gaeta, whose name is another Virgilian memory, for there was the legendary tomb of Caieta, the nurse of Aeneas. Here poetry and landscape go hand in hand.

§ 12

The day of the 'Dance of the Lilies' at Nola – a Sunday – came at last. The mayor of Nola had invited me to the town hall to witness the dance at noon, but having had some experience of public ceremonies, I arrived at Nola, which is only twenty miles from Naples, in time for breakfast. I found the streets almost empty in the early morning sunlight. The cathedral was packed and the sound of High Mass was booming over the piazza from loudspeakers. Selecting a café on the shady side of the square, I had what passes for breakfast in Italy, in this instance some coffee and a veteran bun. I then explored the town.

There is a splendid statue of Augustus wearing the armour of a general and depicted in early manhood when he combed his hair straight down over his forehead. He died in this town at the age of seventy-six in the arms of Livia, begging her to remember their life together. In the side streets I sensed the excitement of the day. Children were running about shouting and singing while exasperated women called to them from balconies. The church bells began to ring. It was interesting to hear them in Nola where it is believed they were first used by St Paulinus to summon his flock to church.

The 'Dance of the Lilies' – a dance which began sixteen

centuries ago – fascinated me from the moment I had heard of it. I thought it one of Italy's most interesting appointments with a venerable past. St Paulinus of Nola was born in A.D. 353, and his tutor, as he grew up, was the poet Ausonius. Paulinus was a patrician and, like many men of his class during the fall of the Empire, he became a Christian and a bishop. He was a friend and correspondent of St Augustine; many of his letters and poems have survived. He was Bishop of Nola when Alaric and his Goths, having sacked Rome in A.D. 410, moved south with their booty. While the barbarians were in Nola they arrested Paulinus and took him away with them, either because he had opposed them or perhaps because he offered himself in place of a widow's son; in any event he was carried off, some say to Africa. How or why he was released is unknown, but he returned to Italy and to Nola, to be greeted by the population of his town dancing with joy and bearing bunches of lilies.

The event became an annual ceremony. The trade guilds began to compete to produce the most spectacular display of lilies. At first, these were carried on poles, as carnations are still carried at Bari during the feast of St Nicholas; then, year after year, the poles, or receptacles for the lilies, became larger and more flamboyant until today, though they are still called 'lilies', they have become huge steeples of wood, about fifty feet or more in height, but the dance, which began in the fifth century, still goes on round them.

In one of the narrow lanes of the town I came upon men nailing painted canvas to a tapering spire or steeple that rose higher than the houses. It was made of an elaborate system of wooden struts and terminated in a painted plaster statue of a saint. The platform on which this steeple was mounted was massive and, I was told, would be carried by relays of fifty men, each team carrying it for twenty yards at a time. The painted canvas depicted various sacred scenes and persons. The process by which in the course of time a lily is transformed into a steeple is well known in the history of religious ceremonies, so is the spiritual virtue to be derived from the muscular effort of carrying immense burdens round a town or up a mountain.

I found that a window had been reserved for me in the town hall. It faced the cathedral so that I was able to look down upon the piazza. Eight 'lilies' dance every year; they represent the lilies carried by the eight trade guilds of Roman Nola when St Paulinus was welcomed home. First, as the sound of distant bands indicated, the 'lilies' perambulate the town before they arrive in the piazza. As noon approached the excitement increased. The piazza began to fill with crowds. Groups of young men and boys joined hands and danced round in circles. No women or girls took part in these dances.

The arrival of the 'lilies' was an extraordinary spectacle. They came one at a time, at intervals of perhaps half an hour. They were all of the same height, and each was played in by a band and carried by sweating men who might have been galley slaves or prisoners condemned to some painful punishment. Each 'lily' had its own band and its own tunes, and as the first came in sight I was surprised to see that twelve large men blowing trumpets and playing other instruments were not marching, as bands usually do, but were seated on the platform of the 'lily', thus adding enormously to the weight carried by their compatriots. This immense, and apparently pointless, physical strain reminded me of the ceremony of the Ceri at Gubbio, in Umbria, when teams of men race up a mountainside carrying huge obelisks of wood.

As each 'lily' slowly tottered into the packed square with its band playing, it took up a position opposite to the town hall when the sweating bearers left it and rested. Then the band struck up a livelier tune, and, to wild shouts of enthusiasm, the bearers lifted platform, band and steeple upon their shoulders, and, by executing a peculiar step, made the steeple rock, or dance. To see such a huge spire with its band executing such a jaunty movement was the oddest sight. The crowd roared its approval and delight. After each 'lily' had performed its dance, it drew up along one side of the piazza until there were four on each side facing each other. Then, carried by another team of fifty men, there arrived in the square a white ship with a golden figure-head which represented the ship in which St Paulinus returned from Africa. A statue of the bishop stood beneath a shrine in the stern, while a figure rarely absent from southern Italian ceremonies, a Saracen turbaned and grasping a scimitar, was the ship's captain. As the galley was played into the piazza by its own band, flowers were showered down upon it from every balcony. The air was loud with 'vivas' and cries of welcome to 'San Paolino' until I thought that emotion could go no further, but I was wrong.

The Church, the great pageant-master of history, added the final touch. The bells of the duomo rang; the shouting crowds fell silent as the double doors of the church opened and from the darkness into the late sunlight came the clergy, the Bishop in cope and mitre, and behind him the silver statue of St Paulinus surrounded by sprays of gladioli. The Bishop went round the square blessing the 'lilies', then the procession returned to the cathedral. The bearers of the statue of St Paulinus circled about before they ascended the steps so that the saint never turned his back on the people. We saw the sun gleaming upon his silver mitre, then he vanished into the darkness of the nave. Nola's appointment with the past was over until next year.

Not surprisingly, the town now became utterly deflated. The streets emptied. Three of the 'lilies' stood abandoned in the piazza with little boys climbing over them. I also felt deflated. For hours the brass bands, the dancing crowds, the rocking 'lilies' had absorbed my attention; and now the party was over. I returned to Naples thinking how extraordinary it is that happiness experienced fifteen centuries ago should be able to explode today in such a burst of exuberance and feeling.

§ 13

There was a slight mist the next morning, and even had the chair-lift been working, I thought it would be more interesting to walk the last part of the way up Vesuvius on foot. I drove therefore into a landscape that became increasingly ominous until on each side of the road I saw horrible elephant-grey rivers of lava lying halted where they had cooled during the last eruption of 1944. I was not prepared for quite such a repellant moonscape, and I wondered, as one does when reading accounts of eruptions, how peasants can continue to live round this keg of gunpowder. The answer is, of course, that when old lava has gathered earth, and has weathered, it is unusually fertile, and is said to grow the best vines and olives.

It was odd to look back and to see the untouched hillsides flourishing with crops and woodland, and with wonderful golden bursts of gorse, separated only by a few feet from the grey, frozen river of death: a slow-moving red-hot porridge that had rolled down from Vesuvius devouring houses, woods, olives and vines as it continued on its way.

A young girl came running out of a hut to tell me that the road had now ended and that I must continue on foot. The hut offered cold drinks, cuff-links and necklaces made of brilliantly iridescent polished lava and such-like rather pleasant mementoes. The climber was advised to change his shoes and put on rope-soled espadrilles and to hire a stout staff. I did both. But I was amused to see a fussy little Frenchwoman, fearing I think that she was being imposed upon, refuse to take this advice and, waving away espadrilles and alpenstock, begin the ascent in a pair of smart town shoes. I was to come upon her about half an hour later, exhausted and defeated, her shoes cut to shreds. I rebuked myself for not having had the kindness to slip a pair of rope-soles in my pocket for her, but, after all, she had a husband with her, but a man I think not accustomed to disputing her decisions.

The path from the hut to the crater of Vesuvius may be a mile, or two or even three in length. All I can say is that it is one of the most trying upward inclines I have ever attempted. I walked on cinders and pulverized lava. The path is soft and in places slippery and it winds about as all mountain paths do, each bend making the summit appear more remote than ever. The mist was still blowing in from the Bay, otherwise I felt sure that the view would have compensated for an ordeal that recalled the most painful moments in *The Pilgrim's Progress*.

I thought that, in spite of our motor-cars and our sedentary lives, we are in some ways tougher than our ancestors. No one these days would consent, as our forebears did, to be pulled up the slopes of Vesuvius hanging on to the belt of a guide. That was the way that Goethe, young, muscular and fit, went up in 1787. 'These guides,' he wrote, 'are girded round the waist with a leathern belt which the traveller takes hold of, and being drawn up by his guide, makes his way easier with foot and staff.' As I plodded on, I cheered myself by remembering my favourite Vesuvius story. When Mrs Piozzi (the ex-Mrs Thrale) went up to the crater in 1786 it was customary to stop at the hermitage and pass a few words with the anchorite who in those days lived there, perhaps turning an honest penny by selling lemonade or lava. Having discussed literature with him, Mrs Piozzi found him to be a Frenchman. He then said to her: 'Did I never see you before, madam?' (It is quite a question to be asked by the anchorite of Vesuvius, but Mrs Piozzi does not go into that.) Yes; they had met before. Gazing into the hermit's face, Mrs Piozzi recognized a once fashionable London hairdresser! After discussing various ladies who had once patronized his salon, Mrs Piozzi said farewell, picking her way up through the cindery lava. As she departed she heard the hermit mutter, 'Ah, I'm an old man now; I remember when black pins first came up!'

How amusing life is, and how unexpected; and how I wished that something like that might happen to me on the slopes of Vesuvius, a hermit London taxi-driver perhaps, or an old repentant publisher; but no, the black path led relentlessly to the summit with no such diversion. There came a moment, as I drew near the crater, when I saw outlined against the sky a number of females being carried through the air in an orderly and efficient manner. The chair lift was, after all, working. This replaces the famous Cook's railway that was a casualty of the last eruption. The mist was still blowing, which made the delivery of a whole chain of these ladies out of it, (and not a single Valkyrie among them,) distinctly odd. As I drew level with the station I rested there, fascinated by the arrival of these tourists on the summit of Vesuvius, each one neatly belted into her chair, each one stepping out as if it were the most ordinary thing in the world to do. The guides claimed their flocks and marched off to the crater.

We stood, perhaps two hundred tourists, as if we were a flight of some small inquisitive birds that had come to rest upon the summit of a vast slag heap. The air was loud with useful information. I heard one of the guides say that the crater is now six hundred and fifty yards across and seven hundred feet deep. There was nothing to indicate that Vesuvius is still alive except the *fumarole*, precisely the same as those I had seen in the Phlegrean Fields. The guides held newspapers at these cracks which instantly burst into flame. People asked hundreds of questions but the most interesting were not asked.

It is curious that until the eruption of A.D. 79, which destroyed Pompeii, nobody thought that Vesuvius was alive. The awful slag-heap into which we were looking was before that time a dense forest famous for its wild boars. Then came the eruption and ever since these have occurred at irregular intervals, sometimes with long periods of inactivity like that from 1500 to 1631, when once again the mountain was cultivated to the summit and the wild boars returned to the wooded crater. At the moment, I thought Vesuvius looked less active than the Phlegrean Fields.

The best eye-witness account of the eruption of A.D. 79 is the well-known description of the Younger Pliny, whose uncle, the Elder Pliny, Admiral of the fleet at Misenum, lost his life during the disaster. August 24, A.D. 79 was probably one of those hot days when it is impossible to feel cool even in the sea. Pliny lived with his widowed sister and her son, the Younger Pliny, whom he had adopted, a young lad of seventeen. After a cold bath, Pliny had retired to his library, perhaps to add to the hundred and sixty volumes of notes on every conceivable subject from which his *Natural History* was compiled. His sister begged him to stop work and to go out and look at a strange cloud, which she compared to a palm tree, that was hanging over Vesuvius. He called for his shoes and went out, then, realizing that this was a natural phenomenon that demanded investigation, he ordered a light galley to take him across the Bay. As he was on the point of setting out, a pathetic appeal for help was delivered from the wife of a friend who lived in a villa at the foot of the mountain. She begged Pliny to send a ship since escape by sea was the only hope. The Admiral then decided to lead a relief expedition and ordered a number of naval vessels to be launched.

As the ships moved in the direction of Vesuvius, burning ash and stones fell upon the decks. Though it was afternoon, a black cloud hung over everything and it was as dark as night. Fearful explosions shook the air and the sea began to retreat as if sucked back by some under-water convulsion. Pliny ordered his galley to land him as near Stabiae as possible, where a friend named Pomponianus had a villa. He found the house in an uproar. The valuables were packed and Pomponianus was on the point of flight. Pliny calmed him down, got the slaves to work and persuaded the cook to produce dinner. After a bath he sat down with his host and enjoyed a good meal, then went calmly to bed and to sleep. They could hear him snoring. As he slept the passage to his bedroom was filling with hot ash. He was awakened. Realizing that the danger was infinitely worse than he had imagined, he saw that the only course for them was to try and fight their way through the falling cinders back to the ships. Tying pillows to their heads, and holding napkins across their mouths, they set off. When they reached the coast they saw that the sea was running mountains high and no ship could approach to take them off. Pliny, a stout man of fifty-six, exhausted by his ordeal, lay down to rest on a canvas sail, but after a time flames and a smell of sulphur caused the party to stagger on in terror. But as Pliny rose to his feet he fell back dead, probably suffocated. (Far off in Rome men and women noticed a strange grey dust that settled over everything; and they wondered what it was.)

The account of the eruption and of Pliny's death was written by his nephew in a letter to the historian Tacitus, who was gathering first-hand accounts of the disaster. Unfortunately that part of his history has never been found.

I descended the wicked mountain to be rewarded on the way by the complete disappearance of the mist, which vanished to reveal the beautiful blue waters far below, and the exquisite curve of coast washed by gentle waves where white houses shone among the oranges and lemons.

§ 14

Our grandfathers and great-grandfathers believed, or at any rate pretended to believe, that the Venus de Medici was the perfect female shape. Oddly enough, our tightly-laced grandmothers and great-grandmothers implied that the same ideal of beauty was not encouraged in real life. The massive, waistless goddess, though she still rouses respect, no longer in replica crowns a thousand bookcases, and would probably provoke no comment upon a modern beach, except, maybe, the whisper that she should diet. The waist was the discovery of the Middle Ages and has determined female beauty ever since.

Perhaps one of the few ancient Venuses who might stand a chance of becoming 'Miss Ancient Rome' is the *Venus Callipygos* in the National Museum at Naples. She was discovered in the ruins of Nero's Golden House in Rome and formed part of the famous Farnese Collection until that was inherited in the eighteenth century by Charles III, and, to the rage of Rome, was eventually moved to Naples. She is among the most admired of the ancient Venuses. She stands removing her single garment, at the same time glancing back over her shoulder to admire her reflection in water. The statue was no doubt intended to be placed on the edge of a swimming pool or on an island in a lake, like the nymphs of Caserta. She is beautifully and cleverly placed in the National Museum so that you come across her suddenly as if you were the wandering shepherd of legend.

This gigantic building, which preserves more of the ancient world than any other museum, was, curiously enough, designed as a cavalry barracks in the sixteenth century. It contains all the well-known Farnese treasures – the Bull, the Hercules, the Flora, the unique Farnese Cup which once belonged to Lorenzo the Magnificent – as well as thousands of less known statues in bronze and marble. There are rooms full of silver, of gold, of jewellery; rooms frescoed by great but unknown artists who lived centuries ago; rooms full of bronze implements once in everyday use, notably surgical probes and forceps of quite modern shapes; rooms full of beautifully designed kitchen pots and pans and of carbonized fruit, bread and meat, as brittle and black as coal, which were fresh and ready to be eaten on August 24, A.D. 79 when Vesuvius destroyed Pompeii and Herculaneum.

It is a pity that some of those who organize the scamperings across Europe which nowadays belong perhaps to the history of movement rather than to that of travel, always take their flocks to Pompeii but often omit the National Museum. I know of no place which gives a greater sense of intimacy with the classical past. Here is the original Dancing Faun from the House of the Faun at Pompeii, also the splendid mosaic pavement from the same building, which shows Alexander the Great and Darius in the heat of battle. In an adjoining room is the finest statue in existence of the Ephesian Diana, a weird figure encased mummy-like in a carapace of symbols, her body festooned with objects which the catalogue calls breasts but are, I believe, the ova of bees. The bee was the symbol of Diana of Ephesus and is to be seen on the coinage. The Goddess was the queen bee – and the Ephesians were among the few in antiquity to know the real sex of the queen – and her temple organization reflected the life of the hive.

I often returned to the museum and found something new to admire every time. What an interesting study are those clean-shaven Roman faces of the Augustan period, so like the Victorians; there is hardly one who could not be imagined in the nineteenth century House of Commons.

The spirit of comedy alighted on this institution in the last century when the author of *The Three Musketeers* was made its curator. The elder Dumas, cruising in the Mediterranean for his health in a yacht whose crew included a charming midshipgirl dressed in bell-bottomed trousers and a neat little jacket, did some mild gun-running for Garibaldi, and asked, as his reward, the curatorship of what was then the Bourbon Museum. His real object was to search for treasures in Pompeii, which that position permitted him to do. The appointment outraged public opinion. Nevertheless Dumas held on to it for four years before returning to Paris, to his creditors and to equally demanding mistresses.

# CHAPTER EIGHT

*Pompeii and Herculaneum – the Sorrento Peninsula – Amalfi and Ravello – Paestum and the Madonna of the Pomegranate – Entering Calabria – Lungro and the Greek Orthodox Albanians – the Ionian Sea – Rossano's Purple Codex – Crossing the Sila – a story of bandits – Cosenza and the tomb of Alaric – Maida Vale.*

## § I

Finding the traffic of Naples too noisy, I went for some days to a charming holiday hotel on the beach at Marina di Equa, north of Sorrento. There was no sound but that of English voices from the sea or the swimming pool; the sun shone all day from the bluest of skies. In the evening we dined out of doors under pine trees beside the sea.

I found that Pompeii and Herculaneum were only about half an hour away by the autostrada and I revisited both several times, finding Herculaneum usually empty and Pompeii always crowded. Goethe wrote the best thing said about these towns when he commented, 'Many a calamity has happened in the world, but never one that has caused so much entertainment to posterity as this one.' That observation would appear to be even truer today than when Goethe wrote it in 1787.

In his day there was little to be seen of Pompeii, while Herculaneum was still buried, though the adventurous traveller was able to explore tunnels and passages by torchlight. These had been made by miners seeking statues for the Bourbon kings. It is only in modern times that the sun has shone again upon the streets and the beautiful villas of Herculaneum, while yard by yard new discoveries are being made as houses in the town of Resina above are demolished. This town still covers nearly half of the ancient city and who knows what wonderful discoveries are still to come, what statues in bronze and marble, perhaps manuscripts. The volcanic mud that hardened into stone locked up Herculaneum as if it were a bank vault, while Pompeii beneath ashes was plundered shortly after the disaster. Many inhabitants who had taken flight in a hurry returned to dig down into their houses for valuables, just as people were seen after an air raid in the last war climbing over rubble in an attempt to find the office safe.

Though the villas of Herculaneum are magnificent, Pompeii has an atmosphere of unique charm and one cannot walk the streets, and note the chariot wheel ruts in the roadway, the little fountains at the street corners and the stepping stones, without remembering the English novel that fired so many imaginations, a book one is afraid to read again in case its magic has departed, *The Last Days of Pompeii*. 'To reconstruct the past in the light of the present was what Bulwer set out to do in *The Last Days of Pompeii*, published in 1834', writes Harold Acton in *The Last Bourbons of Naples*. 'The first idea of the book may have come from his friend Lady Blessington. . . . The master hand in this case was Edward Bulwer's. As soon as he reached Naples in 1833 he imbibed all the knowledge he could from Sir William Gell, listening to erudite details of custom and costume and conjuring up departed inhabitants under the guidance of that best of ciceroni, to whom he duly dedicated one of the most triumphantly successful of all historical novels.' It is pleasant to find that the Italian guide published by Amadeo Maiuri does not forget to mention that the House of the Tragic Poet was the House of Glaucus in *The Last Days of Pompeii*. One wonders how many English visitors still pay a sentimental visit to it.

The two towns had certain differences: Herculaneum was a fashionable seaside place in which a number of rich retired people had built luxurious villas. The humbler inhabitants were chiefly fishermen. Pompeii, on the other hand, was a bustling town of some twenty thousand people of all classes from the poorest ('Share out all the public money, say I', was a familiar note struck by one of its wall scribblers), to rich Romans like Cicero and well-to-do merchants. One fancies that the people of Herculaneum turned up their noses a little at Pompeii as years ago the residents of Hove used to do in the direction of Brighton. But no doubt the people

of Herculaneum shopped in Pompeii and went there if they
wished to see a good show in the theatre. There was a lot of local
industry in Pompeii, and at least one firm exported its product.
This was a concentrated fish sauce, probably made of pulverized
sardines and anchovies, used chiefly in cooking and known as
*liquamen*. In their translation of Apicius, *The Roman Cookery
Book*, Barbara Flower and Elizabeth Rosenbaum state that a small
jar exists with an inscription from Pompeii saying, 'Best strained
*liquamen*. From the factory of Umbricus Agathopus.'

The appeal made by these two towns is that, unlike nearly all
other ancient remains, they belong to a definite moment in time.
In the Roman Forum, for example, only a trained archaeologist is
able to sort out the various periods. It is a puzzling architectural
jumble, and most of it more recent in date than many people imagine. But in Pompeii and Herculaneum one can definitely say 'This
is what they were like on August 24 in A.D. 79'. Calamity overtook
them upon that date; and the municipal overseers had not even had
the time to paint out the offensive graffiti from the walls. Ancient
life had no additions to make to these places after the great volcanic explosion of nearly nineteen centuries ago.

I came upon a pleasant middle-aged woman seated upon a wall
in Pompeii, cooling herself with a paper fan. The moment she
spoke I knew that she came from the Midlands of England. She
told me that she had arrived that morning by coach from Rome;
she had seen a big palace on the way much larger than Buckingham Palace, and that when she had seen Pompeii she would be
taken to Capri and after that, late at night, she would return to
Rome. Pompeii reminded her of Birmingham after an air raid,
but, of course, the weather was much better in Pompeii. I looked
at her in dismay and admiration. It was like meeting someone who
had performed some heroic but pointless wager, like eating
twenty plates of roast beef.


There is now a refreshment room in Pompeii, a cheerful spot in
the centre of the ruins, where I found people of many nationalities
consuming iced drinks in plastic cups. Pompeii forgotten, they

ate and drank and were grateful to be out of the frightful heat. They had no idea what an extraordinary sight they were: the first people to eat under a roof there for nearly two thousand years.

The old Victorian whispering still occurs when crowds come to the squalid little brothel. One would think that English tourists had never read a Sunday paper. Sometimes difficult women will insist on being 'good chaps' and going in with the men, which is terribly embarrassing to the guide and would have shocked their grandmothers, who could walk away swinging their parasols knowing that dear Fred would tell them all about it afterwards.

I intended but forgot to ask whether the custody of the house of the Vettii, with its concealed priapic picture, is auctioned by the guides or whether the tips are pooled. The picture has been a goldmine to the guardians for a century and more. The procedure is always the same. As the tourists are leaving, some of the men become aware that the custodians are making that curious hissing sound accompanied by patting gestures at waist level, the usual ostentatious Italian method of indicating the need for secrecy. Gradually the men loiter in a self-conscious group, aware that some enormity is to be exhibited to them, while the women, with luck, drift away into the street. The guardians then swiftly reveal the ridiculous fresco of a man weighing an impossible deformity in a pair of scales. To some, this absurdity may appear to be an inexplicable contrast to the grave dignity and good taste of the house beyond. How could anyone who could appreciate the one tolerate the other in the entrance lodge? The answer is that the picture was a charm.

It was placed there to avert the Evil Eye. The same emblem in various guises is found all over Pompeii, just as it is sold today in Italy disguised as an ox-horn which hangs on a million keychains, lies in countless handbags, encircles the necks of children or horses, or other objects that require protection. The priapic fresco is the largest and most eye-catching, and therefore the most efficient of its kind to be found in Pompeii. It was placed in the porter's lodge with the idea of trapping the Evil Eye before it had had the chance to cast its malevolence into the house beyond.

Every morning as the sun was coming up behind the cliffs of Vico Equense I would sit on my balcony at Marina di Equa and watch a small motor boat approach from the direction of Naples. It would tie up to our small wooden jetty while three or four people would embark, then off it would go, drawing a white line across the sea, to Sorrento, then across to Capri. This island is now one of the easiest places to visit. You can go there by boat, by hydrofoil, and by helicopter. Like the lady with the fan at Pompeii, many people leave Rome in the morning, visit Capri and return to Rome the same evening.

I was tempted to go there for a day to relive some precious memories, then I decided not to do so. I can recall a time before Capri became Cap-ree when the little piazza was never over-crowded and was always full of people who knew one another; when one drove down to the Marina Piccola in a jaunty little *carrozza* drawn by a pony covered with charms against the Evil Eye that tossed its head proudly with its crown of pheasants' feathers. The Cap-ree of the modern tourist trade is still the true isle of the Sirens who now cast their spell over a more varied and curious assembly of people than ever, though what magic they can absorb in a day I am unable to say. In my experience it takes about a week for the spell to work.

Still, every time the white boat sped over the sea I thought of the Faraglioni rising from smooth water, and I remembered how once a girl dived from a boat in the Blue Grotto and became a silver mermaid as she turned and twisted in the liquid emerald; and I remembered too walking to Anacapri on a hot afternoon and eating purple figs under an olive tree. Those were the days when most people on the island knew Norman Douglas and had known Axel Munthe, long before 'the lassie from Lancashire' had any idea that she would make her home there one day. In a more restrained age than this, life on Capri appeared daring and startling. It was also always witty and amusing.

No, I thought, I would not go to Capri for a day.

§ 2

Leaving Marina di Equa, I travelled along what is probably the most picturesque and among the best known and most dangerous coast roads in Europe, the road round the Sorrentine Peninsula. Someone had told me that there are more than a thousand bends between Sorrento and Ravello, which I can well believe. The speed with which Italians, driving on their brakes, take these corners is terrifying; when the road becomes a cut in the side of the mountain, the motorist is frequently forced to reverse to permit some monster in the form of a coach, or a lorry with a trailer, to edge past inch by inch.

This portion of Campania stands high among those places upon which Nature decided to lavish all her riches. One travels through orchards and gardens with the clear blue sea below. Grapes, lemons and figs grow side by side, while the thrifty gardener often grows a scratch crop beneath them of French beans or zucchini. Before entering Sorrento an inscription on a villa by the roadside, and a superb shower of plumbago, roused my curiosity. I read that Maxim Gorky had once lived there. It was presumably from this house that he went to live on Capri where, stranger still, he was visited by his friend Lenin. I have often thought that those two, who stood for everything that Capri is not, must have been among the oddest visitors that even this island has known. Sir Lees Knowles, in his book *The British in Capri 1806-1808*, when for two years Capri flew the Union Jack, gives a curious pen picture of Gorky, who was, of course, on the island at a much later period.

'In my mind,' he wrote, 'he is pictured as a man of about six feet in height, with a stoop, and a sallow but pleasant face with a blond moustache – a man of about fifty years of age, wearing a slouch hat, a soft white collar, a short yellow jacket, pressed evening trousers, black boots without heels, a ring on the third finger of the left hand with a raised stone. He spoke only Russian . . . Gorky built for himself a charming villa at the side of the pathway leading to the Marina Piccola, overlooking the south side of the island: the top

floor seemed to be a room surrounded by a long narrow window on
each side, giving the maximum of light; flowers, dogs and parrots
were in evidence, and when Gorky returned to Russia, and the
house was being dismantled, I saw in it a fine collection of ancient
and modern weapons. During his residence in Capri, Gorky was
held in the highest esteem by the islanders, and his rare appearances
in public were almost in the nature of royal progresses.'

There was evidently a Russian colony on Capri at the time. In
*South Wind*, Norman Douglas mentions a curious religious sect
whose members bathed naked in a secluded bay.

The road to Sorrento passed through gorges which, as Bernard
Wall noted, are said to be populated with gnomes with the attrac-
tive name of *Monicelli*. Beyond Sorrento the road climbs and twists
until, at a little place called S. Agata, you can look back and see the
Gulf of Naples and ahead is the Gulf of Salerno. And here are more
Russian associations. There are three minute islets in the sea called
li Galli which once belonged to Diaghilev, who left them to
Massine, the present owner.

Coming to Positano where the hills are covered with villas and
their emerald swimming-pools, and where paths meander down
to the beach through grey olive trees, and the coastline sweeps on
washed by the bluest of seas, I thought that Nature and Man have
produced here a perfect reflection of Baiae in the Roman age. It
occurred to me that an English visitor whom I saw picking out a
copy of *The Times* from a newspaper rack was a modern version
of a Roman senator on holiday at Baiae, seeking news of Rome. All
the beauty we read about in the ancient poets has been transferred
to Positano and its immediate coast.

It is unfortunate that one's impression of places is often unfairly
influenced by the weather and various trivialities connected with
personal comfort; and in one way and another I have always had
bad luck in that venerable and beautiful town, Amalfi. I have
known it only in gales of wind and torrents of rain. Now, as I
approached it, I was sure my luck had turned at last, but I found the
town congested with tourists and choked with motor coaches.
People from every country in Europe swarmed over what was
once so simple and peaceful a place. I went to the town hall and

looked at the *Tavole Amalfitane*, the ancient maritime laws which were drawn up in the days when Amalfi was one of the richest of the trading republics, indeed a little Venice that elected its own Doges; then I climbed the long flight of steps to the striped cathedral of St Andrew. The crypt contains the headless body of the Apostle which was brought from Constantinople in the thirteenth century and is said to exude manna like the body of St Nicholas at Bari. This fluid, known locally as the 'sweat' of St Andrew, was collected in a curious machine placed for the purpose above the coffin, but the Apostle failed to sweat for long periods, which was put down to his displeasure.

The beautiful bronze doors inset with silver, which were made in Constantinople about 1066, were, like those I had seen in the underground basilica of St Michael on Mount Gargano, the gift of Mauro di Pantaleone and his son.

I went on to Ravello which I found as beautiful as I remembered it years ago, and marvellously quiet. The bronze doors of the cathedral reminded me of those at Trani, in Apulia, and were evidently made by Barisanus since the method and design are the same: about sixty small bronze panels containing one or more figures in relief attached to a wooden base. The cathedral is dedicated to S. Pantaleone, who was said to have been the favourite physician of the Emperor Maximian. There was great competition for doctor saints in the Middle Ages, particularly in the maritime towns which traded with the East and were so often stricken by plague; and no doubt the bones of S. Pantaleone arrived by way of the usual relic trade or by tomb robbery similar to the pious burglaries which brought St Mark to Venice and St Nicholas to Bari.

I happened to mention to the verger that some thirty years ago a young man had shown me the sacred phial of S. Pantaleone's blood, which is said to liquefy like that of S. Januarius in Naples. He struck an attitude and cried, 'It was I!' and claimed to recognize me. However that may be, we repeated the experience. The sacred phial is kept locked away in a side chapel whose mosaic floor was given in 1925 by an Englishman, Captain John Grant, who had been impressed by the liquefaction ceremony. The pulpits of

Cosmati work from Salerno southward are among the great
artistic treasures of the twelfth and thirteenth centuries, and I think
one of the finest is that of Ravello, supported by six slender twisted
columns whose glittering bands of mosaic rest upon the backs of
four little lions. These Cosmatic pulpits, altars and Easter candlesticks follow the fashion of Rome where in the Middle Ages the
Cosmati family of stone masons collected every kind of coloured
marble to be found in classical ruins and, cutting them into small
cubes, incorporated them in their brilliant and intricate designs. I
think the only example of Cosmatic work in England is the tomb
of the Confessor in Westminster Abbey.

I saw again with delight the ancient trees and walls of the gardens
of the Palazzo Rufolo, timeless and beautiful, with superb views
through pine trees down to the clear blue sea. The gardens are
haunted by many ghosts, among them the rather unusual one of
the only English Pope, Adrian IV, whose name was Nicholas
Breakspear. He celebrated High Mass in the cathedral at Ravello
in 1156 in the presence of six hundred local nobles. A better known
and more recent ghost is that of Wagner, who recognized the gardens as the magic gardens of Klingsor in *Parsifal*. Thousands of
lesser mortals must remember them as a place where they have
known peace and happiness.

I passed through Salerno and was soon on my way to Paestum.

§ 3

The sky had clouded over and there was scarcely a breath of air
as I drove into Paestum. The main street was lined with small shops
which were festooned with pottery and post-cards and all kinds of
hideous garden gnomery or nymphery. One side of the street was
an extraordinary contrast to the other, where, beyond a boundary
wall, were three of the largest and most complete Greek temples
I have ever seen. Descriptions of Paestum, and even photographs,
had not prepared me for the reality. Their size, their massive
strength, their remarkable state of preservation, astonished me. In
the absence of sunlight they stood, a deep reddish-brown in colour,
rising from rough grass and wild flowers, the finest group of Doric

temples in existence and also the most spectacular relic of Magna Graecia in Italy. Far off a clarity in the air seen between their fluted columns proclaimed the presence of the sea, which in the course of time has, like man, deserted them.

As I looked over the wall, a local merchant who had not shaved that week was trying to sell me something when a sharp crack from the sky overhead sent him scurrying to his shop. Soon tropical rain was descending. It formed a mist in which the temples were obliterated. I took shelter in the museum where attendants were running up marble stairs with buckets to catch water from the leaking roof. The electric light then failed, so to flashes of lightning and deafening peals, I looked round at the relics of the city sacred to Hera, Queen of Heaven and, appropriately enough I thought, the wife of the Thunderer.

Among the objects so dramatically revealed were ex-votos showing Hera as a seated goddess cradling a child in her left arm while in her right hand she held a pomegranate. There were others which depicted her without the child but always with the pomegranate, sometimes even with a basketful of them, the symbols of fertility. I wondered whether these humble terracottas were a memory of the famous statue of Hera in Argos, made of gold and ivory by Polyclitus. She was seated upon a golden throne holding a pomegranate in one hand and, in the other, a wand tipped with a cuckoo, a reference to the legend that Zeus, in one of his many odd manifestations, had wooed her disguised as the herald of Spring.

A wall map showed how large a city Paestum had been (the early Greek name was Poseidonia); how massive were the walls that surrounded her; how the temples formed part of a sacred area, as if all the churches in a city had been grouped round a single square. Unknown save to Greek scholars and archaeologists, a discovery was made in 1934 which some would call the greatest archaeological find of the century, certainly the greatest in Magna Graecia. This was a sanctuary town of the Argive Hera a few miles from Paestum, at the mouth of the river Sele, on a site mentioned as that upon which Jason had founded a Heraion during the voyage of the Argonauts. There was nothing to show above ground, though the foundations of a pilgrimage town were uncovered with its temples and shrines from which some thirty thousand ex-votos were taken. The origin of the sanctuary vanished in legend, but the solid foundations have revealed one of the greatest shrines to the Queen of Heaven in the ancient world.

The sun was shining. The storm had vanished. The sky was blue again. Picking my way round pools of water in the road, I approached the three temples, which were now reflected most picturesquely in stray pools around them, and, now in sunlight, were a pale gold brown in colour. The sun outlined the fluting of the columns and cast deep shadows into the tall naves of the interiors. The three buildings stand in the same alignment, separated by varied distances of tough grass and flowers which spring from ancient pavements. Two of the temples are more ancient than the Parthenon.

The tiny figures of men, and of women in brightly coloured dresses, clambered over the huge stones to the entrances, giving life to the tremendous scene and providing a scale of measurement which emphasized the vast size of the temples. Their air of primitive grandeur recalled the Great Hall at Karnak rather than the lighter, more aerial constructions of classical Greece. The note of colour was a reminder that no one in the ancient world saw the temples of Paestum brown and pitted, as we do. They were covered with stucco painted white to imitate marble, while details of the entablature above were picked out in reds and blues. They must have been a dazzling spectacle with the sun upon them and the sea behind them.

Their names are misleading. They were given during the eighteenth century when Paestum was discovered in dense forest and marshes. The so-called Temple of Neptune, and the temple called the Basilica, were both dedicated to Hera, while the so-called Temple of Ceres was apparently dedicated to Athena. So here, as at the mouth of the Sele, was a sanctuary of the goddess of marriage and maternity who presided over the female principle in life. She was also the goddess of flowers and among her servants were girls, known as 'flower-bearers', who took part in temple ceremonies to the sound of a special air played upon flutes.

Opposite the Temple of Neptune I found a number of rose trees in bloom in the garden of a caretaker's lodge. Though they were modern bush roses they drew the mind back to the 'roses of twice-flowering Paestum' which appealed to so many ancient writers, including Horace, Ovid and Martial, though why they should have been so impressed seems to me difficult to understand since surely all roses bloom twice in warm climates. Many have looked for traces of the famous roses of Paestum. The English traveller, Henry Swinburne, who was there in 1785, wrote that 'the wild rose that shoots up among the ruins is of the small single damask kind with a very high perfume, as a farmer assured me on the spot'. But Swinburne did not see and smell one for himself. The indomitable Ramage, who was there in 1828, saw roses which, as he wrote, were 'a pinkish red colour and very delicate looking'. In 1917 Norman Douglas believed that he had found the genuine roses of Paestum, but they were dwarfs not more than a few inches high. He took some away and kept them for three years but they never flowered, though some grew to a height of sixteen feet. It would probably be impossible to find another of these dwarfs, for I was told that the site has been well weeded in the course of the last fifty years and much of the original vegetation destroyed. What a pity this is!

Paestum was founded about six hundred years before Christ by the city of Sybaris on the opposite, eastern coast of the peninsula, which contradicts the impression that the Sybarites did nothing but lie about on scented couches and invent new sauces. The truth is that they were rich, enterprising businessmen and the stories of their luxury, their shaded streets, and their banquets are perhaps the effect of a high standard of living upon frugal contemporaries. Moreover, it was painful for the Sybarites to watch the merchant fleets sailing past them loaded with the exports of Greece and Asia Minor on their way through the Straits of Messina to their terminus at Cumae on the west coast. It occurred to some bright Sybarite that fortunes might be made could exporters and shippers be persuaded to land their goods at Sybaris and allow the Sybarites to send them overland to a caravan city which they would found on the west coast, and so do away with the long and often perilous voyage round the toe of Italy. The point of this plan was that the peninsula is so narrow near Sybaris that from the mountains it is possible to see both the Ionian and the Tyrrhenian seas. The idea caught on and the city of Poseidonia, the later Paestum, was founded. The same motives made the Suez Canal attractive in the nineteenth century. The plan worked. Sybaris became richer than ever and Paestum became wealthy too; and one hopes that the Etruscans paid less for the Greek pots and bronze kettles and whatever else they bought from Greece and the East. But surely it is strange that a city founded on land transport should have called itself Poseidonia. Is it possible that the crafty Greeks hoped in this way to propitiate the sea god for so many lost voyages?

When Sybaris was destroyed by her rival Croton in 510 B.C. the fortunes of Paestum must have declined, yet she was able to survive her parent city for more than a thousand years. As a Roman city she was loyal when many other cities in Magna Graecia backed Hannibal. During the dark moments of the Carthaginian war she even collected the gold vessels from her altars and sent them to Rome as a contribution to the war chest. But glimpses of her become less frequent, and one assumes that the failure of public works, the silting up of harbours, and the spreading of the malarial mosquito were slowing down her life, as they did in other cities of the time. The last glimpse of her, in the Dark Ages, revealed a pathetic band of Christians, pallid with malaria, gathered round their cathedral in the shadow of the great Doric temples, where, above the candles, sat the Madonna of the Pomegranate. The presiding deity of Paestum for so many centuries, converted to the new faith, still had a child upon her knee and held a pomegranate. When the Saracens and the mosquitoes finally made the site intolerable, the people decided to desert the city and, taking the Madonna of the Pomegranate with them, founded a small town called Capaccio upon the slopes of the mountains not far away. When Robert Guiscard came to Paestum in the eleventh century, he found an uninhabited city from which he took as many marble columns as he needed, some of which I had seen in the atrium of Salerno Cathedral and in other churches of the region.

So Paestum vanished from the eleventh until the eighteenth century. Marshes distilling the *mal aria*, which was believed to be the cause of the disease, and great forests, concealed the temples; in addition, the district was notorious for its ferocious bandits. Though it is difficult to believe that even the most exuberant Italian vegetation could completely conceal these temples, that is the accepted fact: they lay concealed like an Italian Angkor-Wat until the mid-eighteenth century when, during the reign of Charles III, road-makers came upon them with amazement.

It was still dangerous to go there, indeed for a century few travellers ventured to do so; and those who did took good care to be on the way home before dark. The first English traveller to give his impressions was Swinburne in the late eighteenth century, and the first to examine the ruins architecturally was William Wilkins, the architect of many Cambridge colleges and of the National Gallery in London, who described them in his book, *Magna Graecia*, in 1807. Visitors to Naples in the nineteenth century were content with Pompeii and Herculaneum; few risked the discomfort and danger of a visit to Paestum, though Shelley did so and admired the glimpse of far-off blue mountains between the fluted columns. Later in the century when the railway arrived, the station master and porter were issued with veils and gloves as a protection against the mosquitoes. Augustus Hare, who noticed this, added that, in his opinion, to be stationed there was a sentence of death.

It did not seem to me that the temples were sad or gloomy, or that they were mourning their past greatness, as some travellers have said; on the contrary, they appeared to me cheerful and bright. I enjoyed the sight of lizards palpitating on the brown stones, the butterflies flickering above the wild flowers, sometimes even fluttering into the vast naves of the temples. I thought that if any ghosts were about they would be of girls strewing flowers or women petitioning the Queen of Heaven for children.

It was remarkable to notice how rapidly the thirsty summer earth had absorbed the downpour, how the pools of water which offered such charming reflections of column and architrave had shrunk and vanished, how swiftly the stones had resumed their warmth. Two men advanced to a small patch of wheat, which was growing up to the entrance of the Temple of Neptune, and began to cut it with sickles. The gold tassels bent and collapsed round them while the rhythmic sound as they cut the wheat joined the hum of insects, the only sounds in Paestum. I walked across to them and asked where the town of Capaccio was, which was founded when Paestum was deserted. One man pointed with his sickle to a hill not far away. He said he had been born there. I asked if there was anything to see in Capaccio. He said no, nothing, and the road was steep. Nevertheless I thought I should like to go there.

The road at first was good, then, as it mounted into the hills, it became a rough and winding track that led finally to a terrace on which stood a large old church. A group of old buildings and houses stood in the background, but there was no sign of life. After eight centuries the inhabitants have descended to the plain to sell postcards, films and pottery to tourists. This was my first hint of the tendency now common (thanks to D.D.T.) to the South of Italy: the movement from the mountains back to the plains.

The church was locked, but by banging upon the door with a stick I roused an old man, who politely welcomed me. I entered a gaunt cathedral of the eleventh century. I noticed one of the spectacular Cosmati pulpits which are a feature of so many great churches of the south. This was the cathedral to which the Bishop of Paestum had moved his throne nine centuries ago. You may, of course, guess what I was looking for; and I found it immediately. Within a glass case above the altar sat the Madonna of the Pomegranate. She is a painted wooden statue, but was so high up that I could not see her clearly. The old man disappeared and obligingly returned with a step ladder. I mounted this, my mind full of pagan memories, and so came face to face with the Madonna.

She is perhaps four feet high, a seated wooden figure, painted and gilt. She is a young woman with a childish mouth and large eyes. Dark hair falls on each side of her face in coils, and upon a folded cloth upon her head rests a large gilt crown tipped by a gold star. The infant Christ, wearing a smaller replica of the same crown, stands upright on her left knee and places His right hand on her shoulder; in her right hand she holds a short staff, or baton, which terminates in a pomegranate. The rind of the fruit is slit to reveal the red seeds inside. The base of the throne carries the words in Latin, 'Hail, Queen of Heaven; hail Lady of the Angels'.

It looked like a seventeenth century work, and I was surprised to find upon the base the date A.D. 1918. When I mentioned this to the sexton, he said he remembered the statue being made fifty years ago by a clever artist in Salerno who had copied it from a picture of a much older statue which had decayed. Thus no doubt the Madonna of the Pomegranate has been refashioned from time to time, always retaining the distinguishing symbol of the Argive Hera. I thought that it may well be that this statue is the only one in existence which reproduces a memory of the lost work of Polyclitus, of which no copy has ever been found. All we know about it is the detailed description of Pausanius, who saw the statue in Argos between A.D. 140–160. It was one of the famous temple statues of the Greek world and is featured on a few coins of the Roman period.

Glancing round the church, I saw that the gilt ceiling was decorated with panels showing the Madonna wearing a spiked gold crown, the Child standing upon her knee, and in her right hand the ancient symbol of her divinity. On the way down the hill I paused at the wayside shrine where the Madonna is to be seen again in coloured tiles, grasping the baton and the pomegranate. Someone who had recently passed that way had left one of the roses of Paestum in a little jar of water.

I was disappointed that none of the clergy was available, since I had many questions to ask. But down in Paestum I met a man who told me that in May and August processions climb the hill to the old church bearing, among other offerings, flowers and votive boats called *cente*, both of which were offered to the Argive Hera centuries before Christ.

This discovery of the Argive Hera at Paestum transformed into the Christian Queen of Heaven seemed to me to deserve the attention of classical scholars, and to repay a thousandfold the fatigue of ascending the hill road to Capaccio.

§ 4

I went southward over mountain roads and came down to the sea at a small town called Agropoli which stands upon a promontory that juts out into the Gulf of Salerno. Here I found a modest bar restaurant whose garden or yard at the back contained a number of vine-covered arbours, in one of which I was brought croquettes of rice and ham with buffalo cheese, an admirable variation of *mozzarella*, which I thought delicious. The family sat opposite in another arbour which opened into the kitchen, eating a hearty meal and sending an emissary from time to time to ask if I was enjoying myself. On one of those kindly visits a son of the house brought a bucket of mussels which had just come up from the sea and offered to prepare *crostini di mare*, which he said was made by spreading mussels cooked in white wine on slices of bread fried in oil; but I was strong-minded enough to resist this offer.

Hearing that an English traveller had arrived, an Italian appeared who told me that he had spent two years in Australia. He was anxious to practice his English, which was fast and fluent. He said he was now a land agent and, as I was to find out later, like nearly everybody in the South of Italy (particularly in Calabria) was dreaming of a golden fairyland of touring cars, lidos, hotels, 'campings', 'dancings', and seaside bungalows. He said with a sigh that tourism now ended at Paestum and that no one explored the beauties of the mountains and the beaches which ran to the frontier of Calabria known as the Cilento. I told him that I was sure his dream would come true.

'I hope,' he said with a sigh, 'I hope!' He was a nice fellow.

I went on through the beauty of the Cilento, sometimes with a view of the sea, and then of blue mountains and forests. Once I looked down from a winding road and saw Cape Palinuro, named after the helmsman of Aeneas, washed by seas as blue as the sky.

Eventually I arrived by devious ways at the deserted ruins of the once great city of Velia. Few people ever visit them and there is nowhere to stay in the neighbourhood. The ruins, which are still fitfully excavated from time to time, stand within a few hundred yards of the sea, but the old harbour has silted up and I could see no trace of it at all. Velia began as a colony centuries before Christ and, unlike most of the cities of Magna Graecia, was founded not by Hellenes but by immigrants from Phocaea in Asia Minor, the same people who founded Marseilles and several sea-ports in Spain. It is quite possible that the Greek pottery and other objects to be seen in French museums found their way to Marseilles by way of Velia about five hundred years before Christ.

Like all the cities of this ancient seaside civilization, the site is marvellously picturesque with the waves breaking nearby upon an immense deserted beach. Some portion of the town walls, as well as the market-place and several streets, have been excavated. But it is impossible to reconstruct the town: most of it lies under the hills or has vanished. Yet in its day it was distinguished for its philosophers and mathematicians, among them Leucippus who, so I have read somewhere, was the first man to teach the atomic theory of matter.

A great number of ancient writers mention this town either under its earlier name of Elea or as Velia. Doctors recommended it as a healthy and invigorating place and Horace made inquiries about it as a possible alternative to Baiae, while Cicero, whose friend Trebatius had a villa there, knew Velia quite well and landed there during sea voyages round this part of the coast.

Among the few modern writers who have visited Velia was the Scot, Ramage, who here had an unpleasant experience with the fleas. The tower is still standing on the hill at the back which Ramage climbed in 1828 and while exploring the ruin was attacked by thousands of fleas. He was in such torment that he ran down to the sea, tore off all his clothes and dashed naked into the waves.

The road south led to an exquisite wood near a place called Laurito, where the bracken was six feet high and the sun came slanting through beech leaves. Here I stopped to admire, far ahead, framed by the boughs of the beeches, a distant gleam of blue water which was the Gulf of Policastro. As I paused, two young women came through the fern and, with the most beguiling smiles and voices, offered me little baskets made of twigs and full of wood strawberries. With delightful effrontery they asked wheedlingly with much eye work and laughter two thousand lire for each tiny basket, which was just about three times as much as any shop would dare to have asked. The robbery was so charmingly staged that I was at first inclined to give what they asked, but then I knew that to do so would only make me a figure of fun. So I laughingly declined and, as they saw me preparing to move on, they cut their price and I bought the baskets. Delighted, they went off into the wood laughing, waist high in the bracken, turning to wave to me until I was out of sight.

I took the road down to the Gulf of Policastro and soon entered the region of Calabria.


§ 5

Calabria is the most romantic, as it is also the least known, of the nineteen regions of Italy. Until recently it was separated from the rest of the peninsula by mountains, the absence of roads, malaria, and, until the last century, by brigands. As recently as 1912 Baedeker warned his readers not to go there unless they were provided with introductions to the local gentry who would put them up, since no hotels existed anywhere except in the larger towns, and even those were of the most squalid description. There are Italians in Lombardy and Tuscany who shudder to this day at the very name of Calabria, and would as soon think of spending a holiday there as in the Congo.

The transformation of Calabria, if the word is not too strong, dates from 1950 when the Italian Government established the Southern Italy Development Fund – the *Cassa del Mezzogiorno* – which has poured millions into the south, and continues to do so, making roads, introducing industries, reclaiming land, draining, irrigating, even restoring ancient castles and cathedrals. Brigandage was put down years ago; even malaria has been abolished – an astonishing achievement – and amazing to relate, hotels, many with air-conditioning and swimming-pools, have been built in places where only a few years ago the three or four writers who ventured into Calabria found only bug-infested hovels. I think two other factors in the awakening of Calabria from its mediaeval coma cannot be exaggerated; they are the 'bus services that now link the mountain villages with the towns and, perhaps above everything, television, which has revealed a new world and has also had a destructive effect on dialect. I should also mention the cheap readymade clothes and washable nylons which have transformed the appearance of the female population.

Englishmen who have written about Calabria are few. The most notable are: Henry Swinburne (1790), Keppel Craven (1821), Ramage (1828), A. J. Strutt (1842), Edward Lear (1847), George Gissing (1901), Norman Douglas (1915 and onwards), Edward Hutton (1915), and E. and B. Whelpton (1957). Not a large list of explorers. These writers rode or walked until the beginning of this century when the railway appeared, a single line laid near the sea and still the greatest blot on the landscape. Ramage, who was twenty-five, walked wearing a travelling costume of his own design, 'a white merino frock-coat, well furnished with capacious pockets, into which I have stuffed my maps and note-books, nankeen trousers, a large-brimmed straw hat, white shoes and an umbrella, a most invaluable article to protect me from the fierceness of the sun's rays'. Ramage was a much greater eccentric even than Edward Lear, who followed him to Calabria five years later. He was a tough Scot who when in peril drew his umbrella and showed fight. He walked, or when able to do so rode a mule, and upon one occasion sat in a cart drawn by buffaloes. Edward Lear travelled with a friend called John Proby and was accompanied by an excellent guide with a gun, and a horse upon which the luggage was carried. The value of Lear's book is not, to my mind, his description of scenery, still less his drawings, which are romanticized beyond the point of recognition, but in his description of the lesser nobility and gentry of Calabria in the middle of the last century. As might be expected of the author of 'The Owl and the Pussy-cat', Lear missed no touch of humour and his pen pictures of dinners, such as that at Stignano, when the youngest member of the family somehow climbed upon the dinner-table and collapsed into a tureen of hot macaroni, provide a humour which is generally lacking in descriptions of this once rather forbidding region of Italy.

All travellers in this century have travelled by train. That was the method used by both Gissing and Norman Douglas, though Douglas also did a lot of walking. Gissing, who was an invalid, saw very little of Calabria; Norman Douglas in the course of more than one visit saw a great deal and his *Old Calabria* will remain a classic, a warm, lovable book illuminated by the writer's charm, humour and scholarship.

§ 2

I motored to the little seaside town of Praia a Mare, which I found to be preparing itself for the Calabrian travel boom in which, as I say, everyone believes. Builders were busy with new hotels and cafés. The Jolly Hotel being full, they advised me to try another which had opened only that very day along the grey volcanic beach.

I must say something about the chain of Jolly Hotels which originated in the south some years ago and has now spread to the north, indeed all over the country. Many a traveller, first hearing of them with perhaps a shudder, envisaging maybe some compulsory form of merriment, will find them no jollier than most hotels, though they still pose an etymological conundrum in a country where the letter J is practically obsolete. I was once so puzzled by this word that I wrote to the head office of the Jolly Hotels to ask if they would kindly explain it to me. They replied that it referred to the lucky card in a pack, known as 'the Jolly Joker', and was used much as the crack Rome–Milan express is called the *Settebello* after the winning card, the Seven of Diamonds, in the popular Italian card game. Not being a card player, this did not mean much to me, and still I cannot remember hearing any of my card-playing friends refer to the 'Jolly Joker'. However, the 'Yolly' hotels, as the J'less Italians call them, in a very real sense inaugurated the reconstruction of the South. They vary from town to town, but they all share one precious virtue: they are all clean and the plumbing really works.

I found the new hotel along the beach open, but only just open. The kitchen staff had not yet arrived; the electricians were trying out the hot-water cylinders and the manager had not yet unwrapped the hotel register. I was welcomed as the first guest. My bags were carried up by an amiable old Calabrian peasant disguised as an hotel porter, a man whose grandfather, wearing a pointed hat, had probably potted at travellers from behind rocks; and he accepted his first tip with delight.

· · · · ·

In the freshness of morning the Gulf of Policastro, bluer, it seemed, even than the Bay of Naples, lay apparently deserted by man. What an extraordinary experience it is in these crowded days to see a road stretching on for miles without a car or a human being on it, to see desolate beaches and rocky coves which it appears no one has ever explored, and to admire a sea, rippling green in the shallows, fading to the deepest of blues, an expanse that might be waiting for Ulysses, for Aeneas, for Jason. How remarkable that ancient Greece should have cast a permanent spell upon the 'toe' of Italy.

While I was thinking of this, I saw two women walk barefoot to the edge of the waves, each carrying upon her head a two-handled amphora of ancient type. They walked in the creamy foam for a little before turning inland, and never once did I see either of them lift a finger to balance her amphora. Such a sight may not be seen often now that tourism is about to claim Calabria but I, at least, have seen it and shall treasure it together with memories of the golden age.

I turned into the hills and ascended a road whose twists and gradients recalled those of the Abruzzo. It led eventually to a remote little village of some four thousand people which has the status of a city. Its name is Lungro. The people are all of Albanian descent who speak a mixture of Albanian and Italian and have remained faithful to the Greek rite. So the village of Lungro is the cathedral city of one of the two Greek dioceses in Italy, the other being near Palermo in Sicily. The arrival of a motor-car in Lungro, and especially one bearing a 'Roma' number plate, was a sensation. A band of tousle-headed youths followed me everywhere rather as sometimes in a field a herd of young bullocks will attach themselves to a stranger out of sheer curiosity. When I turned to smile and say a few words, these lads turned their backs and shambled away to reform again and resume their perambulation.

I entered the little cathedral which, like all Greek churches, was pungent with stale incense, an undistinguished modern building with an ikonostasis decorated with some good modern ikons. My escort followed silently, watching every movement I made, wondering, I suppose, from what threatening region

of bureaucracy I came, and why. There were only a few inscriptions
in the church, the most impressive being a tablet that commemorated the visit to Lungro in July, 1922, of Pope Benedict XV
who had, said the inscription, restored the dignity of the cathedral.

As I was leaving I saw a priest hurrying up, evidently to see why
I had come. He was a striking figure in an Italian scene: tall, swarthy,
square bearded, and wearing the black brimless hat of the Greek
priesthood. I immediately told him my simple and harmless mission
in life, which cleared the air, and we went together into the
*diakonikon*, which corresponds to our sacristy, where we had a talk.
He told me that there are 70,000 people of Albanian descent in the
south of Italy who have remained faithful to the Greek rite. Their
language is known as Albanese. All the towns in the mountains
round Lungro are Albanian. I asked him to give me a list of the
parishes, which are: Vaccarizzo Albanese, Frascineto, S. Benedetto
Ullano, S. Sofia d'Epiro, Plataci, Firmo, Macchia Albanese, Castra-
regio, Eianina, Acquaformosa, S. Vasili, where there is a monastery
and a seminary, S. Demetrio Corone, S. Costantino Albanese,
and S. Giorgio Albanese. The affairs of the Greek Church in
Italy, which is in communion with Rome, are conducted by the
Greek Pontifical College, a few paces from the Spanish Steps in
Rome.

The priest told me that the Mass is celebrated in Greek, though
an official Albanian translation was being prepared. Curiously
enough the Mass was often said in Albanian in past times, he said,
because Albanians in Italy were considered to belong to an oriental
region and under oriental law all languages are liturgical. He said
that twice a year, in April and September, a pilgrimage sets off for
Genazzano, in the hills about thirty miles to the east of Rome, to
the Sanctuary of the Madonna del Buon Consiglio, whose picture
is said to have been miraculously transported from Albania in
1467.

When I asked if Albanians ever married Italians, he said that it
was rare and that the Albanians have retained a strong sense of
separateness, which revealed itself during the Mussolini regime
with its stress upon the glory of being Italian and the heirs of ancient
Rome. Rather than become members of the Fascist Party many

thousands of Albanians emigrated during the 1920s, mostly to the Argentine. He said there were twelve thousand in Buenos Aires alone and a great number in the United States. Long distance emigration is not as common now as it was fifty years ago. The young men go instead to the countries of the European Common Market, particularly to Switzerland and Germany, and most of them return after a time to their own villages.

I mentioned that I was sorry not to have seen the handsome costumes worn by the women and praised by early travellers. He said that many of the older generation still wore them, but the number is becoming fewer every year. The best time to see the costumes is at Easter and the feasts after Easter connected with the victories of the Albanian national hero, Scanderbeg, who died in 1467, which, incidentally, was the year in which the Madonna del Buon Consiglio is said to have taken flight to Italy. He spoke of what he called the 'rhapsodies', or ballads, about Scanderbeg, which are now being collected, but have not yet been printed. The memory of that extraordinary man is still as fresh today in the Albanian villages as it was centuries ago. His real name was Giorgio Castriota. During the Turkish occupation of Albania he pretended to be a Moslem and rose to a position of great authority. Suddenly revealing himself to be a Christian, and rallying the Albanian mountaineers round him, he began a twenty-five year long guerrilla war with the invaders.


I continued across the mountains, winding into valleys and up again into passes where the towns were plastered upon what from a distance appeared to be perpendicular hillsides; I saw everywhere, mile after mile, wild orchids and gladioli and the golden belts of gorse which set Italy alight from north to south and last for months. I did not meet a single car upon these roads. I saw mules with loaded panniers; I saw donkeys piled with sacks; I saw, most characteristic of all, women, as in the Abruzzo, ascending meandering tracks up to mountain villages with waterpots or loads of firewood upon their heads. Some, I noticed, carried the cone-shaped wooden water barrels of the mediaeval water-carrier which were called *coppelle* and in which water was once hawked from door to door.

So I came at length to the town of Castrovillari where the Jolly Hotel gave me a room with a bath. There is a time in life, which I remember well, when to sleep in a cave or a tomb or a hovel or some fearsome shanty seems romantic to a young man; and it is right that this should be so. But in later life, after a hundred miles of switchback mountain roads, how sweet is the sound of bath water, how exquisite the knowledge that the sheets conceal no entomological specimens. How many English travellers in the South have described how, rather than risk the perils of bed, they have sat up all night fully dressed, drinking the local wine!

Bathed and refreshed, I walked out into this mountain town which, subject to earthquakes, wears the uncertain air usual in such places. The Whelptons in their admirable book were reminded of an Irish town, and this I thought to be a good comparison. Castrovillari might indeed, with certain reservations, have been a small country town in Kerry during a heat wave. There were much the same kind of old men leaning on long sticks, similar small shops into whose windows a careless hand has tossed a selection of the goods to be obtained within. I found the people charming and delighted to help and serve a stranger.

The penetrative power of commerce is a fascinating subject. Entering a tiny shop which looked as though it might with difficulty rake up some ancient objects, I found it stocked with most of the best known tubes of tooth-paste, with English and American shaving soaps and, oddly enough, I thought, since I had seen no one in Castrovillari who suggested the use of such a product, after-shave lotion. But, after all, why should this be surprising? Probably some traveller in the fourth century B.C. might have found in such an out of the way spot some of the most popular exports of Athens and Asia Minor, landed maybe at Sybaris or any of the Greek sea-ports and distributed by caravan; for what, after all, was Magna Graecia but a huge commercial concern half of whose income came from importing and distributing merchandise? It was in this shop that I saw a post-card of an ancient Madonna, the *Vera Immagine di Maria Santissima del Castello*, one of the many venerable Greek ikons of the South. Asking where I could see her, I was directed to the old town perched upon a rock about half a mile away.

Here upon a hill-top I found that a number of squalid mediaeval streets were clustered round a stubborn castle, which is now the prison and looks like it, while nearby stands an old church that probably goes back perhaps beyond the Norman age. The view was indescribably splendid. Looking to the north, I faced the whole Pollino range of mountains which divides Calabria from the rest of Italy. It was that time in the evening when the mountains are the colour of blue grapes. Before me lay miles of unknown country penetrated here and there by nothing more than mule tracks. The only account I have ever read of that mountain country is Norman Douglas's description of his climb to the annual festival of the Madonna di Pollino, a two-day journey from Castrovillari, a ceremony that, said Douglas, 'must date from hoary antiquity'. I identified some of the chief mountains, Mount Pollino, Dolce-dorme, Serra del Prete, and a dozen others.

It was an enchanting spot. There was a garden where someone had grown hollyhocks; there were small haycocks in the fields, and the evening light was stealing through the olive groves. Some way below, the smoke of Castrovillari lay like a thin grey veil in the air.

Just inside the door of the church was a holy water stoup with a fish carved inside it, one of the most ancient of Christian symbols. The most precious object is of course the Byzantine ikon of the Virgin, which hangs above the altar and has been retouched century after century. Her miracles are countless. She is celebrated all over the north of Calabria for her ability to solve the problems and per-plexities of life. Peasants visit her for miles around and dedicate their hair to her, one of the most ancient of pagan customs. The ikon is surrounded by tufts of human hair of all colours from ginger to black; even while I stood surprised to see this custom observed a woman entered and tied a tress of her hair as near as possible to the picture as an offering to the Queen of Heaven. The finest collection of dedicated hair which I have seen is in one of the main streets of Merida, in Spain, outside the church of St Eulalia.

I left this enchanted spot with its view of the blue Pollino

mountains and went down to the town where I found some excitement. A touring coach had drawn up outside the hotel. The place
was full of English tourists who had no idea where they were or in
what an unlikely place they were to spend the night. Anyone with
an ear for English accents could tell that the tour had been recruited
in Yorkshire. The courier told me that it was the first conducted
tour to Sicily by road through the South of Italy, and that the
journey as far as Castrovillari had been superb, over the new autostrada which will eventually end at Reggio Calabria. He was fully
conscious that he was blazing a trail.

How fantastic is tourism. It wafts the housewife from Hudders-
field over seas where ancient mariners have striven to survive, it
carries her across old battlefields and the sites of once great cities
and upon the routes of caravans. She complains if the road is a bit
bumpy and in the morning is annoyed if the early morning tea is
late. I met a man from Yorkshire who had landed with the Eighth
Army in Sicily during Operation 'Husky' of 1943, now visiting
the scene of his martial exploits with his wife and daughter.

'I've told them about the country so often,' he said, 'but there's
nothing like seeing for yourself, is there?'

'Perhaps it would have cheered you up,' I suggested, 'had you
known in 1943 that the day would come when you would bring
your wife and daughter to Sicily.'

'By gum, you're right,' he said, 'but I wasn't even married then!'

All that evening the strangers filled the 'Yolly' with the chatter
of North Country starlings (and some puzzled the young barman
by asking for mild and bitter); but in the morning as it was
becoming light there were scurryings and door bangings, then
silence as the tourists sped onwards towards Sicily.

§ 6

When I left Castrovillari I could look down over blue hills and
woodland to the Ionian Sea and the yellow plain upon which the
city of Sybaris once stood. Rich and famous, the parent of Paestum,
a city that could put three hundred thousand men into the field, a
city whose wealth and luxury excited the envy of the Hellenic

world, Sybaris has vanished from the map. Archaeologists have been looking for it for more than a century, and still they continue to search. It disappeared in 510 B.C. in a peculiar way. A group of agitators from Sybaris fled to the rival city of Croton and were given political asylum. When Croton refused to hand them over, Sybaris declared war and was defeated. Her remorseless conqueror decided to stamp out Sybaris, which was done, it is said, by diverting the river Crathis (now called the Crati) over the city, obliterating it beneath tons of mud and silt. Such, it seems, was the end of a city celebrated for its luxury, for its streets shaded with silk awnings, for its landowners who drove round their estates in the finest of chariots, and for its cooks and its epicures.

I found my way down to the plain along mountain roads and by way of picturesque villages, nearly all of them Albanian. In one I was in time to see the conclusion of a Greek Mass. I have always thought this ceremony more mysterious than the Latin Mass, which takes place from beginning to end in view of the congregation, while the *ikonostasis* hides the celebrant and his acolytes from the Greek worshipper for long periods. The sound of chanting and the smell of incense come to him from the holy of holies. Sometimes the priest appears, dark, bearded and clothed in a glittering vestment, to vanish again to his concealed altar. In a way, the Mass is more emotional than in the West. The worshippers often pray standing with their arms held out, the palms of their hands turned outward, an attitude of prayer seen in the frescoes of the Catacombs. I was in time to see the priest give the unconsecrated portion of the eucharistic bread to the congregation – in this instance five old women who held up trembling, veined hands for it at the church door, reverently kissing it.

A mile or so from the old town of Frascineto I saw in the morning light a brilliant group of peasants with their horses and carts grouped outside a fine Byzantine church some distance from the road. I turned into a side lane to see what was happening and found that the church was in ruins and a busy fair was in progress round it, a good example of the vitality of fairs and markets which often survive the buildings round which they originated. It was the most 'mountainy' fair (as they used to say in Ireland) one could imagine. Mountain folk for miles around had come to the old church on foot, on the backs of mules and donkeys and in high-wheeled carts. The unharnessed animals were happily grazing on the sweet green grass round the church while the mountaineers and their women walked between rows of the most commonplace objects set out in rows upon the ground: kitchen chairs, second-hand clothes, shoes and boots, patent medicines, ribbons and gim-crack jewellery and, of course, charms to avert the Evil Eye. There was a fine collection of red and glazed pottery among which I noticed many shapes which have been in use in the south of Italy since the days of the Greek colonies. The two-handled amphora seen everywhere at the village well is still similar to those to be seen in museums. I did not, alas, observe one woman in the gorgeous Albanian dress one reads about; they were all wearing cotton frocks or coats and skirts.

The old church with its tiled domes and semi-domes appeared complete from the outside, but was really only a shell. There were enormous holes in the nave into which it would have been easy to have fallen. These were tombs from which the bodily remains had been removed to a modern cemetery next to the church. The peasants had come to the fair with bunches of flowers and candles to leave in the cemetery. Each tomb was like a small house with its own roof. Photographs of the deceased were framed in every tomb. And I saw the strange and touching sight, so ancient and so pagan, of people lighting little oil lamps on the tombs and leaving offer-ings to the spirits of the departed.

Little by little I descended to the Ionian Sea where the glare of the plain was blinding and the heat intense. A long road runs from Reggio Calabria, on the Straits of Messina, round the southern tip of Italy up the east coast to Taranto, nearly always beside the sea, or never more than a few hundred yards from it. One reads of hundreds of deserted beaches of golden sand waiting to be dis-covered and exploited as a new Italian Riviera. It is true that there are hundreds of such beaches but the sand, not always golden, is more often of a blue-grey, volcanic colour which, to me, is un-pleasing. Here and there in between are stretches of ideally golden beaches each one of which has been claimed by the nearest town as its 'lido' or 'marina', even though there may be nothing there but a wooden hut. Probably the day is not distant when all of these will be well known summer resorts, but before that can happen someone will have to persuade the fairy godmother, the *Cassa del Mezzogiorno*, to move back the railway, which in most places runs between the road and the sea.

I went up and down this road looking for the site of Sybaris. I found the Crati river, which I crossed several times on a girder bridge, a mountain torrent which was almost dry and full of boulders. Like all such torrents, the Crati must have changed its course many times since the end of Sybaris, which makes the search for the lost city extremely difficult. I came with some surprise to a red-brick settlement called Thurio, which is the modern name for the vanished city of Thurii, where Herodotus wrote his history and where it is said he died. Now there is nothing but the wide plain with fields of corn and tobacco shimmering in the heat, and some way off beyond sand dunes, the glitter of the sea.

To a Greek of 600 B.C. it would have been inconceivable that a day would come when a man could go up and down this road looking for Sybaris, asking carters, who shook their heads and moved on, and questioning the odd figure seen in a field of tobacco and receiving in reply nothing but a bewildered negative. I drove into a farmyard where, in reply to my calls, a woman emerged at the top of an outside stone stairway, but I was unable to understand her. However, she seemed to react to the word 'Sybaris' and appeared to wave me along a dirt track towards the sea, which I followed for a mile or so and then gave up in despair.

What a fate for Sybaris! The most melancholy prophecies of Isaiah and Jeremiah, as they foretold the annihilation of great cities, have not only been fulfilled here but exceeded. I seem to remember that the prophets did not rule out lizards, and even dragons, in the abomination of desolation, but upon the Plain of Sybaris there is absolutely nothing to indicate that a great and, one may be sure, beautiful city once stood there. Nothing is left of Sybaris except a word. It exists in all the languages of Europe. In English and French it is 'Sybarite'; in Italian it is 'Sibarita', and also in Spanish; and in German it is 'Sybarit'.

The story I like best about the Sybarites was told by Athanaeus of the Sybarite cavalry, five thousand strong, who wore saffron robes over their armour and whose horses were taught to dance. During the fatal war with Croton the cunning enemy put musicians into uniform who, when they came within earshot of the Sybarite cavalry, struck up the tunes of the musical rides, with the result that the horses began to dance and, dancing, carried their riders into the ranks of the enemy, where they were swiftly despatched. Much the best and fullest account of Sybaritic luxury is also recorded by Athanaeus in his essay on the love of pleasure. 'And some of the roads that led to their villas in the country,' he wrote, 'were covered with awnings all over; and a great many had cellars near the sea, into which their wine was brought by canals from the country, and some of it was sold out of the country, but some was brought into the city in boats. They also celebrate in public numbers of feasts; and they honour those who display great magnificence on such occasions with golden crowns, and they proclaim their names at the public sacrifices and games; announcing not only their good will towards the city, but also the great magnificence they had displayed in the feasts. And on these occasions they even crown those cooks who have served up the most exquisite dishes. And among the Sybarites there were found baths in which, while they lay down, they were steamed with warm vapours. And they were the first people who introduced the custom of bringing chamber-pots into entertainments.' (This custom was revived by Sybarites of the eighteenth century. Many years ago the late Duke of Argyll showed me one *in situ* behind the window panelling of the dining-room in Inveraray Castle.)

Anthanaeus goes on to say that the Sybarites would prepare for a banquet a year ahead, also if one of the cooks invented a new sauce, or a dish, he alone was allowed to make it for a year and to take royalties on it. For some unknown reason those who caught and sold eels were exempt from taxation, as were the dyers who made purple cloth. Noisy trades were removed some distance from the city, coppersmiths, blacksmiths and carpenters. None of this sounds very hedonistic yet the life lived at Sybaris had an extraordinary effect upon contemporaries and near contemporaries who heard about Sybaritic goings on with the avidity with which some people to-day read gossip about Hollywood. One reads Athanaeus, and others who have written about Sybaris, expecting them to reveal some new vice, but there was never any such suggestion. Their greatest excess appears to have been gastronomy, though that qualifies as one of the Seven Deadly Sins only when it becomes gluttony.

I was sorry not to have found the site of Sybaris. The only person who believed that he knew where the city lay was Lenormont, but he said that it was deep down covered with the mud and silt of centuries, and offered rich rewards to those who could discover it. To cheer myself up I remembered an absurd conversation recorded by Orioli in *Moving Along*, which took place in this neighbourhood when he was on a walking tour with Norman Douglas. They were pestered by a tiresome peasant called Tommaso, who kept asking Douglas how much his hat cost, his coat, his walking-stick, and so on.

'And what did your watch cost you?' asked Tommaso.

'I can't say,' replied Douglas, 'it was given me by the Sultan of Turkey.'

'I wish he would give me one too. And your walking-stick?'

'My stick,' said Norman, 'cost eight hundred and fifty lire. It is made of wood that grows in the island of Zamorgla and nowhere else.'

'You must be millionaires.'

'We are.'

'Then Norman turned to me', says Orioli, 'and said, "Never call yourself poor when you talk to these people. Say you are a millionaire, and that you mean to keep every penny of your money and to pay them rather less than anybody else pays. That will make them respect you. And do you want to make them hate you? Never call them robbers and cut-throats: they like that! Say you know they are rich. . . . It makes them furious."'

Douglas must have been an amusing travelling companion. Reluctantly I turned away from Sybaris and was on my way to the town of Rossano.

§ 7

A few miles to the south of the Crati river the hot plain is dominated by a background of blue hills. Some of them hold towns upon their summits like Corigliano Calabro, which is crowned by an old, probably Norman, castle. Behind these hills are the highlands of the Sila, the Switzerland of southern Italy. As I went along, marvelling that the little houses which I passed now and then had no mosquito netting over doors and windows, I came to an orchard in which a man was taking some substance from the trunks of trees. He told me he was gathering manna.

This then was the famous manna that one reads about in the early books on the southern Mediterranean. The accounts of travellers are usually muddled and misleading. For example, George Sandys wrote that 'it falls at night like dew on the mulberry leaves', which caused a modern commentator to add innocently, 'What it was I cannot imagine.' (It was really inaccurate reporting!) In Italy manna does not fall from heaven, neither does it accumulate on mulberry leaves. It is a sugary resin – it tastes sweet – that oozes from the punctured trunks and stems of the ash tree (*fraxinus ornus*), which is indigenous to the southern Mediterranean.

The man was delighted when I climbed over the wall to watch him gather the manna. Cuts are made in the trees and after some hours, when the sap or juice which oozes out has dried, it is gathered. The farmer told me that though the ash tree is common in Calabria, as far as he knew it was cultivated commercially only in Sicily. Manna is a mild aperient which is sold by every Italian chemist and has only recently, I believe, disappeared from the English pharmacopoeia. This antique medicine may be found in any Italian *farmacia* and every Italian mother has administered it to her young. The Biblical manna was evidently something rather different. I remember years ago making inquiries about this in the Arabian desert on the way to Petra and was told that manna was a sticky substance that fell in the night on tamarisk bushes but had to be gathered before the sun was up. In Calabria the ash trees gradually bleed to death. Beginning at the bottom of the trunk, the farmer cuts the tree all the way up, then starts on another side until eventually the tree is covered with gashes and has to be cut down. He gave me a large piece of manna and told me to dissolve it in water and drink it during hot weather. To my annoyance, I lost this lump of the only manna I am ever likely to possess.

I came in a few miles to a mountain road that wound its way up to the ancient town of Rossano. It is grouped upon a hill about eight hundred feet high, with a view downward through olive groves crackling with cicadas to the sparkling sea; north-westward I saw the great golden sweep of the Plain of Sybaris and inland the mountains of the Pollino range whose marvellous purple outlines I had admired from Castrovillari. I drew up in a large, ancient piazza, and, so well does art improve on nature these days, I almost looked round for the film cameras and the technicians.

My car, the only one there, caused some curiosity. Who was I? 'Roma' on the number plate! I could see them wondering what kind of interference I represented. In such situations I try to seek out the most important-looking person, or a policeman, and say clearly 'I am a tourist. I have come here because I have heard that your town is full of interesting things and good people.' After this all is plain sailing. It takes about fifteen minutes for such a remark to get right round a small Italian town.

Rossano has not altered, I should say, since Norman Douglas was there half a century ago. Though fully alive to the beauty and history of the place, he would have preferred his bed to have been uninhabited. He was prompted to count his companions and to add a footnote:

*Guest:* 'Look here, I found two bugs in my bed last night.'
*Innkeeper:* 'What d'you expect to find? Humming birds?'

Rossano is famous for two great possessions, both of them in the cathedral of mottled marble. One is a Madonna *achiropita*, that is to say a picture painted by a supernatural artist, and the other is the unique Purple Codex, known to the learned as *Codex Purpureus Rossanensis*. I found the Madonna enshrined in a baroque chapel, in appearance like all the other supernatural ikons I have seen and evidently the work of a promising angelic art student. The Codex, on the other hand, was quite exceptional, the only purple Greek Codex of the sixth century in existence. It is curious that when

25 Three wooden spires, or 'lilies', in the piazza at Nola, near Naples, during the annual 'Dance of the Lilies'

26A (*above*) Temple of Neptune, Paestum

26B (*below, left*) Church of St Mary of the Pomegranate, Capaccio Vecchio. C (*right*)
Madonna of the Pomegranate

27A (*above*) The Pollino mountains from Castrovillari

27B (*below*) Country fair outside Byzantine church at Frascineto

28A (*above*) Cosenza, Calabria

28B (*below, left*) Memorial to Isabella (d. 1270), consort of Philip III of France, in Cosenz
Cathedral. C (*right*) On the road to Maida Vale

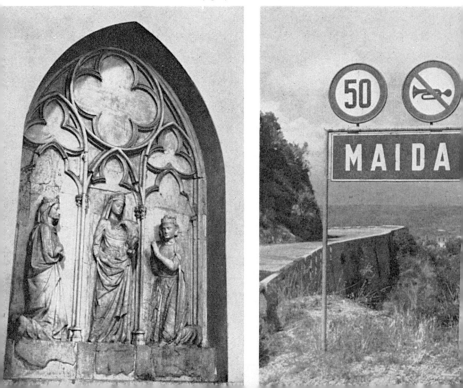

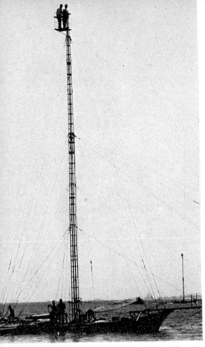

29A (*above, left*) Swordfish boat in the Straits of Messina. The photograph does not show the forward catwalk, which is as long as the mainmast. B (*right*) Woman carries swordfish ashore at Bagnara

29C (*below*) Old type of boat still used at Bagnara

30A (*above, left*) Terracotta ex-voto (500 B.C.) showing Persephone and Hades seated side by side. From Locri Museum, Reggio di Calabria. B (*right*) One of the Dioscuri from a temple near Locri (fifth century B.C.). Museum, Reggio di Calabria

30C (*below*) Coloured terracotta waterspouts from a Greek temple. Museum, Reggio di Calabria

31A (*above*) Reggio di Calabria, facing Sicily and snowbound Etna, across the Straits of Messina

31B (*below*) An eighteenth century impression of a Calabrian earthquake

32A (*above*) The ruins of Locri

32B (*below*) Norman nave of Byzantine columns, the Cathedral, Gerace, Calabria

Ramage was here in 1828 he saw it in the house of one of the canons, whose private property he assumed it to be. Now it is kept in a safe in the diocesan museum.

It is a thick and bulky volume of tough blueish-violet dyed leaves of vellum upon which the Gospel of St Matthew, and nearly the whole of St Mark, are written in Greek letters of silver. There are seventeen brilliant miniatures beautifully drawn and painted and full of details illustrating some of the best known incidents in the Gospels. I noticed the Raising of Lazarus. He is supported by a slave while Christ, already the bearded Christ of Greek tradition, stands clothed in a purple tunic and a golden mantle while Mary and Martha sit at His feet. The Entry into Jerusalem might almost be a modern Christmas card. Our Lord rides from the left, two disciples follow, some boys have climbed a tree in the background, and people are coming out to meet Christ from the Gate of Jerusalem, carrying palms. There is an admirable miniature showing Christ driving the money-changers from the Temple, and I also like the Parable of the Virgins. The five Foolish Virgins are seen in variously coloured dresses holding extinguished torches, while opposite stand the five Wise Virgins all in white, looking excessively virtuous, each one carrying a burning flambeau. The picture of the Last Supper shows Christ and His disciples reclining like Romans at a semi-circular table; a rocky landscape, with a crescent moon and stars in the sky, reveals Our Lord in the Garden of Gethsemane bending over the sleeping disciples.

The priest told me that the history of this treasure is not known. It is believed that it was written and illuminated in Syria and brought to Calabria by Greek monks who fled into exile during the Iconoclastic Controversy, which began in the eighth century. What happened to the missing gospels of St Luke and St John is also unknown.

Rossano deserves a Jolly. There is only one hotel which is graded as fourth class and the restaurants were, to me, invisible. I had some luncheon in an ancient building in which several men were eating at two tables. The room was old and dark, and, had the men been wearing the clothes of a century ago, with those Calabrian hats called *cappelli pizzuti*, I might have imagined myself back in the

age of Ramage and Lear, perhaps even in the time of George
Sandys, who remarked 'no night doth passe without murder'.

The proprietor came forward and led me to a table at which he
immediately seated himself, courteously inviting me to do the
same. He told me that he could see that I was English. He had a
great admiration for England and the English, which spoke well
for our prisoner of war camps, in which he had learned to speak the
language in which he now addressed me. He accepted a cigarette
and began to discuss world affairs, while the men at the table shovel-
ling down spaghetti paused in wonderment to hear their townsman
talking so fluently to a stranger in an incomprehensible tongue.

I ventured to mention the question of food. What would I like,
he asked, as if the kitchens of the Ritz lay beyond. I chose minestrone
and roast kid. The soup was excellent and one might have held a
spoon upright in it; the roast kid, too, was good; then the padrone
appeared carrying a plate of purple figs still warm from his garden.
We drank coffee together and discussed the balance of power in
Europe, the implications of the atom bomb and the possibility of a
third war. I would like to have stayed in Rossano with this warm-
hearted innkeeper but unable to risk the prospect of humming
birds, I decided, late as it was, to cross the Sila and sleep in Cosenza.
The innkeeper thrust a large bag full of figs into the car as he waved
me good-bye.


§ 8

Among the chief geographical facts about Calabria are the
Pollino Mountains which separate the region from the rest of Italy,
the high tableland of the Sila which stretches across the peninsula
from the Ionian to the Tyrrhenian Sea, and in the deep south, at
the very 'toe' of Italy, the mighty mountains with the beautiful
name of Aspromonte. A geologist once told me that the Sila tableland, which is sandwiched between those two mountain formations,
is older than the Apennines, and that a great part of it lies under the
Tyrrhenian Sea. Since the days of Magna Graecia the Sila has been
the lumberjack region of Italy. Here men have felled the mighty
pines for centuries to sell to ship-builders. Among the hoped for

gains that Athens expected from the disastrous Sicilian expedition of 413 B.C. were ships' timber from the Sila.

Though the distance in a straight line from Rossano to Cosenza on the opposite side of the peninsula is only about thirty miles, by road I should think it must be more than a hundred and thirty of the most alarming mountain roads in the south of Italy. There is nothing as trying even in the Abruzzi. Soon I was winding up and down with a hairpin bend in the road every fifty yards, as I mounted to the Sila Grande, as this part of the six hundred square miles of plateau is called. But 'plateau' does not describe this land with its terrific river torrents, dry as a bone in summer, and its mountains, some of which rise 7,000 feet above the sea. The region to the north is the Sila Greca, named after the Albanian settlers there, while to the south lies the Sila Piccola. I was told that bears are no longer to be found there though wolves and wild cats are common.

I admired the hill slopes covered with the finest of olive trees, while in the dry bed of the Colognati the oleanders, once such sinister signs of malaria, were flowering like shrubberies of rhododendrons. I arrived at length at the mountain town of Longobucco, where I found the male population sitting outside the café or upon the walls wearing their best clothes, for it was a saint's day. It is an interesting mediaeval town famed for its weavers, though only a few hand looms are still working, progress having arrived with an organized carpet and rug industry. The word used was *semi-industrializzata*, which I suppose would have been called cottage industry in the early days of the Industrial Revolution.

Having seen this, and other equally inaccessible places in Calabria, I thought more highly than ever, were that possible, of Norman Douglas's explorations as recorded in *Old Calabria*. He came to such places when it was possible to arrive only on foot or by mule. I remembered his description of his long walk to Lungobucco and his reflections on the brigands of the Sila. They lived in the depths of the forests and sometimes shepherds, exploring caves and hollow trees, came upon the loot which robbers had concealed in an emergency and had been unable to retrieve. I was disappointed to see nothing of the feminine finery which I had expected to find in remote Calabria, yet who can blame women for giving up those costly and cumbersome and monstrously hot and uncomfortable dresses with their petticoats, for the sensible washable garments which may be bougnt today for a few shillings? These superb dresses are packed away in camphor balls in a thousand towns and villages, and now is the moment for some enthusiast to collect them and form a museum of southern Italian costume. Even in ten years' time it may be too late.

As I mounted higher into the Sila the olives were left behind, the air became colder and I saw beeches, chestnuts and pines. The wayside shrines had little curtains drawn across them which I do not remember to have seen before in Italy. Some of the roads were lined with red and white striped indication posts to mark the highway during snow storms. The grass was green. The cows with bells round their necks were grey or faun-coloured. Was I in Switzerland or in the Bavarian Alps? The Italian landscape had been lifted so high into the air that it had ceased to be Italian: it was, to all appearances, Alpine. To lift oneself out of Italy in this way, noting how sensitive vegetation is to every upward mile, is a fascinating experience until one comes, at the Lake of Cecita, into a belt of country that might well be the highlands of Scotland, and even the people are unlike the Italians of the sea coast.

There are three narrow lakes in the Sila, all much the same in size and shape, each about eight miles long and two in width. They appear natural but are artificial and are part of the hydro-electrical system that provides Calabria with light and power. South of Lake Cecita, which reminded me a little of Windermere, are the lakes of Arvo and Ampollino. The Swiss chalet, which is the most admired style of architecture, is to be seen in sumptuous form, with balconies, down to the humblest log cabin. There are scores of timber bungalows which are rented in August by those who are able to get away from the heat of the coast. I was told that snow begins to fall in October and often lasts until May.

Eric and Barbara Whelpton, whose admirable travel book I have mentioned, saw the southern Sila, driving up from Catanzaro. They ascended to Taverna, the birthplace of Calabria's only distinguished artist, Mattia Preti, where, in heavy gold frames in the local church, they saw probably the best collection of this artist's rather Spanish-looking religious pictures. The only examples I have seen were in the Capidimonte Museum in Naples. I would like to have seen, as those writers did, the mountain town of San Giovanni in Fiori, of which they wrote: 'The charm of San Giovanni is to be found in the elaborate costume of the women who wear ample black skirts, elaborately embroidered blouses under velvet corselets of rich colours, together with a semi-monastic veil over their heads. During Lent the women veil their faces completely and the men allow their beards to grow.'

How fortunate those travellers were! My own arrival anywhere appeared to be the sign for any woman who might be in regional costume to rush off and change into a flowered nylon dress and an apron! Though ancient finery may be hard to find, it is at any rate possible to travel through the Sila without fear of bandits, although these still exist in Sicily and Sardinia. The newspapers were unable to hush up a story with the authentic old-fashioned ring about it in August, 1966, when Sicilian bandits set up a road block and stopped oncoming cars, forcing the passengers to get out and lie flat in the road. That was the technique of the nineteenth century bandit who advanced with cocked flintlock shouting *a terra, a terra!*, perhaps more effective than the 'hands up!' of the modern gunman.

During the nineteenth century gangs of ruffians, among them escaped galley slaves and murderers, were used politically by anti-Bourbonists to keep the countryside in a turmoil, much as trained terrorists are used today to disrupt established government: but side by side with them the old Calabrian bandit in his brimless gnome's hat still operated but purely for private gain. It is not surprising that only two English writers, so far as I know, ventured into the Sila. They were Henry Swinburne, who travelled with an escort of armed soldiers from Nicastro to Cosenza at the end of the eighteenth century, and a more reckless traveller, Arthur John Strutt, who in 1841, in company with four other young men, went on a sketching holiday, walking and carrying their possessions in knapsacks. Leaving Castrovillari, they mounted into the Sila Grande along the road I had taken, then they branched off over goat tracks, and, crossing the whole of the Sila, reached Catanzaro in the south. This was really, considering the period, a momentous walk and all went well until the party left Catanzaro and struck the wild country south of that town on their way to Caraffa. Here they were set upon by robbers who fired at them and made them lie down, when everything they possessed was taken from them, and they were savagely beaten with axes and mattocks. They might have been killed if a local magnate, Don Domenico Cefaly of Cortale, who happened to have business in the district, had not heard of the attack and rushed up with some armed men.

The villagers, who were Albanians, swore that they believed the young men to be bandits and that they were only doing their duty by capturing them; as for theft, they swore that they had not stolen a thing! The five battered young men were taken by Don Domenico to the house of a friend at San Florio, where their wounds were dressed. Later that night, with the astonishing resiliency of youth, they enjoyed a feast with plenty of wine, and songs sung to the accompaniment of mandolins. One of these reviled the detested 'Greeks' (Albanians) and had the refrain *'O Greco sempre traditore!'*

Don Domenico then took the travellers to his own village of Cortale, where one reads of the almost mediaeval state and lavishness kept by a Calabrian magnate less than a hundred and thirty years ago. 'We entered,' wrote Strutt, 'and Don Domenico, conducting us into an immense saloon, presented us to his wife, Donna Carolina, who received us with much courtesy, and seemed very glad to see her liege lord safe back. The great hall soon filled with the *beau monde* of the village, alike attracted by the desire of paying their respects to Don Domenico, and by their curiosity as to his guests. Here we received the notables in succession, received their commiseration and were required, in turn, to relate and re-relate our adventures . . . and we were heartily glad when, a little after midnight, we were summoned to supper.

'Water is still less in vogue at Cortale than at San Floro, for one beaker sufficed for all the company; perhaps on account of the absence of the ladies; for Donna Carolina and her daughters do not sit down to table with us, but are content with superintending the general arrangements, and the safe arrival of various caravans of dishes, which emerge in savoury solemnity from a vast kitchen, whose oft open door allows us to catch glimpses of a fire, blazing on a stone hearth raised in the centre, and surrounded by toiling servitors, half concealed in steam and smoke; whilst supported on rafters of strong reeds, hams, bacons, *salama*, and salted meats innumerable, enjoy obscurity and fumigation in the upper regions of this scene of hospitable turmoil.'

In the meantime news of the attack upon Englishmen and Frenchmen (for at least two of the young men were French) had reached the authorities at Nicastro and Catanzaro. First, the chief magistrate of Nicastro, accompanied by his clerk, arrived at Don Domenico's palace at Cortale, then came a hundred and twenty militiamen. It was hoped that the young men had not written to their ambassadors, thus drawing the attention of the two most powerful nations in Europe to the misdeeds of Calabria. A swoop on the wicked Albanians of Caraffa was planned and the militiamen arrested several of the villagers. Strutt reports:

'The returning party, as it wound slowly up the steep street (of Cortale) was picturesque and, to us, novel. At the head rode the Capo Urbano, with a great cavalry sabre buckled round him; next came the *élite* of his band, with the prisoners bound, and accompanied by their unhappy wives, in splendid though somewhat faded costumes; whilst in the rear followed the sombre train of Urbans (the militia) looking really quite as desperate as the brigands themselves, with their black dresses, peaked hats and long guns. They marched at once to the prison and ascended the exterior wooden staircase, which led to the apartments of the gaoler, who resides, *al primo*, as it were immediately over his charges. That functionary received the prisoners, and having shown them down an interior flight of stairs, or dropped them through a hole, *à l' ancienne mode*, for we did not observe their method of transit, they soon made their appearance at the bars below.'

The only one of Strutt's delightful water-colour sketches to be reproduced in his book shows this scene: the prisoners at the bars of the prison while their wives stand outside wearing wonderful head-dresses and costumes, all with bare feet.

The end of the affair may seem extraordinary. Almost everything that had been stolen was recovered in various ways except the most serious loss of all, which was fifty-eight golden ducats. However, on the very day that the governor of Catanzaro had ordered the travellers to be reimbursed from parish funds, an urgent messenger from the parish priest of Caraffa arrived with the original gold pieces which had been handed over in the confessional box!

Though not, perhaps, as accomplished a writer as Ramage or Lear, Strutt gives a glimpse of life in Calabria unlike anything else written in English. The author was born in Chelmsford in 1819 and was twenty-two years of age when he made his Italian tour. His father was Jacob George Strutt, painter and etcher, who went to live in Rome when his son was twelve. The boy studied under him and excelled in the painting of animals and trees. He died in Rome in 1888. All through his tour Strutt mentions his sketch-book which he filled with pictures of women in regional costume, for which he had an appreciative eye, of dancers, of fishermen carrying tunny ashore, three men to a fish, and of strange and picturesque characters seen on the roads and elsewhere. I wonder what has happened to this sketch-book? If it still exists it would justify an illustrated edition of Strutt's *Pedestrian Tour of Calabria and Sicily*, which would enrich the scanty personal records of travel in the South.

One of the surprising things about the human race is the change in national character that can occur even in the course of a generation or so, and how odd to reflect that some of the mild-looking inhabitants of the Sila must be the descendants of the ferocious bandits of not so long ago. Norman Douglas mentions a brigand called Caruso, who in 1863 was known to have massacred in one month two hundred persons with his own hands. Orioli in *Moving Along* says that many of the brigands were in their twenties. Nowadays men of this age would probably be working in northern factories or inquiring about emigration to Australia. Orioli goes on to mention a brigand named Scoglio who was shot by national guards in 1868. 'One of them cut off his head,' says Orioli, 'fixed it on a pole and carried it to the village where this young brigand lived. When his mother saw the trophy she fell on her knees and thanked God for delivering her from "this torment of a son".

Young as he was, he had already killed nineteen people, and his greatest joy on killing one of them was to take a piece of bread out of his pocket, dip it in the victim's blood, and eat it, saying "Only now I feel revenged!"'

I passed through scenery which was a faint reflection of Scotland, and descended from pine woods, so silent, straight and mysterious, into the beech and chestnut woods; and so down to warmer orchards and olive groves. Just before I came to a superbly situated town called Spezzano, I saw an old woman holding a black pig by a string and trying to make it jump over a stile. She was the old woman of one's nursery days who was taking a pig to market, and when she came to a stile she said 'pig, pig jump over stile or I shan't get home till morning!' She asked the help, if I remember correctly, of fire, water, a dog, a cow and eventually a cat, before the pig jumped over the stile. I wonder how many children nowadays can recite that long rigmarole, or if any have ever heard of it? From Spezzano I saw, far off, a glimpse of Cosenza.

§ 8

Cosenza is one of the three provincial capitals of the region of Calabria, the others being Catanzaro and Reggio Calabria. Some travellers have found it dull, but to me it is full of interest and beauty. The new town is on the flat land, while the old city clings to the western side of a steep hill where the rivers Crati and Busento meet. Ten miles away is the Tyrrhenian Sea.

I never thought I should visit the town in whose river-bed Alaric the Goth was buried – perhaps the most dramatic funeral in history. When I arrived, I was delighted to find that my window looked down upon the bridge across the Crati, now narrowed to a summer trickle but still visible as a silver ripple in the evening light. I stood there for some time until the lamps were lit and the ancient town was enfolded by darkness.

What changes have taken place in the South of Italy since George Gissing came to Cosenza in 1897, attracted, as I was, by a desire to see the river Busento. He stayed at an inn called, delightfully, Two Little Lions, which, even with his experience of the squalid southern

333

hotels of his day, appeared particularly repellent. 'Over sloppy stones, in an atmosphere heavy with indescribable stenches,' he wrote, 'I felt rather than saw my way to the foot of a stone staircase; this I ascended, and on the floor above found a dusky room where tablecloths and an odour of frying oil afforded some suggestion of refreshment.' At this time the population of Cosenza was about 14,000; today it is more than 82,000.

When Gissing wrote, he was describing the old city on the hill; the new Cosenza, full of typical modern Italian architecture, some of it Fascist, most of it *Cassa del Mezzogiorno*, was still in the future. He never saw the Corso Umberto Primo crossed at right angles by the Corso Mazzini; he never saw the mountain women buying shoes and electric light bulbs; and what would he have said could he have come upon a group of stolid woodmen or shepherds from the Sila seated in a café watching on television a mannequin parade from Milan? And with his painful memories of Two Little Lions, how delighted he would have been with my air-conditioned room and its private bathroom, looking down over the street market to the Crati bridge and the dome of San Francesco di Paola.

Everything written about the South of Italy even thirty years ago, to say nothing of seventy, describes a way of life that is fast vanishing. I have already said but think it worth repeating that good roads, 'bus services, and, above all, television, have brought a new world to once isolated people; probably television has done more than Garibaldi for the true unification of Italy. The speech of announcers has eroded the ancient dialects so that it is rare now to find anyone who cannot understand standard Italian. But even television is unable to make a rocky land fertile, and modern factories, impressive as some may look, often employ surprisingly few people so that emigration continues, either seasonal emigration to other countries in Europe, or to Australia, Canada, and, within the limits of legislation, to the United States.

Hardly a day passed when I did not see evidence of the activities of the *Cassa del Mezzogiorno*: a new dam, a fine new road, a drained marsh, a plain irrigated and sown with field crops, a factory, even a beautiful old Gothic church disinterred from its covering of plaster. This seemed to me almost miraculous: the signs of a southern renaissance. But I noticed that whenever I praised the *Cassa* some knowing-looking Italian would sooner or later place a finger against his nose in the well known cautionary Mediterranean manner which was probably employed by ancient Greeks to warn each other about Phoenicians, and would say, 'Yes, it may seem wonderful to *you*, but please do remember that there is another side to it.' But what precisely this other side is was never quite clear, except that here and there the great pipeline of money may have been tapped, quite legally, of course! However, let an Italian speak on this subject. Luigi Barzini writes in *The Italians*:

'Yet, in spite of all these considerable and sometimes incredible improvements it would be foolhardy to conclude that the *Problema del Mezzogiorno* is definitely on its way to a solution. To begin with, the immense poverty is too old and too deeply rooted really to have disappeared. It has been mostly swept under the carpet. Its pressure still underlies everything. Most of the improvements and modernizations can be observed round a few chosen cities, a few favoured sites, and the most fertile agricultural sections. Everywhere else, where the casual visitor from the north does not usually go, around the corner from a prosperous street, a stone's throw from the resplendent new hotels, factories or workers' housing projects, a short walk up the hills, almost everywhere in the countryside, the *miseria* is still supreme. . . .

'Southerners, of course, naturally want to live better lives, at about the standard of the average Western European, and to solve some of their most urgent material problems. They want all this but they also want something else. They want to see the gap between North and South dwindle. They want to live as well as the northerners. Anything else is not acceptable. Anything else is dishonourable, damaging to their pride. They do not understand why their Nordic countrymen, obviously less clever than they, should have such splendid living conditions, such wonderful factories, such awe-inspiring hospitals, and so much money, and why such things should be less impressive in the South.'

Though I found that southerners might differ widely on almost all the improvements financed by the *Cassa*, on one subject they were united. That is the value of tourism. Most of them believe that one day a golden river of foreign exchange will flow south and then the *Problema del Mezzogiorno* will have been solved. And I think this may be partly so. The southerner, who is asked to step out of the Middle Ages into the industrial world, would, generally speaking, much rather work in a local hotel than in a foreign factory. In addition to which, tourism seems money for jam.

## § 9

Dr Valente, the head of Cosenza's Tourist Bureau, is an historian who has interested himself in the story of Alaric's burial in the bed of the river Busento. One morning he took me along the banks of this river, which divides the old town from the new and flows through a steep and romantic gorge whose rocky sides are covered to the summit with shrubs and trees. I had always imagined that the Busento, or the Bucentinus, as it was known to former ages, was a formidable river, but here I saw a charming little trout stream meandering among boulders and forming pools and cascades as it went on its way. So this was the stream that had been diverted from its course, and after Alaric had been interred in its bed, turned back again so that his grave might remain inviolate for ever: and to think that I had once believed this to have been a mighty engineering feat! Fifty men working with a will could have diverted the Buscento in a few hours as I saw it that sunny morning. The ancient accounts say that when the river had been turned back and the grave covered by its waters, the workmen were slain in order that the spot should remain secret. The local people do not believe this story. They say that the hills provide so much cover that if the ancient inhabitants are anything like the modern, the event would have been the talk of the town.

'At what time of year do you think Alaric was buried?' I asked.

'The Sack of Rome took place in August, 410,' replied Dr Valente.

'And Alaric must have reached Reggio Calabria in September, when a gale wrecked the fleet which he had assembled there to take him and his army to Africa. That was why he decided to retire to Cosenza, where he died, some say of a fever.'

'Do you think the gale meant that the winter rains had started?'
'Not necessarily.'

'So that when the Busento was diverted, it looked much as it looks this morning?'

'Yes, probably it did. Had the rains started in earnest it would have been a raging torrent and it would have been almost impossible to divert it.'

'So we can imagine the burial of Alaric to have taken place on a quiet hot morning like this, with the Busento creaming over the stones as we see it now.'

The path to the river is a narrow track through shoulder-high bamboo and tough river grass. There was a small farm on the hill overlooking the river. A cockerel was crowing, and I could smell crushed fennel as we tramped about before we sat down and talked about Alaric and the Sack of Rome.

If he had been born in A.D. 360, as some believe, he would have been a man of fifty at the time of his death. He was not the shaggy barbarian of popular belief but a Romanized Goth, and an Arian Christian whose ambition it was to hold a high position in the Roman State and to command an army. It is not easy to find a true modern parallel. Even if some Algerian leader, exasperated by the French Government's refusal to make him a Marshal of France, had landed with a powerful army and sacked Paris, the analogy would not be perfect: but it was much that kind of situation. Alaric had been fighting for power in the Roman State for years, leading irregular armies here and there but never achieving his ambition. At last he decided to take what he no longer hoped to be offered. Though technically a barbarian, he was probably a good deal more civilized than, for example, the Normans and Saracens who sacked Rome nearly seven centuries later, or even the fearful ruffians under Charles of Bourbon, who did so in 1527. The sack of 410 was the climax of a series of near attacks in previous years when Alaric had been bought off by the cowardly Romans with gold, dyed skins and pepper, while the miserable and degenerate Western Emperor sheltered in the marshes of Ravenna.

No great buildings were destroyed by the Goths and the churches of St Peter and St Paul were respected. For three days the Goths

337

looted and robbed and no portable treasure was safe from them. The chief places to suffer were the hundred and thirty odd palaces of rich Romans on the Aventine. The Gothic slaves joined their compatriots, forming a valuable fifth column only too eager to lead the raiders to the family jewels. To people alive at that time, this, the first sack of Rome, seemed like the end of the world. Though no longer the Rome of the Republic or even the powerful Rome of the early Caesars, she had ruled the world for so long that news of her humiliation sounded like the death knell of an age. Echoes of the horror and the incredulity inspired by the news may be heard in the writings of St Augustine and St Jerome.

The wagons of the Gothic army, loaded to the brim with gold, gold statues, silver plate, jewels, and some believe the treasures from the Temple of Herod in Jerusalem, which had been on show in a museum in the Forum since they were brought to Rome at the end of the Jewish War, moved south with its captives and with most of the Gothic slaves of Rome. The strangest figure in the procession was Galla Placidia, step-sister of the Western Emperor and cousin of the Eastern Emperor, a young woman of the imperial house in her twenties. Why she did not escape while there was still time, as so many Romans did, is one of the mysteries of history. In the light of her future conduct it almost seems as if she wished to be captured by the barbarians, since after Alaric's death she married his brother Atalphus and, to the scandal of her family and civilized people everywhere, became Queen of the Goths.

Alaric's motive in moving to the south coast was to set sail for Sicily and North Africa and to make himself master of the Roman granary; but, as I have said, he was never to do so. His fleet was scattered by a gale. Perhaps suffering from fever, and possibly haunted by the fear that he had committed sacrilege against the old gods of Rome or the Christian apostles, he retired to Cosenza, where he died.

Dr Valente told me that the tradition in Cosenza is that the chiefs of the Gothic army decided to bury their king in the river bed at the meeting of the Busento with a stream called del Cavallo and in a district known as Vadue. We went to this spot, which was in a romantic glen where, with some reservations, the landscape might have been in Scotland, a place where a trout fisherman would love to have dropped a fly into the pools. It is believed that the Goths, having diverted the stream, dug a deep grave in the river-bed which they lined with stones before they consigned to it the body of their chief, surrounded by the choicest treasures of Rome. Some believe that the Seven Branched Candlestick from the Jewish Holy of Holies and other precious objects may have been buried with him to keep him company in the next world. Having buried their king, the Goths then returned the river to its course.

'I sometimes think,' mused Dr Valente, 'that the whole story may be one of history's picturesque fictions. Yet the ancient authorities tell us that this happened, so what are we to say?'

'Has anybody tried to find the tomb?' I asked.

'Yes, every year an archaeological team arrives from Piacenza, Parma and Bologna to dig in the river-bed at various points. So far they have found nothing. But just think if one day the tomb of Alaric were to be found! Can you imagine the sensation such a discovery would create all over the civilized world? But come, let us not dream; let us, instead, visit our new pasta factory.'

Overlooking the possible site of Alaric's tomb, the financial forces which are reshaping the new South have erected a modern factory for the manufacture of spaghetti in all its forms and shapes. We were soon seated in new deep leather chairs in the manager's office, listening to details of production. Glancing through the window at my elbow, I saw the provocative Busento laughing on its way.

§ 10

The old city of Cosenza crouches upon its mountain, wearing that ill-adjusted air characteristic of earthquake country. The fine marble palaces in which the nobility once lived are now tenements entered here and there by way of a superb Renaissance doorway, and in such places Corinthian columns make fine supports for a clothes-line. Sometimes in a steep and narrow lane one comes across an old palace standing well back behind locked iron gates. Are they still, as they appear to be, inhabited? – do descendants of the old families still move about there beneath the crystal chandeliers? Or are they nursing homes or the offices of associations and institutions?

While wondering about them, I came suddenly to a flight of steps leading to four classical columns which supported a dignified entablature bearing the name of Bernadino Telesio, the most celebrated of Cosenza's sons. He was born in one of the noble palaces in 1509 and he died in Cosenza in 1588 – the year of the Spanish Armada. One of the most distinguished scientific investigators of the Renaissance, his work had a great effect upon the thought of his time. He founded the academy which I now saw at the top of a flight of steps, still thriving after four centuries.

The secretary greeted me as if I were a visiting philosopher and took pleasure in showing me the library, the reading-room, and the room where members once staged plays.

The cathedral of Cosenza, which was consecrated in 1222 in the presence of the Emperor Frederick II (he was then twenty-eight), is a dark Gothic building which has been stripped of its baroque covering of plaster and restored to its original austerity. I was taken to the archbishop's palace, where a courtly monsignore unlocked a safe and, apologizing for having to go off on urgent affairs, left me with the most beautiful treasure of its kind in Calabria. It is a Byzantine reliquary cross which is said to have been the gift of Frederick II. The body of the cross is of gold filigree work with jewels of red, green and yellow, each one standing out in a little cup of gold. The two sides of the cross are different. The most beautiful side, which contains a minute splinter of the True Cross, has five Byzantine medallions of perfect enamel work, one in the centre and the others at the terminal arms of the cross. Each of the five medallions, though no larger than a big coin, is a finished ikon in pale pastel colours, the work of some superb master jeweller or enameller.

I thought the cathedral had been possibly tidied up a little too much. I looked in vain for a tomb which I had believed to be there, that of Henry, the eldest son of Frederick II, who committed suicide in 1242. Frederick's domestic life was full of unhappiness,

Henry being one of his greatest disappointments. The young man rebelled and plotted against his father, who tried him and sentenced him to prison. This was equivalent to a death sentence to Henry. He endured seven years of confinement, then one day, when in the castle at Nicastro, near Cosenza, he went out riding and suddenly spurred his horse over a precipice and was dashed to death. He was buried in a shroud of gold and silver tissue in which eagles' feathers had been woven. 'We mourn the doom of our first-born,' wrote Frederick. 'Nature bids flow a flood of tears, but they are checked by the pain of injury and the inflexibility of Justice.'

Though I failed to find his tomb, I found another and an unexpected one, or rather a memorial. It commemorates the death of a Queen of France, Isabel of Aragon, wife of Philip III, who died in Cosenza in 1271. She was returning with her husband from the abortive Tunisian Crusade. While crossing the river Savuto, her horse stumbled and threw her into the water. She was six months pregnant, and her child lived only for a few hours after her. The memorial is the work of a French artist who, so tradition says, was sent from France to Cosenza to execute it. It is a beautiful, simple and touching work. It shows Our Lady in the centre and on one side Isabella, on the other, Philip.

Even an age familiar with many violent tragedies must have been shocked when the King arrived home in France from Tunis bringing with him three corpses, those of his father Louis IX (St Louis), who had died during the Crusade, his brother, John Tristan, Count of Nevers, and his brother-in-law, Theobald, King of Navarre. When he left Cosenza the funeral train was increased by the body of his beautiful young wife and her prematurely born infant. The day after he returned to Paris, Philip conducted a state funeral at St Denis, but he was not crowned until the following year.

I left the town of Cosenza with regret and went south to Nicastro.

§ 11

The road, which was excellent, ascended in a series of hairpin bends for something like twenty miles. There are few places left in the world where the appearance of a motor-car stampedes mules

and goats, but this is one of them. The mules are ridden by old
women in black who wear scarves almost like yashmaks. They sit
sideways and have little control if the mule suddenly decides to
mount a bank.

Here I saw for the first time women in regional costume riding
mules or donkeys or striding along the road balancing jars or boxes
upon their heads. They wore black bodices and black skirts looped
back into a kind of bustle, revealing scarlet petticoats. They walked
like queens. Those who carried burdens did so upon turban-like
head-pads. I noticed, as in other parts of Calabria, the little wooden
casks like miniature torpedoes containing, perhaps, water, precisely
the same in shape as the cask held by *il Faccino*, the old wall fountain
in the Via Lata in Rome.

The countryside was a lush compromise between Kerry, as I
recall it thirty years ago, and Cornwall, with blue hills in the background which might have been the lowlands of Scotland on a
sunny day; there were clumps of blazing gorse and woods of oak
and chestnut. Low hedges of rosemary scented the air for miles.
There were also snakes, quite large ones, which streaked across
the road.

I stopped at a small town called Soveria Mannelli to buy some
petrol and noticed an obelisk which commemorated the arrival
there of Garibaldi in 1860. I looked into the church for a moment,
where I saw women kneeling wearing black lace mantillas.

Nicastro, some tortuous miles to the south, a busy agricultural
place in the mountains, was half destroyed, and many of its inhabitants killed, in an earthquake in 1638. It has regained its spirits
and rebuilt its churches, while a population of about 30,000, many
of them wearing red petticoats, gives an air of gaiety and vitality
to its streets. Upon the top of the mountain is all that is left of the
castle built by Robert Guiscard, and enlarged by Frederick II, where,
as I recalled when I was at Cosenza, the unfortunate Henry, Frederick's heir, spent his last days.

All the way down from Nicastro, at various bends and turnings
in the road, I had magnificent glimpses of the Tyrrhenian Sea glittering in the west; then I saw the huge plain of Maida, planted now
with olives, which gave its name to Maida Vale in London. Could

any two places appear more unlike than the Plain of Maida and the Edgware Road and Maida Vale? The story is a strange one.

The Battle of Maida Vale, which was fought in 1806, was one of those incidents in the war against Napoleon during that rather operatic period when Nelson and Lady Hamilton were preserving the Bourbon dynasty, when Capri flew the Union Jack for a short period, and when England had a fleet and a small army based on Sicily.

The battle of Maida was a simple operation. A British force of fewer than five thousand men landed on the Plain of Maida at the end of June. They managed to land their field guns, although the surf was heavy. The French army, rather larger in numbers and with some cavalry, was strongly established in the mountains where some advised it to remain and to allow the malarial mosquito to deal with the British. However, the French decided to attack and, impetuously descending to the plain, were soundly defeated. It was the end of the French army in Calabria. The officer in charge of the victorious army was Sir James Stuart, who was born in Georgia in 1759 and had served with the British in the American War of Independence.

The news of the victory at Maida, proof that Napoleon's armies could be beaten, although quite a minor action, exhilarated London so much that the new district then being developed beyond the Edgware Road was called Maida Vale. There is still a memory of the battle in a public house called 'The Hero of Maida', a large red-brick building which stands about a quarter of a mile north of the Edgware Road underground station. It is decorated inside with enlargements of old prints of the battle, but how many of the patrons know who 'the Hero' is, I cannot say.

Sir John Stuart was one of Britain's most fortunate generals. Not only was he immortalized by a public house, he was also thanked by both Houses of Parliament and granted a pension of a thousand pounds a year for life. His grave is to be found in Bristol Cathedral.

It was an odd experience to read 'Maida' on a road sign and to find myself in a hilly little Calabrian town. It was a saint's day. The town band was assembling near the church, someone had let off the usual premature rocket. The church was full. I asked a pleasant-looking man who formed one of a group seated upon a wall if he knew that his town had given its name to a district in London. Yes, he replied, everybody knew that; in fact a friend of his had been to Maida Vale in London and had driven all through it seated in a red omnibus.

# CHAPTER NINE

*Pizzo and the Death of Murat – Why Richard Coeur de Lion Stole a Hawk – Earthquake Country – Fishing for Swordfish – Reggio Calabria – Bergamot Country – Relics of Magna Graecia – Calabrian Briar Pipes*

§ 1

The first place I arrived at after crossing the Plain of Eufemia was the fishing town of Pizzo, mounted upon a cliff, with white sandy beaches below. Before the tunny fleet sets off in the spring the nets are blessed by the priests, then church bells ring as the boats put out to sea.

Pizzo is celebrated in the history of nineteenth century Europe as the town where Napoleon's brother-in-law, Joachim Murat, was shot. That brave soldier, but unfortunate ruler, had married Caroline Bonaparte, and in conformity with Napoleon's policy of placing a relative on every possible European throne, was created King of Naples. This went to Murat's head. Though one of the most fearless of soldiers, he had a silly streak which delighted in show and in the wearing of flamboyant uniforms, designed by himself. He was a mixture of Porthos and the late Field-Marshal Göring. He had not been King of Naples for long before the *lazzaroni* called him 'the King of Feathers'.

Napoleon's summing up of his character was, as usual, concise and accurate. Murat, he said, was brave on the field of battle but weaker than a woman or a monk when not in the presence of danger: he had physical but not moral courage. Napoleon said after Waterloo that had Murat commanded the French cavalry defeat might have been transformed into victory. As a king he was good, honest and sincere, and one of many rulers who wished to unite Italy. By what strange fate did an inn-keeper's son, who became the best cavalry leader of his time,

345

and then a king, come to die in this remote fishing town in Calabria?

During a reign of seven years Murat broke with Napoleon, but was no match for the plots and counterplots of the Allies. After Waterloo he found himself driven from Naples, while Ferdinand IV returned joyfully from Palermo to occupy his old throne and the Palace. In his vanity and self-deception, Murat still believed that he had only to land in Italy in one of his finest uniforms, using the words 'unity', 'freedom' and 'reform', to be the leader of an army that would drive the Bourbons out of Italy for ever. He gathered a few officers and about two hundred and fifty men and set sail in seven small three-masted ships in October, 1815. His plan was to land at Salerno and march on Naples. However, a storm arose which blew his flotilla past Salerno and down the west coast. He never saw his fleet again and his own ship had to put into the little fishing harbour of Pizzo. He must have had in mind Napoleon's escape from Elba and his triumphant march to Paris: but he was not Napoleon, neither was Pizzo in France.

Climbing the steep streets, I came eventually to all that is left of Pizzo Castle, an old building with an archway entrance and crumbling towers. The view down to the harbour is superb. I entered the castle and, mounting a stone stairway, found that the building is now a club house and hostel. It was here that Murat was imprisoned for five days and then shot. The affable manager, realizing that he controls the only place in Pizzo which any historically-minded stranger would wish to see, has the story ready in all its details. He led me to a window and pointed down dramatically to the sea. . . .

It was 8th October, 1815, which was a Sunday. The people of Pizzo were strolling about the piazza after Mass when they observed a small ship entering the harbour. Out stepped a gorgeously attired officer glittering with gold lace, wearing a feathered hat. His spurs were gilt. Together with his few companions he climbed the cliff path to the town where, appearing in the crowded piazza, his followers called for cheers for King Joachim Murat. Instead of cheers, there was an uneasy silence in which many people, scenting trouble, prudently vanished from the scene. Murat tried to buy a horse, but, such is the irony of fate, no one would sell a horse to the man who had commanded the cavalry of the Grand Army at Austerlitz and Jena and had led the great cavalry charge at the Battle of the Pyramids. Instead, they turned hostile and a policeman attempted to arrest Murat. In the end the Frenchmen had to turn and run for the harbour, but when they reached it they found that their ship had sailed away, the captain having also scented trouble. With some difficulty, and while a screaming mob was rushing down the cliffs, they managed to launch a fisherman's boat that was drawn up on the sand. They might have got away if Murat's spurs had not been caught in a fishing-net, and before he could be released the crowd was upon them.

Then followed a frightful display of Calabrian ferocity. The Frenchmen were beaten and scratched. Among their fiercest assailants were old women: one of them dug her nails into Murat's face, screaming, 'You orate about liberty yet you had four of my sons shot!' The policeman managed to get them, half dead and in tatters, to the castle, where they were all flung into a cell so small that they could scarcely sit down on the mud floor.

The manager led me to this cell. It is a dark, cave-like evil room with one small window high in the wall, a horrible little Black Hole of Calcutta. In the meantime the Italian general commanding the district semaphored the news to Naples and sent a detachment of troops to Pizzo. The officer removed Murat from the cell and gave him better quarters in a room nearby, which is now a refreshment bar. He also sent a doctor, food and wine. Murat was able to write letters appealing for help to the British and Austrian ambassadors in Naples, but these were intercepted by the agents of Ferdinand IV and were never delivered.

Ferdinand was at the opera when he received the semaphored message. He left the theatre and held a council at which it was decided to order the military commander to court-martial Murat. The King added an ominous postscript to the effect that he was to be allowed only half-an-hour with the priest after his sentence. Murat was found guilty of incitement to civil war and conspiring against the rightful king and was sentenced to be shot. The sentence was carried out at once. He showed not the slightest fear. All he asked was that the firing party should 'aim at the heart but spare my face'. The space in the little courtyard, where the manager of the hostel described the scene, is so small that the barrels of the muskets must almost have touched Murat's body. He refused to let them bandage his eyes and died, as Napoleon had said, fearless in the face of danger. He was buried in the local church, but all attempts to find his remains have failed. He was forty-eight years of age.

I went into the bar where the manager recommended a glass of his home-made *orzata*, which was excellent. While we were talking, we were joined by a tall, bearded, apostolic-looking young man who wore shorts and carried an immense knapsack. The moment he opened his mouth I knew that he was a Canadian. He told me that he had hitch-hiked from Rome to Pizzo in two days. I could scarcely believe it.

'Well,' he said, 'I guess one has good days and bad days.'

'Where are you making for?' I asked.

'Johannesburg,' he replied.

'But do you expect to hitch-hike across Africa?' I asked.

He shrugged his shoulders and looked more apostolic than ever. I expected him to say, 'The Lord will find a way'; and I am sure he was thinking so.

I, who rarely give anybody a lift, having had friends who have been robbed or hit over the head, and slashed with razors while performing this kindly act, began to think that I may have left St Paul stranded by the roadside on many an occasion. Wondering how a man can set out to travel enormous distances in the cars and lorries of others, I waited for the right moment to ask him how much money he carried. He said that when he left London he had about a hundred and fifty dollars.

When I left the castle, I turned to look back at it and saw an inscribed stone which I had not noticed before. It is inset above the entrance gate, and reads:

To
the blessed memory of
KING GIACOMO MURAT,
a prince glorious in life and
fearless in the face of death,
who was shot here.
This stone records a day saddened by the
ferocity of a mad government.
The Municipality of Pizzo erected it,
A.D. 1900.

I thought that this was the most barefaced attempt at an *amende honorable* that I had ever read. The government may have been ferocious, but what of the ferocity of the ancestors of those who put up the stone; what of the old woman of Pizzo who tore off enough of Murat's moustache to keep in a newspaper as a happy memory of that sad day.

§ 2

As I travelled south the road left the sea and passed between hills planted with olive trees and oranges. Sometimes they grew in the same groves, alternating, as I had so often seen olives and figs planted together in Apulia. In this part of Calabria it is the custom for black pigs to be taken out to scrounge or scavenge by their owners, with a cord or rope tied to a hind-leg, and I saw such groups in nearly every village. The Southern Italian habit of growing the oleander as a tree is to be seen along this road. I passed avenues of them and, as malaria has been defeated, they carried no menace with them. Ox wagons came along drawn by grey-brown oxen the colour of Jersey cows, big, strong animals but lacking the spread of horn and the gentle majesty of the white oxen of Tuscany.

This is fearful earthquake country. There is hardly a town which has not some story of disaster in its past or recent history. The ancient town of Mileto, which is now mainly a long, straggling street near the ruins of the early Mileto, was destroyed in 1783, and again in 1905 and 1908, yet, with the optimism of those who live in volcanic country, the survivors have always returned to make a fresh start. It is difficult to remember that Mileto was Roger of Hauteville's favourite stronghold, the place where he was married and where he died, and a town of great consequence in Norman Italy; it was also in Mileto that Richard Coeur de Lion stayed when on his way south to the Crusades to join the English fleet at Messina. There are still a few Greek columns from a temple, which formed part of the ruined abbey where he once spent a night, but nothing now recalls the splendour of earlier times.

It is recorded by Roger of Hovenden that soon after leaving Mileto, accompanied by only one knight, Richard attempted to steal a hawk from a peasant's house and was nearly killed for it. The villagers attacked him with anything that came to hand. 'One of them then drew his knife against the king,' wrote Roger, 'upon which the latter giving him a blow with the flat of his sword, it snapped asunder, whereupon he pelted the others with stones, and with difficulty making his escape out of their hands, came to a priory called Le Baniare.' This would have been the abbey of S. Maria at Bagnara, which had been founded by Roger of Hauteville and was later destroyed in an earthquake.

I wondered, as I went on, where that bizarre episode had occurred. Why should the King of England have wished to steal a hawk? The answer is interesting. Hearing the bird cry out, Richard immediately rushed not to steal it but to rescue it from (according to the laws of England) its illegal owners. He either did not know, or did not care, that in spite of the Norman background falcons and hawks were not allotted only to the nobility and gentry in the Kingdom of Sicily, but could be owned even by peasants. Writing of hawks in his *Sports and Pastimes*, Joseph Strutt said that these birds were regarded as emblems of nobility and that it was felony punishable by imprisonment for a person unqualified by noble blood to own one or hide one in his house. So presumably Richard would have been just as impetuous had the hawk's cry been that of a damsel in distress.

. . . . .

South of Rossano the road crosses a plain golden, as I saw it, with stubble fields, then bends towards the coast. Coming to the town of Gioia Tauro, I wished, and not for the first time, that I had the courage to try a fourth-class hotel simply to see if they are still as crude and uncomfortable as they were in the days of Gissing and Norman Douglas: but set back from the road in an olive grove was a delightful-looking Jolly Hotel, where I was given a bedroom with an alcove containing a writing table.

I have seen the olive tree in Greece and Cyprus, in Turkey and the Near East, and in many parts of Italy, but never have I seen such splendid and romantic trees as in this part of Calabria, from the Plain of Eufemia southward to Gioia Tauro. From my window I looked into one of the most beautiful groves I can remember, a place which appeared to sum up the romance of the Mediterranean world.

Among the few other guests was an Italian, well dressed and wearing horn-rimmed glasses, who seemed to me to be perhaps an important commercial traveller or possibly an official of the *Cassa*. He was neither. He was an agricultural scientist. We met after dinner, drawn together by solitude. He was a talkative man and soon told me of a fantastic mission on which he had been engaged. Solemnly gazing at me through thick lenses, he said that he had been introducing impotent male fruit-flies into the island of Capri.

I though it was perhaps to my credit that I kept a straight face.

'The experiment,' he explained, 'is to introduce a number of male fruit-flies which have been subjected to sterilization radiation and cannot breed. So the balance of nature is disturbed. It is hoped that a proportion of female fruit flies will mate with the impotent males with the result that there should be a drop in fertility.'

'But is this more effective than the usual chemical sprays?'

'It is an experiment,' he said, 'and it will take years to prove.'

'Nature is a crafty old dame,' I suggested. 'Suppose the females will have nothing to do with the sterilized males?'

He gave a magnificent Italian shrug.

'Who can say? After all, it is only an experiment.' He sighed and allowed his glass to be refilled.

'Why should Capri have been selected for your experiment?'

'The reason is that the island is far enough from the mainland to be free from a mass emigration of fruit-flies, so that we can study the problem knowing that the only flies involved are indigenous. The perfect outcome would be the rejection of the fertile males in favour of the infertile!'

I went to bed later than usual, glad to have been told the latest chapter in the long and variegated sex history of Capri.

Opening my window, I saw that the olive grove below was lit by moonlight; each tree stood in its own shadow and the green wash of light picked out the trunks and shimmered upon the leaves. Though the trees were old, there was no hint of deformity about them, no witchlike arms were thrust into the night; they had retained the firm lines of youth. It is strange how at times, un-expected and unsought, the spirit of a land appears to manifest itself in a single feature, maybe a mountain or a stretch of coast, a forest or a valley, affecting one for a moment with the im-pression that one is about to be admitted to some ancient secret of the earth. Here I felt that all the spirits of the South had gathered in this grove, that somewhere in the silence lived a memory of Greater Greece, the coloured temples and the ships.

§ 3

Nature has somehow reserved an unusual beauty for those parts of Calabria which she has most frequently destroyed. From Pizzo southward there is an additional clarity in the air, a bluer sea, beautiful clouds, while the mountains of Aspromonte mass them-selves with such nobility and charm that one thinks a landscape like this could produce only poets and artists. Though Edward Lear romanticized and exaggerated everything he drew in the south, he did manage to convey an impression of the characteristic Calabrian town which crouches so closely upon a mountain top that from a distance it would be possible to mistake it for a con-tinuation of the geological formation. This is most striking when these towns cover the top of a rock that juts into the sea, or rise above a deserted bay of yellow sand upon which fishing boats are drawn. The air in South Calabria seems to have an added silkiness, while the water, where it meets the sand, is the clearest green ribbed with sun ripples fading to the darkest of blues. The wind blows scented with orange blossom and jasmine. Yet this exquisite corner of Italy is earthquake country.

In the Abruzzi earthquakes might conceivably be thought of as a tragic but not entirely unexpected chastisement of a sombre landscape, but in Calabria they affect one rather as though someone exceptionally talented and attractive had gone mad. I noticed and understood among the Calabresi a supersititious reluctance to talk about earthquakes, and it is not a topic that one would naturally bring up. The only person with whom I discussed it was a seismologically-minded citizen of Cosenza, who was interested in the phenomena and had read a great deal about it.

He had been in two bad earthquakes when a child, but he said that as his parents were not apparently frightened he accepted without alarm that pictures should suddenly swing about and furniture move. He also told me that during an earthquake on the Plain of Eufemia the earth suddenly opened, swallowed a monastery, and closed again. He said that one of the most painful effects of a bad earthquake is the effect on the human mind. During a really bad shock a number of people go mad temporarily or permanently.

The year 1783 was a bad earthquake year. The movement began on 5th February, and continued until the end of May. It was estimated that 30,000 people lost their lives in the South of Italy. Then epidemics followed. Sir William Hamilton carried out a number of observations at the time. He noted how horses and oxen stood braced with legs apart as if 'sensible of the approach of each shock'. Lenormant mentions a woman who could never again be induced to enter a building and spent the rest of her life under a tree.

The earthquake of Messina in 1908, which destroyed that city and also Reggio di Calabria on the opposite side of the Straits,

353

claimed 96,000 lives and lowered the coastline by twenty-six inches at Messina and twenty-one inches at Reggio. During that disaster the two volcanoes, Etna and Stromboli, remained unchanged throughout the shocks, which were caused, so experts say, by the dislocation of mineral masses far below the surface of the earth. Orioli, in *Moving Along*, mentions a rich woman who became so deranged by her experiences that she insisted on being suspended outside a window of her house by a rope; and there she stayed and was fed by her servants.

It was extraordinary to travel through this lovely country and to know that century after century it has been subject to sudden chaos. So I came to the charming little fishing town of Bagnara, of which Norman Douglas wrote: 'The calamities that Bagnara has suffered in the past have been so numerous, so fierce and so varied that, properly speaking, the town has no right to exist any longer.' Not only does it exist, however, but it looked radiant in the early sunlight, with the red roofs shining and the sea curling over like liquid emerald upon the sand. 'It never struck me,' wrote Douglas about Bagnara, 'that the time might have been profitably employed in paying a flying visit to one of the most sacred objects in Calabria and possibly in the whole world, one which Signor N. Marcone describes as reposing at Bagnara in a rich reliquary – the authentic Hat of the Mother of God.'

If this revered object is the 'Hat' preserved in the Carmelite Church, its appearance is now that of a golden crown. It is kept under lock and key and is visible only on the most solemn occasions. However, the obliging verger lit up the church and showed me a replica.

Another oddity about Bagnara is the story that the men look after the houses while the women do all the work and business. All I can say is that I saw a lot of women buying and selling in the market, and perhaps the men had skimped the housework since a great number of them were playing cards in cafés.

Just above Bagnara I caught my first glimpse of Sicily, only a stone's throw, so it seemed, on the other side of the Straits of Messina, and one of the finest views in Europe. The air was so clear that I could see the Sicilian towns sparkling in the morning light, while on the far side of the island the white cone of Etna, gently smoking, was lifted into the sky.

A few miles from Bagnara a signpost on the side of the road bore the word 'Scilla', while, jutting out to sea a short distance away, I saw the famous rock of Scylla where the monster lay in wait to devour those sailors who had escaped the whirlpool of Charybdis on the opposite coast. I have been told that on windy days the narrow entrance to the Straits of Messina can make a nervous sailor remember the old legends and recall the fear of Odysseus as he passed through and saw six of his best oarsmen snatched up by the monster of Scylla.

The ancient castle on the rock is now a ruin, but part of it has been transformed into probably the most elegant and attractive youth hostel anywhere in the world, certainly no other can compete with it for romantic interest. The entrance is an old gate studded with hundreds of nails, and a bell hangs near; a lantern above the archway illuminates the arms of the Princes of Ruffo, the owners of the castle. Seated at a refectory table beneath a vaulted ceiling, guests can now watch television upon the Rock of Scylla!

It is always sad, after having admired an idyllic scene, to hear of some awful happening there. Below the castle is a beautiful beach of yellow sand to which, so I was told, all the inhabitants of Scilla flocked in terror when their town was completely destroyed in the earthquake of 1793. The aged Prince Ruffo of Scilla, who was praying in his chapel, joined the terrified crowds on the beach and knelt with them in prayer. As they prayed the earth shook and, to a sound like thunder, a portion of Monte Baci, the next headland, crashed into the sea. As it did so, a huge wave came sweeping up and carried Prince Ruffo and fifteen hundred people out to sea, where all perished.

§ 4

The first thing I noticed when I came to the town of Reggio di Calabria was an odd-looking boat about half a mile off shore. It carried an enormously tall single mast made of open steel girders. I thought it must be a marker of some kind, indicating a rock or some other obstruction. Then I saw that a similar steel projection stretched from the bows as long, it seemed, as the boat itself.

While I watched this peculiar craft, a man climbed the steel mast and took up his position on a small platform there, while another moved forward on the steel catwalk protruding from the bows. As the boat began to move forward, steering an erratic course, it seemed to me that it must surely capsize. Suddenly the man on the forward platform lifted his arm and something shining – a spear, a harpoon – shot through the air and fell ahead into the sea. Instantly the water was lashed into foam as a huge fish surfaced and fought for its life. That was my first sight of a swordfish boat and the only time, for the fishing season had ended, that I saw a man spear a swordfish as the ancient Greeks did in these waters centuries before Christ.

Swordfish boats, which closely resemble their prey in shape, are a characteristic sight of Reggio and the Straits of Messina. There is a primitive kind, which is a rowing-boat, with a tall pole in the centre with a number of cross-trees on it which offer a precarious foothold for the look-out man, and a dangerous-looking wooden walk forward for the harpoonist: but the larger boats with their steel masts, from which the boat can be steered, are taking their place.

On most of the beaches between Reggio and Bagnara you can see these boats drawn up on the water's edge. Some of the larger have masts sixty feet high and forward platforms of the same length. The look-out man can see the swordfish in the clear water and immediately steers the boat in its direction, and manoeuvres it so that the spearman can get a good shot. The spears which I saw were twelve feet long and ended in a double prong. I saw only one trident.

The swordfish come down from colder water to spawn in the Straits of Messina and generally travel singly or in pairs. While I was talking to a fisherman on the beach at Scilla, two elderly Englishwomen, who happened to be on their way to Sicily with a conducted tour, came up with a guide, a young Italian.

'You see, ladies,' he said, 'the swordfish come here to make love.'

'What did he say, dear?' asked one of the ladies.

'He said the swordfish come here to spawn, darling,' shouted her friend.

The other looked with the bright, interested eyes of the very deaf, and asked:

'They come to do *what?*'

'They come here,' shouted her friend, 'to propagate – to *breed*!'

'Oh, I see. Thank you, darling.'

They walked away, the guide profoundly shocked.

A fisherman told me that the swordfish is one of the swiftest fishes in the sea and one of the most nervous. Even the drip from an oar is sometimes enough to send him off at thirty miles an hour. Once mated, the fishes remain together and behave with the greatest fidelity, indeed the young guide was not being delicate when he spoke about the swordfish 'making love', since it is believed by the fishermen that they feel affection for one another. When a female fish is speared the fisherman say that her mate will never leave her but will swim round frantically as if trying to help her, and is often speared as well. There is a moving popular song on this theme by Domenico Modugno, 'Lu pisce spada'.

The fishermen have a language of their own. Their boats are called *ontri*; the spear is a *triccia*; the look-out man is the *guadiano*; the spearman is the *allanzatore*, sometimes the *fariere*, and some believe that the hoarse, guttural cries when the look-out man sights a swordfish, and his directions to the spearman, have been handed down in the Straits of Messina since the age of Magna Graecia.

The swordfish season lasts from March until July, which is the time that the epicure should visit Reggio. The average weight of a good fish is about a hundred and twelve pounds, but occasionally a monster is speared. Each boat carries a crew of five and the fishing is as profitable as it is sometimes dangerous. A wounded swordfish armed with a sharp proboscis two feet long is a formidable object to land. It is sometimes the custom, should the harpoonist miss a good shot, to throw him overboard.

I have never eaten swordfish in other parts of Italy. There is always such a demand for it that most of it is consumed locally and only a small quantity is preserved in brine or oil. The fish is expensive, but people are always ready to pay for it. *Ziphias gladius* in Latin, *pesce spada* in Italian, and *pez espada* in Spanish, for it is also caught off the coast of Spain, is valued everywhere.

The best way to cook *pesce spada* is the Sicilian way, which is first carefully to prepare this mixture: a quarter of a cup of olive oil, the juice of two lemons, a teaspoonful of freshly chopped mint, two teaspoonsful of origano, and salt and pepper as you like it. Mix this well. Before you place your slice of swordfish under a grill, brush it generously with this mixture and keep on brushing it as the fish is cooking. It takes about seven minutes when cooked about four inches from the flame. If the fish is about an inch thick, there is no need to turn it.

First get your slice of swordfish however! If you cannot do so, the above mixture, without the mint but with a clove of crushed garlic and some chopped parsely instead, is excellent when brushed from time to time over a quartered chicken, indeed there is no more delicious way to grill a chicken; and before you serve it pour the rest of the mixture over it. Then use your fingers.

§ 5

To live in an Italian city with a population of a hundred and fifty thousand whose history goes back far beyond the Christian era, yet to see no building earlier in date than 1908, is an unusual experience. There is, in fact, only one building in Reggio which has survived earthquakes, the Aragonese castle near the cathedral, and it is worth visiting for the magnificent view. The new city is as rectangular as New York, and though there is nothing distinguished about the buildings, the site is superb, facing Sicily across the Straits. I found it a delightful and restful place where I should like to spend a long holiday one day. I thought too that the people of Reggio were amiable and charming. I could never forget that nearly everyone I met who was of over sixty years of age would probably be a survivor of the earthquake of 1908. The city was completely destroyed and even buildings which were still habitable had to be pulled down. Out of a population of thirty thousand, about five thousand lost their lives.

When Norman Douglas was writing *Old Calabria* he saw Reggio so soon after the disaster that people were still living in wooden huts and old railway trucks, while architects were planning the present city. He heard many horror stories, but his account also includes the only comic earthquake experience I can remember. Three friends of his happened to be staying in Reggio. 'On the first shock they rushed together, panic-stricken, into one room; the floor gave way, and they suddenly found themselves sitting in their motor-car which happened to be placed exactly below them. They escaped with a few cuts and bruises.'

The new city was planned with care and skill. A beautiful sandy lido is tucked away on a point; a fine promenade planted with palm trees and shrubs faces the sea, and behind it are the rectangular streets crowded, as all Italian streets are, with traffic. They empty only in the evening when the life of Reggio converges for the *passeggiata* upon the Corso Garibaldi. The cathedral, standing impressively above a long flight of steps, has been lovingly rebuilt. Nothing remained after the 1908 earthquake except the outer walls still bearing the Latin quotation that impressed George Gissing so much, *circumlegentes devenimus Rhegium*. This comes from *Acts* (28:13), 'And from thence' (Syracuse) 'we fetched a compass and came to Rhegium.' The rest of the verse – a reference to St Paul's journey to Rome – is 'and after one day the south wind blew and we came the next day to Puteoli'. The phrase 'fetched a compass' has puzzled some commentators, but surely it simply means 'tacking'? Then after St Paul had spent a day in Rhegium, the south wind blew and they covered the hundred and eighty miles to Puteoli in a day. A statue of the Apostle stands outside the cathedral, together with that of St. Stephen, who was the first bishop. Inside, the church is large and impressive, and I thought the care with which ancient memorials and inscriptions had been salvaged from the ruins of the former building and re-erected, though seared and cracked by the earthquake, was a touching sight.

One's impressions of a strange city are influenced, certainly in later life, by the comfort enjoyed there, or the discomfort suffered.

My hotel, which had just been opened, was one of the best in Italy, indeed I cannot recall one in Rome or Milan which I would consider superior. It was air-conditioned and the staff were efficient, with that kindly Italian friendliness which has now vanished from the tourist routes; the cooking was faultless and Italian. Such hotels are being built all over the South. The day will soon come when the miseries suffered by travellers in wretched inns even thirty years ago will be forgotten.

Among the memories I shall always treasure about Reggio are the evenings when I sat on my balcony and watched the lights come up in Sicily. Sometimes the soft south wind was blowing, the wind that took St Paul so swiftly to Pozzuoli, bringing with it a warm musky scent of herbs, of fennel, of jasmine, of rosemary. I would see the lights sparkle across the water in little coast towns and villages and appear on the hills, then, as night fell, I would see a red glow far off, which was Mount Etna.

§ 6

Two of Reggio's unique possessions are the Fata Morgana and the bergamot. The Fata Morgana is a mirage of great beauty that occurs at certain times in the Straits of Messina. Though it is said to occur frequently, I never came across anyone who had seen it. That of course, was just chance; thousands must have seen it. The vision hovers above the water and appears to be so real, with its towers and castles, its roads and its mountains, that those who see the enchanted landscape feel that they have only to take a step or two to enter it.

As interesting as the optical delusion is the name, which was given to it by the Normans. 'Fata' in Italian means 'fairy', and the Fairy Morgana was no other than King Arthur's rather difficult sister, Morgan le Fay. Having seen King Arthur upon the pavement of Otranto Cathedral, to meet Morgan le Fay in the Straits of Messina was not as surprising as it might have been. There is a story that Roger of Hauteville stood one day upon the Reggio side of the Straits and wished for a fleet in order to conquer Sicily. Suddenly, from her palace beneath the waves, rose up Morgan le Fay and spread the mirage before him, bidding him to cross. But Roger, full of Norman commonsense, declined to do so, saying something to the effect that he would conquer Sicily with his strong right arm and not by the black art of sorcery.

The bergamot is just as romantic as the Fata Morgana. No one knows where it came from, how it originated, or why it should grow nowhere else in the world but round Reggio di Calabria. It looks like a small yellow orange and is bitter. An oil is extracted from the skin which is highly prized by the makers of scent; indeed I was told that no costly perfume is made without it. A great number of the people of Reggio owe their Fiats to this mysterious and profitable fruit. You see it growing everywhere, sometimes in large plantations, sometimes just a dozen trees in a garden. A thousand bergamot trees can produce an annual income of a million lire. The professor in charge of the *Stazione Sperimentale delle Essenze*, which studies everything to do with perfumes, told me that Reggio exports two hundred tons of bergamot oil every year. He showed me a bergamot, which looked like one of those small unripe oranges about the size of a golf ball which fall from a tree during drought. The smell was strong and musky and reminded me of the oil of citronella which not so long ago was used to repel insects.

The Moors, he said, introduced the 'Seville' orange into Spain and used the oil from its rind medicinally and for perfumes. They also made the famous oil of Neroli, distilled from orange blossom, which is still used today, but they never had the elusive bergamot. I asked why the bergamot produced such a superior oil and, in answer, I was asked to smell phials containing distillations of roses, violets, lemons, lavender and a dozen others until my sense of smell was unable to register anything, and when the bergamot was presented to me I was unable to recognize its superiority. In fact I much preferred the rose!

An odd thing about the bergamot is that it appeared only about two centuries ago and that attempts to grow it elsewhere have failed. Henry Swinburne must have made the earliest reference to it in English when, during his travels in 1772–80, he wrote, 'The Rheggians carry on a lucrative traffic with the French and Genoese in the essence of citron, orange and bergamot. This spirit is extracted by paring off the rind of the fruit with a broad knife, pressing the peel between wood pincers against a sponge; and as soon as the sponge is saturated the volatile liquor is squeezed into a phial and sold at fifteen carlines an ounce.' Norman Douglas told his friend Orioli that bergamot oil was first made at Reggio by a secret process known to one family, who made an immense fortune out of it.

'The first child of the bergamot,' said the professor, 'was Eau de Cologne, which was the invention of an Italian.'

He was Giovanni Farina, who was born in 1685 and settled in Cologne in 1709, though some say that the original prescription was that of Farina's uncle, Paul de Feminis, who left Milan to settle in Cologne at the end of the seventeenth century. Eau de Cologne remained a secret in the family and was passed from father to son. It was Napoleon's favourite scent; I have read that he used to drench himself in it.

Another pleasant occupation of Reggio is the production of jasmine oil. Forty per cent of the world's production of this oil comes from this scented tip of Italy.

§ 7

The four museums south of Naples which should be seen by all who are interested in Magna Graecia are those at Paestum, Bari, Taranto, and Reggio di Calabria. Each has its special treasures: Paestum, the relics of the sanctuaries of Hera; Bari, its Greek vases; Taranto, its wonderful Tanagra figures; and Reggio, its complete survey of South Italian archaeology from neolithic times onward, with emphasis, so far as I am concerned, on the exquisite terracotta ex-votos from Locri.

The museum is a large modern building in the Corso Garibaldi in which everything is beautifully displayed upon three floors. This is the first time that one comes face to face with the visible antiquity of Reggio, or rather Rhegion, or Rhegium as one must think of it in this building. Here and here only are to be seen relics of the Greek colony founded about 715 B.C. on the advice of the Delphic Oracle.

The aged female medium at Delphi, often an unlettered peasant dressed as a young girl (a reference to an earlier time when the Pythia had to be a virgin, said Diodorus), spoke, so men believed for centuries, with the voice of the god Apollo. It was usual for Greek cities which desired to create a colony to send a deputation to ask the advice of the Oracle and, like so many other cities of the Greek world overseas, Rhegium was planned in the far-off sanctuary of the Pythia.

How did the Delphic Oracle possess such an intimate knowledge of geography? It not only sent a party of Chalcidian emigrants to Rhegium, a group of Achaeans to the admirable site of Croton, and another group of Achaeans to Metapontum, but it also directed others to Cyrene in North Africa and to most of the early settlements in Sicily. There were one or two recorded failures when the settlers returned to Delphi in disappointment and were given a new site, after which all was well. But, generally speaking, the Delphic Oracle appears to have been the colonial office of the Hellenic world, and the founder of some of the most famous cities of antiquity. So well known was this that one of the names given to Apollo was 'the Great Founder'.

There does seem to have been something inexplicable about the Delphic Oracle, whose name lives on today when all the other oracles have been forgotten. The most famous story is that of Croesus, King of Lydia, who decided to test six of the most famous oracles of his day, including, of course, the Delphic Pythia. He sent out messengers even as far as the Oracle of Jupiter Amon, in the Oasis of Siwa, ordering them on a certain hour of the hundredth day after their departure from Sardis to ask the various oracles what Croesus, King of Lydia, was doing at that particular moment. Telling nobody, he had devised a task which no one could have invented. Upon the appointed hour, and with his own hands, he had cut up and was boiling a hard-shelled land tortoise with the flesh of a lamb in a brass vessel with a brass lid.

The messengers returned to Sardis with the oracular responses written out. All the oracles had failed except Delphi. Even before the Lydians entered the sanctuary the Pythia answered the question in the following hexameter verse:

*I can count the sands, and I can measure the ocean;*
*I have ears for the silent, and know what the dumb man meaneth;*
*Lo! on my sense there striketh the smell of a shell-covered tortoise*
*Boiling now on a fire, with the flesh of a lamb, in a cauldron –*
*Brass is the vessel below, and brass the cover above it.*

Delighted, Croesus sent magnificent gifts to Delphi which were still the glory of the sanctuary in the days of Herodotus. The story has the ring of truth because, having accepted the Pythia's omniscience, Croesus then put the real question: would it be advisable to go to war with Persia? The Pythia replied that if he did so he would destroy a mighty kingdom: but the Oracle's ambiguity had heartlessly lured him to his doom. It did not occur to him that the destroyed kingdom could be his own.

Discussing the curious story of the testing of the oracles, T. Dempsey in *The Delphic Oracle* asked: 'And if it is genuine, whence the Pythia's knowledge? She could not have gained it by any purely physical means. Those were not the days of wireless telegraphy or wireless telephony. How then, must we explain it? It is impossible to say with any degree of certainty. Perhaps it is to be explained by the laws of telepathy, for, especially under abnormal psychic conditions, persons have shown themselves endowed with a knowledge truly marvellous. These abnormal psychic conditions in the case of the Pythia, would probably be induced to a certain extent by the course of mantic preparation which she had to perform. The fasting, the drinking from the sacred spring, the chewing of the laurel leaves – these combined above all with a *strong belief in the reality* of the inspiration, might, in a guileless, uneducated soul – especially a woman – produce such an abnormal psychic state, which could induce even the physical phenomena of trance and agitation such as were associated with the Delphic priestess.'

The highly-developed mediumship of the Pythia was supplemented by a priesthood which probably possessed the best intelligence service of antiquity. The priests of Apollo must have known the secrets of courts and countries everywhere, and it is perhaps not too fanciful to suggest that their card index system has probably never been bettered. And if one asks why the priests of Apollo were interested in colonization, surely the answer is that every group of settlers who departed overseas with the god's blessing would, the moment they reached their new home, erect an altar to him; and so the cult of Apollo would spread over the Hellenic world. Also, though I do not think that this was obligatory, it was the custom when the new cities became prosperous for them to send offerings of gold to the sanctuary at Delphi, thus colonization would increase its fabulous wealth.

So one looks up from the glass cases in this admirable museum at Reggio to ponder the mysteries of the ancient world. One sees the pottery and the bronze handled by the citizens of Rhegium and other neighbouring settlements centuries before Christ, and while one feels a bond of common humanity with them, especially in their affectionate love of animals, one is also aware that they inhabited a world in which, setting aside basic humanities, we should have been strangers. Reggio possesses a fine little statue which today would be accepted as the Good Shepherd. It shows a man with a lamb carried upon his shoulders: but he is a man on his way to a temple to offer the animal as a sacrifice. Not until compassion entered the world with Christianity was the lamb carried upon the shepherd's shoulders not as a sacrifice but as a symbol of life, distressed and maybe wounded, that needed comfort and help.

Among the treasures of the museum are the marble statues of two horsemen – the Dioscuri – about half the size of life, which once decorated a temple, or temples, at Locri. One of the horsemen is galloping over a sphinx; the other over a figure, half man and half fish, which probably represents Poseidon, and indicates that the Twin Brethren had come by sea to Locri. I was a little surprised to read in a learned work published recently that 'the Greeks rode without saddle and bridle', a curious slip of the pen. Though they rode bareback, even the earliest vase paintings show the use of the bridle, while chariot harness was so sophisticated, and the arched necks of the horses so pronounced, that one wonders if the Greeks did not also use the curb-chain.

The Dioscuri are seen in the act of dismounting, or sliding, down the flanks of their horses to the ground, as bareback riders in a circus are seen to do before they run forward and leap upon the back of the horse ahead. The statues must have looked striking in full colour, mounted upon a temple. The obsession of Locri with Castor and Pollux is an extraordinary story. When the city was still making its way, about 550 B.C., it was threatened by its rich and pugnacious neighbour, Croton. Locri could put only 10,000 men into the field, while the army of Croton numbered 100,000. What was Locri to do? Obviously, consult the oracles. An embassy was accordingly sent to Sparta to ask for aid, but the Spartans, unwilling to become involved in an overseas war, advised the Locrians to consult the Dioscuri. Having sacrificed in the temple of Castor and Pollux in Sparta, the ambassadors were assured that the great Twin Brethren were on their side and would fight in their ranks. The delighted Locrians then fitted out one of their galleys with a magnificent temple-cabin for Castor and Pollux, and so sailed home with their invisible passengers. When it was known in Locri that the ambassadors had brought back the heavenly twins, the morale of the city rose and one may fancy that any strange horsemen seen in the neighbourhood were closely scrutinized.

However, the people of Croton had not been idle. The city sent an embassy to Delphi to ask Apollo how best to win the war. The Pythia replied that piety and not armaments would bring victory. The ambassadors recognized this as the first move in a financial deal and quickly offered Apollo a tenth of the spoils. By way of mysterious channels, Locri learnt of the bargain and instantly sent ambassadors to Delphi, in the greatest secrecy, to make a better offer, which was a ninth part of the spoils of the immensely larger and richer city. Apollo changed sides.

So, with powerful celestial backing, Locri, with her small but well-trained army, went with confidence to encounter the huge, luxurious army of Croton with its untrained levies. Selecting an admirable site for the battle upon the banks of the river Sagra, the ten thousand men of Locri vanquished the one-hundred-thousand strong army of Croton. Needless to add, during the heat of the fight two splendid warriors mounted upon white horses, wearing each a purple chlamys and a Lacedaemonian hat, were

366

seen fighting with the Locrians. The result of this battle was talked about all over the Greek world. It was said that the news of the victory was miraculously conveyed the same day to Greeks gathered at Olympia and the phrase 'the battle of Sagras' became a saying, or proverb, to describe something that was almost incredible, but true.

Colour must have been everywhere on temples, on houses, on statues. A great variety of terracotta decoration is to be seen in the museum to which ghostly hints of red, blue and green still cling. Most beautiful of all, I thought, were the ex-votos – *pinakes* – which are about ten inches square and were designed as temple offerings. Each one is pierced by two holes by which it was suspended on the walls of a sanctuary. These must have been made by the finest artists, though the moulds from which they were made have never been found. Each scene is in slightly raised relief; some show Persephone and Hades seated side by side on a high-backed seat, holding offerings; others depict various gods and goddesses; and one is a charming little scene in which a girl bends over a decorated box, which looks like her wedding chest, placing inside it a carefully folded garment. On the wall at her back, hanging from nails, are two vases, a bronze mirror and a basket. It is an intimate glimpse into a home of Magna Graecia four hundred years before Christ.

§ 8

An unexpected activity in Reggio is the export of briar for pipes, and also the manufacture of the completed article. This industry was started at the end of the last century by a British Vice-Consul named Kerrick, who was impressed by the great number of gigantic briar roots to be found in the mountains. He had them collected and sawn into blocks, which he exported to pipe makers in England, France and the United States.

I was invited to visit a pipe factory a few miles from Reggio, beside a beach where they were drawing up the swordfish boats. There was also a strange character who by no great flight of the imagination might have escaped from a Greek vase. He was drifting in a rowing-boat, holding in his left hand a bucket with a glass bottom through which he examined the limpid depths, while in his right hand he grasped a trident. Every now and again he would plunge the trident into the water but without result until, coming near some rocks, he brought it up with an octopus writhing on its points. It was difficult to leave this son of Poseidon for a pipe factory, nevertheless I did so.

I stepped, it seemed, into the nineteenth century when Mr Kerrick first sawed up his briar roots. The little factory with its flapping belts and its unprotected saws and wheels would give an English factory inspector a fit, yet everybody seemed to have the correct number of fingers and to be in the best of spirits. On the ground floor were sacks full of giant briar roots which had been collected by peasants in the Aspromonte. Eight men sawed them into neat blocks about five inches square, setting aside the best for export to England.

The actual manufacture of a pipe seemed to me a rapid and simple process. A block of briar was held in a machine for a few moments and withdrawn as a pipe bowl and stem. In a matter of minutes forty or fifty of these had accumulated on a wooden tray which was carried up a ladder to an upper room where a number of young girls fitted the vulcanite mouthpieces, polished the bowls, and dyed them.

In the course of my visit I was generously presented with ten pipes of various shapes, and I was to find out during the next few days how difficult it is to give away a pipe. One produces it with a flourish only to be told, 'I do not smoke.'

A pipe is also a personal possession which a man likes to choose himself. Most smokers have suffered from pipes selected lovingly by women. In the end, keeping two as curiosities, I concealed the others in a wardrobe, hoping that they would someday fall into appreciative hands.

During a walk down the Corso Garibaldi one day I remembered how Craufurd Tait Ramage delighted in Calabrian honey when he was in the Reggio neighbourhood in 1828. I went into a grocer's shop and bought a jar, thinking it would be a pleasant change from the inevitable apricot jam of what is miscalled 'breakfast'. The honey was indeed delicious. I thought I could detect the rich-smelling herbs and the lovely flowers of the Aspromonte transformed into sweetness while still retaining something of their former beauty. Happening to examine the jar one morning, I saw that the honey came from Milan. This is typical of the commercial scene in Southern Italy. It is probably simpler and cheaper to deal with an efficient firm in Milan than with some difficult old bee-keeper in the mountains.

# CHAPTER TEN

*The 'Jasmine Coast' – Marinas and Lidos – Locri – Gerace – A Norman Cathedral – The Town of Cassiodorus – Catanzaro – Crotone and the Lone Column – Return to Sybaris.*

§ 1

The road, accompanied by its inseparable companion the railway, runs beside the sea from Reggio round the 'toe' of Italy and up the east coast to Taranto. It is a good road nearly all the way, but the railway is an eyesore which is embarrassing to those towns which are anxious to create lidos. In spite of the excellent road-making that has gone on in the South of Italy in the last fifteen or twenty years, there are parts of the Aspromonte, as of the Sila, which can never be approached save by mule tracks or helicopters. There are still mountain villages which will never be invaded by the motor-car.

Southern Italians are fond of selecting romantic names for the coastline. East from Reggio, and stretching round the coast, the Jasmine Coast changes its name to the Coast of the Saracen, as it moves north along the Ionian Sea. And these names seem to be well chosen. The smell of jasmine from gardens and plantations followed me to Locri and beyond, while the swarthy fishermen and mountaineers with their black hair and black eyes looked remarkably like my conception of a Saracen. It is lonely country. Only in the vicinity of the small towns do you meet another car. Miles of lonely beaches succeed one another, while the gentle foothills of the Aspromonte rise behind in terraces to the high mountains, the last of the Apennines.

The most southerly town in Italy is a small fishing port of about nine thousand inhabitants called Melito di Porto Salvo, famous as the place where Garibaldi landed twice from Sicily during the Risorgimento. The only road across the Aspromonte runs north

from this town; on each side of it wild mountain country is crossed
by tracks leading to villages with Greek names, whose inhabitants
speak a dialect which some claim to be a legacy of the last age of
Byzantium while others consider it to be the speech of Greek
refugees from the Morea in Turkish times. The shepherds and
mountaineers, speaking their strange dialect, are as separate as the
Albanians though, I fancy, they are more acceptable to the Italians:
at least I heard no one say of them, as they used to say of the
Albanians, 'If you meet a wolf and an Albanian, shoot the Albanian
first!'

Garibaldi had been temporarily forgotten in Melito when I was
there and everyone was obsessed by a witch. Having always thought
of witches as old women, I was surprised to find that this one was a
little girl of nine called Nicolina. Apparently the moment the child
arrived to pay a visit to her uncle and aunt, things began to go
wrong. Tables and chairs were overturned, jugs shot across the
room and a barrel of grain, which was too heavy for a strong man
to move, was easily transported through the air. Worse still, the
hens stopped laying and rabbits killed each other in their hutches.
The priest tried to exorcise the poltergeist, but without success.
The villagers then called in a wizard from the mountains who was
familiar with werewolves and all forms of black magic, and he,
after having sealed the house, called upon the evil spirit to depart:
but his charms also failed. The villagers chased the poor child across
the fields with pitchforks, while her contemporaries stoned her. I
asked if I could see her, but she had since returned home when peace
had descended immediately upon Melito and life had become
normal again.

When I came to the village of Bova I remembered how highly
Edward Lear had praised its mountain honey during his Calabrian
tour. I wondered whether this superlative honey had come into
his mind when he wrote:

*The owl and the pussy-cat went to sea in a beautiful pea-green boat,*
*They had some honey and plenty of money wrapped up in a five-*
*    pound note. . . .*

On the spur of the moment I went into the village shop and asked for some honey, but they had none. A young man in the shop told me that he could find some for me. In the obliging way in which Italians will drop whatever they are doing in order to help one, sometimes walking miles out of their way, the young man, wheeling a bicycle, led me up hilly streets until we came to a house in a row of stone houses, where a flight of steps led to the first storey. I was soon seated at a table opposite an old lady in a dark little room crammed with furniture. She could not understand a word I spoke. The young man explained that the stranger wanted some honey. The old lady called out for two middle-aged women, probably her daughters or granddaughters, who came in to listen while the young man began again and explained our mission. 'They have honey,' he said to me in a reassuring aside: but they made no attempt to produce it. Instead, they asked innumerable questions, looking at me with curiosity and compassion. Unable to understand what they were saying, I felt fairly sure that they had come to the conclusion that I was mad. Eventually one of the women went out and returned with a gallon tin full of honey which she asked me to accept. I told the young man to explain that a few spoonsful were all I needed. This was the most unfortunate thing I could have said. They were now convinced that I was out of my mind. An argument started which went on and on, and all I could do was to sit silently, thinking how Edward Lear, who was responsible for the situation, would have enjoyed it. The argument having at last come to a full stop, the women began to look at me with the sympathy which they would have expended upon an idiot child. Eventually one of them rose and left the room, to return with a small glass jar which she filled and handed to me with a kindly smile. I thanked them and could sense them thinking 'poor fellow' as I stumbled down the dark stairs, grasping my pot of honey. When I turned to thank my companion, I found that he had mounted his bicycle and was already half-way down the hill on his long-suffering tyres. I looked back at the house and saw the curtains twitching. I thought that the story of the stranger from a far country who had come to Bova for a spoonful of honey would be built into quite a saga. No doubt that is the way many a legend has started.

The honey was excellent, but no sweeter than other honey I have tasted in Calabria, which confirmed my suspicion that Lear often exaggerated.

§ 2

Pleasant waves of jasmine scented the air for miles. It grows as a small bush, sometimes in plantations, at others varied with berga-mot. Dry river-beds led down from the hills to the sea, and now and again there was a pool where kneeling women were washing clothes. Once, when I stopped to look at the immense boulders rounded and polished by the winter torrents, I saw a black snake curled up there so perfectly disguised as a shadow that I did not notice him until he moved.

All along the road, only a few miles apart, I came to a succession of little marinas bearing the name of some parent town or village a mile or two away in the hills. There was Bova Marina, Marina Palizzi (Palizzi being a village of some four thousand inhabitants a few miles away), Marina di Brancaleone (whose parent village lies in the hills at the back), then Ardore Marina, the parent Ardore being a diminutive hill town of olive groves and orchards; and so on all the way up the Ionian coast. Some of the marinas have well-designed bathing pavilions and strips of matting leading across the sand to the sea; others are merely a few sheds and half a dozen beach umbrellas. It is a strange contrast: the old hill village where mules still press with panniers up the steep streets, and a few miles away a brightly painted marina, bearing the same name, where young people in bathing costumes tinker with a motor-boat or play the latest music. This is characteristic of the coastline of Calabria: it has emerged from the Middle Ages into a world of television and lidos: the Fata Morgana is no longer a city hanging in the air but an hotel and cars full of millionaires. After talking to many Calabrians, I came to the conclusion again that the creation of a holiday land was more to their liking than that of industrial life.

I came at last to the straggling main street of Locri, a town noted for making mattresses, bitumen and garden ornaments – painted gnomes and suchlike – which are set out on wayside stalls. A young man who was cleaning a Vespa told me that I had overshot the ruins of Locri by a mile or so, but he offered to go back with me. His name was Limitri, which is dialect for Demetrio. We found the unobtrusive entrance to once mighty Locri by way of a lane and a farmyard. I asked my companion if Greek names were common in Locri. He said that he had a friend called Dionigi (Dionysius) and another named Achille; and I thought it interesting that the old gods and heroes, chastened no doubt at the baptismal font, should nevertheless still be able to bestow their names upon young men with motor scooters.

We came to the ruins of Locri in an olive grove where the crickets were snapping. There was nothing much for the untrained eye to see but mighty blocks of grey stone from which weeds and grass were sprouting. A huge black pig was asleep under an olive tree near the foundation of what looked like a temple. Like some awakened Bacchus, it glanced up acutely with bloodshot eyes, grunted angrily, and went to sleep again.

Limitri told me that the boundary walls of Locri have been traced for about five miles and though there was more to be found excavation had stopped because of a land dispute. I found the ruins confusing, but was glad to have seen the site of so many happenings. The city had been built on flat land from which three hills rose, which were fortified and were called by Livy and others 'citadels'.

As we tramped across the rough ground, on the edge of fields of root crops and through olive groves, I tried to rebuild Locri in my imagination, but failed, even though I had seen the statues of Castor and Pollux and the exquisite *pinakes* in the Reggio Museum. Yet it was here that the army of ten thousand, convinced that the gods were on their side, went out and defeated the hundred thousand from Croton. How quickly nature can obliterate the work of man. I once knew a street off Cheapside in the City of London which was destroyed by air raids in the last war. I often passed that way before the City was rebuilt and stopped to look into the cellars which were all that was left of the street, but they seemed to bear no relation to the place I had once known so well. Only a bottle or a bicycle wheel among willow-herb, or an old hat lying on cellar steps, were memories of better times. Had they been an ancient Greek bottle or a Roman hat they would have had an honoured place in a museum, and it is from such debris, and from vaults and cellars and foundations, that we try to recreate the brilliance of a lost civilization.

There is one curious story about the origin of Locri. It was said by Polybius, who knew the city well, that it was founded by slaves from Greece who had run off with their mistresses while their masters were away at war, and in support of this story, the historian mentions that nobility in Locri was conferred by the mother, not the father. As we walked on, we came to a ravine outside the city wall in which the remains of the famous temple of Persephone were discovered, which seems to have been a gold deposit vault whose treasure was protected not by steel bars but by the fear and reverence inspired by the goddess. Nothing is now left of this treasure house but a disturbance in the ground, since all the stones discovered were carried away by local farmers.

When Locri was faced by war with Croton it was proposed to move the temple of Persephone inside the city walls, but at dead of night a voice was heard in the sanctuary forbidding them to do this, declaring that the goddess would herself protect her shrine. And she proved to be an efficient guardian. Her bank was not robbed until the First Punic War when a Carthaginian fleet made off with the sacred gold. Persephone immediately consulted Poseidon with the result that the ships were wrecked a day or so after and all the treasure recovered.

The next robbery occurred during the Second Punic War when most of the cities of Magna Graecia changed sides with the war news. After the battle of Cannae, it seemed to many that Hannibal must win, and pro-Carthaginian parties, anxious to be on the winning side, sprang up in most of the southern Greek cities. During a period when the Roman party came back to Locri and a Roman garrison took over, the commander allowed his troops to commit frightful atrocities including the theft of the temple gold, as a reprisal for Locrian disloyalty to Rome. This caused the Locrians to send envoys to Rome, who appeared in Greek suppliant fashion, said Livy, in rags and tatters, holding branches of olive, and, after prostrating themselves with tears before the Consuls, humbly asked

375

permission to address the Senate. They gave a detailed account of the misdeeds of the Roman commander and roused such indignation that a court of inquiry was sent to Locri. One senator was so enraged by the sacrilege committed in the temple of Persephone that he argued that the gold should be recovered from the thieves and double the amount deposited in the Treasury. Most, if not all, of the gold was recovered and returned to the goddess. The Roman officer commanding was sent in chains to Rome, where he died in prison. The later history of Locri is one of steady decline. The city lingered on into Byzantine times, when probably Saracens and malaria brought life there to its end, and the few remaining inhabitants fled to the mountains and founded the town of Gerace.

As a ruin, Locri is in the eighteenth century tradition, like a Piranesi drawing. Trees and shrubs spring from ancient stones; Nature has spread a carpet of grass and flowers over places where men once prayed to the immortal gods and where they once argued and bargained. Passing through an olive grove and an opening in a hedge, I emerged into a small clearing in which stood a small farmhouse, almost a hut. Lying near by was an immense amphora, intact, a jar that may have contained oil or wheat, and was large enough to have concealed some of Ali Baba's men. It lay there, a memorial to the capricious forces of survival.

I left the obliging Limitri, who had business with a friend locally, and continued along the main road by the sea, reflecting how much more difficult had been Ramage's visit to Locri in 1828. He arrived across the mountains by what is still called *Il Passo del Mercante*, accompanied by four armed guards because of the brigands. He rode a pony. 'As for myself,' he wrote, 'my only weapon of defense, if weapon it could be called, was my dilapidated umbrella, which I fear the Italian brigands would not be inclined to consider very formidable. If we met them, however, I intended to flourish it in the way we sometimes alarm cattle; and as they are probably unacquainted with such an article, they might imagine it some deadly weapon of war, and take to flight.'

Fortunately, they met no brigands.

§ 3

The town of Gerace lies in the mountains about five miles from Locri. The road has a series of mountainous hairpin bends, but fortunately there is little traffic upon it. An infrequent bus runs from Locri up to Gerace, then continues across the mountains to Gioia Tauro, on the Tyrrhenian coast, one of the most picturesque journeys in Calabria. It is to me a saddening reflection that had one encountered a solitary traveller in this part of the world a century ago, he would almost certainly have been an Englishman. Now he would be a German. I met a young man in a steep and lonely part of the mountains carrying an immense pack, and stopped to ask if I could give him a lift, but he thanked me and said no: he was bound for a village off the road. His English was as rudimentary as my German, so I was unable to ask what enthusiasm, scholarly or physical, had attracted him to such an out of the way place.

The snakes appeared to be particularly active, or it may have been the time of day when they wished to cross the road. Like the lizards of Gargano, they selected the last possible moment to do so and streaked across, generally, I think, intact. They were not diminutive adders, but large black reptiles, some at least three feet long.

The town of Gerace stands 1,500 feet above the Ionian Sea in a situation aptly described as a '*posizione panoramica stupenda*'. It really is a fantastic site and, as a survival of a former age, Gerace is one of the most striking towns in the region. I thought that had it been in north or central Italy it would have been known to every-body and be as famous as San Gimignano. It was founded in the ninth century by Greek-speaking refugees from Locri who had been driven from what was left of their ancient city by the Saracens. The town did not appear to possess a restaurant or an hotel, and I think that if one were stranded there like a nineteenth century traveller, one would be hospitably received by the mayor or a leading citizen.

The town has been repeatedly shaken and disrupted by earth-quakes, though fortunately the wonderful Norman–Gothic cathe-dral, the largest church in Calabria, has survived and has recently been restored. It is an austere and lovely relic of the Norman age in Southern Italy. The soft light, as I saw it, turned the venerable

Greek nave pillars to silver-grey. I hope the legend is true that they came from the temple of Persephone in Locri; if so, they are a survival as dramatic as they are spectacular.

I had the good fortune to meet a local historian who was only too happy to talk to me about Gerace. He kindly invited me to his house, where we sat in a room pleasantly littered with books and drank the strong red Calabrian wine which, as in classical times, should be diluted with water. At the time of the Norman conquest of Italy Gerace was one of the strongest Byzantine fortresses in the south. In the tenth century a large Arab army from Sicily, which had captured Reggio without any trouble, was foiled by Gerace. The size of this Arab army was, if the figures are accurate, fifty-two thousand infantry, two thousand cavalry and a camel corps of one thousand, eight hundred. During this period the town was ruled by the Strategos, whose title was later changed by the Normans to Governor.

The charge of the Norman knights must have been shattering. Half a century or so later, in 1059, Robert Guiscard cut his way through a Greek army commanded by the Bishops of Gerace and Casignana, which was fought on the plains of San Martino, and succeeded in capturing the city. My acquaintance told me a story which has been preserved by the Norman monk, Geoffrey of Malaterra, who wrote a history of the Normans in Italy. It seems that the clashes of temperament between Robert Guiscard, the eldest son of the Hauteville second marriage, and Roger, the youngest, were often violent, and many were caused by Robert's reluctance to keep his word and hand over Calabrian territory to his brother. Gerace, it appears, considered Roger to be its lord, though there were some Greeks who were loyal to Robert. During one of these brotherly disputes, Robert was besieging Roger in his favourite town of Mileto, on the west coast. One night Roger slipped away across the mountains to Gerace to seek reinforcements, pursued by the furious Robert: but the gates were shut in Robert's face. However, he had a friend in Gerace named Basil and so managed to enter the town in disguise. Here he was recognized by servants, was arrested and flung into prison. His host, Basil, was killed and his wife suffered the appalling agony of impalement.

(One wonders why feeling ran so high among these Byzantines.) However, Roger demanded the right to punish Robert Guiscard and the brothers were brought together in the main square of the town. Here, instead of drawing swords, they embraced and settled their differences. The piazza is still called the *Piazza del Tocco*, the Piazza of the Touch.

Gerace remained Byzantine until late in the Middle Ages and the Latin rite did not displace the Greek until 1480, twenty-seven years after the capture of Constantinople by the Turks. I asked if any Greek words have survived in the everyday speech of Gerace, and my acquaintance replied that the local dialect is dying, but a few words derived from the Greek may still be heard, such as 'giramida' (a tile) from *keramis*, 'catoiu' (a basement room) from *kat-a-ion*, 'pappu' (grandfather) from *pappos*, 'catarrattu' (a trapdoor) from *katarros*. Sometimes, he said, one heard such words as 'poma', an oven-lid, and 'rizza', the core of an apple; but, generally speaking, people who go away to work, and who own a wireless or a television set, drop the ancient dialect, and probably the last to use such words are the old people who still live in Gerace. Such words, though maybe not the last accents of Greek Locri, are certainly an authentic echo of Byzantine Italy.

The town still bears traces of having been a mediaeval stronghold. Three of the gates have become archways while retaining their old names, the Arch of the Lombards, the Arch of the Bishops, the Arch of the Barghetto, and a fourth, which once had a drawbridge, is still called the Street of the Bridge. The old castle, now so badly shaken by earthquakes that one is forbidden to enter it, stands on the highest part of the rock. When I stood and looked down into a distant valley whitened by the course of torrents and to the hills and mountains beyond, receding in every shade of blue, I thought I had never seen a finer site for a castle. I was told that it is built upon Byzantine foundations and has been altered and added to ever since. How strange it is that they still remember that about nine hundred years ago Roger Hauteville made a great room there which he called the *Sala di Mileto*.

History and fame have ebbed away from this place, whose population is now said to be about four thousand. The younger people have gone to the factories at Locri, some have emigrated, others have sought work in Germany or Switzerland, so that Gerace today seems to be inhabited by old people, some of whom may be seen industriously engaged in basement rooms or sunning themselves on balconies. Even the Bishop of Gerace departed when in 1954 Pope Pius XII commanded that in future the diocese should be Gerace-Locri. Probably for the last time the spirit of ancient Gerace flared up as crowds surrounded the episcopal palace in order to deplore and, if possible, oppose the departure of their bishop, and also, my informant whispered, the removal of the precious patrimony which the cathedral treasury had accumulated in the course of a thousand years. Those who take any pleasure in the ironies of history might place among them Gerace's return to Locri.

Both Ramage and Lear visited Gerace. Ramage was there in 1828, and Lear in 1847. Ramage was not much impressed and was in any case more interested in the tangled ruins of Locri. His wish to examine some silk cocoons was refused by the owner, who thought that he might have the evil eye. On the other hand, Lear and his walking companion John Proby visited Gerace twice and enjoyed themselves in the hospitable home of Don Pasquale Scaglione, then one of the chief citizens. One of the things which impressed Lear was that the women 'wear the skirt of their outer dresses turned over the head'. They do so no longer. It is a tradition in Gerace that this fashion goes back to the times of the Saracen invasions and made it easy for women to cover their faces.

'Why?' I asked.

'Who can say?'

§ 4

Forty miles from Locri to Copanello the road turns into the mountains to Squillace. I kept count of the marinas and lidos upon this road and recorded ten, which is one every four miles. Their names, starting from Locri, are, Marina di Gioiosa Ionica, Marina di Caulonia, Riace Marina, Monasterace Marina, Marina di Badolato, Isca Marina, Marina di Davoli and Marina di Copanello.

I have already said something about these sprouting seaside

places, but, as I passed one after the other, it seemed to me that I had not done them justice and that they are more historically significant than I had at first imagined. What one is witnessing today is really the re-colonizing of the coast of Magna Graecia: thus a process which began seven centuries before Christ has been resumed. As I have already said. Saracens and malaria drove the surviving inhabitants of the sea-coast cities into the mountains during the eighth and ninth centuries A.D. Now that malaria has been abolished, sun-bathing, motor-boats and the promise of profit are drawing men down from the mountains. There will be no more great cities with their walls and their towers, but almost certainly there will be a succession of ugly concrete hotels, swimming-pools, dance bands, striped pavilions, waiters in white jackets, deck chairs and an empire of sun umbrellas. One has only to think of the coast round Rimini to know what the Ionian coast is likely to be. It will also doubtless become residential again, the shore dotted with villas whose remote predecessors were those of Greeks and Romans.

From the headland at Staletti I looked down over an enchanting stretch of coast where – it was Sunday – hundreds of people were bathing, sun-bathing and paddling canoes. This is the only day of the week when many of these infantile lidos are crowded or even open. One hears a great deal of the frightful poverty of southern Italy yet every Sunday hundreds of motor-cars descend to the coast from near-by towns from which cheerful and prosperous-looking families emerge to invade the local marina. Who are these unimpoverished Southerners? No doubt the *gente bene*, as the phrase is, the best people, the bureaucrats, the doctors, the lawyers, the gentry of the small towns.

I descended a steep road to the sunny beach at Copanello, which might have been Juan les Pins in the days of its innocence. Cars were parked in the shade of trees, pleasant little bungalows surrounded a swimming-pool, though I wondered who would use it when miles of emerald green Ionian Sea were only a few yards away. Three large concrete buildings in the background, one still a skeleton, were hotels or flats. I was given an admirable lunch in the restaurant and studied the crowd with interest. Knowing their background in one of the austere Calabrian mountain towns, their Sunday transformation was a curious one. Every young person was wearing the latest in Italian 'beach wear' as advertised or seen on television. It was odd to reflect that many of the young women now in a state of near nudity probably possessed grandmothers, or some other elderly female relatives, who still wore the heavy regional dress with red petticoat and blue overskirt. I had the impression that a two-piece bathing costume was considered rather daring, and I saw for myself that most of the girls were closely watched, or perhaps it would be kinder to say attended, by an elderly marine version of the duenna.

Gissing certainly, and Norman Douglas probably, would have deplored the transformation of this lonely and beautiful coastline into another Riviera; but such things are inevitable. The South of Italy possesses two of the finest sea-coasts in Europe, and it is difficult to say which is the more attractive, the Tyrrhenian or the Ionian. I have mentioned, probably more than once, that many southerners are really more interested in tourism than in factories. It seems to them easy money, as perhaps it is. At any rate one hopes, as one observes the beginning of new seaside places, that they may someday help to solve the economic problem of the *Mezzogiorno*. At one of the marinas a young man showed me with pride over a new hotel in which he said his father had invested all his savings, having first sent his son on a course of hotel management in Switzerland.

Leaving this sophisticated scene, I went into the mountains and was soon in the venerable town of Squillace, whose claim to fame is that it was the birthplace of Cassiodorus, and the place to which he retired in his old age to found a monastery on the family estate. To many it will recall several chapters in Gissing's *By the Ionian Sea* in which the writer described a visit there by carriage in a torrential downpour of rain. He thought Squillace a miserable ruin, and his time was spent in a squalid wine shop where he and the young driver of the carriage were given something to eat and were villainously cheated. Altogether an unfortunate day.

Gissing must have been an odd and difficult character, and I have an idea that the popular conception of him as the prophet of despair, always in tragic need of money, a poor fellow badly treated by life, is not entirely accurate. He was on his way to popularity and was already showing signs of that commercial acumen which he deplored in others, when he was stricken down in middle age. His friendship with H. G. Wells, who was his junior by nine years, lasted until his death. They were temperamental opposites: Wells, self-confident, aggressive, becoming a success; Gissing, poor, diffident, sensitive, educated, and at odds with life. They must have been an odd couple. I knew Wells slightly in his later years and I wish I had asked him about this friendship, and why such a romantic Philhellene as Gissing should have chosen as the subject of an historical novel not Magna Graecia, which he loved and of which he wrote so beautifully, but the period of Roman decline during the first barbarian kings – Odoacer and Theodoric and their successors. The title of this novel, his last, was *Veranilda*, which was inspired, apparently, by reading the letters of Cassiodorus. Hence his desire to visit Squillace.

Like many cultivated Romans of the fifth century, Cassiodorus thought that Italy would be better off under intelligently-guided barbarian rule than under the taxation and the bureaucratic tyranny of the Byzantine East. All the successful barbarian kings had Roman secretaries, sometimes a Roman civil service, and Cassiodorus was no doubt one of those idealists who believed that the barbarians could be quickly civilized. After a long and distinguished career at the Gothic court at Ravenna, he retired at last, disheartened by intransigence and savagery, and founded a hermitage and a monastery upon his estates at Squillace. In his old age, or rather the first period of his old age since he lived to be nearly a hundred, he performed there his greatest service to posterity. He was the first churchman in Italy to establish the *scriptorium*, the writing-room, as a regular feature of a monastery where monks could be trained in copying manuscripts. To him, and to those who adopted his system, scholarship owes many of the classical texts that have survived. In his spare time Cassiodorus made water-clocks and sundials; possibly he also invented the self-filling lamp by which his scribes worked on winter evenings and sometimes at night.

I had rather better luck than Gissing. First of all, the sun was shining and I liked the old town, which now shelters about three thousand people. I did not meet any rapacious innkeepers, neither was I offered any undrinkable wine. Instead, I was taken to see a ruin said to be that of the monastery, called the Vivarium because it included the fish ponds of the family villa. I found that the name of 'Cassiodoro', or 'Cassiodorio', is as frequently invoked at Squillace as 'Tibberio' in Capri; but the landscape has been twisted and contorted by earthquakes so that probably many a landmark familiar to past generations has vanished. It seemed to me interesting that in a remote mountain town with no bookshop and no literary tradition, a place unvisited by tourists, the name of Cassiodorus should have been kept alive simply by having been passed from lip to lip for fourteen centuries.

I went on through beautiful, gentle country, the air scented with rosemary and thyme; there were olives, oaks, chestnuts and fields of yellow stubble. Along the road came women wearing a slight variation of the local dress: red skirts, white petticoats and blue cloaks, most of them barefoot. They carried upon their heads either amphorae or other objects, their arms swinging freely, their attitudes those of figures on Greek vases. The men were invisible. I thought this a poor district, but nothing is more difficult for a casual visitor to judge than poverty, especially in a warm country. One would have to live there, speak the language and be intimate with a great number of people before one could know the truth about this.

I came to a mountain town called by the delightful name of Girifalco, which is the Italian for 'gerfalcon', and probably, if one could delve into its history, one would find that the name goes back to the Normans or maybe to that greatest of falconers, Frederick II. Entering the church, I saw a life-sized statue of a young woman in a green dress who was holding out upon a golden plate, as if offering someone a biscuit, a pair of bulging eye-balls. This was Santa Lucia of Syracuse, the patron saint of all those who suffer from ophthalmia and other diseases of the eyes. According to the legend, she was offended by a young man who said that her beautiful eyes gave him no peace by day or night. Remembering the words

of Christ, 'if thine eye offend thee, pluck it out', Santa Lucia plucked
out both of hers and sent them to her admirer with the message,
'Now you have what you desired; so leave me in peace!' The poor
fellow was so stricken with remorse that he was converted to
Christianity: and it is good to relate that the story ended happily
since God would not allow Santa Lucia to suffer, and one day, while
she was at prayer, her eyes, more beautiful than ever, were restored
to her.

I went on deeper into the mountains, thinking how monotonous
in its uniformity life must be in these remote towns and villages.
The sexes are segregated, as far as one can see, and there is an
enormous surplus female population. Such men as are visible,
either old or young boys, sit about on walls or in the café, but the
women are always at work, fetching and carrying, cooking and
sewing. Though the dullness of peasant life must be almost unbearable, these people are not boorish: they are kindly, quick-minded,
and swift to laugh and smile. I have heard it said that the people in
these Calabrian mountains resemble Greeks, but I would hesitate
to say this. What precisely does one mean by a 'Greek type'? Is it the
Praxitelean type so rarely seen in Greece? Carlo Levi, who lived
among southern peasants in a neighbouring region, has this to say
of them:

'I was struck by the peasants' build: they are short and swarthy
with round heads, large eyes, and thin lips: their archaic faces do
not stem from the Romans, Greeks, Etruscans, Normans, or any
of the other invaders who have passed through their land, but
recall the most ancient Italic types. They have led exactly the same
life since the beginning of time, and history has swept over them
without effect. Of the two Italies that share the land between them,
the peasant Italy is by far the older; so old that no one knows
whence it came, and it may have been here for ever. *Humilemque
videmus Italiam*; this was the low-lying humble Italy that first met
the eyes of the Asiatic conquerors as the ships of Aeneas rounded the
promontory of Calabria.'

Just as night was falling, I came to a town upon a mountain top.
This was the provincial capital of Catanzaro.

§ 5

So little has been written about the South of Italy since the beginning of this century, when all travellers described the fearsome and verminous hovels in which they were often obliged to stay, that once again I must mention that in Catanzaro I found an air-conditioned hotel and a bedroom with a bathroom. There was also another first-class hotel slightly larger than the one I selected. Readers fresh from Gissing and Douglas will scarcely believe this, but it is a sign of southern advancement which I think cannot be mentioned too often.

From my balcony I looked across to the old city spread upon the summit of an adjacent mountain top which, though only a thousand feet above the Ionian Sea, gives the impression of being an alp. It is an earthquake city which has been torn and twisted by convulsions throughout its history, in addition to air raids during the last war. Catanzaro is an odd name with a rather Arabic look about it yet its derivation is entirely Greek – *cata anzos* – which means above the gorge or ravine. This ravine, now spanned by a gigantic steel arch which carries a girder bridge, is the meeting place of two rivers, but when I saw it the river-beds were dry and covered with grass and even with shrubs which had grown since the last rains. No city in the South of Italy has a more spectacular site: the blue sea is only a few miles away to the east, while, inland, the equally blue mountains of the Sila recede into the distance, fold upon fold.

They say of Catanzaro that it is the city of the three V's – *il Vento* (the wind) *i Velluti* (velvet) and *Vitiliano* (the local saint). While I was there the celebrated wind failed to blow, but I found that S. Vitiliano was a seventh century bishop of Capua and that the making of velvet, an industry introduced from the Byzantine East during the Middle Ages, has now become a specialized handicraft. The city, which has a population of seventy thousand, wears that distressing air, so familiar to the traveller in southern Italy, of a place repeatedly patched-up after earthquakes. One climbs a steep road to the old city to find oneself in narrow streets of massive stone houses and minute shops in whose tiny windows are sometimes surprisingly displayed the last word in electrical equipment, television sets and tape-recorders. It is typical of southern Italy that one should look through mediaeval window-frames at radio equipment. 'Where am I? What time is it?' are often the first words a patient speaks after an operation, the words probably also of the Sleeping Beauty when she was awakened; and I have often thought that it would be quite appropriate to hear them in so many places throughout the *Mezzogiorno*.

The cathedral is a vast and dignified modern church which has been rebuilt after its destruction in an air raid during the last war. It was by a happy chance that a fine sixteenth century bust of San Vitiliano survived.

I thought the Catanzaresi were particularly lively people. Like the Neapolitans, they are small, dark and excessively talkative, and it was the first city in which, so it seemed to me, the men out-numbered the women, though that is a dangerous generalization. There may have been some special reason unknown to me why the town was full of vivacious men gesticulating in the streets and in the cafés, all of them apparently with something to do.

Waiting at a bus stop was a countrywoman wearing the most spectacular dress I had seen in the course of my journey. This was obviously not the working dress which I had seen in the mountains but full dress for a gala occasion, such as a visit to Catanzaro. She wore a bodice of bottle-green velvet, a scarlet petticoat that came to within six inches of the ground, over which, looped back rather in the style of a nineteenth century bustle, was an elaborately frilled and starched overskirt of salmon-pink. The effect, though striking, was spoilt, I thought, by her shoes, which were ordinary slippers without heels, and by the absence of a headdress, which such splendour required. I noticed that beside her stood a child of about twelve, perhaps her daughter, who was wearing a dress made from the same delicate salmon-pink material as the woman's overskirt but cut in a modern fashion. The little girl, a white satin bow in her hair, might indeed have sat as a model for juvenile fashions. It was curious to see the two generations together, so different, one proclaiming the last splendour of the Middle Ages, the other conforming to the conventions of the present day.

Readers of Gissing will recall that Catanzaro was the windy town to which he retired with such delight after his depressing illness in the Concordia Inn at Crotone on the coast. But of the few writers who have visited Catanzaro I think the most unexpected was Stendhal, who, after attending the re-opening of the San Carlo Opera House in Naples in 1816, went on a brief tour through the South. He was too urban in his tastes to say much about it, and indeed probably detested every moment of it; however, he appeared on horseback in Otranto holding a sunshade. Of Catanzaro, he had only this to say:

'My latest experience was to watch a peasant woman in a fit of temper hurling her child against a wall not two paces distant, and using all the strength she had. I was certain that the child had received a fatal hurt; it is about four years old, and is rending the air with agonizing screams beneath my very window; but apparently no serious damage has been done.'

My own memory of Catanzaro (apart from the beautifully-dressed woman) is less dramatic but more pleasant. It is of two young men seated together outside a café in the old city, talking together with the utmost animation as they consumed ices in which whole wood strawberries were embedded. And this was at ten o'clock in the morning! Glancing into the window of the café, I saw trays of the most delicious ice-creams, some green filled with pistachio nuts, others even more exotic in appearance, which gave me the impression that possibly the Sicilian art of making frozen sweetmeats, which dates back to the days of the Arabs, had survived in this city, and had managed to defy the mass productions of Milan.

§ 6

I always find what is sometimes called mediaeval hospitality an embarrassing ordeal. I refer to the dinner guest who secretly arranges with the manager to pay the bill, thus at one blow sweeping aside whatever desire you may have entertained of making some courteous return for kindness received. This happened to me in one of the southern towns and the memory rankled for days.

One calls for the bill, the waiter comes up smirking and bowing to say that the signore has nothing to pay, while one's guest puts on an expression of ludicrous innocence, or else smiles and shrugs his shoulders, saying, 'It is nothing: you are now in my town.' I have met this misguided type of generosity in other parts of Italy, but generally among friends, and the incident is passed off with laughter.

Gissing once went into a shop with a mere acquaintance when, after making a number of purchases, he found that the other man had already paid for them. And I think it was Gissing also who, having ordered a bottle of wine in a Southern restaurant, found that a complete stranger had paid for it. I am well aware that the idea at the back of this misguided generosity is that the payer considers himself the host, as it is his territory, and in former days he would no doubt have invited the stranger to stay in his house.

I am getting wily about these 'bill snatchers'. I found one in Catanzaro, a person full of old-world courtesy, who, having been of help to me, and, wishing to make some slight return, I invited to dinner in a restaurant: but I took the precaution beforehand of leaving sufficient money with the cashier to pay the bill. I am almost certain that I managed to circumvent my guest, who had a whispered conversation with the manager and seemed a little puzzled and distraught throughout the meal. Only once have I had the disconcerting experience, which I had once believed was confined (to use a graceful old-world phrase) to ladies of easy virtue in night clubs, of having a bottle of wine sent over to me by a stranger. The only thing to do is to lift one's glass and bow. These manners belong to another age.

How little the stranger knows of what really goes on in the places he visits. Sometimes there is a hint that things are not quite what they seem; it may be that someone comes along with a surprising story, and in this way a curtain is lifted. This happened in a shocking way in Catanzaro when the Press reported that the police had received an anonymous letter advising them to dig in a certain spot for the body of Antonio Agostino, who had been missing for eighteen years. They did so and found his remains. Then a peasant, aged eighty, came forward to say that three men, who had since emigrated, had murdered Agostino at a place called the 'sacred rock', and that he had actually witnessed the murder. The legend is that if sufficient human blood is poured upon it the rock will part, to reveal an enormous fortune in golden nuggets.

The old man said that he saw the three murderers cut their victim's throat and hold him down on the rock so that his blood poured out over it. The men waited for hours but the rock did not move: but the men did. The last heard of this ancient sacrifice was that Interpol was being asked to trace them.

As I looked at the Calabrian mountains, I wondered how many other sacred rocks there may be, known only to the peasants. The lovely but enigmatic landscape, in spite of an occasional factory, seemed to be linked with dark and ancient forces.

§ 7

Thirty miles along the coast I came to the seaport of Crotone, upon the site of ancient Croton, which was one of the Greek colonies decreed by the Delphic Oracle. I noticed that the town arms show a tripod from which two serpents' heads are lifted, the tripod of the Pythia. The town, which is quite a large one, is untidy, partly mediaeval, and hot. A huge castle composed of ancient masonry dominates it and were it to be pulled down no doubt a wonderful museum might be built from the fragments. In the centre of the town, approached by a stately flight of steps, is the cathedral upon whose walls I read the words: 'It is forbidden to spit in the House of God.' (Livy mentions that it was sacrilege to spit near the house of the high priest in the Forum.)

Large chemical works bind Crotone to the modern world, giving the town employment. My disappointment with Crotone, which may be a little unfair, is based on the contrast between its modern commonplace condition and its former splendour, when its walls had a circuit of twelve miles. It had the reputation of being the healthiest city of Magna Graecia; its athletes were always winning more than their share of prizes at the Olympic Games, and the reputation of its men, as well as its women, for physical beauty

may have had something to do with the course of training laid
down by the Medical School, which at one time was considered
the best not only in colonial Greece, but also in the Hellenic world.
Herodotus has a lot to say about this School and tells us that the
doctor of Darius, King of Persia, was Democedes of Croton. He
was such a good doctor that the King kept him practically a prisoner
in Persia, but being a Greek and full of subterfuge, he managed to
escape.

I have already said something about Pythagoras at Croton, of
Croton's extermination of its rival, Sybaris, and of Croton's subsequent defeat, from which it was eventually to recover, at the
hands of Locri's much smaller army. It is a long and fascinating
story lived when the world was young. We see these people in the
sunlight beside the Ionian Sea, rich, powerful, and gifted; then a
shadow passes across the picture and after many centuries a traveller
wanders about modern Crotone saying to himself, 'Can this really
be the place?'

Ramage did not think much of Crotone when he was there in
1828 and, like the few who have written about the town, he compared its present condition with its ancient splendour. He seems to
have met the ancestress of Gissing's slatternly hostess as she presided over 'a low-roofed chamber, the gloom of which was only
heightened by a few glimmering lamps. . . . The landlady offered
me macaroni and *triglia*, a fish plentiful on the coasts of the
Mediterranean, and if she and her cooking utensils had been a
little more cleanly, I should have found little fault with her
supper.' He was eventually driven away from Crotone by what he
described as 'legions of flies brought out by the mid-day sun'.

The best chapters of Gissing's *By the Ionian Sea* describe the
squalid hotel at Crotone, the 'Concordia', in which he fell so ill
that it was feared he might die. Yet through it all ran an uncouth
kindliness which he managed to convey admirably. Coming from
Gissing, who was a connoisseur of poverty and in his early years
knew how grim life could be even for the hale and hearty, this is a
fascinating piece of writing. The moment he could totter about he
left Crotone for the breezy heights of Catanzaro. I was surprised to
read in a recently published English book that Gissing died at

Crotone in 1901 and is buried in the cemetery: this is not so. He died in 1903 in the south of France and is buried in the English cemetery at St Jean de Luz.

Years later, Norman Douglas found that the 'Concordia' had improved since Gissing's day, indeed he seemed quite fond of it. He discovered that most of the characters mentioned by Gissing were dead except for the little waiter, then married and grey-haired, and Doctor Sculco, who had attended Gissing.

'I called on this gentleman,' wrote Douglas, 'hoping to obtain from him some reminiscences of Gissing, whom he attended during a serious illness.'

'"Yes," he replied to my inquiries, "I remember him quite well; the young English poet who was ill here. I prescribed for him. Yes-yes! He wore his hair long."

'And that was all I could draw from him. I have noticed more than once that Italian physicians have a stern conception of the Hippocratic oath: the affairs of their patients, dead or alive, are a sacred trust in perpetuity.'

Gissing was deeply upset by his inability to visit all that is left of Greek Croton, the Doric column that has given its name to Cape Colonna. It is only six miles away and in Gissing's time it was easier to reach it by boat; now there is a hot but tolerable road to it.

Here the beautiful fluted column, as massive as any at Paestum, stands in lonely majesty above the sea. It rises from a few blocks of the temple pavement and is one of the most dramatic and evocative survivals in the South of Italy. It is the sole relic of the greatest temple in Magna Graecia, the Sanctuary of the Lacinian Hera, the Queen of Heaven, which stood in a sacred grove of trees with superb pastures where sacred herds of cattle bred by the priests were to be seen grazing. Like most of the great temples, it was a gold deposit vault which was protected by the awe inspired by the deity. Even Hannibal, badly in need of money and longing to steal the golden column which stood in the temple, did not dare to commit such sacrilege.

The temple is of unknown antiquity. Virgil says it was there in the time of Aeneas. The third book of the *Aeneid* gives a description of navigators steering their galleys from temple to temple as they came down the Ionian coast of Magna Graecia, each one a landmark where the crews sometimes disembarked and sacrificed before continuing their voyages. The Greeks assembled once a year at the Temple of the Lacinian Hera to take part in a procession in honour of the goddess and to vie with one another in the splendour of their offerings. The inside of the temple was decorated with paintings by the greatest artists of the time, the most famous being the picture of Helen by the rich and celebrated Zeuxis, who lived about 400 B.C. It is said that the government of Croton allowed him to study five of the most beautiful local girls naked in order to combine their beauty in his painting.

Livy has left perhaps the best description of the temple. 'It had an enclosure surrounded by dense woodland,' he wrote, 'with lofty firs, and, in the centre, rich grassland where cattle of all kinds, sacred to the goddess, grazed without any shepherd to attend them. At night the various flocks and herds used to return each to their own stalls, unharmed by lurking beasts of prey or by marauding men. Thus a great deal of money was made out of these cattle, and from the profits a column of solid gold was dedicated to the goddess. The temple, too, was as famous for its wealth as for its sanctity, and, as often happens with well-known places, stories of supernatural things are connected with it: for instance, it is said that in the entrance court there is an altar on which the ashes are never stirred by wind.'

I have described how I found a Christian version of the goddess Hera, holding a pomegranate and called the Madonna of the Pomegranate, in the village of Capaccio Vecchio above Paestum; and here at Cape Colonna is an equally surprising survival. There is a little chapel on the point dedicated to the Madonna of Cape Colonna, sometimes called by the country people Santa Hera. Once every seven years, upon the second Sunday in May, crowds gather, as they did centuries before Christ, to pay homage to the Queen of Heaven. There is a procession as there used to be long ago; and in the May sunlight the Doric column of the Sanctuary of the Lacinian Hera stands above the sea, linking the old world with the new.

§ 8

My failure to find Sybaris preyed uneasily upon my mind even
though I knew that qualified archaeologists have been looking
vainly for it since 1879. The curator of the museum at Reggio di
Calabria had told me that a great amount of time, skill and money
have been spent in the hope of discovering Sybaris, and the present
attempt is a joint Italian–American venture aided by every kind
of electrical detecting device. A book in English and Italian, *The
Search for Sybaris, 1960–1965*, has just been published by the Lerici
Foundation of Rome and the University Museum of Philadelphia,
United States of America.

The two large volumes, one consisting of maps, are an imposing
record of (so far) unrelieved failure. Such determination deserves
to be rewarded. Year after year the archaeologists arrive to employ
techniques which must astonish the old-fashioned archaeologist to
whom a spade was a spade. The searchers for Sybaris roam the
plain with vans full of electrical equipment, or they may be seen
carrying strange devices with such names as 'the Varian Associates
cesium magnometer', 'the Geohm Conductivity apparatus', or the
'Proton magnometer'. So far the electrical probes sent down into
the plain have aroused no answering echo. Sybaris, so famed in the
ancient world (the book contains sixty-eight references to the city
by ancient authors), has now become silent.

If the original authorities for the destruction of Sybaris in 510 B.C.
are reliable, the people of Croton, having defeated the Sybarites,
changed the course of the river Crathis so that it flooded and
eventually wiped out the city. Thus the problem of finding Sybaris
would seem to be a simple one, yet it has defied expert explorers
for years. The area is not a large one. If, as I say, the ancient writers
can be believed, a Greek city whose walls had a circuit of more than
eight miles must lie at the most eighteen feet under the present plain,
probably about five miles from the sea.

Why Sybaris should be so fascinating is difficult to say. Perhaps
the words 'sybaritic' and 'sybarite' give it a certain interest, though
when one has read all the ancient references to 'sybaritism', how
commonplace they are: the feasts, the street awnings, the honour

paid to cooks, the chariots in which men visited their estates, the Maltese lapdogs which women carried, the pet monkeys, the purple cloaks, the scented hair bound by gold fillets, the confinement of smoky and noisy trades to certain quarters (the earliest noise and smoke abatement scheme), all this appears merely to reflect a standard of living that one would expect to find in any rich community of the time. Why the writers of antiquity should have picked upon Sybaris as the symbol of excessive luxury is difficult to understand. Can it have been a kind of early Greek Aberdeen, the butt of humorists? Some of the stories about Sybaris, like that of the man who suffered a rupture when seeing labourers hard at work, are just as silly as many of the Aberdonian stories about economies.

Oddly enough, one of the great events in the history of Sybaris, which, as I mentioned earlier in this book, denotes not effeminacy or love of ease, but sheer hard-headed commercial energy was the establishment of their trading depot, Paestum, on the Tyrrhenian coast. No effete people could have devised and carried out such a scheme.

I have sympathy with Professor Froelich G. Rainey, Director of the University Museum of Philadelphia, who writes in his introduction to the book I have mentioned: 'Many times during these past years of searching for concrete evidence of Sybaris I have felt that the famed city was a myth. Ruins of contemporary Greek cities bordering the Ionian Sea, such as Locri and Metapontum, are found on the surface of the ground or buried less than a meter deep. Why should Sybaris, largest and most famous of them all, still be lost to us?'

The answer, of course, is that perhaps it is not there. An ingenious theory is that of Robert L. Raikes who suggests that earthquakes and a tidal wave may have overwhelmed Sybaris and that this flooding 'became in subsequent legend translated into wilful destruction (but be it noted by water) by the inhabitants of Croton'.

Though the book is too technical for the general reader, with its emphasis upon plans and diagrams and the adaptation to archaeology of electronics primarily devised for space satellites, still the difficulty of finding this elusive city decided me to return to the plain and, if possible, to see the Americans at work.

It was a run of about eighty miles from Crotone along the excellent coast road, a more desolate stretch of country than that further south, the railway as usual keeping the road company on the seaward side. Sometimes road and railway would curve a mile or so inland, then approach the sea again and run for miles beside deserted bays and beaches. Girder bridges crossed the beds of torrents every few miles, towns and villages were few, indeed signs of life were infrequent except for the little railway stations whose staffs even thirty years ago considered it exile to be sent there for duty. It was scarcely believable that the malarial mosquito had been defeated, though everywhere I was shown windows without netting. This extermination of the mosquito is, I think, perhaps the greatest miracle in the south of Italy.

A landscape which has been haunted for centuries by malaria has a stricken look and probably it will be some time before this part of Calabria is farmed by those who do not sleep elsewhere. I was reminded of another once malarial coast, that of Turkey south of Izmir. I well remember how the frogs croaked in the marshes round Ephesus and how anxious those who knew the country were to get indoors before dark.

I saw Rossano again upon its hill, and I climbed into the mountains to Corigliano where during my first visit a farmer had given me a piece of manna. Then I descended to the Plain of Sybaris where heat was pulsing from a sky of brass. The harvest had long since been gathered and the plain was streaked with yellow stubble. I had been advised at Reggio to go to the railway station, Sibari, and ask for the *Americanos*; but the station was closed and there was not a soul to be seen. I came at length to some red brick bungalows. Upon the porch of one a woman sat at a table so absorbed in some task that she did not hear me unlatch the garden gate and walk up the short path. She was sitting with a number of wooden boxes full of broken pottery in front of her, which she was fitting together as if they were parts of a jigsaw puzzle. She was a Dutch archaeologist who had been working with the team from Pennsylvania University, whose work had just ended. The Americans had left only a few days before and, alas, no one remained to show me how a 'Geohm Conductivity apparatus' works!

The bungalow housed a small collection of objects found upon the plain, mostly fragments of pottery, some Greek, some later in date, and little of it meaning much save perhaps to an expert. Being what Rose Macaulay would have called 'ruin-minded', I thought of the savage ironies of time: that the path to a city whose name is synonymous with luxury should be paved with broken kitchen pottery!

The archaeologist asked if I had noticed, when I was in the museum at Reggio di Calabria, a bronze tablet which had been discovered in the neighbourhood of Sybaris in 1965, written in archaic Greek, and reading from right to left. As it happened I remembered this well, and had made some notes about it. It is a small, thin sheet of bronze pierced at the four corners where nails had attached it to a wall. It records the exploits of an athlete called by the ringing Spartan name of Kleombrotos, the son of Dexilaos, who had dedicated the panel to Athena in fulfilment of a vow. Evidently he promised the goddess this ex-voto if she would grant him victory in the games. Unfortunately he did not think of giving the name of his town.

'Why do you ask if I have seen this?' I asked.

'Well – I happen to have found it,' replied the archaeologist modestly. The only voice from the Sybaritic plain had been found by this charming Dutchwoman, now so diligently mending the kitchen pots. We discussed the life and death of Sybaris, she with professional enthusiasm, I with melancholy. There was one man, however, who foresaw the doom of Sybaris. His name was Amyris. The story is that the Delphic Oracle had prophesied fame and fortune to the city as long as her people did not pay greater respect to a mortal than to the gods. One day a master pursued a slave into the temple of Hera where, his anger getting the better of him, he beat him. The slave then ran from the temple and hid in the tomb of his master's father; but there the man refused to follow, so great was his respect for his father's memory.

When Amyris heard of this he began to sell his property and to convert everything he possessed into money. Then he emigrated to the Peloponnese. He had interpreted the incident as the sign of the approaching annihilation of Sybaris, and the fulfilment of the Delphic prophecy. His fellow Sybarites laughed at him, indeed their jokes inspired a popular saying of the time, 'Amyris is mad'. But Amyris was the only one, so far as we know, who saved his fortune and deliberately removed himself from the doomed city at what was apparently the height of its prosperity.

## § 9

I retraced my steps southward down the Ionian coast to Reggio di Calabria, where I had left a suitcase and some books. I spent a night at Crotone where Gissing would be interested to know there are now three hotels of the third class and two of the fourth. Those familiar with the Italian scene will be able to imagine them. There was no air-conditioning and no private bathroom, but I was comfortable enough and there were no intruders in my bed.

I went to the cathedral which I found enveloped in festive hangings of red and gold. Here I sat through a long service, watching the incense rise in blue clouds round the high altar while candlelight gleamed upon gold vestments. How incredible to sit in a cathedral in a square called the Piazza Pythagoras and to see incense rising in a temple where a projection of the goddess Hera is revered as the *Madonna di Capocolonna*. It is not really necessary to have a 'Geohm Conductivity apparatus' to discover Magna Graecia: all you have to do is to go to church.

I walked back to the hotel admiring those gifted travellers who, after a hurried glance at a foreign country, are able to solve problems which have defeated experts. As I sat in the dusk watching the people of Crotone passing beneath loops of coloured electric lights, while the usual festal rocket exploded prematurely in the background, I thought that any lecturer of the London School of Economics, who had seen what I had seen, would be able, at length and in the jargon of his institution, to say whether Southern Italy is moving towards a 'viable' economy or not. But this I was unable to do. I simply did not know.

I had seen an ancient peasant society rooted in beautiful but unprofitable highlands in the process of being converted to an industrial age. Here and there factories were presumably spreading their local 'viability'; though how few workers can run even a large factory. Such gigantic concerns as the Bari oil refinery and the Taranto steel-works are, however, in a different class: they are really Big Business, and they look to the European Common Market as the destination of their products.

More appealing to me were the land schemes, among them the spectacular Plain of Metaponto. Here, where long ago Greek millionaires grew their wheat and bred their horses, thousands of small farmers, aided by the State, each farm with its water-rights and its tractor, have now brought this rich land back to life. It is green as far as one can see with crops of fruit, vegetables and tobacco. There is energy and cheerfulness in the air, a feeling of problems solved and crops moving smoothly to their markets through a co-operative society.

It may not be widely known that the South of Italy has been the scene of a land reform more striking than any carried out by a non-Communist country. About twenty years ago some three thousand square miles of agricultural land were taken over by the State, mostly from absentee landlords who, with a superb touch of official humour, were paid out at their own valuations . . . based on their income tax returns! The land was divided into twelve-acre farms, which the labourers were encouraged to own under a State mortgage scheme. This enormous area, of which the Plain of Metaponto is a part, is now thriving. But, in a poor and mountainous country such rejuvenation is limited, and there cannot be many more schemes of this character.

While so many surprising things are happening in the South, *La Cassa* continues to budget for more and ever more billions for the *Mezzogiorno*; and still old women in black mount the rocky mountain tracks with loads of firewood upon their heads: they still tramp the roads barefoot to the public fountains, ancient priestesses of fire and water who have probably never heard of the *Cassa del Mezzogiorno*. But even they must be aware of change. They have seen the mosquito vanquished; they have seen people leaving the hill towns and going down fearlessly to live in the plains; some may even have seen a moon probe on television; more important, perhaps, all have travelled in a motor-bus to the nearest town.

The complexity of the South is increased by the paradox that this depressed area very largely runs the Italian State. Most of the governors and prefects, most of the professors, lecturers, government officials and, in general, that huge class of powerful but moderately salaried persons covered by the word *professionisti*, are southerners. Signor Luigi Barzini writes in *The Italians*: 'Southerners think mainly in political, not economic terms.' He notes that the northerner is devoted to the acquisition of wealth, *la richezza*. 'Only wealth can, he believes, lastingly assure the defence and prosperity of the family. The southerner, on the other hand, knows that this can be done only with the acquisition of power, prestige, authority, fame.'

This astute observation perhaps explains what I had sometimes noticed in the South: a reluctance among educated people to say a good word for material prosperity; the cynical shrug which greeted the report of a great industrial scheme; the unwillingness to admit that the North has anything to teach the South. Barzini again seems to hit the nail on the head when he writes that industrialization 'assumes that southerners would be northerners if only they were surrounded with the proper political and economic structures'.

Not only is the southerner different from the northerner, but there are also a variety of southerners, from the gregarious, ebullient Neapolitans to the grave Calabrians, sometimes upon cold mountain evenings wrapped to the eyes in cloaks like black togas, impassive, dark men who turn the mind to El Greco and to Spain. Upon slight acquaintance, a stranger, not always, of course, the best judge, may smile to think that the southerner is indifferent to money; that indeed, as far as avarice goes, there is nothing to choose between North and South. Gissing went so far as to say 'in all the South of Italy money is the one subject of men's thoughts'. It seemed to me that the attitude of the southerner to the northerner resembled the exasperated bewilderment of one who sees someone whom he does not think of as in any way more gifted than himself – rather to the contrary in fact – growing rich and successful, while he remains poor.

'If only there were some way of making money without working in horrible, ugly factories!' Though no one ever said that to me, I was always expecting to hear it, and more than once I seemed to detect such a sentiment behind dark, intelligent eyes. Of course there *is* a way, and every southerner knows it. It is emigration. Like the Scots and the Irish, the Italian often thrives and blossoms away from his own land and achieves a success and a distinction which he could never hope to have enjoyed at home. Even if the South were able to offer all its sons a living, I think the pull of emigration, the lure of distant opportunity, and the invitation of relatives established abroad to share their prosperity, would be too strong.

One is inclined to forget how much countries other than the United States owe to Italian emigration. I received a letter from a friend in Melbourne, Mr Alfred Stirling, who was for years the Australian Ambassador in Italy.

'Next, of course, to the Scots, the English and the Irish,' he wrote, 'the Italians have made the largest and most important contribution to Australia, and are still doing so. They have been coming since the gold rush of over a century ago, and even earlier. Verdi's *Attila* was given in Sydney in 1846 only a year after its première at *La Fenice*, in Venice. (Rome only got it for the first time in 1965.) All told, nearly a million Italians have come here – 350,000 in the last twenty years. Perhaps eight per cent of the population is of Italian origin. In my State, Victoria, alone, there are 250,000 Italians, 200,000 living in Melbourne.

'One of the greatest Italian success stories is the firm of Transfield, the constructing engineers operating all over Australia, built up in a decade by two young engineers, one from Turin, the other from Milan. Italians have contributed greatly to the hydro-electric work of the Snowy Mountains Authority – comparable to the Tenessee Valley Authority. Wherever there is concrete work to be done you will find Italians – skyscrapers, bridges, roads, power transmission, tunnels. The Aliscafi of Rodriguez of Messina fly across Sydney Harbour as they do from Messina to

Reggio di Calabria. In another sphere Italians have revolutionized the eating habits of Australians. Restaurants, pizzerias and gelaterias everywhere offer good Italian food and specialities. Italians run grazing properties, dairy farms and grow tobacco, oranges, lemons, grape-fruit and other *agrumi*, also a wide range of vegetables. The Australian motor-car industry has over twenty per cent of Italians on its staff. One of the founders of Australian surgery was General Tomasco Fiaschi (half Scottish), who is now commemorated by a statue-fountain, a replica of Florence's *Porcellino*; and Melbourne owes its five-track boulevards to the Surveyor-General Catani, a town planner of well over a century ago.'

Emigration is rightly called one of the tragedies of Italy, and particularly of the South; on the other hand, it is well known that dynamism and ambition that might never have developed at home respond to new surroundings. Many countries will continue to benefit in the future, as in the past, from the inherent skill and artistry of the most talented nation in Europe.

In the morning, with no breath of wind stirring, the sky as blue as the sea, I went on south past the little marinas grouped round the Gulf of Squillace. The mountains rose inland where every hill lifted its ancient town into the sunlight; romantic to look at from a distance, but I knew how many were moribund, inhabited by women and old men. Every half mile or so the winter torrents had carved a white bed of sand and boulders aimed at the sea; the mountains were clothed sometimes to the top with trees, bushes and a flora that is probably the same as that familiar centuries before Christ to the colonists from Greece.

I spent some days in Reggio di Calabria, which is one of the most cheerful and pleasant of southern cities. I went again to the museum to see the objects beautifully displayed there from the cities of Magna Graecia. They meant more to me now that I had climbed over the stones of Locri and had seen the honey-gold column of the Lacinian Hera at Croton. The museum staff must be the most polite in existence. When it was seen that I was genuinely interested, the curator himself came to show me round, even insisting upon opening cases and placing into my hands some object that had attracted me. In the evening I would look from my balcony across the Straits of Messina to Sicily. Sometimes there would be only the faintest redness far off in the sky, which indicated Etna, but at other times a deep and angry light reflected volcanic fires. The lights of towns and villages upon the opposite shore sparkled invitingly. I was sorely tempted to cross the narrow straits, and once I even consulted the time-table. I should like to have stood at the tomb of 'Stupor Mundi' in Palermo and to have seen the Hauteville tombs at Monreale, but one cannot, alas, do everything. Seated alone in the scented night, I watched the lights come out upon the Sicilian shore and hoped that perhaps someday I might be fortunate enough to cross those tempting waters.

# BIBLIOGRAPHY

Acton, Harold, *The Bourbons of Naples* (London, 1956)

Acton, Harold, *The Last Bourbons of Naples* (London, 1961)

Bartlett, Vernon, *Introduction to Italy* (London, 1967)

Blessington, Countess of, *The Idler in Italy*, 2 vols (London, 1839)

Blunt, Rev. J. J., *Vestiges of Ancient Manners and Customs Discoverable in Modern Italy and Sicily* (London, 1823)

*Cambridge Ancient History* (Cambridge, 1928–39)

Canziani, Estella, *Through the Apennines and the Lands of the Abruzzi* (London, 1928)

Collison-Morley, Lacy, *Naples Through the Centuries* (London, 1925)

Comnena, Anna, *The Alexiad*, translated by Elizabeth A. S. Dawes (London, 1967)

Craven, R. Keppel, *A Tour Through the Southern Provinces of the Kingdom of Naples* (London, 1821)

Craven, R. Keppel, *Excursions in the Abruzzi* (London, 1838)

Crawfurd, F. Marion, *The Rulers of the South*, 2 vols (London, 1900)

David, Elizabeth, *Italian Food* (London, 1955)

Dini, V., and Magrini, F., *Gli Antichi Sports e i Giuochi Popolari nel Folklore delle Manifestazioni Italiane* (Arezzo, 1966)

Douglas, Norman, *Old Calabria* (London, 1956)

Douglas, Norman, *Siren Land* (London, 1957)

Douglas, Norman, *Alone* (London, 1940)

Freeman, Kathleen, *Greek City States* (London, 1950)

Gissing, George, *By the Ionian Sea* (London, 1901)

Goethe, Wolfgang, *Goethe's Travels in Italy* (Bohn's Standard Library, London, 1885)

Gunn, Peter, *Naples, a Palimpsest* (London, 1961)

Hamilton, Sir William, *Observations on Mount Vesuvius etc* (London, 1774)

Hare, Augustus, *Cities of Southern Italy* (London, 1911)

Hutton, Edward, *Naples and Campania Revisited* (London, 1958)

Hutton, Edward, *The Cosmati* (London, 1950)

Jackson, Hamilton, *The Shores of the Adriatic* (London, 1906)

Kantorowicz, Ernst, *Frederick the Second 1194–1250* (New York, 1957)

Lear, Edward, *Edward Lear in Southern Italy* (reprinted, London, 1964)

Lenormant, François, *La Grande-Grèce*, 3 vols (reprint, Cosenza, 1961)

Livy, *The War With Hannibal*, translated by Aubrey de Sélincourt (Penguin Books, 1965)

MacIver, R. D., *Greek Cities in Italy and Sicily* (Oxford, 1931)

Martino, Ernesto de, *La Terra del Rimorso* (Milan, 1961)

Masson, Georgina, *Frederick II of Hohenstaufen* (London, 1957)

Monaco, Franco, *Manifestizioni Italiane* (Rome, n.d.)

Norwich, John Julius, *The Normans in the South* (London, 1967)

Orioli, G. I., *Moving Along* (London, 1934)

Ovid, *The Fasti of Ovid*, 5 vols, edited and translated by Sir James George Frazer (London, 1929)

Parke, H. W., *A History of the Delphic Oracle* (Oxford, 1939)

Pausanias, *Pausanias's Description of Greece*, 6 vols, translated with a commentary by Sir James George Frazer (London, 1913)

Rainey, F. G., and Lerici, Carlo F., *The Search for Sybaris* (Rome, 1967)

Rogers, S., *Italian Journal* (London, 1814–21)

Ross, Janet, *The Land of Manfred* (London, 1889)

Ramage, Craufurd Tait, *Ramage in South Italy* (reprint abridged and edited by Edith Clay, London, 1965)

Runciman, Steven, *The Sicilian Vespers* (London, 1958)

Stendhal, *Rome, Naples and Florence* (reprint translated by Richard N. Coe, London, 1959)

Strutt, A. J., *A Pedestrian Tour in Calabria and Sicily* (London, 1842)

Swinburne, Henry, *Travels in the Two Sicilies*, 2 vols (London, 1777–80)

Thucydides, *The Peloponnesian War*, translated by Rex Warner (Penguin Books, 1954)

Wall, Bernard, *Italian Life and Landscape*, 2 vols (London, 1950–51)

Warner, Oliver, *Emma Hamilton and Sir William* (London, 1960)

Whelpton, E. and B., *Calabria and the Aeolian Islands* (London, 1957)

Wood, Casey A., and Fyfe, F. Marjorie, *The Art of Falconry, being De Arte Venandi Cum Avibus of Frederick II of Hohenstaufen* (Boston, 1955)

Woodhead, A. G., *The Greeks in the West* (London, 1962)

I found Baedeker's Touring Guide *Italy*, 1962, disappointing compared with Baedeker's guide to *Southern Italy*, 1912. Muirhead's Blue Guide to *Southern Italy*, 1959, is good but is obviously due for revision and expansion. The best and most complete guides to the South of Italy are those (in Italian) of the Touring Club Italiano, Milan. The titles of the five guides which cover the five southern regions are: *Abruzzo e Molise, Campania, Napoli e Dintorni, Puglia, Basilicata e Calabria*.

The reader who wishes to have a concise and accurate survey of Italian history should get *Italian Life and Landscape*, 2 vols, 1950–51, by Bernard Wall (a masterpiece of expert condensation); and *Introduction to Italy* by Vernon Bartlett, 1967.

# INDEX

# The Rulers of Southern Italy

## THE NORMAN CONQUEST

At the beginning of the 11th century Norman knights returning from pilgrimages to the Holy Land saw in the disturbed state of Southern Italy, torn between Lombard, Byzantine and Saracen, a profitable field for military adventure. The first Norman to make his name there was **Rainulf** (c. 1030), who was rewarded for his military aid with the town of Aversa, near Naples. He became the first Count of Aversa (1030–45); and his town developed into a market for Norman mercenaries.

The greatest conquerors were the Hautevilles. They were the sons of a modest landowner Tancred de Hauteville of Hauteville-la-Guichard in Normandy. He had twelve sons by his two marriages. His three eldest sons laid the foundations of Norman power in Southern Italy. They were:

| **William** (Iron-Arm) | **Drogo** | **Humphrey** |

William became Count of Apulia (1042–46) and was succeeded by Drogo (1046–51) and Humphrey (1051–57).

The two most notable sons of the second marriage were:

| **Robert, the 'Guiscard', or wise** (c. 1015–85) | **Roger** (1031–1101) |

Robert was the eldest son of the second marriage, Roger the youngest. Between them they built upon the foundations laid down by their half-brothers. At their deaths they controlled the whole of Southern Italy. Robert Guiscard died (1085) Duke of Apulia and one of the most powerful men in Europe; Roger subdued the Saracens in Sicily and founded a royal dynasty there. He died in 1101, known as 'the Great Count'.

## THE NORMAN KINGS OF SICILY (NAPLES)

| | |
|---|---|
| 1112–54 | Roger, son of Roger 'the Great Count' |
| 1154–66 | William I, 'the Bad', son of the above |
| 1166–89 | William II 'the Good', son of the above. (His wife was Joan of England, daughter of Henry II and sister of Richard Lionheart.) He died childless and willed the kingdom to his aunt Constance (daughter of Roger II), whom he married to Henry of Hohenstaufen, who became the Emperor Henry VI. After William's death the throne was usurped by: |
| 1189–94 | Tancred, an illegitimate cousin of the late king |
| 1194 | William III, infant son of the above, who was deposed and murdered. Henry VI and Constance claimed the kingdom and established their capital at Palermo |

## THE HOHENSTAUFEN

| | |
|---|---|
| 1194–97 | Henry VI, Holy Roman Emperor (son of the Emperor Frederick I, 'Barbarossa') |
| 1197–1250 | Frederick II, only son of Constance, who became Emperor and was known as *Stupor Mundi*, 'the Wonder of the World' |
| 1250–54 | Conrad IV, Emperor, son of Frederick II |
| 1254–66 | Manfred, illegitimate son of Frederick II |

# THE ANGEVINS

The Pope, anxious to destroy the Hohenstaufen as foes of the Papacy, offered the Kingdom to **Charles of Anjou**, the brother of Louis IX of France. Charles slew Manfred in battle (1266) but unable to conquer Sicily made his capital at Naples. The Sicilians, having proved their hatred for French rule in the revolt called 'the Sicilian Vespers (1282), offered the throne to Peter III of Aragon, the husband of Constance, daughter of Manfred. Thus two rival houses ruled at the same time in Southern Italy, one French at Naples with no hereditary claim, the other Spanish, at Palermo, founded on the claims of Constance as a descendant of the Hohenstaufen.

## HOUSE OF ARAGON (Sicily)

| | |
|---|---|
| 1282–85 | Peter III of Aragon, 1st of Sicily |
| 1285–91 | Alfonso |
| 1291–98 | James |
| 1296–1337 | Frederick II of Aragon |
| 1337–42 | Peter II |
| 1342–55 | Louis |
| 1355–77 | Frederick III |
| 1377–92 | Maria |
| 1392–1409 | Martin I |
| 1409–10 | Martin II of Aragon |

## HOUSE OF ANJOU (Naples)

| | |
|---|---|
| 1266–85 | Charles d'Anjou |
| 1285–1309 | Charles II |
| 1309–43 | Robert 'the Wise' |
| 1343–81 | Joan I (deposed) |
| 1381–86 | Charles III |
| 1386–1414 | Ladislaus |
| 1414–35 | Joan II |
| 1435–42 | René of Anjou (father of Margaret of Anjou, Queen of Henry VI of England) |

From 1410 to 1458 Sicily was ruled from Spain.

In 1442 Alfonso V, 'the Magnanimous', subdued Naples which was then ruled by Spanish monarchs until 1501. This was succeeded by rule by Spanish Viceroys, which lasted until 1713. After the War of the Spanish Succession Naples came under Austrian rule until 1734. In that year, after some minor warfare, Naples and Sicily accepted Charles, son of Philip V of Spain and Isabella Farnese, as king. He founded the Neapolitan House of Bourbon.

## HOUSE OF BOURBON

1734–59    Charles III.

In 1759 he succeeded to the throne of Spain. His third son became King of Naples and Sicily.

| | |
|---|---|
| 1759–99 | Ferdinand IV (of Naples) |
| 1799 | *The French Parthenopean Republic* |
| 1799–1806 | Ferdinand IV (restored) |
| 1806–08 | *Joseph Bonaparte* |
| 1808–15 | *Joachim Murat* |
| 1815–25 | Ferdinand IV (and 1st of the Two Sicilies) (2nd restoration) |
| 1825–30 | Francis I |
| 1830–59 | Ferdinand II of the Two Sicilies |
| 1859–60 | Francis II |

From this period the Kingdom of the Two Sicilies formed part of united Italy.